D1612467

LAW AND BODY POLITICS

Law and Body Politics

Regulating The Female Body

Edited by
JO BRIDGEMAN
Feminist Legal Research Unit
The University of Liverpool
and
SUSAN MILLNS
Feminist Legal Research Unit
The University of Liverpool

Dartmouth

Aldershot • Brookfield USA • Singapore • Sydney

© Jo Bridgeman, Susan Millns 1995

Published by
Dartmouth Publishing Company Limited
Gower House
Croft Road
Aldershot
Hants GU11 3HR
England

Dartmouth Publishing Company
Old Post Road
Brookfield
Vermont 05036
USA

British Library Cataloguing in Publication Data
Law and Body Politics: Regulating the
Female Body. - (Socio-legal Studies)
  I. Bridgeman, Jo II. Millns, Susan
  III. Series
  342.0878

Library of Congress Cataloging-in-Publication Data
Law and body politics : regulating the female body / edited by Jo
  Bridgeman and Susan Millns.
      p.   cm.
  "Socio-legal studies series."
  Includes bibliographical references and index.
  ISBN 1-85521-515-2
    1. Women–Legal status, laws, etc.–Great Britain. I. Bridgeman,
  Jo. II. Millns, Susan.
  KD734.L34 1995
  346.4101'34–dc20
  [344.106134]
                                  95-102
                                     CIP

ISBN 1 85521 515 2

Printed in Great Britain by Antony Rowe Ltd,
Chippenham, Wiltshire

Contents

List of Contributors

Fiona Beveridge is a Lecturer in Law at the University of Liverpool.

Lois S. Bibbings is a Lecturer in Law at the University of Bristol.

Jo Bridgeman is a Lecturer in Law at the University of Liverpool.

Marie Fox is a Lecturer in Law at Manchester University.

Kirsty Keywood is a Lecturer in Law at the University of Liverpool.

Elizabeth Kingdom is a Senior Lecturer in the Department of Sociology, Social Policy and Social Work Studies at the University of Liverpool.

Christina M. Lyon is Professor of Common Law at the University of Liverpool.

Susan Millns is a Lecturer in Law at the University of Liverpool.

Susan R. Moody is a Lecturer in Law at the University of Dundee.

Anne Morris is a Senior Lecturer in Law at the University of Liverpool.

Siobhan Mullally is a Lecturer in Law at the University of Hull.

Susan Nott is a Senior Lecturer in Law at the University of Liverpool.

Sally Sheldon is a Lecturer in Law at the University of Keele.

List of Cases

List of Statutes and Other Documents

Acknowledgements

The Feminist Legal Research Unit at the University of Liverpool has provided much valuable support for this collection which was inspired by the first conference held by the Feminist Legal Research Unit in March 1993 entitled "Body Politics: Control Versus Freedom: The role of feminism in women's personal autonomy". Our thanks go to our colleagues in the Unit, Fiona Beveridge, Kirsty Keywood, Christina Lyon, Anne Morris, Debra Morris and Sue Nott for their help and support throughout the busy period during which this book was written, and to Lois Bibbings, who, although no longer at Liverpool, has been involved in the work of the Unit since its beginnings.

In addition we acknowledge the work of those who generously gave their time and expertise to produce the final text: Ann Porter, Carol Prescott and Brian Thompson for their much needed computing advice, David Arnold and Eric Lafrenière for assisting with preparation of the text and Rachel Chapman for compiling the bibliography and index.

Finally we acknowledge the debt owed to our students taking the "Law and the Sexes" and "Body Politics" courses on which we teach. Discussion with them on many of the issues raised by this collection has helped clarify our thoughts and convinced us of the necessity for creating a vital space for the debate of feminist perspectives in legal studies.

Introduction

In the old metaphor of the Body Politic, the state or society was imagined as a human body, with different organs and parts symbolizing different functions, needs, social constituents, forces, and so forth - the head or soul for the sovereign, the blood for the will of the people, or the nerves for the system of rewards and punishments. Now, feminism imagined the human body as *itself* a politically inscribed entity, its physiology and morphology shaped by histories and practices of containment and control - from foot-binding and corseting to rape and battering to compulsory heterosexuality, forced sterilisation, unwanted pregnancy...[1]

The metaphor of the Body Politic found in the works of Plato, Aristotle, Cicero, Seneca, Machiavelli, and Hobbes, amongst others, has been drawn upon by feminists and reformulated to permit investigation of the politicisation of the body and the saturation of the body with political meaning. By exploring the politics of the body, feminists contribute to an analysis of the processes whereby women's bodies are sexualised, objectified, regulated and violated by the institutions of patriarchal society amongst which the legal system takes its place. Feminists have shown that whilst the female body has emerged as a site of struggle and a focus of legal fascination, the legal system has at the same time played a role in silencing women and rendering our needs, if not our bodies, invisible.

In unmasking the alleged impartiality and neutrality of law[2] and in exposing the extent to which the legal subject is gendered, women have been shown to be alien to the legal system; foreign bodies inhabiting a hostile terrain. This has led in some quarters to an expression of concern as to how, when, indeed whether at all women should resort to law.[3] The chapters in this volume emphasise that it is not necessary to accept or reject wholesale legal rules and procedures; the dichotomy - whether to use law or not - has been dismantled so that different strategies can be advocated in response to different issues. Each chapter is concerned with an exploration of points at which law and the female body make contact and with strategies through which the nature and meaning of that contact can be reformulated. Contact between law and the body is achieved through various mediums. It may be mediated through medical practices, for example through abortion, new reproductive technologies, sterilisation, and the treatment of anorexia, or through the criminalisation of acts practised upon the female body such as female circumcision, physical violence and rape, or through the specific regulation of women's bodies as we engage in activities in the public sphere, such as paid employment. These areas of activity reveal that body politics is concerned with both the engagement of law and the female body, notably in the regulation and policing of motherhood, and their failure to engage at other times such as when the female body is violated.

In "Body Politics and Rights" Elizabeth Kingdom considers feminist body politics in the context of the use made by feminists of appeals to rights. She provides an overview of feminist critiques of rights discourse and suggests a "bodyright strategy" based upon Foucault's analysis of power. Elizabeth Kingdom argues that there is no easy solution to the question of whether or not to employ rights discourse, explaining this through an outline of the reservations which feminists have about, as well as strategic reasons for, adopting rights discourse in their campaigns. She stresses that it ought not to be expected that feminists will agree over the use of a rights-orientated strategy, over the adoption and choice of slogans and over bodyright strategy. Rather she suggests a "conversion strategy" which demands that attention be given to current legal politics, to the specific jurisdiction and to the international context in which the use of rights is contemplated. She suggests that this approach removes the dichotomy of abstention from, or engagement with, law and opens up the possibility of the strategic use of rights discourse. Warning that preoccupation with rights can marginalise wider economic and social issues, Elizabeth Kingdom argues that a "conversion strategy" avoids the risk of seeing law as an exclusive area in which to resolve rights disputes and an exclusive focus of feminist politics.

Jo Bridgeman, in "They Gag Women, Don't They?", considers the law's engagement with the anorexic woman in the context of the wider social and cultural implications of anorexia. She explores the social position of women in western societies of the late twentieth century and particularly the constraints imposed by ideals of femininity. In examining the link between the conflict that all women experience about our place in the world and normal female practices of dieting and exercise, she argues that anorexia can be understood as a condition situated at one end of a continuum of normal feminine behaviour. Using Luce Irigaray's analysis of the feminine as excluded, as repressed in patriarchal society, as the "other" in legal discourse predicated upon the male subject, Jo Bridgeman argues that whilst the feminine is repressed and while woman is without an identity in patriarchal society, she has no voice; as a consequence, the anorexic woman seeks to express herself through her body, taking to the extreme society's ideals of femininity. An outline of the rights which Luce Irigaray argues must be enacted to ensure respect for sexual difference and to enable women to create the conditions in which we can accede to identity suggests that Luce Irigaray's work may be illuminating in the many instances in which the law engages with the female body.

In the chapters by Anne Morris and Susan Nott, Susan Millns, Sally Sheldon and Kirsty Keywood, different aspects of women's reproductive lives are explored which serve to show how it is vital for feminist campaigns to avoid universalisation and to respect the very real differences in the lives of women. Anne Morris and Susan Nott in "The Law's Engagement with Pregnancy" explore the treatment which women encounter at the hands of law during pregnancy. "Pregnant Woman", they argue, is treated differently from "non-pregnant humanity". Assumptions about her "difference" are used to her detriment so that she is perceived as two persons rather than one and her freedoms are curtailed in the interests of the foetus. In this chapter Anne Morris and Susan Nott explore the effects which the potential of women to become pregnant and actual pregnancy have in both the private and the public sphere. The concept of foetal personhood and the recognition of competing claims are examined, notably in the context of the medical treatment which Pregnant Woman receives. It is argued that pregnancy is seen as conflict rather than integration and in this conflict law represents the voice of the foetus. In the public sphere of employment Anne Morris and Susan Nott assess legislation protecting the pregnant worker, noting that little account is taken of her specific situation. In neither the public nor the private sphere is Pregnant Woman permitted to make decisions regarding the health and safety of herself and her foetus.

In the following chapter Susan Millns considers the position of women who seek access to new reproductive technologies in their efforts to achieve a pregnancy. She considers the legal construction of women who are deemed suitable recipients of these technologies, and the control which the medical profession exercises over the decision to grant access to the technologies. Susan Millns argues that the ideology underpinning access is one which seeks to reconstruct the heterosexual family in that those considered suitable for treatment are those women who fit within a model of heterosexual family life. Without greater self-determination in reproductive choices she suggests that a reproductive revolution in which autonomous motherhood is guaranteed cannot be realised. The power of the medical profession is further explored by Sally Sheldon who investigates the way in which the debate on abortion has been formulated to facilitate medical control of the practice. Through an analysis of the development of legislation governing abortion it is argued that the current perception of abortion as a medical issue is problematic because it operates to exclude accounts of others, most particularly those of women seeking an abortion, accounts which are perceived as having no place within the medical framework.

Against the anorexic woman, the pregnant woman, the childless woman and the aborting woman appears the doctor determining and articulating her fate. These examples serve to highlight how women are denied a voice when it is vital they be heard. The silencing of the female voice is nowhere more apparent than in the case of the woman with learning disabilities. Kirsty Keywood explains in "Sterilising the Woman with Learning Difficulties - In her Best Interests?", that because of their life-circumstances, some women are simply never expected to be mothers. She suggests that the law on the sterilisation of women with learning difficulties currently privileges paternalism at the expense of women's autonomy and that in striking this balance many wider social, moral and political questions have been ignored. Kirsty Keywood argues that learning difficulties and the sexuality of women are social constructs, and that the medical profession and the judiciary perpetuate myths about the sexuality of women with learning difficulties so that sterilisation is justified on the grounds of intellectual subnormality and gender. Kirsty Keywood, in asking whether it can ever be justifiable to sterilise women with learning difficulties, argues that this question demands consideration of areas which extend beyond the law to wider social and political dimensions, but that ultimately resolution of the issue should be based upon the obtaining of consent from the woman in question.

The issue of consent is raised by Lois Bibbings in "Female Circumcision: Mutilation or Modification?". Situating the practices which are variably described as female circumcision not only within a cultural context but also within the context of other body modification techniques she explores the arguments which have been made to deplore the practices referred to. Lois Bibbings argues that a frequent feminist response to the practices of female circumcision is to perceive them as violence inflicted upon women and as an extreme example of patriarchal oppression. She suggests that by viewing the practices within the context of other forms of body modification an alternative feminist analysis is possible.

The infliction of abuse upon the female body is explored in the subsequent two chapters on responses to violence against women in the private sphere. Marie Fox examines the response of the legal system to women who react against such violence by killing their abusive partner. Through a discussion of the merits or otherwise of resorting to the defences of provocation, diminished responsibility and self-defence, Marie Fox outlines broader strategies to provide an analysis which goes beyond the limiting confines of these defences and the question of law reform. She argues that only by looking at the particularity of the experiences of the battered woman who kills her abuser and by shifting the focus to the abuser can justice ever be achieved for battered women. Christina Lyon in the following chapter examines the practical response to violence against women from the perspective of her experiences working with a Domestic Violence Forum. She outlines the reasons for the City Council's establishment of the Forum and describes the efforts of the working groups making up the Forum and their various responses to the issues raised by violence against women in the private sphere.

A further aspect of the engagement of the criminal justice system with the female body is discussed by Susan Moody in the context of sexual assault. She analyses the constructions of women which are called into play at the sentencing stage of sexual assault trials. Through an examination of recent sexual assault cases in Scotland and the sentences passed on the perpetrators Susan Moody pieces together legal perceptions of women, be they the victims, spouses, or acquaintances of the man committing sexual assault. Together with the preceding chapters on domestic violence this chapter emphasises the need to ensure that women's voices are heard as they articulate their experiences and describe the violence perpetrated upon their bodies. Only by hearing the accounts of such women can the context of the violence and the woman's response to it be understood.

Finally Fiona Beveridge and Siobhan Mullally discuss the account taken of women's experience within the framework of international human rights law. Through an examination of the claims made to gender neutrality, they examine the difficulties of articulating the harms done to women and the consequent marginalisation of women's human rights in the public sphere of international law. The possibilities of a "right to bodily integrity" are explored as a strategy for resolving the problems identified when international law is called upon to deal with issues relating to the female body.

Each chapter in this book, by investigating legal and non-legal strategies to the various instances of law's interaction with the female body, seeks to add our own voices to debates on feminist politics of law. To the extent that the chapters reveal the way in which the Woman of Legal Discourse[4] is a singular construct, it is apparent that a multiplicity of voices is called for in order to articulate the diverse experiences of women and to acknowledge the different realities of our lives. It is evident that, whilst on one level law engages with women in the regulation of our bodies, on another level our experiences are not acknowledged by the legal system and the concrete realities of our lives are not addressed. It is hoped that the different strategies explored in this book may go some way towards increasing not only our visibility but also our audibility within the legal system.

NOTES

1. S.Bordo, *Unbearable Weight: Feminism, Western Culture and the Body* (1993) at p.21.
2. See, for example, N.Naffine, *Law and the Sexes: Explorations in Feminist Jurisprudence* (1990).
3. See generally C.Smart, *Feminism and the Power of Law* (1989). These concerns operate at two levels. First, on a general level should feminists engage with law to achieve societal reform? Whilst Smart is sceptical about the possibilities of using law to bring about social

change, Catharine MacKinnon, for example, has explicitly used law as a tool in her attempts to eradicate pornography and sexual harassment (see C.MacKinnon, *Feminism Unmodified: Discourses on Life and Law* (1987)). A second and very much linked question concerns the confidence women may have in the effectiveness of the legal system in dealing with their complaints. A paradigmatic example of this is the area of sexual offences. For example, for an analysis of the rape trial, often characterised as a further violation of the rape victim, see J.Temkin, *Rape and the Legal Process* (1987) and for an analysis of the female as "other" in `the legal discourse of sexual offences see S.Duncan, "'Disrupting the Surface of Order and Innocence': Towards a Theory of Sexuality and the Law" (1994) 2 *Feminist Legal Studies* 3.

4.   The construction of the "Woman of Legal Discourse" is explored by C.Smart in "The Woman of Legal Discourse" (1992) 1 *Social and Legal Studies* 29.

1 Body Politics and Rights

ELIZABETH KINGDOM

INTRODUCTION

With justification, feminists regularly express grave concern over horrifying and disturbing examples of the apparent collusion of medicine and law in imposing new forms of intervention in women's medical decisions. Similar concern is expressed at the continuing threats to progressive legislation, such as attempts to undermine *Roe v. Wade* in the United States,[1] a restrictive interpretation of the Midwives Act 1951,[2] and unabated attempts to undermine the Abortion Act 1967 in the UK.[3]

Janet Gallagher collects several such examples under her critique of the concept of foetal rights:

> The claim has been made, for example, that if doctors judge that an unborn child is seriously at risk, a pregnant woman may be forcibly subjected to a Caesarian section despite her explicit refusal; that government restraints may be placed on a pregnant woman's physical activities and lifestyle; that mothers can be held liable in tort for injuries to children occasioned by their 'prenatal negligence'; and that terminally ill women should be excluded from the protection of 'living will' statutes.[4]

To this catalogue Gallagher adds cases concerning coerced organ donation and searches involving bodily intrusion.

There are other issues to include in the catalogue. Dorothy Roberts documents the abuse of "crack Black mothers" who suffer disproportionately from the State's failure to provide drug treatment and pre-natal care for pregnant women.[5] Noel Whitty analyses the legal regulation of abortion in Ireland, culminating in the infamous case in which a young woman's right to life was pitched against a foetus' right to life, the conflict being resolved initially by refusing the young woman the right to travel out of the Irish jurisdiction to terminate her pregnancy.[6] Laurie Nsiah-Jefferson documents the negative experiences of poor women and women of colour concerning reproductive choice, in particular mass programmes for contraceptive injections of Depo-Provera, sterilisation abuse, and coercive birthing practices, such as forced intrauterine transfusions.[7] Lastly, though not to exhaust the catalogue, Patricia Williams records that:

> recently, in Massachusetts, a woman who suffered a miscarriage in a drunk-driving accident was charged with vehicular homicide when the fetus was delivered stillborn.[8]

This catalogue of unwelcome interventions should not be taken to mean that feminist body politics is concerned exclusively with the points at which law and medicine coincide in their treatments of women. Clearly, feminist body politics need not be restricted in this way. It also includes assault, rape, domestic violence, trespass against the person, abduction and kidnap, habeas corpus, and health and safety legislation.[9] Equally, it is salutary to note that feminist body politics in law is not exclusively about interventions and intrusions. Dorie Klein and June Cress note:

> the *lack* of criminal law to deal with activities most harmful to women: production of unsafe birth control devices, profitable medical experimentation, industrial pollution, military violence, and economic injustice.[10]

Accordingly, in this chapter feminist body politics in law is not exhausted by a critique of the coincidence of unwelcome legal and medical interventions. It extends to other debates, such as the potential for feminist politics of written constitutions, in which the deployment of rights discourse is at issue.

As with all politics of resistance, the first recourse of feminist body politics has typically been to formulate feminist politics in terms of rights, such as a woman's right to choose, the right to self-determination, and the right to bodily integrity. But there is an extensive feminist literature on how rights discourse has operated in law and on the limitations of that strategy, particularly where it has been based on what I shall refer to as "right over body". This dissatisfaction has been variously theorised, and feminists are not united in their conclusions. This chapter is an overview of key arguments and an assessment of some of the most promising directions for what I shall refer to as "bodyright strategy".

In section one, *Right over Body*, I examine key theorisations of rights which have formed the basis of feminist critiques of rights discourse. The title refers to the theorisation of rights discourse in connection with bodies according to which legal subjects are defined as the possessors of rights over their own bodies. Feminists have argued that this sort of theorisation is gendered, in the sense that women do not enjoy that right in the same way as men. Further, they see an affinity between such theorisations of right over body and the way in which this type of rights discourse can obscure economic and social inequalities between men and women and consequently legitimate them, virtually by inattention. Other feminists, however, have reservations about the easy acceptance of these critiques, since they would appear to preserve a concept of legal power which is not conducive to the development of feminist strategies.

Section two, *Bodyright Strategy*, begins with an assessment of the potential for feminist politics and strategy in law of a different analysis of power. This is the concept of "bio-politics" found in the work of Foucault. Crucial for feminists is the question of whether Foucault's emphasis on the body as the target for the exercise of power relations undermines the possibilities of active resistance. One persuasive argument is that the successful deployment of Foucault's analysis of power may involve an emphasis on the concept of the self which, far from undermining the use of rights discourse, makes it difficult to distinguish between campaigns in terms of Foucauldian resistance and campaigns presented in the discourse of the legal subject possessed of rights.[11] This argument reopens the possibility of what I call "bodyright strategy", that is the calculation of the strategic use of or avoidance of rights discourse for feminist body politics. Here I review the circumstances under which, despite feminists' reservations about rights discourse, in particular "right over body", they may deem it strategic to present feminist body politics in law in terms of rights.

It is sensible at this point to guard against two misinterpretations of the term "bodyright strategy". First, "bodyright" should not be understood as assuming or proposing a category of law which defines rights over bodies. Bodyright here is not analogous, then, with copyright as a category of law dealing with rights restricting reproduction of original works. Secondly, bodyright is to be contrasted with the concept of right over body as used in the previous section. Bodyright makes no *presumption* of a legal subject possessing a right over its body. Equally, the term is used without prejudice as to whether feminists should conduct body politics in law in terms of any type of rights discourse. Rather, the term "bodyright strategy" is a convenient way of bringing together debates on the use or repudiation of rights discourse as a strategy for those areas of feminist politics which can be loosely designated "body politics of law".

This review of feminist debates concerning right over body and bodyright strategy is not a retrospective analysis. The debates are recent and unresolved. My conclusion is that the debates are not capable of resolution for immediate feminist body politics, particularly where feminist body politics in law involves the assessment of bodyright strategy beyond the immediate context of UK political circumstances. This conclusion offers neither intellectual nor political reassurance that bodyright strategy can be worked out according to preconceived principles or analyses.

RIGHT OVER BODY

Alarmed by what would appear to be increasing opportunities for the abuse of women afforded by new reproductive technology, feminists have sought to resist them through the assertion of women's rights, such as a woman's right to choose, the right to control one's own body, or the right to bodily integrity. Yet there is a voluminous progressive and feminist literature, in the UK, the US, Canada and Australia which is critical of this strategy.[12] In this section, I review some of the ways in which these critiques have been theorised.

A useful starting point is the proposition that rights discourse forms part of the broad Enlightenment political discourse in which freedom and power are properties of the human individual. Here the human individual is typically conceptualised in Cartesian terms as a duality of soul/consciousness/mind and body, and it is the mind which exercises rationality and autonomy and which controls the body. Rights are typically seen as inhering in the mental, or ideal, part of this autonomous human individual. Anthony Carty describes the Enlightenment project in terms of:

> the virtues of clarity and lucidity which were to have made possible the foundation of society upon natural reason [and] the self-evident rights of man.[13]

Similarly, C.B. Macpherson identifies these concepts of freedom and rights in the political individualism of the Levellers. He documents their insistence on the derivation of civil and political rights from natural right and on the fundamental postulate that "every man is naturally the proprietor of his own person", that "natural right is derived from property in one's own person".[14] He explains that for the Levellers, property is characterised as:

> property *in* a thing, meaning a right to use, enjoy, exclude others from, or dispose of, that thing. Thus they could speak of a property in land, in estate, in right to trade, in the franchise, or in one's own person.[15]

The radical nature of the rights discourse of the Levellers and of the Enlightenment is no warrant, of course, for continuing to use rights discourse in the form of right over body. Bernard Edelman has shown how contemporary legal texts operate with the concept of man's self-possession, with the concept of the free legal subject. For the law, man's freedom is derived from his ownership of his body. Man's disposal of his body and of the product of his labour is confirmation of that freedom. In this way, the wage contract, in which man disposes of himself and of what he produces, is confirmation of man's freedom. Legal subjects enter law as individuals, the sale of whose labour power is the object of a contract freely entered into, irrespective of their social and economic circumstances and regardless of the material effects of the contract. So, Edelman argues, the law identifies the legal subject as an agent appropriate for commodity circulation and in this way provides the conditions necessary for exploitation in the sphere of production. It follows that rights which are the possession of this legal subject are similarly constructed within the law without reference to prevailing social and economic possibilities and practices of exploitation.[16]

Each component of these theorisations - the Cartesian concept of the human individual, the law's construction of the legal subject with right (and by implication control) over body, and the law's creation of the conditions of exploitation - has been subjected to a feminist critique, culminating in a devastating attack on right over body for purposes of bodyright strategy.

First, feminists have claimed that the Cartesian dualism of mind/body is gendered. Liz Stanley and Sue Wise argue that the epistemological oppositions of science/nature; reason/emotion; objectivity/subjectivity are mapped on to the binary categories of mind/body, and that all these oppositions are gendered according to masculinity/femininity.[17] Judith Butler, too, shows that in the Western philosophical tradition from Plato through Descartes and Husserl to Sartre:

> the ontological distinction between soul (consciousness, mind) and body invariably supports relations of political and psychic subordination and hierarchy.[18]

For Butler, the distinction corresponds to masculine disembodiment and feminine corporeality and supports the domination of women by men.

Secondly, feminists have argued that the law's construction of the legal subject as possessing the right to dispose of its body and in terms of self-possession, or ownership of its body, is gendered. A familiar example here is the work of Catharine MacKinnon, proposing that the law and the rights it confers are male.[19] In a similarly essentialist analysis, Jocelyn Scutt points to the differential experiences of men and women in their capacity to enjoy their status as legal subjects in control of their bodies. In her analysis of the patriarchal principles operating in the legal and medical profession, Scutt alerts feminists to the prevalence of rights of "ownership" and "property" in debates on genetic and reproductive engineering, rights which are "bolstered within the legal system, through the application of copyright, patents and commercial laws".[20] Scutt is particularly incensed at the way women's participation in IVF programmes is the result of male coercion, deploying ideologies of wifeliness and motherhood, whilst the response of the legal and medical profession to a woman's failure to conceive is that doctors are absolved from responsibility, since "the woman was a fully, freely consenting party to the treatment meted out".[21]

In a less essentialist way, Frances Olsen argues that "rights theory conceptualises a society composed of self-interested individuals whose conflicting interests are mediated by the state". She analyses statutory rape laws to claim that they treat women's sexuality as a thing, as an object to be guarded, that the law does not construct women as legal subjects on a par with men, and that it treats women's and men's bodies differently.

> By refusing to grant women autonomy and by protecting them in ways that men are not protected, the state treats women's bodies - and therefore women themselves - as objects. Men are treated differently. Their bodies are regarded as part of them, subject to their free control.[22]

It is a short step from the argument that right over body is gendered to the argument that the very language of rights is an instrument of law's creation of the conditions of exploitation. Just as, for Edelman, the social and economic conditions of the parties to the wage contract are irrelevant to the determination of its validity,[23] so feminists have argued that preoccupation with rights, and in particular, with conflicts between rights in the context of abortion politics, facilitates the suppression of wider economic and social issues, such as the availability of contraceptive education.[24] Similarly, Dorothy Roberts has shown that while *Roe v. Wade* would appear to give all women the formal right to abortion it is an empty right for poor women and women of colour. Roberts links the "negative right to privacy", that is, the woman's right not to experience State intervention (the right on which the decision in *Roe v. Wade* turned) to racial inequality, since by being "left alone" women of colour are removed from State support.[25]

All these arguments are persuasive, and they point to avoidance of any slogan or strategy which is formulated in terms of right over body, thereby obscuring economic and social inequalities between men and women. But, for a number of reasons, feminists should be wary of accepting these arguments without qualification.

First, feminists recognise that the use of right over body is a double-edged sword. On the one hand, its use brings feminist politics into the arena of legitimate politics, at the risk of "defeminising" the issues at stake. For example, claiming the right to reproduce is likely, in the present climate of legal and medical opinion on the desired form of family life, to be transformed into a general human right to reproduce which men too can claim. That general right can then be interpreted as a husband's right to reproduce and a wife's duty to do so.[26]

But those feminists who have reservations about the unwelcome legitimising effects of right over body recognise that there may be political contexts in which it is necessary to "play the game", to present campaigns in terms of right over body, to deploy the terms which law recognises. This may well involve recourse to the concept of the officially ungendered (however arguably gendered) legal subject. As we shall see, the gendered legal subject and her right over *her* body still make an appearance in feminist bodyright strategy.

At the same time, feminists should be wary of the demarcation of law, as'the field in which the subject is the bearer of rights, from broader economic and social institutions and practices. This demarcation risks preserving the concept of law as the exclusive arena in which rights disputes are to be resolved and as the proper arena for the resolution of feminist politics. This in turn preserves a concept of legal power which some feminists have found unsatisfactory for purposes of feminist legal politics and strategy.[27] They have accordingly turned to a different type of analysis of power, legal and otherwise, which they find more conducive to the development of feminist strategy in the context of law. The following section is, first, an account of why feminists have been impressed with Michel Foucault's analysis of power and bio-politics and, secondly, of how their perception of its limitations for purposes of feminist strategy in law reopens the question of the use of rights discourse, including right over body, for body politics.

BODYRIGHT STRATEGY

Foucault's concept of bio-politics refers to the specific configuration of power relations which have developed over the last two centuries and whose domain are the phenomena of life, whether through the macro policies of populations or through the micro "anatomo-politics of the body". The techniques and tactics of power which focus on the body, such as the deployment of knowledges of sexuality, child-rearing, and hygiene, treat it as a living organism to be constructed through the operation of norms. On this analysis, the exercise of power is no longer predicated on the concept of the legal subject and is no longer identified with the imposition of law.[28] Further, the exercise of power in relation to the body is no longer equivalent to simple repression and control; the body is produced by the operation of diffuse and frequently competing disciplinary techniques. Lois McNay cites the nineteenth century proliferation of discourses pronouncing truths on deviant sexualities which legitimated normal heterosexuality but which created a counter-discourse pronouncing truths on homosexuality as natural.[29]

For Foucault, it is the productive nature of diffuse discourses - to produce and reinforce power and also to make it transparent and opposable - that underlines the indistinct nature of repression and resistance. The concept of resistance is no longer predicated on the legal subject as a discrete entity external to social phenomena, as possessing the extra-social right to accept or refuse attention to its body, and as striving for freedom. Resistance becomes the critique of the claimed truths of disciplinary techniques, just at the point where the discourses seek to produce effects on the body. In this way, the possibility of resistance is built into the very operation of power.

Foucault's reconceptualisation of power and the body is both problematic and attractive for feminists. As Vikki Bell notes, it dispenses with precisely the concept of "juridico-discursive power" which has been adopted by feminists in order to explain the persistent dominance of men's possession of power over women.[30] In the context of bodyright strategy, Foucault's analysis would call into question any appeal to the concept of a legal subject's extra-discursive right to control its body. On the other hand, Foucault's coupling of power and resistance is attractive for its usefulness both in undermining the dichotomy between abstention from and engagement with the law as a feminist strategy and in providing a theorisation of resistance conducive to bodyright strategy.

A striking application of Foucault's analysis of power is Alison Young's deconstruction of the media representations of women's political protests as exemplified by coverage of the women's peace camp at Greenham Common. She acknowledges her debt to Foucault's account of the body as the object of operation of technologies of power and control, but at the same time being the site of potential strategies for resistance.[31]

> Through the parody and implosion of commonplace notions of the body and through the discovery of new or different significations of bodily relations and representations, the Greenham women 'live out' the tension Foucault noted within the place of the body; constructed and manipulated under the strategies of agencies such as the police or the press, yet working from the same place to invert, displace and rewrite our understanding of the female body in contemporary culture.[32]

Young documents the Greenham women's challenge to natural, justifiable, or reasonable sex roles for women, for example by using symbols of motherhood to convert the perimeter fence into a gallery of creative work by women. Of particular interest for this chapter is Young's account of how the women, charged with breach of the peace, subverted court procedures, for example by giving speeches on the evils of the arms race. They also resisted being defined as the objects of law's repression and control by engaging with the law as litigants, for example by bringing a lawsuit against the United States government for its failure to uphold its obligations under the Genocide Act 1969. Young records how, as legal subjects, the Greenham women were attempting the revalorisation of the body within political dissent, and she acknowledges their considerable achievements, such as exploiting the confusion of the criminal justice system over what charges to bring and what sentences to impose. She concludes, however, that there is a limit to how far law can accommodate protest. The Greenham women's achievements have been "circumscribed by the ineluctable form [such as questioning title to land] and contours of the law which prevent it from supporting their demands."[33]

In emphasising the active nature of resistance, Young's work can be seen as rectifying what some feminists identify as a serious weakness in Foucault for feminist politics. For example, McNay argues that, despite his claim that power and resistance are inseparable, Foucault tends to analyse the body as docile, the passive recipient of disciplinary techniques.[34] For McNay, this tendency to reduce individuals to docile bodies is unsatisfactory, because it fails to explain how individuals can act as autonomous agents, because it fails to explain how women have been able to act as autonomous individuals, and because it underestimates the importance of freedoms which women have won through appeals to law and through the use of rights discourse.[35]

McNay allows that Foucault's emphasis on the docility of bodies is to some extent corrected by his concept of the self as developed in his final, and neglected, works *The Use of Pleasure* and *The Care of the Self*. Here Foucault complements his study of disciplinary techniques with a study of "technologies of subjectification". These are the practices and techniques through which individuals can be active in shaping their own identities. An example is the capacity, however limited by a cultural reality laden with sanctions, taboos and restrictions, to dislocate gender norms, and, through the rejection of the static model of sexual difference consonant with the concept of the docile body, to choose gender identity.[36]

Even if feminists accept this modification, however, problems of bodyright strategy are far from resolved. McNay herself argues that Foucault's work is not free of "cryptonormativism", in the sense that, although he attacks the notion of rights, he nonetheless assumes that his audience is familiar with the ideals of autonomy, dignity and human rights. McNay illustrates this argument by reference to Foucault's work on freedom of speech. On the one hand, Foucault argues that the liberal discourse of rights must be abandoned, since it has the ideological function of obscuring disciplinary domination; rights discourse must be replaced with the notion of free speech as a practice, in the sense of being a political obligation to question the claimed truths of those in authority. On the other hand, McNay suggests that:

> when Foucault exhorts individuals to challenge governments in the name of free speech, it is difficult to see how his definition of free speech as a practice substantially differs from the liberal notion of free speech defined as a right. The difference appears to be rhetorical rather than substantive.[37]

If feminists find McNay's argument persuasive, it means that in their formulation of bodyright strategy they cannot, after all, dismiss the possibility of employing rights discourse, even that form of rights discourse predicated on right over body. As I have argued elsewhere, there is no automatic solution to the question of whether to employ rights discourse.[38]   Whatever their reservations about rights discourse, feminists may well reach the decision that their campaigns have to be presented in terms of rights discourse.

There are at least three strategic reasons which provide grounds for deciding to adopt rights discourse. The first, which I call the ineluctability of rights discourse, is where the legal-political context in question is so firmly defined in terms of rights discourse that for any intervention to be successful it too must be cast in those terms. The second, which I call the re-assertion of rights discourse, is where the limitations of rights discourse are judged to be less important than its political effectiveness. The third, which I call the conversion strategy, is where feminists can devise ways to convert conventionally conceived "women's rights" into rights which genuinely improve women's position.

1. The ineluctability of rights discourse
The absence in the UK of a formal bill of rights and a written constitution presents UK feminists with different possibilities of involvement in legal-political issues from those experienced by feminists in Canada and in the US. The existence of the Canadian Charter of Rights and Freedoms and of the American Constitution can be seen as requiring feminist interventions in legal politics at the level of the State to formulate their strategies in terms of the prevailing rights discourse. As we shall see, feminists are by no means agreed on the progressive nature of this type of rights discourse.   Similarly, Hilary Charlesworth, noting this disagreement, observes that in Australia "the politics of federalism and legalism have produced a culture wary of rights discourse."[39]

It is arguable, then, that the experiences of feminists involved in American and Canadian constitutional politics cannot easily be translated to the UK. On the other hand, UK feminists cannot afford to postpone assessment of the best ways to intervene in legal politics of this sort. Debates on the desirability of a UK bill of rights are intensifying, as are demands for the incorporation of the European Convention on Human Rights into British Law. More generally, at a time when the balance of power between European Community law and that of its Member States is far from static, the potential of the European Social Charter could become more of a feminist issue if the UK government is forced into greater European involvement, or indeed seeks it out.

In this respect, Anne Hilbert's work is important for feminists. She documents how, in the debates surrounding access to abortion procedures, the package of rights guaranteed under the 1937 Irish Constitution is not the same package of rights as those protected by the European Court of Justice. The Irish judiciary sought to analyse the content and the priority of the rights, such as the competing right to life of the mother and the foetus, to be protected under the Constitution: the "substantive rights" model. The European Court of Justice, in contrast, did not inquire into the moral, philosophical and ethical content of the substantive right to abortion but identified nonpersonal economic rights, such as the right to travel to another Member State to receive an abortion and the right to information about abortion: the "affecting commerce" model. As a result of the 1992 Irish referendum on abortion, the package of rights protected by the substantive rights model has recently, though not necessarily permanently, been displaced by the package of rights protected by the affecting commerce model.[40]

Hilbert's analysis should have the effect of bringing to the attention of UK feminists the pitfalls and the potential of rights discourse in contexts where the parameters of State legal-politics are defined by a written constitution or bill of rights. Compulsory reading will also include the continuing disagreements occasioned by the critique of rights discourse developed by the Critical Legal Studies movement, to which I now turn.

2. The re-assertion of rights discourse

From the early 1980s, representatives of the Critical Legal Studies movement (henceforth CLS) have sustained a critique of rights discourse which is conveniently summarised into four main points by Mark Tushnet:

> (i) Once one identifies what counts as a right in a specific setting, it invariably turns out that the right is unstable; significant but relatively small changes in the social setting can make it difficult to sustain the claim that a right remains implicated. (ii) The claim that a right is implicated in some settings produces no determinate consequences. (iii) The concept of rights falsely converts into an empty abstraction (reifies) real experiences that we ought to value for their own sake. (iv) The use of rights in contemporary discourse impedes advances by progressive social forces.[41]

One might illustrate these points with the previously mentioned debate over access to abortion procedures in Ireland. Tushnet could argue that the mother's right of self-determination under the Irish Constitution was destabilised in *Attorney General v. X*[42] by public reaction to the plight of a fourteen year-old pregnant girl, the victim of rape, who was refused the right to travel to Britain for an abortion through the invocation of the right to life of the unborn. Further, the clash of claimed rights produced consequences which, given the scope for reinterpretation of relations between decisions of the European Court of Justice and the legislation of Member States, are clearly indeterminate. Tushnet could then point to the way in which the clash of rights and interpretations effectively relegated the experience of the pregnant girl, and that of all women whose pregnancy is unwanted, to the sidelines of the legal-political wrangle. Finally, the complexity of those rights wrangles becomes dominated by the competing interests of powerful institutions, such as the European Union and the Catholic Church, thereby undermining the attempts of progressive forces to improve women's situation in relation to access both to abortion procedures and to information about abortion. It is on this last point, however, that Tushnet's critique of rights discourse has attracted criticism. The criticism levelled against CLS work is that, far from impeding progressive politics, rights discourse is an essential strategy of particular importance both for feminist politics in general and for feminist bodyright strategy as it involves poor women and women of colour.[43]

At the general level of minority critiques of the CLS position on rights discourse, Patricia Williams argues against the CLS tendency to abandon rights discourse in favour of the discourse of needs. She cites the "restyling" of arguments about rights to shelter for the homeless into arguments about the needs of the homeless. This restyling overlooks both the fact that blacks have been campaigning, with dismal failure, in terms of needs for generations and the fact that there is a "long history of legislation against the self-described needs of black people".[44]

Williams argues that this restyling of arguments is inadequate to the situation of those minorities who have never had rights; blacks do not need to deconstruct rights which they have never had.

> The argument that rights are disutile, even harmful, trivialises this aspect of black experience specifically, as well as that of any person or group whose vulnerability has been truly protected by rights.[45]

For Williams, this black experience cannot be assimilated to Marxist analyses of the exploitation of the proletariat by the bourgeoisie. Its basis is in racism, conscious or not. On this analysis, the location of the origin of rights as emanating from the history of slavery and its laws or as the product of bourgeois society has no political meaning for black people, since they have never had the rights which such analyses identify. Accordingly, Williams contrasts the symbolic importance of rights assertion with what she identifies as a failure of rights commitment on the part of those who are able to confer rights.

> From this perspective, the problem with rights discourse is not that the discourse itself is constricting but that it exists in a constricted referential universe.[46]

On this argument, a vital weakness of the CLS position is that it neglects the motivational power of rights discourse.

> For the historically disempowered, the conferring of rights is symbolic of all the
> denied aspects of their humanity: rights imply a respect that places one in the
> referential range of self and others, that elevates one's status from human body to
> social being.[47]

In the light of previous discussion about predication of rights on the abstract juridic
subject, it is worth noting that Williams sees the conferment of rights not as
predicated on the Enlightenment and post-Enlightenment separation of mind and
body, with the concomitant right over body. Rather she sees the conferment of
legal rights as the transformation of mere body into social being. Accordingly,
although she does not give practical advice on how to achieve the expansion,
Williams argues for an expanded concept of privacy and property, so that:

> privacy is turned from exclusion based on self-regard into regard for another's
> fragile, mysterious autonomy; and so that property regains its ancient connotation
> of being a reflection of the universal self. The task is to expand private property
> rights into a conception of civil rights, into the right to expect civility from
> others.[48]

Elizabeth Schneider recognises the force of Williams' type of position, but is more
sympathetic to the CLS arguments on the limitations of rights discourse. She
proposes an analysis of the relation between rights and legal argument which she
characterises as dialectical. For Schneider, it is important to have "a view that
allows us to acknowledge both the universal, affirming, expressive, and creative
aspects of rights claims and at the same time, maintain a critical impulse toward
rights".[49] She is emphatic on the importance of the sheer experience of rights
assertion for feminism. Her point is that, without the assertion of women's rights,
the women's movement has no position from which to evaluate the advantages and
limitations of rights discourse.

Schneider claims that this approach is represented by the outcome of *State v.
Wanrow*.[50] Here a black woman, with a cast on her leg and walking with crutches,
killed Wesler, a white man whom she believed to have tried to molest her children.
Initially, Wanrow was convicted, mainly on the strength of the court's instruction to
the jury to apply "the equal force standard", the test requiring that self-defence must
involve only force equal to the force used by the assailant. Wanrow shot Wesler,
who was not armed. The progressive lawyers involved developed a legal argument
for Wanrow's right to equal trial by challenging sex-bias in the law of self-defence.
On appeal, the Supreme Court reversed the conviction, challenging the court's
failure to direct the jury to consider the reasonableness of Wanrow's action from *her*
perspective.

Schneider's comment on the case stresses what she sees as the dialectical elements of legal process. On the one hand,

> the political insights into sex-bias in self-defense ... arose out of legal formulation
> and argumentation. But the legal argument concerning the 'right to equal trial'
> grew out of a political analysis of sex discrimination.[51]

The advantage of characterising the outcome of *Wanrow* as the result of a dialectic approach is open to debate. The term "dialectic" suggests a formulaic approach, requiring the initial separation of feminist involvement in legal politics from feminist extra-legal analysis, a separation to be collapsed at a point which, as a case proceeds, is unknown to the parties involved and can be identified only in retrospect. Feminists involved in legal politics do not need to be saddled with an approach which requires them to be vigilant for key points in a dialectical process somehow transcending the actual circumstances of a case or a campaign. They need only to remember that legal outcomes are produced by a variety of conditions, some of which may be formally legal, others emanating from feminist politics, others again a function of the personalities and particular circumstances of the parties involved.

Support for this position can be found in the work of Frances Olsen, Martha Minow and Didi Herman. At first sight, Olsen's work on the dilemma between rights-oriented and non-rights strategies is like Schneider's: a formulaic approach according to which feminists must decide either to use rights discourse or not to do so. In fact, Olsen emphasises the immensely complex ways in which rights discourse can both restrict feminist thinking and support campaigns for important social reforms.[52] Consonant with this observation, Martha Minow argues for using rights discourse as a tool of communal dialogue in which conflict is made audible and unavoidable; she knows the limitations of rights discourse but sees its potential too: "rights rhetoric bears traditional meanings, but it is capable of carrying new meanings."[53]

Didi Herman also recognises this potential. In the context of the emergence of new social movements, she analyses the wins and losses associated with the appeal to rights in the campaigns and struggles for legal equality waged by Canadian lesbians and gays. Her view is that the "lesbian and gay rights problematic" cannot be restricted to an abstract debate about the pros and cons of rights discourse: "[m]ore often than not, rights claims are neither radical rearticulations nor dangerous and diversionary."[54] Herman is correct to expose the artificiality of an all-or-nothing approach to the use of rights discourse, not least since that limited view precludes what I shall now discuss, the conversion strategy.

3. The conversion strategy

In the previously discussed disagreement between the CLS critique of rights and those feminists who press for the use of rights discourse as a strategy for Black politics, Kimberlé Williams Crenshaw acknowledges that gains effected through the deployment of rights rhetoric now make it possible for persisting economic inequalities to be presented in terms of the particular circumstances of an individual or a group. In this way, it becomes more difficult to attribute racial inequality to racism and to establish a broader vision of racial equality.[55] Whilst the political commitment of Crenshaw's argument is not in doubt, feminists can also note that Crenshaw does not provide any concrete proposals for how rights discourse can continue to be a useful strategy. Feminists will surely sympathise with her suggestion that rights discourse should be used in such a way as to minimise the costs and maximise the gains of engagement in a discourse which is inherently legitimating, in the sense that it leaves underlying economic and political inequalities untouched. But feminists will also be looking for definite strategies which they can consider adopting.

In this regard, feminists will find Katherine Culliton's work of considerable interest. She proposes that strategies for strengthening women's right to life and their right to physical integrity might include the interpretation of domestic violence and rape as torture. The effect of this conversion would be to bring these offences under the sway of considerable portions of international law, such as the European Convention on Human Rights.[56]

To back up this proposal, Culliton refers to an important recommendation of CEDAW. This is the Committee on the Elimination of All Forms of Discrimination Against Women, the body set up to monitor the United Nations 1980 Convention for the Elimination of All Forms of Discrimination Against Women. CEDAW recommended that gender-based violence constitute torture. As such, it would be a violation of women's fundamental rights, and any State adopting the Convention could be prosecuted and held responsible even for private acts of domestic violence. Culliton suggests that:

> even women who have not attempted to use the domestic legal system can make a persuasive case that the state is at least partially responsible for their injuries because the state's tolerance of domestic violence creates and perpetuates an environment in which women feel they cannot turn to the legal system for aid.[57]

Culliton is aware of the daunting prospect of using international law for such a case. In the Inter-American System, however, a woman can bring an individual petition before the Inter-American Human Rights Commission and Court. Culliton claims that the Court has a good track record over battered women's petitions, and she points to the advantages of international litigation: cases attract publicity, they have value as precedent across States, they assist recognition of the world-wide epidemic of violence against women, and they bring support for women's rights as "fundamental, non-derogable human rights".[58]

Culliton's proposal is a clear example of the conversion strategy. It shows how critical examination of rights discourse otherwise fixed at the level of indignant rhetoric can produce a reconceptualisation which gives directions for clearly identifiable bodyright strategy, in this case in the context of international law. To formulate a conversion strategy like this is inevitably a complex task, requiring attention to very different types of documents and analyses. The range can be illustrated by the work of Zaim Nedjati, Anne Hilbert, Adrien Katherine Wing, Anne Hellum and Joyce Outshoorn.

First, the conversion strategy demands familiarity with exploitable shifts in rights discourse. Nedjati analyses the changing jurisprudence of the concept and scope of individual human rights in the European Commission.[59] He notes that the Commission is taking a more liberal approach by its willingness to take into account the economic and social conditions of the High Contracting Party involved in the case in question. For example, in a case brought against compulsory sex education in Denmark, the Commission ruled that, given the social development of Denmark, it could reasonably be held that compulsory sex education could help to combat unwanted pregnancies and should not therefore be banned.[60]

Next, the possibilities of international feminist bodyright strategy are also considered by Hilbert. Her work on the Irish abortion debate is a valuable reminder that one type of rights discourse can be supplanted by another and that the appeal to rights has no *a priori* radical *or* reactionary status.[61] The implication here is that, as they develop strategies for feminist politics in law, feminists have to consider in detail how various rights discourses are already operating, and what the chances are of supplementing or replacing anti-feminist rights discourse either with feminist rights discourse or with alternatives to rights discourse. In these respects, feminists will benefit from the work of Wing on Egyptian family law and Hellum's review of feminist bodyright strategies in reproductive technology.

Wing's research shows how the Egyptian Family Law Amendments of 1979 can be treated as a paradigmatic caution on the vicissitudes of rights discourse. The Amendments were passed by the Presidential decree of Anwar Sadat and included a number of progressive rights, such as strengthening a mother's right to custody of minor children, a wife's right to work without spousal permission, and a first wife's right to automatic divorce should the husband take a second wife. Fundamentalists designated these "Jihan's law", after the First Lady of Egypt, Mrs Jihan Sadat, because she had overstepped her proper customary role to influence Sadat and Parliament to make unsuitable laws. In 1985, the Constitutional Court revoked all those rights, except the right to automatic divorce on the husband's second marriage. Wing claims that, because the judiciary would take a conservative line should any such case be brought, the outcome was to retain the law's fundamental bias in favour of polygamy. She suggests that these events are a lesson in the dangers of "tinkering" with law reform to advance women's rights and of failing to take account of culturally based resistance to international rights standards.[62]

As well as demanding familiarity with variations in rights discourse, the conversion strategy is aided by scrutiny of different feminist approaches to bodyright strategy. A useful source is Hellum's work on new reproductive technology, the variety of positions advanced by feminists and the corresponding slogans they have adopted. Her discussion brings to mind the feminist critique of the legal subject as having a right over its body discussed in *Right Over Body*. She cites rights-based positions, such as the demand of the Norwegian Association of Childless Persons that childlessness be seen as a disease entitling women, including lesbian and single women, to statutory rectification. Hellum suggests that this position is not merely optimistic. It underestimates the extent to which reproductive technology treats women's bodies as fertility machines. In contrast, FINRAGE (Feminist International Network Against Reproductive and Genetic Engineering) adopted the slogan "we are our bodies, we are our eggs" to deny the dichotomy between body and soul [sic] and that between fertility and body.[63] These dramatically opposed positions surely make it otiose to observe that unity among feminists over whether to adopt a rights-orientated strategy, over the choice of feminist slogans, indeed over bodyright strategy in general, is not to be expected.

To underline this point, Outshoorn provides an informative description of the different slogans adopted by the women's liberation movement in different countries to express its demand for women to be the moral judges over abortion and to take responsibility for their decision.

> In a country with a strong natural rights tradition, such as the United Kingdom or the United States, abortion was defined as a woman's right. In the Federal Republic of Germany and in the Netherlands the demand was phrased in terms of control over one's body enshrined in the German feminist slogan 'Dein Korper gehort dich' [Your body belongs to you] or the Dutch 'Baas in eigen buik' [Boss of your belly].[64]

As noted previously, despite feminist critiques of the notion of the legal subject and the ease with which law assimilates it into its preferred category of ownership, the feminists whom Outshoorn describes here have clearly decided to play the legal game and deploy the discourse of right over body. As she observes, however, the result has been that the resolution of the opposition between pro-choice and anti-abortion movements is inevitably moved into the parliamentary arena, leading to extended and frequently acrimonious political hostilities.

The foregoing analyses could be used to draw up a preliminary checklist of the different types of inquiry which would have to be made for the development of any specific conversion strategy. What is the jurisprudential tradition informing the jurisdiction which provides the context for bodyright strategy? In what ways have specific bodyright strategies been defeated under that jurisdiction?   Does that jurisdiction favour feminist interventions drafted in terms of right over body? Are campaign slogans expressed in terms of right over body always counter-productive? Are there any alternatives to slogans which are based on right over body?   How have feminist campaigns in comparable jurisdictions progressed? Is it possible to circumvent a jurisdiction and operate in a more favourable jurisprudence? What are the likely obstacles to draft legislation?

   The conversion strategy, as exemplified by Culliton's work, obviously requires a gradual refinement of this checklist, but it is precisely this sort of process that makes the conversion strategy the most promising approach to bodyright strategy. It demands attention to the peculiarities of prevailing legal politics, both in a specific jurisdiction and increasingly in international contexts, but it crucially comprises a research programme for devising draft legislation which would improve the scope for feminist bodyright strategy.

CONCLUSION

The debates reviewed in this chapter are not capable of final resolution. The very notion of bodyright strategy points to the absence of a mechanical bodyright strategy. Feminists are not likely to agree on bodyright strategy in the areas of feminist legal politics discussed here, regardless of whether bodyright strategy has to be developed in the context of single issues, such as abortion in the UK, or whether it has to be developed in the context of constitutional or international law. For UK feminists in particular, new constitutional debates about the introduction of a bill of rights and new questions of how European Community law will affect UK legislation open up uncharted zones of bodyright strategy.   For some time, bodyright strategy will be a contested feature of feminist body politics.

NOTES

1.   *Roe v. Wade* (1973) 410 U.S. 113. See also the Special Double Issue of *Women's Rights Law Reporter* (1989) 11; *Webster v. Reproductive Health Services* for selected amicus briefs on this attempt to restrict or reverse *Roe*.

2.   J.Bridgeman, "Demanding Reproductive Control?" in *Body Politics: Control versus Freedom: the role of feminism in women's personal autonomy*, Feminist Legal Research Unit, The University of Liverpool, Working Paper No.1 (1993) 31.

3. G.Williams, "The Fetus and the 'Right to Life'" (1994) 53 *Cambridge Law Journal* 71.

4. J.Gallagher, "Prenatal Invasions and Interventions: What's Wrong with Fetal Rights?" (1987) 10 *Harvard Women's Law Journal* 9.

5. D.E.Roberts, "Punishing Drug Addicts who Have Babies" (1991) 104 *Harvard Law Review* 1419, and "The Future of Reproductive Choice for Poor Women and Women of Color" (1992) 14 *Women's Rights Law Reporter* 305.

6. N.Whitty, "Law and the Regulation of Reproduction in Ireland" (1993) XLIII *University of Toronto Law Journal* 851.

7. L.Nsiah-Jefferson, "Reproductive Laws, Women of Color and Low Income Women" (1989) 11 *Women's Rights Law Reporter* 15.

8. P.Williams, *The Alchemy of Race and Rights* (1990) at p.183.

9. For example, there is scope for feminist research into the gender body politics of nervous shock (R.Graycar and J.Morgan, *The Hidden Gender of Law* (1990) at pp.177-183); constructions of female and male disability (M.Oliver, *The Politics of Disablement* (1993) at p.72); treatment of prisoners of war (A. Roberts and R. Guelff eds., *Documents on the Laws of War* (1994)); testing for invalidity pensions (Child Poverty Action Group, *Rights Guide to Non-means-tested Benefits* (1994/1995)); and the difference which the weight of female and male body fluid may make in the formula for making charges under the drink driving legislation (N.J.Ley, *Drink Driving Law and Practice* (1993)).

10. D.Klein and J.Kress, "Any Woman's Blues: a Critical Overview of Women, Crime and the Criminal Justice System" in *Crime and Social Justice*, eds. T.Platt and P.Takagi (1981) at p.161.

11. L.McNay, *Foucault and Feminism* (1992) at p.145.

12. For example, H.Charlesworth, "The Australian Reluctance about Rights" (1993) 31 *Osgoode Hall Law Journal* 195; J.Fudge, "The Effect of Entrenching a Bill of Rights upon Political Discourse" (1989) 17 *International Journal of the Sociology of Law* 445; E.Kingdom, *What's Wrong with Rights?: Problems for Feminist Politics of Law* (1991); C.MacKinnon, *Toward a Feminist Theory of the State* (1989).

13. A.Carty, "Introduction: Post-Modern Law" in *Post-Modern Law: Enlightenment, Revolution and the Death of Man*, ed. A.Carty (1990) 1; and see E.Kingdom, *supra*, n.12, at p.51.

14. C.B.Macpherson, *Possessive Individualism* (1962) at pp.137-142.

15. C.B.Macpherson, *ibid.*, at p.143.

16. B.Edelman, *Ownership of the Image: Elements for a Marxist Theory of Law* (1979) at pp.68-87. For an account of Edelman's work, see, P.Hirst and E.Kingdom, "On Edelman's *Ownership of the Image*" (1979/80) 20 *Screen* 135.

17. L.Stanley and S.Wise, *Breaking Out Again* (1993) at pp.194-195.

18. J.Butler, *Gender Trouble* (1990) at p.12.

19. C.MacKinnon, *supra*, n.12.

20. J.Scutt, "Women's Bodies, Patriarchal Principles" in *The Baby Machine*, ed. J.Scutt (1990) 185, at pp.185-186. Feminists will therefore be concerned at the proposal put forward by Judith Jarvis Thomson in *The Realm of Rights* (1990) at pp.205-226, that we possess rights in

respect of our bodies which may be characterised in terms of ownership of the body. Thomson makes no attempt to place such a notion in a social context which would draw attention to the differences in people's capacity to enjoy such a right. For related discussions, see, C.C.Farsides, "Body Ownership" in *Law, Health and Medical Regulation*, eds. S.McVeigh and S.Wheeler (1992) 35, and S.Marshall, "Whose Child is it Anyway?" in *Constituting Families: a Study in Governance*, eds. D.Morgan and G.Douglas (1994) 127.

21.   J.Scutt, *ibid.*, at p.199.

22.   F.Olsen, "Statutory Rape: A Feminist Critique of Rights Analysis" in *Feminist Legal Theory: Readings in Law and Gender*, eds. K.T.Bartlett and R.Kennedy (1991) 305, at pp.306-308.

23.   For a more recent version of this argument see A.Norrie, *Crime, Reason and History* (1993). Norrie also argues that, in the context of sexual crime, law and psychiatry operate with a concept of individual, responsible choice to the exclusion of the social context which creates an offender such as Peter Sutcliffe.

24.   E.Kingdom, *supra*, n.12, in note to chapter 3.

25.   D.E.Roberts, *supra*, n.5, *Harvard Law Review*, 1480.

26.   E.Kingdom, *supra*, n.12, in note to chapter 4.

27.   C.Smart, *Feminism and the Power of Law* (1989) chapter 8.

28.   A.Hussain, "Foucault's History of Sexuality" (1981) 5&6 *m/f* 169.

29.   L.McNay, *supra*, n.11, at p.39.

30.   V.Bell, *Interrogating Incest: Feminism, Foucault and the Law* (1993) at p.39. Bell provides one of the clearest and most reliable accounts of Foucauldian analysis and its potential for feminism.

31.   A.Young, *Femininity in Dissent* (1990). For a rigorous analysis of the tensions between power as productive and power as relational in Foucauldian feminism, see D.Cooper, "Productive, Relational and Everywhere?: Conceptualising Power and Resistance within Foucauldian Feminism" (1994) 28 *Sociology* 435.

32.   A.Young, *ibid.*, at p.15.

33.   A.Young, *ibid.*, at p.29.

34.   L.McNay, *supra*, n.11, at p.3.

35.   L.McNay, *ibid.*, at pp.43-47.

36.   L.McNay, *ibid.*, at pp.70-73.

37.   L.McNay, *ibid.*, at p.145.

38.   E.Kingdom, *supra*, n.12, chapter 8. A similar argument is put forward by Nicola Lacey, not in connection with rights discourse as such, but in terms of the attribution of individual responsibility and blame as an answer to the social practice of rape. Her point is that the discourse of individual responsibility may compound pre-existing social injustice on many occasions, but that, given the prevailing oppressive attitudes, that discourse may have value in enunciating normative judgments about socially acceptable conduct (N.Lacey, "Abstraction in Context", review of A.Norrie (*supra*, n.23) (1994) 14/2 *Oxford Journal of Legal Studies* 255, at pp.265-266).

39.   H.Charlesworth, *supra*, n.12, at p.195.

40. A.M.Hilbert, "The Irish Abortion Debate: Substantive Rights and Affecting Commerce Jurisprudential Models" (1994) 26 *Vanderbilt Journal of Transnational Law* 1117.

41. M.Tushnet, "An Essay on Rights" (1984) 62 *Texas Law Review* 1375, at pp.1382-1384.

42. *Attorney General v. X* [1992] I.L.R.M. 401.

43. A key collection of these debates are the papers presented at the tenth National Critical Legal Studies (CLS) Conference: "Minority Critiques of the Critical Legal Studies Movement" (1987) 22 *Harvard Civil Rights/Civil Liberties Law Review*.

44. P.Williams, *supra*, n.8, at p.151.

45. P.Williams, *ibid.*, at p.152.

46. P.Williams, *ibid.*, at p.159.

47. P.Williams, *ibid.*, at p.153.

48. P.Williams, *ibid.*, at pp.165-166.

49. E.M.Schneider, "The Dialectics of Rights and Politics" in *At the Boundaries of Law: Feminism and Legal Theory*, eds. M.A.Fineman and N.S.Thomadsen (1991) 301, at p.316.

50. *State v. Wanrow* (1977) 88 Wash. 2d. 221, 559 P. 2d 548. E.M.Schneider, *ibid.*, at p.305. Also see M.Fox, "Legal Responses to Battered Women who Kill" in this volume, n.55.

51. E.M.Schneider, *supra*, n.49, at p.307.

52. F.Olsen, *supra*, n.22, at p.305.

53. M.Minow, "Interpreting Rights: an Essay for Robert Cover" (1987) 96 *Harvard Law Journal* 1860.

54. D.Herman, *Rights of Passage: Struggles for Lesbian and Gay Legal Equality* (1994) at p.149.

55. K.W.Crenshaw, "Race, Reform and Retrenchment: Transformation and Legitimation in Antidiscrimination Law" (1988) 101 *Harvard Law Review* 1331.

56. K.M.Culliton, "Finding a Mechanism to Enforce Women's Right to State Protection from Domestic Violence in the Americas" (1993) 34 *Harvard International Law Journal* 507.

57. K.M.Culliton, *ibid.*, at p.522.

58. K.M.Culliton, *ibid.*, at p.561.

59. Z.M.Nedjati, *Human Rights under the European Convention* (1978) at p.241.

60. European Commission of Human Rights, Report of 21 March 1975, in Appl. No.5095/71, at pp.35-40.

61. A.M.Hilbert, *supra*, n.40.

62. A.K.Wing, "Custom, Religion and Rights: the Future Legal Status of Palestinian Women" (1994) 35 *Harvard International Law Journal* 149.

63. A.Hellum, "New Reproductive Technology in an Ecological Perspective" in *Birth Law*, ed. A.Hellum (1993) 125, at p.131.

64. J.Outshoorn, "Abortion Law Reform: A Woman's Right to Choose?" in *Women, Equality and Europe*, eds. M.Buckley and M.Anderson (1988) 204, at p.207.

2   They Gag Women, Don't They?

JO BRIDGEMAN

SPECULATIONS

The purpose of this chapter is to speculate upon the law's engagement with a phenomenon of our time, anorexia.   Anorexia is a condition historically and culturally situated in advanced industrial societies[1] and one disproportionately high amongst women.[2]   In recent years, media coverage of the sufferers of eating disorders and, most particularly, anorexia has provided images of skeletal frames of young women "starving amidst plenty";[3] newspaper stories accompanied by photographs;[4] documentaries;[5] magazine articles providing graphic accounts of calorie-intensive hospital diets compared with the "half a biscuit and glass of water" to which the anorexic limited herself.   The case of *Re W (A Minor) (Medical Treatment: Court's Jurisdiction)*[6] was thoroughly reported in the press.[7]   However much I thought about this case, however many times I discussed it with students, read about different approaches to treating anorexia and the experiences of anorexics, any conclusion I reached about the case was achieved by dismissing a certain amount of ambivalence.[8]   This chapter considers the case of *Re W* and that of *Riverside Mental Health NHS Trust v. Fox*[9] to explore the engagement of the law with the anorexic woman.   I will then draw upon the work of French feminist, Luce Irigaray,[10] to provide a theoretical insight into the issues.

Luce Irigaray is concerned with the project of bringing about social and cultural transformation.   From the origins of her work in psycho-linguistics, psychoanalysis and philosophy, she has, in recent years, become more concerned with the law as a means of changing the existing social order.[11]   She takes up Simone de Beauvoir's idea of woman as "other", developing it further.   Whereas Simone de Beauvoir emphasised access to the world of men (*equality*), Luce Irigaray focuses upon the recognition of two distinct genres (*différence*). De Beauvoir's "other" is, in Irigaray's terms, the "other of the same":

> Irigaray ... is positing an 'other' which would not simply be the 'other of the same' (and so a state to be transcended in the pursuit of 'the same'), but a self-defined woman who would not be satisfied with sameness, but whose otherness and difference would be given social and symbolic representation. Each sex would then be 'other' for the other sex.[12]

Within the particular symbolic system known as patriarchy, the only possible subject-position is masculine, "the only feminine identity available to women is that of 'defective' or 'castrated' men; women are not symbolically self-defined."[13] Luce Irigaray argues that women's identity has yet to be created, the problem is "how to locate the means whereby the female speaking subject has been excluded from philosophy/discourse/culture and to work out the conditions for her accession to speech and social existence."[14] In her later work, she makes it clear that big shifts in society and culture are necessary if woman is to accede to identity and subjectivity. Consequently, her attention has shifted from psychoanalytic theory to other discourses, whilst maintaining her stress on sexual difference:

> The direction her work is taking involves a more direct focus on women's civil status, their position as a sex before the law, the need for *woman*kind to be recognized as a genre distinct from *man*kind, and the importance of translating sexual difference into specific social forms, both to mediate relations between women themselves, and also to lay claim to an existence embodied in distinct and concrete instances as a basis for relationships with and negotiations with the world of men.[15]

Through a brief consideration of the work of Luce Irigaray, in the context of the cases concerning the medical treatment of women with anorexia, I will suggest the value of her work to our understanding of law's engagement with women. Through this understanding we may begin to conceive of the use which may be made of the law as a means of transforming the existing social order.

THE ANOREXIC IN LAW

Increasingly the courts have been asked by the medical profession to determine, prior to carrying out treatment, the lawfulness of the treatment proposed. Particular legal and ethical problems arise for the medical practitioner, which the courts are asked to resolve, in cases where the patient lacks competence (either through mental incapacity or age), or refuses to give her consent.   Given both the increased prevalence of eating disorders in contemporary society and the nature of anorexia which presents particular treatment difficulties, it was inevitable that doctors seeking to impose medical treatment upon an anorexic would seek judicial guidance as to their legal position.

1. W[16]

The first occasion was *Re W.*   In the Court of Appeal, Lord Donaldson MR outlined the series of sad and unfortunate events which had occurred to W during the course of her life.   In 1984, at the age of eight, W was orphaned by the death of her mother from cancer, her father having died three years earlier from a brain tumour.   W, her older sister and younger brother were taken into the care of the local authority because their aunt, who had been named as testamentary guardian, was unable to care for them.   At the home of their first permanent foster parents, W was bullied by an older child of the foster family.   In 1987 she was referred to a family consultation clinic suffering from depression and a nervous tic and, the following year, the family were moved to new foster parents as it was felt that this fostering arrangement could not continue.   In December 1989 the new foster mother had to undergo surgery for breast cancer and, early the following year, W's grandfather, to whom she was greatly attached, died.   Lord Donaldson MR suggested that this was "the last straw" for W, as, in June 1990, "W became obsessive about her schoolwork, wanted to leave school and began losing weight."[17]   Later that year, W was referred to a clinical psychologist at the clinic where she had been treated in 1987.   Her condition did not improve and so, in January 1991, W was admitted to a specialist residential unit for children and adolescents under the care of a consultant psychiatrist.   In March, the clinical psychologist treating W left the area and was not replaced for five months.   Little progress was made; in August she was fed by nasogastric tube and her arms were encased in plaster to prevent her from injuring herself by picking at her skin.   The following month, the consultant psychiatrist had a heart attack and, consequently, W had no contact with him for three months.   It was during this time that her foster parents indicated that if W were discharged they could not continue to offer her a home.

The local authority applied for leave, under s.100(3) of the Children Act 1989, to make an application for the exercise by the court of its inherent jurisdiction.   Initially the local authority sought an order of the court, not to provide W with any particular treatment, but to remove her power to control her treatment because "it was clearly possible that she might at any time decide to refuse consent to some form of treatment ... because one of the symptoms of anorexia nervosa is a desire by the sufferer to 'be in control' and such a refusal would be an obvious way of demonstrating this."[18]   By the time the case came before Thorpe J the local authority had identified an alternative placement at a London hospital and sought leave to move W to this unit or another establishment approved by the Official Solicitor and to give her medical treatment without her consent. W did not refuse all treatment but wished to remain at the residential unit where she was being treated when the hearing of the appeal began.

The legal issue, according to Lord Donaldson MR, was whether, in the light of the provisions of s.8 of the Family Law Reform Act 1969, the common law "authoritatively considered and defined"[19] in *Gillick v. West Norfolk and Wisbech Area Health Authority*[20] and the fact that W was sixteen years old, the court had any jurisdiction to make orders concerning W's medical treatment which conflicted with her expressed wishes. The secondary issue was what treatment should be authorised if the court had the necessary jurisdiction.[21]   In short, the Court of Appeal held that:

> there is ample authority for the proposition that the inherent powers of the court under its parens patriae jurisdiction are theoretically limitless. ... There can therefore be no doubt that it has power to override the refusal of a minor, whether over the age of 16 or under that age but '*Gillick* competent'.[22]

> ... [T]he legal 'flak jacket' ... protects the doctor from claims by the litigious whether he acquires it from his patient who may be a minor over the age of 16, or a '*Gillick* competent' child under that age or from another person having parental responsibilities which include a right to consent to treatment of the minor. Anyone who gives him a flak jacket (that is, consent) may take it back, but the doctor only needs one and so long as he continues to have one he has the legal right to proceed.[23]

Therefore, not only was Lord Donaldson MR in no doubt that the court could give consent to medical treatment in the face of a refusal by a minor, but further that doctors can obtain the consent which protects them from legal liability from anyone with parental authority (such as a parent or the local authority). On the secondary issue, the choice was between leaving W where she was or transferring her to the clinic in London - each of which was supported by a responsible body of medical opinion. Lord Donaldson MR considered "if ever there was a case for respecting the discretionary decision of the judge who has heard the witnesses, including W, this was it."[24]   Taking what Judith Masson describes as an "uncritical approach" to the medical opinions Lord Donaldson MR upheld the decision of Thorpe J that W should be transferred to the London clinic.[25]

2. Carolyn Fox[26]

Carolyn Fox, aged twenty-eight, and suffering from anorexia nervosa, was detained under the Mental Health Act 1983 at the Riverside Mental Health Trust. The hospital made an application for a declaration that, in the circumstances, it would be lawful to force-feed her. If, as was Carolyn Fox, the patient is liable to be detained under the 1983 Act, s.63 provides that the consent of the patient is not required for any *medical treatment*[27] given for the *mental disorder* from which she is suffering. The issue was whether anorexia was a *mental disorder* for which forced-feeding was *medical treatment*. Stuart-White J, in the Family Division, accepted the evidence of Carolyn Fox's consultant that anorexia nervosa was a mental disorder, that forced-feeding was treatment within s.145 of the Mental Health Act as an essential part of nursing and care and that until there was a steady weight gain no other treatment could be offered for her mental condition. His Lordship concluded that forced-feeding, if needed, would be medical treatment for her mental disorder under s.63 of the Mental Health Act 1983. By the time her case reached the Court of Appeal it was concerned with technical issues: she appealed against the refusal of Wall J to discharge the order made by Stuart-White J arguing that the order was, in effect, an interim declaration and that the court "had no power to make an interim declaration". The Court of Appeal accepted her argument and set aside the order expressing relief that "some of the stress" from the appeal had been removed because "happily ... the condition of this patient has not, in fact, required the forcible feeding which had been contemplated and ... she has, in fact, put on some weight." Having said that, Sir Stephen Brown P emphasised that if her condition did not continue to improve it might be necessary for the hospital to consider making a further application.

Thus the scene is set of the anorexic in law. The cases raise many questions, some of which have been explored elsewhere.[28] In many ways, these two cases raise very different questions given that W was a competent minor who refused her consent to a proposed treatment regime whilst Carolyn Fox was compulsorily detained under the Mental Health Act 1983 and, therefore, her consent was not required for any medical treatment administered for her mental disorder.[29] Consent is the legal expression of the principles of Western political philosophy - autonomy, self-determination and personal integrity. Liberal political theory assumes an independent, isolated, autonomous self, and likewise, it is assumed that the individual who engages with the legal system is independent, isolated, and autonomous. Thus a pragmatic approach is taken, case by case, to individual problems. But, as Celia Wells comments:

> [f]reedom, autonomy and self-determination are expressions of a noble aspiration
> that human beings should be able to maximise control over their own lives. None
> of these, however, can be regarded as absolute or unproblematic. Any expression

of autonomy or self-determination which fails to recognize that individual lives are partly determined by social, economic and cultural conditions is deficient.[30]

A conventional, autonomy-respecting approach provides an inadequate response to both *Re W* and *Fox*, failing to take into account the wider issues of culture, gender and medical authority. In this chapter, I propose another reading of these cases - a reading which does not assume that the anorexic woman is an island but which aims to further our understanding of the engagement of the law with a woman suffering from a condition culturally and historically situated in western society of the late twentieth century.

BODY TALK

The first medical description of anorexia as a discrete syndrome was made by W.W. Gull in an address in Oxford in 1868, but it is in the last twenty years that the incidence of anorexia has risen dramatically.[31] For the first six years, W.W. Gull called the syndrome he had identified *hysteric apepsia* only later using the term *anorexia nervosa*. In *Unbearable Weight: Feminism, Western Culture and the Body*, Susan Bordo describes anorexia as the "sister-phenomenon" of hysteria of the second half of the nineteenth century.[32] Our understanding of this culturally and historically specific condition, and our reactions to women who suffer from it, can be furthered by examining its "sister-phenomenon", hysteria.

Susan Bordo explains that the late nineteenth century was, in many ways, very like the present especially in terms of the conflicting demands women were confronting: the opening up of possibilities versus the established hold of old expectations. It was the era of the first major feminist wave but it was an era "when the prevailing ideal of femininity was the delicate, affluent lady, unequipped for anything but the most sheltered domestic life, totally dependent on her prosperous husband, providing a peaceful and comfortable haven for him each day after his return from his labors in the public sphere."[33] Hysteria did cross class and gender lines, also occurring in lower class women, who likewise internalised normative prescriptions of proper womanly behaviour, and in men. But in the mid to late nineteenth century, hysteria was predominantly suffered by middle and upper class women, by women who were expected to do nothing of any social or economic consequence but be the social ornament of their husband.[34] Clearly not all women, and not all middle and upper class women, were hysterics, as anorexia does not affect all women today. However, as Carroll Smith-Rosenberg explains, the parallel between the hysteric's behaviour and stereotypical femininity was too close to be simply a matter of coincidence. An examination of hysteria reveals the complex relationships existing between cultural norms and individual behaviour, between defined disease and behaviour considered normal.[35]

Non-domestic opportunities for working women were opened up by the industrial revolution which provided work in the factories on the production lines of mass-produced goods.   But, as a consequence, "female" skills were removed from the home to the factory, making the lives of middle class and upper-middle class women emptier than before.   The role of the wife of a successful man was to do nothing:

> Her delicacy, her culture, her childlike ignorance of the male world gave a man the 'class' which money alone could not buy. A virtuous wife spent a hushed and peaceful life indoors, sewing, sketching, planning menus, and supervising the servants and children. The more adventurous might fill their leisure with shopping excursions, luncheons, balls and novels. A 'lady' could be charming, but never brilliant; interested, but not intense.[36]

The ideal woman was gentle, refined, sensitive, emotional, dreamy, delicate, loving and sexually passive. Aggression, independence, self-assertion and curiosity were male traits. She was not expected to achieve in any area considered male (and, hence, valued by society). She might be intelligent, creative, energetic, independent and highly educated but she was condemned to a life of boredom, isolation and intellectual frustration. Such notions of femininity were invoked, at this time, by the judiciary in the "Persons" cases to deny women their claims to recognition as persons and, hence, access to public life. The issue in these cases was whether women should, by virtue of their sex alone, be barred from public functions or professional life. The various claims, such as that of Sophia Jex-Blake and her associates, were denied. These women claimed that they were entitled to graduate from the University of Edinburgh Medical School if they passed their examinations, after the University had terminated their studies when they refused to provide an undertaking that if they were successful in their examinations they would not ask to be awarded a degree.[37] A middle class woman was expected to run the household of her husband, produce sons for professional or business life and daughters for good marriages, and display graciousness and refinement. She was, as Carroll Smith-Rosenberg explains, "in essence, to remain a child-woman, never developing the strengths and skills of adult autonomy."[38] Was there not a connection "between the monotonous domestic lives these women were expected to lead after they completed their schooling, and the emergence of compulsive daydreaming, hallucinations, dissociations, and hysterical conversions"?[39]

> In this context, the dissociations, the drifting and fogging of perception, the nervous tremors and faints, the anaesthesias, and the extreme mutability of symptomatology associated with nineteenth-century female disorders can be seen

to be concretizations of the feminine mystique of the period produced according to rules that governed the prevailing construction of femininity.[40]

The exaggeration of stereotypically feminine characteristics, which were the symptoms of hysteria, expressed the frustration of women with their role in late Victorian society.[41] Women are still confronted with conflicting expectations but, in industrialised societies of the late twentieth century, are far more likely to develop an eating disorder than hysteria.[42]

Victorian women learnt the norms of femininity through their schooling, conduct manuals and the literature of the time. In the late twentieth century, the era of mass media, advertisements, television soap-operas, women's magazines, newspapers:

> the rules for femininity have come to be culturally transmitted more and more through standardized visual images. ... We are no longer given verbal descriptions of what femininity consists. Rather, we learn the rules directly through bodily discourse: through images that tell us what clothes, body shape, facial expression, movements, and behaviour are required.[43]

Susan Bordo argues that the cultural representations of masculinity, femininity, beauty and success which surround us not only homogenise but these homogenised images normalise functioning as models against which the self continually measures and judges. In "Whose Body is This?" she analyses media images arguing that contemporary disciplines of diet and exercise and eating disorders arise out of, and reproduce, normative feminine practices of our culture:[44]

> These [images], no less than the Victorian conduct manuals offer a virtual blueprint for disordered relations to food and hunger. The representation of unrestrained appetite as inappropriate for women, the depiction of female eating as a private, transgressive act, make restriction and denial of hunger central features of the construction of femininity ...[45]

Dieting, slimming, food restriction and exercise regimes are normal feminine behaviour. One study has revealed that on any day of the year at least twenty-five per cent of women will be dieting, and that at least sixty per cent go on diets at least once a year.[46] Susan Bordo questions the understanding of anorexia as a pathological condition. She argues that it is at one extreme of a continuum of normal feminine practices which, at that extreme, sets in play physiological and psychological dynamics leading to addictive patterns and medical and emotional problems outside the "norms" of behaviour:

> [M]any of the 'non-sociocultural' factors that have been dominantly conceptualised

as 'distortions' and 'delusions' specific to the 'pathology' of anorexia and bulimia have been revealed to be prevalent among women in our culture.[47]

One example of the supposedly pathological delusions of the anorexic is Body Image Distortion Syndrome. In her *Teenage Diary*, Julie, having gained twenty-four kilograms to reach her target weight of fifty-seven kilograms, looked at her body in the mirror:

> Everyone can see I'm fat but no-one dare tell me in case I stop eating again. They don't seem to understand. I bet Dee's secretly laughing. She's made me fat and horrid. I was nice. I was thin but now I'm horrid. I'm ugly.[48]

How many women do the same and feel the same about their bodies? Drs Wayne and Susan Wooley of the University of Cincinnati College of Medicine carried out a survey in 1984 of 33,000 women which found that seventy-five per cent of those aged between eighteen and thirty-five believed that they were fat. A small number were medically overweight (225) but forty-five per cent of those who were actually underweight considered themselves to be too fat.[49] Susan Bordo also explains how "faulty thinking" about the power of forbidden foods, "dichotomous reasoning" (if I eat anything, I'll eat everything),[50] and personalisation[51] are considered to be delusions of anorexia but are prevalent amongst women in our culture. Reasoning like "if only I could lose some weight, then it would be alright, life would be different, I would be happy" is not entertained by only the anorexic woman. This sense of self value, that by changing the shape of our bodies we can transform ourselves into worthy selves is common amongst women: the survey referred to above found that the respondents chose losing ten to fifteen pounds above success in work or in love as their most desired goal.[52] Media images make apparent the association between attaining the ideal body image and success or acceptance for women. These "distorted attitudes" are, in fact, a fairly accurate representation of the biological realities, psychological and physiological dynamics of dieting and social attitudes toward slenderness.[53]

To argue that there is a continuity between anorexic behaviour and normal female behaviour is not to deny how serious that condition is. It is to suggest that the anorexic is not pathologically different in her make-up from all women and that cultural dictates undermine the full potential of all women. In *Hunger Strike*, Susie Orbach suggests that the anorexic embodies, in an extreme and painfully debilitating way, a psychological struggle characteristic of the contemporary situation of women. She argues that anorexia represents one extreme on a continuum on which all women today find ourselves, in so far as we are vulnerable, to one degree or another, to the requirements of the cultural construction of femininity:[54]

> The emaciated body of the anorectic, of course, immediately presents itself as a caricature of the contemporary ideal of hyperslenderness for women, an ideal that, despite the game resistance of racial and ethnic difference, has become the norm for women today.[55]

The successful woman in the media imagery of our culture may have gained access to the public world, she may be a successful career woman but she is also 'expected to be a mother, wife, lover and, whilst fulfilling these roles, find the time and energy to keep herself slim, tight and young.[56] The images which portray slenderness as the ideal are not simply portraying a meaningless fashion ideal. This cultural ideal is not merely aesthetic and, as such, the question which needs to be explored is why slenderness?

Feminist claims for equality did have their formal successes; gaining for women the vote, access to education, to employment with legislative protection against sex discrimination, and the right to equal pay. The lives of sexually active heterosexual women no longer have to be limited to the role of reproducer and mother due to available contraception and abortion. But a closer look at the effects of these gains on the reality of women's lives, on the position of women in contemporary society, suggests at least that their success is limited, if not that the claim for equality needs to be reappraised.[57]

Female political gains have been countered by emphasis on an appropriate body size which grows ever smaller so women are constantly engaged in trying to mediate the effects of culturally induced body insecurity. All women experience pressure to make our body conform to the ideal, and to do so women must feed others whilst denying own desires. Women experience contradictory pulls, having been culturally and psychologically prepared for a life in which we service the needs of others, but also being presented with the possibility of living a life for ourselves. Yet, despite the rhetoric of female equality, feminine values have not been assimilated outside the domestic sphere and entry to the public world is on the condition that women conform to the prevailing masculinist values.[58] Anorexia is a graphic picture of the internal experience of contemporary females in which all women live with tension about our place in the world: "[a]norexia symbolizes the restraint on women's desires. In the most tortuous denial of need and dependency and the most persistent and insistent expression of independence, women with anorexia live out the contradictions of contemporary cultural dictates."[59]

Susan Bordo explains that a fairly moderate dieting regime often precedes anorexia. The condition, therefore, begins in a conventional feminine practice which becomes pushed beyond the parameters of moderate dieting:

> The anorectic's ability to live with minimal food intake allows her to feel powerful

and worthy of admiration in a 'world' as Susie Orbach describes it, 'from which at the most profound level [she] feels excluded' and unvalued.[60]

She is admired for her strength of will and self-confidence and, at home, she realises, through the resulting battles over food, the power she can have over the lives of those around her.[61] Like the hysteric, the anorexic takes to the extreme the "ideological construction of femininity emblematic of the period in question."[62] The anorexic by her response, which is both ultra-feminine and a rejection of femininity, embodies the contradictions of contemporary society, in which women have been allowed access to the public world but must not abandon femininity or the female roles of wife and mother. Susan Bordo argues that the "relentless pursuit of excessive thinness" is an attempt to embody certain values, to create a body that will speak for the self in a meaningful and powerful way. The slender body has numerous meanings, "it is capable of being used as a vehicle for the expression of a range of (sometimes contradictory) anxieties, aspirations, dilemmas. Within such a framework, interpreting anorexia requires ... awareness of the many layers of cultural signification that are crystallized in the disorder."[63] She suggests that this includes:

i.   the promise of transcendence of domestic femininity and admission to the privileged public world;

ii.   symbolic and practical control of female hunger, continually constructed as a problem in patriarchal cultures and internalised in women's shame over their own needs and appetites;

iii.   the symbolic recircumscription of woman's limited "place" in the world;

iv.   the ideal of a perfectly managed and regulated self, within a consumer culture which has made the actual management of hunger and desire intensely problematic.

Luce Irigaray has never been interested in equality, she is interested in examining the role of women as mothers as the unacknowledged foundation of Western civilisation, and the obliteration of women as women. As Margaret Whitford explains, in "The Bodily Encounter with the Mother" Luce Irigaray put forward the idea that western culture is founded not on parricide (as Freud hypothesised) but on matricide:

> [T]he major cultural taboo is on the relationship with the mother. The stress on Oedipus, on castration, serves to conceal another severance, the cutting of the

umbilical cord to the mother. This relationship with the mother needs to be brought out of silence and into representation ...[64]

The substratum of the culture, the language, the imaginary and the mythology in which we live, the whole of our western culture is based upon the murder of the mother. In order to take power, the mother was killed by the "man-god-father". If the foundations of this social order are shaken, fundamental social change will follow:

> That is why they are so careful to keep us on a leash ... And why they gag hysterics ... there is a revolutionary potential in hysteria. Even in her paralysis, the hysteric exhibits a potential for gestures and desires ... A movement of revolt and refusal, a desire for/of the living mother who would be more than a reproductive body in the pay of the polis, a living, loving woman. It is because they want neither to see nor hear that movement that they so despise the hysteric.[65]

Luce Irigaray argues that it is necessary to put into words and symbolic representations the primitive relation with the mother's body. If women are to create a new identity for ourselves within the symbolic order, it is essential to invent new ways of speaking about relations between women. By *parler-femme*, by *speaking (as) woman*, one may attempt to provide a place for the "other" as feminine:[66]

> Does the hysteric speak?[67] Isn't hysteria a privileged place for preserving - but 'in latency', 'in sufferance' - that which does not speak? And, in particular (even according to Freud ...), that which is not expressed in woman's relation to her mother, to herself, to other women? Those aspects of women's earliest desires that find themselves reduced to silence in terms of a culture that does not allow them to be expressed. A powerlessness to 'say', upon which the Oedipus complex then superimposes the requirement of silence.[68]

Luce Irigaray considers that the drama of hysteria is that it is inserted between the gestural system, that desire paralysed and enclosed within its body, and a language that it has learned in the family, in school, in society. The problem of *speaking (as) woman* is precisely that of finding a possible continuity between that gestural expression or that speech of desire - which at present can only be identified in the form of symptoms and pathology - and a language, including a verbal language.[69]

Hysteria had the practical consequence of preventing women from functioning in the role of carer of husband and children, becoming in that respect a silent protest. Not only functionally but symbolically American and French feminists alike:

have heard the hysteric speaking a language of protest, even or perhaps especially when she was mute. Dianne Hunter interprets Anna O's aphasia, which manifested itself in an inability to speak her native German, as a rebellion against the linguistic and cultural rules of the father and a return to the 'mother-tongue': the semiotic babble of infancy, the language of the body. For Hunter, and for a number of other feminists working with Lacanian categories, the return to the semiotic level is both regressive and, as Hunter puts it, an 'expressive' communication 'addressed to patriarchal thought', 'a self-repudiating form of feminine discourse in which the body signifies what social conditions make it impossible to state linguistically'.[70]

Likewise, feminist writers have interpreted anorexia as a species of unconscious feminist protest. Susie Orbach describes it as a hunger strike, in which the action of food refusal and dramatic transformation of body size "expresses with her body what she is unable to tell us with words" - her indictment of a culture that disdains and suppresses female hunger, makes women ashamed of our appetites and needs, and demands that women constantly work on the transformation of our bodies.[71] Like the hysterical woman, the anorexic woman speaks. Gagged, her protest is written on her body, not embraced as conscious politics.[72]

SILENCING WOMEN

Typically, doctors would recommend that the hysteric took bed rest or withdrew into domestic life. As a remedy for a condition brought about by isolation, boredom and intellectual frustration, this was about as effective as fattening-up cures are for anorexia.[73] I do not wish to dwell upon the range of alternative treatments recommended for either hysteria or anorexia, but upon the response evoked by women with these conditions. Caroll Smith-Rosenberg analysed the writings of nineteenth century doctors, concluding that doctors felt that the hysteric presented a threat to their prestige and authority. Many doctors became locked in a power struggle with their hysterical patients. Such women, doctors claimed, used their symptoms as weapons in asserting autonomy in relation to their physician; as long as they remained ill they were winning.[74] Indeed, the literature on both anorexia and hysteria is strewn with battles of will between the sufferer and those trying to "cure" her.[75]

In the cases of *W* and *Fox* the court was enjoined, as arbiter, in the battle of wills.[76] The judges could either respect the autonomy of the anorexic woman, accepting the consequences this may have or, by making the order sought in W's case and the declaration in Carolyn Fox's, override this, enabling her to be moved to a different treatment centre or force-fed. The assumption that the legal subject enters the law as an independent autonomous being, able to exercise self-determination and with personal integrity deserving of respect, provides an inadequate position from which to consider the judicial approval of the treatment of young women with anorexia. There is no position from which to understand anorexia as the response of a woman experiencing the conflicts about her role in contemporary society with which all women live.

1. Controlled

The local authority in *Re W* applied for leave to seek orders under the inherent jurisdiction of the High Court, not with any particular course of treatment in mind, but to remove from W power to control her treatment. Lord Donaldson's judgment portrays W and her doctors as engaged in a battle for control:

> [I]t was clearly possible that W might at any time decide to refuse consent to some form of treatment ... because one of the symptoms of anorexia nervosa is a desire by the sufferer to 'be in control' and such a refusal would be an obvious way of demonstrating this.[77]

Lord Donaldson cited with approval the judgment of Thorpe J who thought that W was refusing her consent to be moved to the London hospital because of a "desire to be in an environment where, as she thought, she was in control and could cure herself if and when she thought it right to do so".[78] However, it was apparent which side Lord Donaldson supported: "[t]hat she might leave it too late, does not seem to have occurred to her."[79]

Not only was W, a young woman, challenging the authority of the medical profession as to what was in her best interests, but she fitted into the accepted view of anorexics as manipulative and crafty (which might explain why the consultant, in whose care she was, supported her wish):

> The past year has not been a year of successful treatment or progress. ... W is manifestly in control and the unit is reduced to proposing that they should move away from psychological coercion to offering reward for good behaviour. That announcement to W could, in my judgment, only serve to underline to her the extent to which she is in control. ... Although I have great respect for W's consultant and for the dedication of the staff, it seems to me that they have been manoeuvred into a position from which a change is necessary, even if it is a change that carries the risk of interpretation by W as 'yet another adult rejection and failure'.[80]

The Court of Appeal overrode her refusal to consent to be moved to the London unit - making it clear that W was not in control.

As Carolyn Fox was compulsorily detained under the Mental Health Act 1983, she had no claim to control the medical treatment which she received for her mental disorder.   However, by refusing food, Carolyn was in fact in control.   The application sought to take this from her.   In the Family Division of the High Court, Stuart-White J thought that it was impossible to say if she would co-operate with the forced-feeding and consequently, made a declaration which stated not only that it would be lawful to spoon-feed Carolyn Fox without restraint, and lawful for her to be spoon-fed by a nurse with another female nurse restraining her, but also, if she refused to accept food by spoon-feeding or sufficient food to improve her weight to BMI level, that it would be lawful to sedate her and feed her by a nasogastric tube under the direction of appropriately qualified medical staff.[81]   Thus, to wrest control from her the High Court sanctioned actual physical restraint.

2. Pathologised

The courts accepted the view of anorexic behaviour as pathological not as part of a continuum of normal female behaviour.   Pathologising the anorexic legitimates medical authority: a medical solution is required for a medical problem.   Carolyn Fox was compulsorily detained under the Mental Health Act 1983, thus any medical treatment for her mental disorder could lawfully be carried out without her consent.   To be detained for a period longer than twenty-eight days an application for admission for treatment had to be made under s.3 which requires that the patient:

> (a)   ... is suffering from *mental illness*, severe mental impairment, psychopathic disorder or mental impairment and his mental disorder is of a nature or degree which makes it appropriate for him to receive treatment in a mental hospital; and
> (b)   in the case of psychopathic disorder or mental impairment, such treatment is likely to alleviate or prevent a deterioration in his condition; and
> (c)   it is *necessary for the health and safety of the patient* or for the protection of other persons that he *should receive such treatment* and it *cannot be provided unless he is detained* under this section. (my emphasis)

For s.3 to apply to an anorexic patient, anorexia must come within the definition of mental illness.   Whether it does is entirely a matter of clinical judgment as mental illness is not defined under the Act (although anorexia is classified as a mental illness by the World Health Organisation).   Additionally, it must be necessary for the anorexic's health and safety that she receive treatment which cannot be provided unless she is detained.   Margaret Brazier emphasises that the number of patients eligible to be detained under the Act, and thus who can be treated without consent, is small, so that "only the most dangerously disordered and profoundly handicapped patients will be detained in hospital under the Act."[82]   This is not how I would describe a woman with anorexia.

In *Re W*, Lord Donaldson MR explained that the Mental Health Acts had not been considered in any detail in the course of argument, that they may not have been applicable to W, but that "even where they are applicable it may be in the long-term interests of the minor that if the same treatment can be secured upon some other basis, this shall be done" because the uninformed sometimes view mental illness as different from physical illness, and knowledge that she had been treated under the Acts might be used, in the future, to her disadvantage.[83] Whilst avoiding reference to the Mental Health Act, it was clear that Lord Donaldson MR understood anorexia to be a pathological condition which demanded medical intervention:

> It should be stressed that anorexia nervosa is an illness which is not the fault of the sufferer. In this it is no different from pneumonia or appendicitis. It is, however, much more difficult to treat and cure, not least because one of its clinical manifestations, which is part and parcel of the disease, is a firm wish not to be cured, or at least not to be cured unless and until the sufferer wishes to cure herself. In this sense it is an addictive illness although, unlike other addictions such as drug taking, the sufferer is not to be blamed for having allowed herself to become addicted.[84]

Lord Donaldson questioned whether W was in fact competent to make an informed decision about her treatment:

> [W]hat with all respect I do not think that Thorpe J. took sufficiently into account (perhaps because the point did not emerge as clearly before him as it did before us), is that it is a feature of anorexia nervosa that it is capable of destroying the ability to make an informed choice. It creates a compulsion to refuse treatment or only to accept treatment which is likely to be ineffective. This attitude is part and parcel of the disease and the more advanced the illness, the more compelling it may become.[85]

This view is itself not uncontroversial, especially given that W's anorexia was not considered severe. It is interesting to note that Balcombe LJ referred to the evidence of Dr G, a consultant psychiatrist specialising in anorexia nervosa, which supported the finding of Thorpe J that W *was* competent to make an informed decision:

> I am convinced that she has a good intelligence, and understands what is proposed as treatment. ... She is by no means so severely undernourished that her thinking is physically impaired. (The starving people in Belsen, and Ethiopia recently, were noted to be clear in mental powers, which are preserved above all else.)[86]

Without comment Balcombe LJ continued, "it was conceded, in answer to a question put by the court, that it is a feature of anorexia nervosa that it is capable of destroying the ability to make an informed choice."[87] The court selectively used the facts available to construct W's pathological state, justifying the imposition of the medical treatment against her consent.

3. Gagged

At the initial hearing, Carolyn Fox was not heard. She was literally absent. She had consulted solicitors, but did not have legal aid. Although notice was given to the solicitors by the Riverside Trust that the application was to be made, they did not appear at the ex parte hearing. Accordingly, Stuart-White J dealt with the application upon the basis of the evidence of her consultant, Dr Robinson, and the brief submissions of counsel for the Riverside Trust. Thus, it may not be very surprising that Stuart-White J accepted the evidence of the consultant that forced-feeding was medical treatment within s.145 of the Mental Health Act 1983 and that it was treatment for the mental disorder of anorexia nervosa. In the Court of Appeal, Sir Stephen Brown P expressed the view that it was unfortunate that the application came before the judge ex parte, without the advantage of representation on behalf of the patient, particularly as there was some reason to believe that there was a conflict over the facts. However, "I do not in any way criticise the action taken by the Health Trust and the doctors. I believe that in the circumstances it was a very proper course to take; that is to say, to seek the assistance of the court."[88] It would seem that he considered that it was of greater importance that the doctors were assured of the legal position before forcing treatment upon her than that she be given the opportunity to argue her case. That Sir Stephen Brown P's focus was upon the needs of the doctors is apparent:

> [The proceedings] reflect the sensitive and difficult nature of the responsibilities of members of the medical profession. ... A case of this nature raises difficult and sensitive considerations. This court appreciates, as do all the Divisions of the High Court, that the position of doctors treating patients in certain circumstances is exceptionally difficult. The dilemmas which confront them are very real.[89]

The court understood the dilemma of the medical profession. No attempt was made to understand the difficulties facing Carolyn Fox. Sir Stephen Brown P appreciated the urge of the doctors to provide treatment, as they were trained to do. The court understood the reaction of the medical profession, while Carolyn Fox was not even guaranteed a hearing.

I can understand the need of the doctors to feel that they were doing something, and the court's endorsement of this. I can appreciate the doctors' desire to change what was causing them so much stress, to seek to control, by medical intervention, the behaviour of the woman who is starving her body and the court's willingness to interpret legal principles to provide legal sanction for such intervention. But still the silencing of Carolyn Fox and W, and the apparent brutality of what that involves, (forced-feeding and submission), fills me with horror. The reason I disagree with the decisions in *W* and *Fox* is not because to determine that the medical profession can lawfully treat young women suffering from anorexia without their consent denies them self-determination, or because to hold that anorexia is a mental illness for which forced-feeding as medical treatment is a brutal, autonomy-denying, application of the Mental Health Act 1983. The decisions give legal force to the response of the medical profession which is assumed to be the response of the rational individual (and which assumes that doctors are autonomous, independent individuals, unaffected by societal and cultural expectations or by those imposed upon them by their profession). The decisions fail to see anorexia as the response of a woman experiencing tension about her life, given conflicting messages regarding her role in society and the requirements of the cultural construction of femininity. The decisions assume an individual dissociated from cultural conditions, when she is not.

Clinical literature tends to explain culture as provoking, exacerbating, or giving a distinctive form to an existing pathological condition - contributory rather than productive of eating disorders. In comparison, the cultural context productive of hysteria in the late nineteenth century is now understood:

> Thanks to the benefit of historical distance and the work of feminist scholars, almost all clinicians and theorists today agree that the ultimate sources of hysteria and neurasthenia as characteristic disorders of elite Victorian women are located in Victorian culture, and especially (although not exclusively) in ideology and upheavals related to gender. Most Victorian physicians, we should remember, lacked this perspective. It is only as hysteria has shed its symbolic, emotional, and professional freight, as it has become a historical phenomenon, that it has become possible to *see* it, in some ways, for the first time.[90]

It is now possible to understand the role played by Victorian ideals of masculinity and femininity and the styles of behaviour that regulated them in the production of hysteria and thus see hysteria as a gendered and historically specific condition of Victorian culture:

> It is one thing, apparently, to acknowledge the role played by culture in the production of a virtually extinct disorder, wrestled with by long-dead physicians who were working with now-discredited models. It is another thing altogether for contemporary medicine similarly to interrogate the status of disorders it is still trying to subdue. Researchers do now acknowledge the pre-eminent role played

by cultural ideology in the production of hysteria, but they still resist applying that historical lesson to the understanding of anorexia and bulimia.[91]

Of course, culture alone does not cause anorexia, but this does not mean that there must exist an underlying pathology to explain why some women develop anorexia. Biological factors may play a role in determining which individuals will prove most vulnerable to eating disorders; genetic and other factors do play a role in determining an individual's level of vulnerability. Of course the sad series of events in W's life can explain her vulnerability, can explain something of the conflict which she was experiencing about her life. But that she developed anorexia is not due to individual pathology:

> [W]e *are* all exposed to ... homogenizing and normalizing images and ideologies
> concerning femininity and female beauty. Those images and ideology press for
> conformity to dominant cultural norms. But people's identities are not formed *only*
> through interaction with such images, powerful as they are. The unique
> configurations (of ethnicity, social class, sexual orientation, religion, genetics,
> education, family, age and so forth) that make up each person's life will determine
> how each *actual* woman is affected by our culture.[92]

If we accept the pre-eminent role of cultural images, the contradictions with which women are faced, and that anorexia is an unconscious protest against these, we can see how inadequate is the response which sees the individual before the law as an independent, autonomous self. If we force-feed her, if we force a different treatment regime upon her, or if we let her determine her own treatment, she may die, she may live, who knows, eventually, she may even be cured. Medical treatment may change the shape of her body, it won't alter the social position of women, the conflicts and ideal prescriptions embodied, in the extreme, by the anorexic woman.

THROUGH THE MAGNIFYING GLASS·

As Luce Irigaray's attention has shifted to women's position before the law,[93] her focus has shifted from the mother-daughter relationship and relationships between women to having an effect on and in the world of men and *parler-femme* has been replaced by the sexuation of discourse and culture.[94] She warns against displacing the male/female binary before the female side has acceded to identity and subjectivity: "[t]o omit the question of the woman-as-subject and her identity in thought and culture is to leave in place a tenacious and damaging imaginary structure."[95] In "Women-Amongst-Themselves: Creating a Woman-to-Woman

Sociality" she stresses the necessity for collective and public recognition of women's difference and for symbolic forms which correspond to women's specificity, the need for an *identity*:[96]

> The symbolization of sexual difference, of two *genres* or kinds, is presented as a possible force for renewal against the destructive tendencies which Irigaray sees in our society: in thought, in culture, in science ... But, '[f]or the work of sexual difference to take place, a revolution in thought and ethics is needed'. This is a project which would require a massive upheaval in the ways in which we conceptualise the world, including a revolution in the modalities of space and time as they are at present conceived. Woman has always been for man his space, or rather his *place*, but has no place of her own. This deprives her of identity-for-herself.[97]

The way forward is by political action, and the presentation of concrete and practical proposals to help women to achieve a cultural identity.[98] Luce Irigaray constantly criticises the notion of the same, of unity which she considers is grounded in the experience of one sex, "such a notion of semblance, however, is intrinsic to the reason of law."[99] She sees the law of the western legal tradition as founded upon a masculine identity. The feminine, her values, her specificity has been denied or repressed. To create a feminine public sphere in which to think, act, speak or live, a culture appropriate to the feminine genre must be identified and protected by legal rights. In "The Necessity for Sexuate Rights"[100] Luce Irigaray put forward the idea that each *genre* or sexual kind should have rights and responsibilities which correspond to its specificity:

> Her main point is that what she calls 'the people of men' has appropriated women's bodies, children's bodies, nature, space, symbolism, the divine, and representation in general. To define rights for women, therefore, is to try and imagine what it might be like for women to share in culture *as* women and to become full citizens in their own right.[101]

Having reached the position where she feels that certain difficulties cannot be resolved unless an equitable legal system is established for both sexes, she argues that a first step in creating the conditions for woman's accession to identity is the enactment of legislation which respects sexual difference.[102] The law needs to be rethought to take into account the needs of the two genres. Notably her focus remains on sexual difference not equality and it must be emphasised that this is not another rehearsal of the equality/difference debate. Both equality, which claims access for women to the spheres occupied by men, as their equals, and difference, which demands valorisation of those characteristics and roles which have been traditionally ascribed to women, depend upon the male as the touchstone for comparison. For Luce Irigaray, it is not a question of the differences between the sexes, sexual difference focuses on two distinct genres and, as the only possible subject position in patriarchy is masculine, this requires the creation of feminine identity. In the equality/difference debate woman is oppressed as woman, for Luce Irigaray woman is repressed - in patriarchal society she has not yet acceded to subjectivity, women are not symbolically self-defined:[103]

> Women and men are not equal. And the equality strategy, when it exists, should always aim at the recognition of difference. For instance, equal numbers of women and men could take part in all social activities, so as to make them evolve. At one level that solution is obviously perfectly desirable. But it is not enough. And its inadequacy leads to regressions and scepticism about the existence of difference between men and women, which are perpetrated by women themselves.[104]

Luce Irigaray considers that the equality strategy is inadequate because contemporary social order is not neutral from the point of view of the difference between the sexes. Working conditions, production techniques, the goals of work and the systems of work are not defined equally by, or for, women and men. There is hardly any kind of work which enables a woman to earn her living, as a male does, without alienating her identity in working conditions and contexts developed to suit men alone. Access to the public world and the guarantee of equal pay for equal work within it do not ensure respect for the human identity of women. Social organisation needs to be rethought, otherwise, "we sanction the fact that, in order to acquire a minimal freedom, women must submit to the imperatives of a culture which is not theirs."[105] To create the conditions in which the female subject can accede to social existence it is necessary to recognise that "there are different rights for each sex and that equality of social status can only be established when these rights have been codified by the civil powers."[106]

In "How to Define Sexuate Rights?"[107] Luce Irigaray outlines what she believes have to be asserted as *rights* for women:

i.   The right to human dignity, including:
a.   An end to the commercial use of our bodies or their images;
b.   Valid self-representations of women, in gestures, in words and in images, in all public places;
c.   An end to the exploitation of motherhood by civil and religious powers.

ii.   The right to human identity, that is:
a.   Legal encodification of physical and moral integrity as a component of

female identity;

b.   The right to motherhood must be recognised as a component of female identity. Women must enjoy a civil right to choose to be pregnant and to choose how many pregnancies to have.

iii.   Mother-child duties will be defined in a code, ensuring that the mother can protect her children, supported by the law.

iv.   Women will have a civil right to defend our lives, the lives of our children, our dwelling places, traditions and religion against any unilateral decision based on male law.

v.   At the financial level:

a.   The unmarried will not be penalised by taxation;

b.   If the state grants family allowances, they will be the same value for each child;

c.   Women will pay the same taxes as men for the media and half of the coverage will be adapted to them.

vi.   Systems of exchange (for example, linguistic exchange) will be revised so as to ensure women and men a right to equivalent exchange.

vii.   Women will have equal representation in all places where civil or religious decisions are taken.

Luce Irigaray emphasises that it is necessary to work through the written law in order to define rights appropriate to each genre. In *J'aime à toi: équisse d'une felicité dans l'histoire*[108] she maintains her focus on law, identifying the legal rights necessary to protect the ethical and cultural dimensions of women's civil identity: "[t]he definition of feminine legal personality begins with the listing of rights appertaining to the dignity and inviolability, physical and moral integrity, of the feminine body."[109] Importantly this extends beyond the right to protection from physical abuse, as the right to existence implies the autonomy of all individuals, of whatever age and within or without the private sphere:

> Much of the discussion of moral integrity thus concerns the representation of feminine identity in public space. Rights of moral integrity or dignity are concerned with the public use and circulation of linguistic and visual images of women that violate the autonomy or devalue the integrity of feminine personality. Pornography is the prime example of such devaluation but Irigaray adds commercial exploitation of the feminine form, together with a right to positive

representation in public space, to an economy of signs or images that neither exploits nor reduces the feminine to its function or its social utility.[110]

The substantive content of the feminine rights which she advocates include:

i.   Inscription in law of the minimum conditions necessary for woman's personal development as an autonomous feminine subject;

ii.   Maternity rights and freedom of choice with economic protection for the mother and specific legal definition of the separate rights and duties of mother and child;

iii.   Cultural integrity and aesthetic sensibilities of the feminine genre. This requires the creation of a public sphere appropriate to feminine identity; a public culture, languages, arts and civil and religious institutions in which feminine speech and desire would play an intrinsic role;

iv.   Extension of the latter inscription of the feminine genre within the public sphere in which the relation of mother to child would become the basis of a feminine genealogy: "associated with the institution of a feminine genealogy would be a wider cultural valuation of feminine rites, traditions and mythologies as forms of cultural transmission. ... [T]he law [would] be used, in short, to protect relations between women and, particularly, between mother and child."[111]

Irigaray emphasises that a positive cultural identity for women depends not only upon laws but also the reinvention of a genealogy of the feminine, the creation or reinstitution of feminine traditions, because "this civilization has no philosophy, no linguistics, no religion, no politics of the feminine. All these disciplines are adapted to a masculine subject".[112]

All women in contemporary western society grapple, to some degree, with culturally induced body insecurity. Our laws do not ensure positive representation of feminine identity. All women experience the contradictory pulls between public and private spheres. Contemporary social order is not defined equally by both men and women. The anorexic responds in a particularly graphic way to the alienation all women feel in a society where the female is denied identity. Women's health suffers from lack of self-affirmation, from the impossibility, or denial, of a definition of women as subjects and objects by and for themselves.[113] At this extreme, our laws engage with the female. But within legal discourse, women exist as "other of the same", other to the male subject who is represented as the universal. Sexual difference is untheorised and unrepresented and for so long as this is so, women remain without subjectivity.[114] Gagged, symbolically and, literally:

> their words are not heard. What they say is illegitimate in terms of the elaboration
> of diagnoses, of therapeutic decisions that affect them. Scientific discourses and
> serious scientific practices are still the privilege of men, as is the management of
> the political in general and of the most private aspects of our lives as women.
> Their discourses, their values, their dreams and their desires have the force of law,
> everywhere and in all things. Everywhere and in all things, they define women's
> function and social role, and the sexual identity they are, or are not, to have. They
> know, they have access to the truth; we do not.[115]

CONCLUSION

Luce Irigaray's proposals - outlining the civil rights to be legislated to create the
conditions for change to a social order respectful of sexual difference - are
presented in the context of the civil law tradition. The problems of rights discourse
have been explored elsewhere.[116] I do wonder whether these reservations are the
same given that the project is to seek to create the conditions in which the terms of
our thinking can be altered. I also wonder whether, concerned with the creation of a
public sphere appropriate to feminine identity and the representation of feminine
identity in the public sphere, here is one instance where strategically an appeal to
rights is appropriate. However, without having to determine that issue, at least for
the moment, I believe, in agreement with Peter Goodrich, that the importance of
her work, of equal validity to our common law tradition, is philosophical:

> It plays with a conception of a plurality of forms of legal personality in such a way
> as to force the existence of difference into the consciousness of jurists: feminist
> ethics requires a dialectical relation between laws and their objects. It shows that
> the question of justice and more specifically the ethics of difference is intrinsic to
> the question of legitimacy which is equally a matter of legality.[117]

It is not necessary to accept Luce Irigaray's appeal to rights to engage with her
work. Her focus on sexual difference and on law that recognises the potential
cultural and political identity of women can act as a magnifying glass through
which to consider our own legal system. By no means am I suggesting that Luce
Irigaray's proposals represent a blue-print for a utopian society, as I'm sure she
herself would not. But we do need to further our understanding of the position of
women before the law and this can be achieved by making comparisons with other
eras, other societies, and by supplementing our understanding with her "radical
theoretical speculations" on "the construction of sexuality in law".[118] Luce Irigaray

is concerned with "a cultural politics which potentially alters the ground of possibility and opens the future to a history and law of difference."[119] The decisions in *W* and *Fox*, explored through the context of the expectations and realities of women's roles and the ideals of femininity in contemporary society, show the need for both.

Such speculations are not limited to the engagement of the law with the medical treatment of the anorexic woman but may reveal what has to be changed in the numerous areas where law engages and upholds the cultural dictates of expectations of women. We need to reconsider, for example, laws on contraception, abortion, reproductive technologies, pornography, rape, domestic violence, prostitution and the killing of an abusive partner. Through these speculations we may locate the means by which the female subject has been excluded and, from there, work out the conditions for her accession to social existence by arriving at a "concept of feminine legal personality" and obtaining a "vision of legal processes and laws appropriate to women".[120]

NOTES

1. Only in societies where food is plentiful is dieting or food refusal an option. S.Bordo, *Unbearable Weight: Feminism, Western Culture and the Body* (1993) writes at p.192, "[t]he moral requirement to diet depends on the material preconditions that make the *choice* to diet an option and the possibility of personal 'excess' a reality." C.Chinkin and S.Wright, "The Hunger Trap: Women, Food and Self-determination" [1993] *Michigan Law J.* 262, explore the many cultures in which women, for social, economic and personal reasons, are denied or deny themselves food, the claim of a right to food and the right to be free from hunger and the role which international law and human rights have to play in securing these rights.

2. N.Wolf, *The Beauty Myth* (1990) at p.183, estimates that ninety-five per cent of those suffering from anorexia in Britain are women. P.Garfinkel and D.Garner, *Anorexia Nervosa: A Multidimensional Perspective* (1982) at p.112, estimate that close to ninety per cent of all anorexics are female. Although it is noted that in the last decade more cases of men with anorexia have been reported.

3. The cadaveric body of the anorexic attracts more attention than does either the bulimic - who may hide well both her bulimic episodes and the inner turmoil to which they give expression and whose slim, but not emaciated, body does not broadcast that something is wrong - or the compulsive eater whose overweight body, with its associations with lack of control, does not hold the same fascinations.

4. S.Boseley, "The seeds of a double agony" (1994) *The Guardian*, July.

5. "Julie Through the Looking Glass" *Teenage Diaries*, BBC 2, (1992) 26 August.

6. [1992] 3 W.L.R. 758.

7. W's anonymity was protected by the Children and Young Persons Act 1933, s.39(1), which

gives the court, in relation to any proceedings, the power to direct that no report of the proceedings should reveal the name, address, school or include any particulars calculated to lead to the identification of the child/young person concerned.

8. In "Old enough to know best?" (1993) 13 *Legal Studies* 69, whilst acknowledging that the facts presented particularly difficult issues, I argued that the "paternalistic" decision of the court enabled those who could not bear to stand by to act but denied W self-determination in so doing.

9. [1994] 1 F.L.R. 614.

10. I cannot pretend to do justice to her work. I do, however, hope that by drawing upon aspects of it I can suggest the particular use of her work to a feminist analysis of the law.

11. In her introduction to *The Irigaray Reader*, Margaret Whitford emphasises the importance of reading Luce Irigaray's later work in the light of her earlier work (M.Whitford ed., *The Irigaray Reader* (1993) at p.12).

12. M.Whitford, *ibid.*, at p.24.

13. M.Whitford, *ibid.*, at p.3.

14. S.Duncan, "Law as Literature: Deconstructing the Legal Text" (1994) V *Law and Critique* 3, at p.12.

15. M.Whitford, *supra*, n.11, at p.10.

16. *Re W (A Minor) (Medical Treatment: Court's Jurisdiction)* [1992] 3 W.L.R. 758.

17. *Ibid.*, at p.761.

18. *Ibid.*, at p.762.

19. *Ibid.*, at p.763.

20. [1986] A.C. 112.

21. *Supra*, n.16, at p.763.

22. *Ibid.*, at p.769.

23. *Ibid.*, at p.767.

24. *Ibid.*, at p.770.

25. J.Masson, "*Re W*: appealing from the golden cage" (1993) 5 *J.C.L.* 37, suggests that the court's decision was no more likely than W's to promote her welfare.

26. *Riverside Mental Health NHS Trust v. Fox* [1994] 1 F.L.R. 614.

27. The Mental Health Act 1983, s.145, provides that medical treatment includes nursing care, habilitation and rehabilitation under medical supervision.

28. See R.Thornton, "Minors and Medical Treatment - Who Decides?" [1993] *C.L.J.* 34; J.Eekelaar, "White Coats or Flak Jackets? Doctors, children and the Courts - Again" (1993) 109 *L.Q.R.* 182; J.Masson, "*Re W*: appealing from the golden cage" (1993) 5 *J.C.L.* 37; N.Lowe and S.Juss, "Medical Treatment - Pragmatism and the Search for Principle" (1993) 56 *M.L.R.* 865.

29. Section 63 authorises non-consensual treatment only for mental disorder not for any treatment required by the patient for physical injury or disease.

30. C.Wells, "Patients, Consent and Criminal Law" [1994] *J.S.W.F.L.* 65, at p.69.

31. N.Wolf, *The Beauty Myth* (1990) at p.183, estimates that there are now some 3.5 million

sufferers of anorexia in Britain, with 6,000 new cases every year.

32. S.Bordo, *Unbearable Weight: Feminism, Western Culture and the Body* (1993).

33. S.Bordo, *op.cit.*, at p.157.

34. C.Smith-Rosenberg, "The Hysterical Woman: Sex Roles and Role Conflict in 19th-Century America" (1979) 39 *Social Research* 652, at p.660.

35. C.Smith-Rosenberg, *ibid.*, at p.654.

36. B.Ehrenreich and D.English, *For Her Own Good: 150 Years of the Experts' Advice to 'Women* (1979) at p.95.

37. *Jex-Blake v. Senatus of Edinburgh University* (1873) 11 M. 784.

38. C.Smith-Rosenberg, *supra*, n.34, at p.656.

39. S.Bordo, *supra*, n.32, at p.158.

40. S.Bordo, *ibid.*, at p.169.

41. The "Persons" cases and the campaigns of the suffragettes arose out of the same frustrations. See A.Sachs and J.Hott-Wilson, *Sexism and the Law: A study of male beliefs and legal bias in Britain and the United States* (1978) chapter 1.

42. S.Bordo, *supra*, n.32, at p.51.

43. S.Bordo, *ibid.*, at p.169.

44. S.Bordo, *ibid.*

45. S.Bordo, *ibid.*, at p.130.

46. L.Gammon, "Fat is a Fetishist Issue" (1993) *The Guardian*, 2 December.

47. S.Bordo, *supra*, n.32, at p.54.

48. "Julie Through the Looking Glass" (1992) *Teenage Diaries*, *supra*, n.5. Dee is Dr Dee Dawson.

49. W. and S.Wooley, "33,000 Women Tell How They Really Feel About Their Bodies" (1994) *Glamour*, February, quoted in N.Wolf, *supra*, n.31, at p.185.

50. In J.Shute, *Life-size* (1992), Josephine is receiving treatment for her anorexia: "'I can't. I just can't. Not ... cake.' The very word is difficult for me to say: obscene, taboo. *Cookies, cake, chocolate, and other sweets - avoid them like Satan!* 'It's food, Josephine. There are no "good" foods and "bad" foods.' I know this isn't true. But how can I convince her? There are certain ... things ... that, once you put them in your mouth, force you to keep going, keep cramming, keep chewing, in a frenzy of horrified craziness" (at p.169).

51. An example of which, hatred of being seen eating, is shown in the film *Life is Sweet* (director, Mike Leigh). The family are seated around the kitchen table eating Sunday lunch, except for Natalie, who is the anorexic daughter. Her mother asks, "What's it like in the first class dining compartment, then?" To which Natalie replies, "Listen, if I choose to eat in my own space, that's my prerogative, right."

52. W. and S.Wooley, *supra*, n.49.

53. S.Bordo, *supra*, n.32, at p.58.

54. S.Orbach, *Hunger Strike: The Anorectic's Struggle as a Metaphor for Our Age* (1993).

55. S.Bordo, *supra*, n.32, at p.170.

56. S.Bordo, *supra*, n.32, asks at p.140, why our culture is so obsessed with keeping our bodies

slim, tight, and young? In a note she explains, "[m]y use of the expression 'our culture' may seem overly homogenizing here, disrespectful of differences among ethnic groups, socio-economic groups, subcultures within [western] society, and so forth. It must be stressed here that I am discussing ideology and images whose power is *precisely* the power to homogenize culture."

57. For an assessment of employment legislation, see A.Morris and S.Nott, *Working Women and the Law: Equality and Discrimination in Theory and Practice* (1991) and "Law's Engagement with Pregnancy" in this volume. On the provision of contraception and abortion, see R.P.Petchesky, *Abortion and Women's Choice: The State, Sexuality and Reproductive Freedom* (1986) and S.Sheldon, "The Law of Abortion and the Politics of Medicalisation" in this volume.

58. At the time of writing this has been exemplified in the unfair dismissal and sexual harassment case of Samantha Phillips. See I.Wolff, "Bulls, bears and bimbos" (1994) *The Observer*, 14 August.

59. S.Orbach, *supra*, n.54, at p.9.

60. S.Bordo, *supra*, n.32, at p.180.

61. These responses are explained by Aimee Liu in her autobiographical account of anorexia (A.Liu, *Solitaire* (1979)).

62. S.Bordo, *supra*, n.32, at p.168.

63. S.Bordo, *ibid.*, at p.67.

64. M.Whitford ed., *The Irigaray Reader* (1993) at p.25.

65. L.Irigaray, "Women-mothers: the silent substratum of the social order" in *The Irigaray Reader*, ed. M.Whitford (1993) 47, at p.47.

66. L.Irigaray, "Questions" in *The Irigaray Reader*, ed. M.Whitford (1993) 133, at p.137.

67. Barbara Ehrenreich and Deirdre English explain that, "[a]side from fits and fainting, the disease took a variety of forms: hysterical loss of voice, loss of appetite, hysterical coughing or sneezing, and, of course, hysterical screaming, laughing, and crying" (B.Ehrenreich and D.English, *For Her Own Good: 150 Years of the Experts' Advice to Women* (1979) at p.124).

68. L.Irigaray, *supra*, n.66, at p.138.

69. L.Irigaray, *ibid.*

70. S.Bordo, *supra*, n.32, at p.175, referring to D.Hunter, "Hysteria, Psychoanalysis and Femininsm" in *The (M)Other Tongue*, eds. S.Garner et al. (1985) 114.

71. S.Orbach, *supra*, n.54, at p.83.

72. Compare this with the suffragettes who consciously employed food refusal as a political protest to further their cause. See J.Bridgeman, "Hunger Strikes and Children's Rights" (1992) 25 *Trouble and Strife* 36.

73. "Despite countless theories about why young women succumb to anorexia, the in-patient treatment has remained much the same: a high-calorie diet reinforced by a strict behavioural regime, aiming to get the patient back up to normal weight in as short a time as possible. At its worst this means total bed-rest, solitary confinement and the removal of anything that might give pleasure or comfort. ... The patient trades weight-gain for 'privileges' in an

elaborate system of rewards and punishments" ("First Person" (1992) *The Guardian*, July).
Of course, this does not represent the only way in which anorexics are treated.

74.   C.Smith-Rosenberg, *supra*, n.34, at p.674.

75.   S.Bordo, *supra*, n.32, at p.180.

76.   This battle is starkly apparent in B's case. B, a twenty-four year-old woman, was
compulsorily detained under the Mental Health Act 1983 suffering from borderline
personality disorder coupled with post-traumatic stress disorder. She claimed that she was
being unlawfully detained under the Mental Health Act but her application that she be freed
and for leave to seek judicial review of her detention was denied. The health authority
renewed it's application to the Family Division of the High Court that it was lawful to force-
feed her by nasogastric tube, against her will ((1994) *The Times*, 17 June). Thorpe J made
the declaration sought "despite accepting she was capable of deciding to refuse treatment and
that forced-feeding would reduce the chances of success for psychotherapy, the only
treatment which in his opinion might help her condition" ((1994) *The Guardian*, 26 July).
The battle of wills is summed up by the acting manager of the hospital: "[o]ur primary
concern is to keep her alive against her wishes."

77.   *Re W (A Minor) (Medical Treatment: Court's Jurisdiction)* [1992] 3 W.L.R. 758, C.A., per
Lord Donaldson MR, at p.762.

78.   *Ibid.*, at p.769.

79.   *Ibid.*

80.   *Ibid.*, at p.771.

81.   In the Court of Appeal Leggatt LJ was alone in addressing the issue of restraint. His
objection was not to the fact that physical force would be employed to restrain her and
facilitate the forced-feeding but that the order was defective because the paragraphs which
addressed forced-feeding were only applied for as alternatives. See [1994] 1 F.L.R. 614, at
p.622.

82.   M.Brazier, *Medicine, Patients and the Law* (1992) at p.105.

83.   *Supra*, n.77, at p.771.

84.   *Ibid.*, at p.761. That Lord Donaldson MR thought that people addicted to drugs should be
blamed for allowing themselves to become addicted suggests that he has not considered the
wider social context in which drugs are used.

85.   *Ibid.*, at p.769.

86.   *Ibid.*, at p.772.

87.   *Ibid.*, at p.773.

88.   In the Family Division, Wall J was of the opinion that the court did have jurisdiction, *where
matters of life and death are concerned*, to make what is in effect a final declaration ex parte:
"[s]uch a declaration was made by the President in the case of *Re S (Adult: Refusal of
Treatment)* [1993] Fam. 123 ... In that case the President heard only one side, but in my
judgment had no alternative but to grant the declaration sought. Clearly, once made, the
order was final: the operation was carried out and could not be reversed. My common sense
rebels at the proposition that the court has no jurisdiction to act when it is faced with an

emergency in which exercise of its powers to make a declaratory judgment will preserve life and a refusal to exercise them is likely to result in death or permanent injury" (*Riverside Mental Health NHS Trust v. Fox* [1994] 1 F.L.R. 614, at p.616). Rather than providing approval for granting a declaration ex parte, the decision in *Re S* and the subsequent criticism of the case suggest why the court should be reluctant to do so. See A.Morris and S.Nott, "The Law's Engagement with Pregnancy" in this volume.

89. *Ibid.*, per Sir Stephen Brown P at pp.618,621.
90. S.Bordo, *supra*, n.32, at p.50.
91. S.Bordo, *ibid.*, at p.51.
92. S.Bordo, *ibid.*, at p.62.
93. In Luce Irigaray's work, post 1985: *Sexes et parentés* (1987); *Le Temps de la différence* (1989); *Je, tu, nous* (1990); *J'aime à toi: équisse d'une felicité dans l'histoire* (1993), she engages with political change. However, it must again be emphasised that her later work has to be understood in the context of her earlier work.
94. M.Whitford ed., *The Irigaray Reader* (1993) at p.11.
95. M.Whitford, *ibid.*, at p.13.
96. M.Whitford, *ibid.*, at p.160.
97. M.Whitford, *ibid.*, at p.157.
98. P.Goodrich, "Writing Legal Difference: Helena Kennedy's *Eve was Framed: Women and British Justice* and Luce Irigaray's *J'aime à toi: equissé d'une felicité dans l'histoire*" (1993) 4 *Women: A Cultural Review* 317, points out that Irigaray has offered several classifications of the necessary doctrinal legislation. In *Le Temps de la différence* (1989) the primary emphasis was upon social and welfare rights; in *Je, tu, nous* (1990) aesthetic rights and rights of language; in *J'aime à toi* (1993), she is concerned with ethical and cultural dimensions of women's civil identity.
99. P.Goodrich, *ibid.*, at p.320.
100. L.Irigaray, "The Necessity for Sexuate Rights" in *The Irigaray Reader*, ed. M.Whitford (1993) 198.
101. M.Whitford ed., *The Irigaray Reader* (1993) at p.162.
102. Language also needs to be transformed as an essential tool of production for the liberation of the female subject. See L.Irigaray, "The Cost of Words", "The Neglect of Female Genealogies" and "Linguistic Sexes and Genders" in *Je, Tu, Nous* (1990).
103. The equality/difference debate is obviously much more complex than this would suggest. For a fuller consideration see H.Eisenstein and A.Jardine eds., *The Future of Difference* (1990); A.Phillips ed., *Feminism and Equality* (1987).
104. L.Irigaray, "How to Define Sexuate Rights?" in *The Irigaray Reader*, ed. M.Whitford (1993) 204, at p.206.
105. L.Irigaray, *ibid.*
106. L.Irigaray, *ibid.*, at p.207.
107. L.Irigaray, *ibid.*.
108. Although I would like to have been able to consider this work in greater depth, unfortunately,

I am limited to the translations of Luce Irigaray's work presently available. Thus, any reference to this work relies solely upon P.Goodrich, *supra*, n.98.

109.   P.Goodrich, *ibid.*, at p.323.

110.   P.Goodrich, *ibid.*

111.   P.Goodrich, *ibid.*, at p.324.

112.   P.Goodrich, *ibid.*, at p.322.

113.   L.Irigaray, "Your Health: What, or Who, is it?" in *Je, tu, nous* (1990) at p.105.

114.   S.Duncan, *supra*, n.14.

115.   L.Irigaray, "The Bodily Encounter with the Mother" in *The Irigaray Reader*, ed. M.Whitford (1993) 34, at p.35.

116.   See E.Kingdom, *What's Wrong with Rights? Problems for Feminist Politics of Law* (1991); E.Kingdom, "Body Politics and Rights" in this volume which reviews the feminist literature concerning rights strategies.

117.   P.Goodrich, *supra*, n.108, at p.327.

118.   P.Goodrich, *ibid.*, at p.320.

119.   P.Goodrich, *ibid.*, at p.321.

120.   P.Goodrich, *ibid.*, at p.321.

3 The Law's Engagement With Pregnancy

ANNE MORRIS AND SUSAN NOTT

In an ideal world biology would not dictate an individual's destiny and in particular women's capacity to bear children would not colour the way in which they are treated and the opportunities that are available to them. In reality, however, the fact that they bear children has adverse consequences for the treatment which women receive within society. Some women would undoubtedly argue that any disadvantages are more than compensated for by the pleasures associated with motherhood. Regrettably such pleasures are not quantifiable, whilst the negative effects of pregnancy and motherhood are well-documented. Woman's ability to bear children is at once her privilege and her burden.

The desired outcome of any wanted pregnancy is the birth of a healthy child and, since a woman's behaviour prior to and during the course of her pregnancy can affect the foetus, this raises the possibility of conflict between woman and foetus. Liberal tradition respects individual freedoms and grants rights to those recognised as competent to exercise them, but this idea of competence carries within it a powerful mechanism of control: to whom will rights be given, what will they consist of and who will judge competence to exercise them? Prior to pregnancy the adult woman is an individual deemed capable of exercising choices, taking decisions about her body and what she will do with it and to it. Confirmation of her pregnancy alters this view of her individual autonomy in terms of her behaviour and her right to live her life as she chooses, especially where this puts her and the foetus at risk. She becomes "no longer just a woman, she is a woman ... with child."[1] Her pregnancy differentiates her from her workmates, her family and the rest of non-pregnant humanity. A pregnant woman is popularly perceived not as one person but two - mother and foetus[2] - and society may expect, even demand, that her freedom is curtailed in the interests of the foetus. The same attitude is not displayed towards men even though their behaviour before and during pregnancy could prove equally damaging to a foetus.[3]   The biological potential to bear children has, moreover, been perceived as endowing women with particular qualities such as caring and nurturing skills and, these in turn, have been alleged to affect the way in which women think and tackle moral dilemmas, giving rise to a distinctively female way of reasoning.[4]   Certainly, it is often assumed that a woman's ability to function efficiently is impaired during pregnancy.[5]   For women the consequence of these assumptions, whatever the truth of them, is detrimental, and in particular their ability to make rational decisions concerning their own well-being and that of the foetus may be challenged.

Identifying women primarily by their procreative functions leads also to the apparently ingrained assumption that because women bear children, they should also assume prime, if not total, responsibility for rearing those children.   This has important consequences for the ability of women to compete with men in the labour market.   Women are assumed to be suited to certain types of employment which leads to segregation of the sexes in the workplace as well as the undervaluing of skills perceived as feminine, and it is well-known that women's work is generally lower paid than those occupations traditionally associated with men.[6]   The birth of a child will have little, if any, effect on a man's pattern of employment, but the reverse is frequently true for women where the need to care for a child may force a woman to give up paid employment.   As one study has concluded:

> [r]esponsibility for child-rearing is the major correlate of female labour force participation. It matters not so much how many children a woman has to care for, but how young is her youngest charge. The mother of an infant is very unlikely to have paid work, however many other children she has.[7]

A woman's departure from the workplace in these circumstances may result not from choice, though it may be represented as such,[8] but because there is no institutional framework to allow women to combine child care with full-time employment. Alternatively, since women are on the whole less well-rewarded for their paid work, a dual-earner couple may decide that it is logical that the woman is the partner who subordinates her career to the demands of child care.

Increasing numbers of women are choosing not to abandon paid employment,[9] but they may be forced to adopt unsatisfactory strategies to combine motherhood with employment. A woman may have to work part-time instead of full-time or take a job that is inappropriate to her level of skill and education.[10]   Employers may take advantage of a woman's weak bargaining position in order to pay her less.[11]   Nor is this inability to match the working patterns of men merely a short-term phenomenon:

The effects of caring responsibilities in the past also have an impact on a woman's current rate of pay, even after she becomes more of a free agent in the labour market, for the market rewards accumulated employment experience just as it penalises workers with interrupted employment records.[12]

It is not only pay which suffers: a woman may also jeopardise work-related benefits such as a pension.[13]   In short, her ability to maintain financial and thus social independence is often dealt a serious blow by the consequences of child-bearing.

Pregnancy and motherhood have undeniably adverse practical consequences for women because of the manner in which society internalises this biological fact. This is not chance but rather a reflection of the various perceptions of what it means to be a Pregnant Woman[14] or a Mother.   The law has a key part to play in this process.   This is because the law constructs its own notion of Woman, and in particular of Pregnant Woman, which is at odds with the way in which real women wish to lead their lives.   As a consequence women are forced by the law into behaving in certain ways and making certain choices:

> There are a number of legal rules that function to compel or encourage women to bear children and to assume disproportionately larger responsibilities for rearing children than men do.   Of these rules, those that regulate biological reproduction or the structure of the family are explicitly engaged in such functions; rules that regulate the wage market or wage market subsidies maternalize the female body more indirectly.[15]

The suggestion that the law is guilty of upholding a particular ideological view of women's roles and of maternalising their bodies seems at odds with the current legal emphasis on equal opportunities.   In the United Kingdom, for example, the protective legislation which subordinated women to their procreative functions by restricting the hours which women worked and the industries in which they might be employed purportedly to safeguard their role as mothers, has been largely repealed.[16]   The decision of the United States Supreme Court in *Muller v. Oregon*[17] legitimising the regulation of women's working hours, but not those of men,[18] in order to have healthy women producing healthy offspring, certainly *seems* out-dated in its idea that women were subordinate even to a *potential* foetus. Legislation now in force in Europe and the United States accords pregnant workers various rights which can include a return to work after the birth of a child.[19]   How then can the law be accused of forcing women to adopt stereotypical roles?

Understanding how the law engages with pregnancy and constructs the "Pregnant Woman" demands more than a consideration of single issues such as the treatment of pregnant workers.   Even the most positive strategy, (which incidentally few would claim accurately describes the law's current treatment of pregnant workers), will fail if contradictory laws exist elsewhere in the system.   Laws are not compartmentalised, but form part of a continuous narrative.[20]   Just as a reader cannot understand the plot of a book by reading a single chapter, the same is true of the law.   By examining how Pregnant Women are treated by the law both in the private sphere of their personal lives, as well as in the public sphere of the workplace it is possible to build up a fuller picture of what it means in the eyes of the law to be a Pregnant Woman.

THE PRIVATE POLITICS OF PREGNANCY: ONE PERSON OR TWO?

Questions surrounding the legal status of the Pregnant Woman are often phrased in terms of conflict between mother and foetus[21] which serves to underline the idea that where there was one person there are now two.   Although the "foetus as a person" debate is not concluded and is not, as such, the subject of this chapter it is highly relevant to the extent that it exemplifies the difficulties faced by legal systems based on respect for personal autonomy.   When considering the "conflict" between a woman and her foetus, and the extent to which the courts will countenance control of the woman, it should be borne in mind that, to date, English law has denied the status of a legal "person" to a foetus.   In a number of cases it has been held that an unborn child has no legal existence until it is has a physical existence independent of its mother[22] and in *Re F*[23] a court refused to make a foetus a ward of court, despite evidence that the mother who was in late pregnancy, was mentally disturbed, abusing drugs and had a propensity to go missing.   Other jurisdictions tend, in general, to take a similar view though the issue is far from settled.[24]   Whilst not debating here the legal personhood or otherwise of the foetus, this section will consider how recognition of competing claims of the foetus entails control of the Pregnant Woman in her private life and especially in her medical treatment.

    It is a fundamental tenet of the law relating to medical treatment that no person may be treated without his or her consent: "Every human being of adult years and sound mind has the right to determine what shall be done with his own body ... "[25] and this extends even to refusal of life-saving treatment.[26]   This is simply to express the individual's right to self-determination.   There is no shortage of authority illustrating that the courts will go to great lengths to protect the individual against the well-meant but unauthorised intervention of the medical profession.   In *Malette v. Shulman*[27] a seriously injured woman was diagnosed as needing a blood transfusion to save her life.   Despite a card found in her purse indicating that she was a Jehovah's Witness and did not wish to receive blood products she was transfused.   Having recovered, Malette sued the doctor for treating without her consent. The Canadian court took a markedly self-determinative approach holding that the doctor was liable for the tort of battery and stating that:

> [a] competent adult is generally entitled to reject a specific treatment or all treatment, or to select an alternate form of treatment, even if the decision may entail risks as serious as death and may appear mistaken in the eyes of the medical profession or of the community ...
>
> The principles of self-determination and individual autonomy compel the conclusion that the patient may reject blood transfusions even if harmful consequences may result and even if the decision is regarded as foolhardy. ... To transfuse a Jehovah's Witness in the face of her explicit instructions to the contrary would, in my opinion, violate her right to control her own body and show disrespect for the religious values by which she has chosen to live her life.[28]

The right of a patient to refuse even life-saving treatment has been recognised in English law in *Airedale NHS Trust v. Bland*[29] where it was stated (by Lord Keith) that an adult who is conscious and of sound mind "is completely at liberty to decline to undergo treatment, even if the result of his doing so will be that he will die."[30] Although these comments seem to uphold unconditionally the right of the competent adult to control her own body and destiny, the position is, on closer examination, not so clear cut. The judges are always conscious of the conflict between self-determination and the sanctity of life. This is present in all cases where an individual chooses to die rather than to accept life-saving treatment and the dilemma that faces doctors (trained to treat) in this situation should not be under-estimated. It is, however, especially acute in the case of a pregnant woman who, by refusing treatment endangers both her own life and that of the foetus. In general, where the courts have felt unable to countenance the assertion of self-determination, the issue has been side-stepped by concentrating not on the conflict between sanctity of life and self-determination but on the question of the validity of the withholding of consent. If the competence of the individual to consent or to refuse is successfully questioned the issue of autonomy is shelved: the individual concerned is incapable of deciding for herself and, like a child or someone with a mental disorder, may be treated in what another decides are her best interests. This ambivalence towards self-determination is apparent in *Re T*:[31] a woman who was not a Jehovah's Witness but who had been brought up by her mother who adhered fervently to those beliefs, instructed, after a conversation with her mother, that she was not to be given blood if that should prove necessary. When it did become necessary the High Court declared that it would not be unlawful to administer a transfusion as it was in her best interests to do so. The judges in the Court of Appeal were clear that a person has the right to refuse treatment, regardless of the consequences. Nevertheless it was held that on the particular facts it was not unlawful to treat even in the face of her refusal because of the influence exercised over T by her mother: T's decision was not her own and she had not meant what she said.

Whilst the courts must be vigilant on behalf of those who are truly incapable of making their own choices, by admitting these vague "outside influences" as a challenge to the capacity to give a valid consent, the courts have delivered a considerable weapon to those who find it difficult to accept that for some individuals their beliefs or wishes lead them to choose death rather than life. That is not, however, the only reason why *Re T* may be seen as less than whole-hearted support for self-determination. As it happened, T was pregnant: her baby was delivered still born by caesarian section before her condition deteriorated. No question arose as to her consent to that procedure but in deciding the lawfulness of transfusion Lord Donaldson MR held that while the competent patient has the right to refuse treatment, this right may possibly be qualified in "a case in which the choice may lead to the death of a viable foetus ... if and when it arises the courts will be faced with a novel problem of considerable legal and ethical complexity."[32]

Here self-determination and sanctity of life collide most obviously and, from the point of view of pregnant women, most troublingly. The law is not unused to the need to balance competing interests: few cases are, after all, entirely one-sided. The law therefore falls easily into the practice of considering both sides even when dealing with the most fundamental of questions including the right to bodily integrity and protection from unauthorised treatment. It has been suggested that in the case of self-determination there are a number of competing interests including the preservation of life and the protection of an innocent third party.[33] In the case of an adult woman who is not pregnant, sanctity of life seems unlikely, on the strength of most authority, to override her right to refuse treatment. For a pregnant woman, however, the position is very different. It becomes apparent that Woman and Pregnant Woman are legally very different - a distinction which many (pregnant) women struggle to accept. The question: "one person or two?" is designed to highlight the supposed conflict between woman and foetus and is arguably a typically (male) legal approach to Pregnant Woman. It sees and objectifies the pregnancy in terms of the woman as a vessel for a new person: Woman becomes invisible. There is no room for the experience of pregnancy as integration rather than competition. The law cannot cope with such a "self-centred" idea since it is wedded to balancing the rights of one against the rights of another. From the point of view of law, Pregnant Woman is no longer Woman but is a means, albeit to whom certain duties are owed, to an end. That end is the production of a healthy child who must be protected against her mother if necessary. The foetus, on this basis, since it has no independent voice, must be heard through the protection of the law.

The result of this is to deprive women of their right to refuse treatment where to do so endangers the foetus. Instances of court authorised forcible caesarians occur in a number of jurisdictions.[34] One of the most infamous and poignant is that of *Re AC*.[35] Angela Carder was twenty-six and a half weeks pregnant and was dying from cancer, the evidence being that she would live only another forty-eight hours. Although she was sedated, her family maintained that she had been opposed to a caesarian section. Evidence was presented to the court that the foetus had a fifty to sixty per cent chance of survival if delivered, though the procedure could well hasten Angela's death. The court ordered a caesarian, the child did not live and Angela died two days later. The decision was later overturned,[36] the appeal court noting that the lower court had proceeded by balancing the rights of the mother against the interest of the State in protecting the rights of third parties i.e. the foetus. The majority decision of the appellate court was that it would be an extraordinary case indeed in which a court might ever be justified in overriding the patient's wishes and authorising a major surgical procedure such as a caesarian section.[37]

This appears to uphold the right to self-determination of pregnant women: the law sees Woman rather than Pregnant Woman. It is, however, one decision, in one State, in particularly unusual circumstances. Angela Carder was going to die, no matter what was or was not done to her, while the foetus had some chance of survival. By far the more usual case is that where the mother or, more typically, the foetus may die without treatment, but with it both will almost certainly live. In the one reported English case, *Re S*,[38] S was having her third child and had been in labour for a considerable time. The court heard that without a caesarian the baby could not be born alive and that the mother's life was also endangered. Based on their religious beliefs, both S and her partner refused the procedure. The court declared that the operation could lawfully proceed against the couple's wishes, referring in a brief, hurried judgment to *Re AC* as giving support for intervention, presumably on the questionable basis that this was an "extraordinary" case. *Re S* encapsulates the problems inherent in the law's engagement with pregnant women underlining the different legal status of Pregnant Woman and the perceived conflict between mother and foetus. The depth of the problem is shown in a dissenting judgment in *Re AC* in which the judge states that:

> a woman who carries a child to viability is in fact a member of a unique category of persons ... A woman carrying a viable unborn child is not in the same category as a relative, friend, or stranger called upon to donate bone marrow or an organ for transplant. Rather the expectant mother has placed herself in a special class of persons who are bringing another person into existence, and upon whom that other person's life is totally dependent. Also uniquely, the viable unborn child is literally captive within the mother's body.[39]

Note the assumption that pregnant women are no longer "merely" women and the inevitable consequence that they no longer have the rights of women. The extent to which this departs from the usual position can be gauged by comparing the general rules as to a person's legal duty to help another. In the Anglo-American tradition it is a general principle of law that there is no liability for failure to act and thus a person who sees another drowning will not be under any legal compulsion to attempt a rescue - no matter how easy that may be. There are some exceptions to the rule on omissions, notably where there is a special kind of relationship between the parties, and of particular relevance in this context are those cases where there is a parent-child or doctor-patient link. Even here, however, the parent/doctor has no obligation to risk life or injury. If a child requires a kidney transplant or bone marrow donation, and the only good match is her father there is no *legal* compulsion on the father to undergo the necessary surgery.[40] Since the courts will not order invasive surgery in these cases, on the basis that to do so would offend against fundamental principles of bodily integrity and autonomy (and according to one case[41] would raise the spectre of the swastika and the Inquisition) it begs the question as to why the law should distinguish between a parent and Pregnant Woman. There are undoubted similarities between the cases and in particular it is impossible to escape the conclusion that a parent is under a heavy moral responsibility to take steps to preserve the life of a child, but the presence of an ethical imperative is by no means a *sufficient* justification for the imposition of a legal obligation (as the rescue principle indicates). A woman who refuses a caesarian may be morally responsible for the death of her foetus, just as a father who refuses to rescue a drowning child may be. But if the father cannot swim and the current is strong he will not be subject to legal coercion. A caesarian is a major invasive procedure: it is routine and comparatively safe but it does carry risks for the woman.[42] It does mean that the chance of a subsequent vaginal delivery is reduced and there is also evidence that incidence of post-natal depression is higher following caesarians. The procedure may limit the number of pregnancies which are medically advised. These are reasons which a woman may take into account in refusing the procedure. She may also have religious reasons for her refusal and in other contexts these are respected, even though, as the judges comment, many would find them incomprehensible or irrational.

There is, too, another aspect to the issue of forcible delivery by caesarian. The argument appears to be that the means (subjugation of the woman's personal autonomy and subjection to risk) is justified by the good consequences (delivery of healthy baby). Such a consequentialist argument is unlimited: if a woman may not exercise her right to personal autonomy at the end of the process, the same may well be true from the start of her assumption of this special status of Pregnant Woman.[43] Pregnant women are advised not to smoke, drink, take drugs, eat certain foods, engage in certain activities, work in certain environments. If they may be compelled to undergo invasive surgery, they may also be ordered to do or to abstain from doing other things with penalties should they not comply. So far, there has been little evidence in the UK of such intervention in what might be described as a woman's private life.[44] This is not the case, however, elsewhere. In the USA it is possible to find examples of the legal control of pregnant women even to the extent of criminalising these women. In 1986 a woman was charged under the California Penal Code with "child" abuse for wilfully failing to provide medical care in relation to the foetus she was carrying.[45] She had ignored medical advice regarding drug use, abstention from sexual intercourse and the need to call for medical assistance if she began to bleed. Her baby was born with brain damage and died within two months. She was not convicted because it was held that the relevant statute was not intended to punish women for conduct during pregnancy. Since then, however, prosecutions have continued and in Florida, for example, a young crack addict has been convicted of exposing her babies to drugs while pregnant. Although that statute did not apply to foetuses either, the court convicted on the basis that the cocaine passed to the infants during the short period after birth and before the cord was cut.[46] Other cases exemplify the idea that a woman's freedom of choice during pregnancy will be suspended in order to prefer the "rights of the foetus". To this end, the courts have been willing to order women to undergo monitoring and even the detention of pregnant women.[47] In one case a woman who was convicted of dishonesty involving $700 was sent to prison for the length of her pregnancy expressly because the judge wanted to protect the baby from the mother's drug abuse.[48] Even if the courts stop short of direct action, indirect control is evident where the courts allow pre-natal conduct to influence decisions as to custody of the child once it is born or to allow the baby to sue the mother for damage caused by her conduct during pregnancy.[49]

In the private politics of pregnancy, the law creates a Pregnant Woman who is forced to compromise her autonomy in favour of that of the foetus. Instead of being credited by the law with the capacity and intelligence to make their own decisions women may have their opinions ignored as being misguided or misinformed. Pregnant women who indulge in anti-social behaviour, such as drug-taking, or ignore the advice given to them by "medical experts" may be viewed as deviating from proper maternal behaviour to such an extent that in some jurisdictions they may be subjected to criminal sanctions.

THE POLITICS OF THE WORKPLACE: WORKER OR PREGNANT WOMAN?

It is against the background of her treatment in the private sphere that the law's construction of the pregnant *worker* must be assessed. A woman's status as a worker may be threatened by her pregnancy for a number of reasons. She may, for example, be physically unable to carry out her work because of the pregnancy. In particular, the duties she is called upon to perform or her working environment may pose a danger to her health or the well-being of the foetus. Even if she is capable of performing her job, an employer may wish to dismiss her in the belief that her continued presence at work will involve a degree of disruption, for example absence for ante-natal appointments, that will upset the smooth running of the enterprise. Every woman will need time off work immediately before and after the birth of her child and the inconvenience that this may represent may persuade the employer not to hold open her job for her.

The law's treatment of these issues will dictate how it perceives and hence constructs the Pregnant Woman as worker. In the private sphere the rights of women are weighed against those of the foetus. In the workplace the situation is more complex since a great deal depends on what approach the law takes towards a particular issue. Is the pregnant worker to be regarded first and foremost as an employee so that any specific problems that she experiences are subsumed into the wider context of employment law? Is pregnancy primarily a health and safety issue with employers being charged with the responsibility of adopting policies that ensure a safe working environment for the employees as well as a due regard for the foetus? Alternatively, is the treatment of pregnant workers most accurately perceived as an opportunity for sex discrimination, using a woman's procreative functions as an excuse for treating her less favourably than a man?

1. Threats to the pregnancy

Women in paid work are restricted in both their employment choices and opportunities by policies designed to exclude them from the workplace on the basis that there are potential risks not to them but to a foetus. The danger typically arises from agents, such as lead, used in manufacturing and other processes and from radiation used in x-rays.[50] Two approaches can be taken towards such hazards. On the one hand an employer can adopt a "hazard-based approach", which requires that the hazard be reduced or eliminated. The alternative is a "worker-restricting approach", which may necessitate the removal of those employees who are vulnerable to a particular hazard.[51] The former approach is likely to involve higher costs but will place fewer restrictions on workers than the latter. At first sight, the law in the UK appears to require employers to eliminate hazards, since the Health and Safety at Work Act 1974 obliges them to provide working conditions which ensure, as far as is reasonably practicable, the health and safety of their employees.[52] Conversely, however, regulations that deal with specific substances, such as lead, are couched in terms of control measures designed to restrict the exposure of employees.[53] In reality, the emphasis in the legislation on an employer doing what is reasonably practicable in the circumstances means that materials that pose a threat to pregnant workers but not to their non-pregnant colleagues are unlikely to be eliminated because the costs and other burdens associated with eliminating a risk posed simply to this group are unlikely to be seen as reasonably practicable.[54] Until recently, therefore, an employer might legitimately have dismissed a pregnant worker on the grounds that her continued employment contravened safety regulations and was unlawful.[55] As a result of a European Union initiative,[56] new health and safety regulations have been introduced in the United Kingdom[57] and women in occupations deemed a threat to the foetus may not now be dismissed. Instead their employers must either eliminate the threat, or transfer the worker to more suitable employment, or where that is not possible, suspend her without loss of pay.[58]

This new approach to dangers facing pregnant women in the workplace has the advantage over the old of ensuring women keep their jobs or at least their pay. The harsh pragmatism of the old law - if the pregnant worker is prevented by law from doing her job, then dismiss her - has been replaced by a more benevolent paternalism. What the pregnant worker is still not allowed to do is make her own choice about the dangers facing her and her unborn child in the workplace. In the same way that the laws surrounding medical treatment seem to give priority to the foetus, so too does the law regarding health and safety at work. In *Habermann-Beltermann v. Arbeiterwohlfahrt, Bezirksverband Ndb/Opf eV*[59] the European Court of Justice decided that the termination of a pregnant woman's contract of employment was contrary to European law. The woman was a nurse specifically employed to work nights, but German law on the protection of mothers prohibits a pregnant woman from undertaking night-work. However, although it was held unlawful to end the contract of employment, there was no argument about the justification for the German protective legislation. Although her employment rights may be preserved, the woman's freedom to choose when she will work was removed (in this case she could not work days because of existing dependant children) even though the question of the harm caused by night-work either to a woman or a foetus was not specifically addressed in the judgment.

Exclusionary policies that take effect once a worker is *pregnant* are short-term in their effect. After the birth of her child a woman may presumably return to her original job. In some workplaces, however, the agents used may threaten a woman's ability to conceive or to bear a child. Alternatively, the slightest exposure of the foetus may carry a risk of serious harm and it may be several weeks before a woman realises she is pregnant. In these circumstances can an employer justify the exclusion of *all* female employees of child-bearing age? Such policies which seek to exclude women from work on the basis of their potential for child-bearing are unacceptable on the basis that they discriminate against women, reduce their employment opportunities and refuse to see women as independent from their procreative function: women workers are defined by their biology. Differences between women are ignored and it is assumed that all women are potential mothers, not wage-earners. *All* workers are entitled to safe working environments in which risks are minimised. A woman is entitled to expect that should she become pregnant, she will not be forced to work in conditions which threaten the health of the foetus but she is also entitled to take control over her own body. To subordinate the woman to the foetus or the potential foetus is unacceptable:

> One can forget that however important the life of the foetus is, it exists within 'another human being, and if one forgets to respect her life, all the advances in individual freedom, autonomy and human dignity that have been made are negated. She is cast back in the role of second class citizen which the human rights movements of the last century have done much to obliterate.[60]

There has been one occasion in the UK, in *Page v. Freight Hire (Tank Haulage Co) Ltd*,[61] where an exclusionary policy of this nature was challenged. Mrs Page was twenty-three, divorced and employed as a tanker driver. Her employer told her she could no longer drive lorries carrying dimethylformamide (DMF) because the makers had warned them that it was dangerous to women of child-bearing age. It should be noted, however, that whilst DMF has a variety of unpleasant side-effects for both women *and* men no attempt was made to prevent men from driving the lorries. Page told her employer that she was aware of the risk, accepted it, did not want children and was prepared to grant an indemnity to the employer should injury in fact occur. This offer was rejected and Page lost her job. Her complaint that she had been discriminated against on grounds of her sex was accepted by the court, but declared to be lawful on the basis that the Sex Discrimination Act 1975 allowed discrimination based on laws which pre-dated the Act. The court accepted that the Health and Safety at Work Act 1974 provided the employer with a defence since it requires employers to take all reasonably practicable steps to protect the health and safety of employees. Subsequently much general "protective" legislation was repealed and the relevant section of the Sex Discrimination Act was amended[62] but still expressly permits discriminatory treatment of women provided this is sanctioned by earlier legislation (including regulations made under those Acts) where it is necessary for the protection of *women* as regards maternity, pregnancy or other risks specifically affecting women. It is likely therefore that the amendment would not have assisted Page: she is within the protected class whether she wants to be or not.

If the workplace poses a threat to a woman's pregnancy or her reproductive potential the law in the United Kingdom is prepared to sanction her removal from the workplace on the grounds of health and safety. Her personal autonomy is compromised and her financial independence may be threatened because in this situation the law sees women primarily in terms of their reproductive role and not as independent actors. This becomes even clearer when the situation of men is compared: first, there does not appear to be the same degree of concern for male reproductive health (even though evidence shows that this is at risk from the working environment); second, if men *were* excluded from a particular job because of such a threat, but women were not, there would be unlawful sex discrimination because the exception in the Act only relates to women. It is instructive to note that in other jurisdictions this whole issue has been approached not from a health and safety perspective but as raising questions of sex discrimination.

In the USA the legitimacy of foetal exclusion policies was considered by the Supreme Court in *International Union, United Auto Workers v. Johnson Controls*.[63] Prior to that decision it was estimated that the enforcement of foetal protection policies in the USA could close up to twenty million jobs to women.[64] The case involved the USA's largest producer of car batteries in the manufacture of which lead plays a large part. It is known that exposure to lead is potentially harmful and that this includes exposure of the foetus through the mother. Johnson decided that women should be excluded from any job involving exposure to lead unless there was proof that the woman had been sterilised or was infertile. This applied regardless of intention, contraception or age, including women over fifty and those whose husbands had been sterilised. The policy did not, however, apply to men, even though it is also known that lead affects male reproductive capacity as well. In the Supreme Court it was held (reversing the lower courts) that the policy was sexually discriminatory and unlawful under Title VII of the Civil Rights Act 1964 as amended by the Pregnancy Discrimination Act 1978.[65] The Court noted that fertile men, but not fertile women were given the choice as to whether they wished to risk their reproductive health for a particular job. Justice Blackmun in giving the Court's opinion stated that decisions about the welfare of future children must be left to the parents who conceive, bear, support and raise them rather than to the employers who hire those parents and that the law simply did not allow the dismissal of a woman because of her failure to submit to sterilisation. He noted that concern for a woman's existing or potential offspring has been used historically as the excuse for denying women equal employment opportunities but that it is no more appropriate for the Courts than it is for individual employers to decide whether a woman's reproductive role is more important to herself and her family than her economic role.

Even before *Johnson* it had been pointed out that foetal exclusion policies seemed only to apply to jobs and industries traditionally seen as male-dominated and which thus also paid higher wages. The same concern was not manifested for those women in "women's work" who were exposed to the same chemicals and radiation in hospitals, dry cleaners and dental surgeries. Neither was there a similar drive to protect potential fathers even though a toxin may affect both men and women.[66] Furthermore, even though the decision may have outlawed the policies themselves the thinking behind them may be harder to dislodge: employers are liability conscious and their response may be to ensure not that risks are minimised to make the environment safer for men and women but that women sign away rights they or the foetus may otherwise have to sue the employer for negligence should an injury in fact occur. A woman who chooses to keep her job, having been warned that exposure to certain substances is potentially harmful, should, however, not be denied the right to expect that the risks are minimised and that she is protected so far as is practicable. The same applies to her male colleagues.

Employers may argue at this point that women are asking too much: they want to be free to work at the occupation of their choice, but expect compensation - from the employer - should something go wrong. It is true that every employer owes a duty of care to the individual employee but this duty is broken only if the employer fails to take reasonable care. Total exclusion from the workplace is a particularly draconian response to the problem. It is moreover one which seems to be more common in traditionally male areas of work. Women of child-bearing age are not routinely excluded from hospitals, textile factories or childcare jobs even though these all involve risks to a foetus.[67] Even if one considers the problem from the point of view of liability to the child who is born damaged, the law in the UK provides in the Congenital Disabilities (Civil Liability) Act 1976 that a child may sue for injuries as a result of an occurrence before its birth, but it is a defence for the employer to show that the employee was aware of the risks and had accepted them. There is always a problem in employment in deciding how voluntary such assumption of risk may be said to be: if the choice is between a highly paid and a low paid job or between a job and no job, the worker may be over-influenced by economic necessity. At this point paternalism takes over in that women will simply be prevented from exercising their choice in the interests of any child they *might* bear. This underlines the view that women are perceived principally in terms of their responsibility for producing the next generation of workers: that is what they are for and that is the sum of their identity. Their wishes are subordinate if they wish to act in a way which may threaten a foetus - even if they do not intend to become pregnant. On this model women are valued as child-bearers (not workers) and cannot be trusted to make sensible decisions about their own life-styles. Furthermore, their work is perceived as secondary. In a lower court in the *Johnson* case in the US, it was said that women want to work only "to better the family's station in life"[68] a statement which epitomises the stereotypical idea of a male breadwinner whose wife works only for the extras. Not only does this philosophy discriminate against women, it also prejudices the working conditions of men. Many agents which threaten the foetus also pose risks to the reproductive health of male employees: exclusion of women from that workplace means that employers are less likely to introduce measures which would minimise or eliminate risks. Removing one section of the workforce is considerably cheaper than having to take precautions for all workers.

2. Threats to the pregnant worker

Threats posed by the workplace to a woman's pregnancy can be viewed by the law in a variety of ways with radically different outcomes; some of which are more beneficial to women than others. The same is true of threats to the pregnant worker. These refer to actions taken by an employer, such as refusing to hire a pregnant worker or deciding to dismiss her because her presence is seen as potentially disruptive or as involving the business in additional expense. It might seem that the obvious way for the law to construct such behaviour is as sex discrimination against a pregnant woman. The United Kingdom courts have, however, consistently rejected the argument that to refuse to offer a pregnant woman employment or alternatively to dismiss her because she is pregnant automatically amounts to direct discrimination.[69] The wording of the Sex Discrimination Act requires a woman to compare her treatment with that accorded to a man.[70] In its early jurisprudence the UK courts simply dismissed such pregnancy discrimination claims on the basis that no such comparison was possible in the case of pregnancy.[71] In later cases the UK courts have been prepared to equate pregnancy with illness. The court would ask whether a sick man would have been treated in a more favourable fashion than the pregnant woman had been treated. Only if the answer was yes, might this amount to sex discrimination.[72] This comparative approach was criticised on various grounds.[73] First it equated pregnancy with illness, giving the impression that a pregnant worker was in a "delicate condition" as described in Victorian novels. The formula also worked to the advantage of employers who treated all their employees, pregnant or not, in an ungenerous fashion. Far more seriously, it forced a pregnant worker to comply with a male standard when her experience is uniquely female.[74]

The United Kingdom was not alone in its refusal to treat the adverse behaviour directed towards a pregnant worker as automatically constituting sex discrimination. Courts in the United States, for example, have been prepared to adopt very similar reasoning. Disability insurance plans that specifically excluded pregnancy from the risks insured have been held not to be discriminatory[75] on the basis that pregnancy is a condition restricted solely to women. An exclusion would be discriminatory only if the condition in question applied to both sexes, and one sex was covered against the risk and the other was not. Later legislation, the Pregnancy Discrimination Act 1978, has adopted the comparative approach by providing that "women affected by pregnancy, childbirth or related medical conditions shall be treated the same for all employment-related purposes, ... as other persons not so affected but similar in their ability or inability to work."[76]

The interests of women are far better served by the purposive approach of the European Court of Justice. In a series of decisions it has reasoned that "[a]s employment can only be refused because of pregnancy to women, such a refusal is direct discrimination on grounds of sex."[77] This acknowledges that it is misleading to ask how a similarly situated man would be treated. Pregnancy is incontrovertibly associated with a woman's sex so discrimination on these grounds must constitute sex discrimination. In the light of this clear ruling from the European Court of Justice, the UK courts might be expected to have abandoned their comparative approach and in *Webb v. EMO* the House of Lords did decide that to dismiss a woman because she is pregnant *is* unlawful direct discrimination[78] holding that child-bearing is a characteristic of the female sex and to base dismissal on that is to base it on gender. In this case, however, the pregnant worker had been hired to replace another worker who was about to go on maternity leave, and the House of Lords determined that the employee was not dismissed because she was pregnant but because her pregnancy meant that she would not be available for work at the time she was required. Since a man hired for the same reason would also have been dismissed if absent at the crucial time, this was not sex discrimination in the view of the House of Lords. The European Court of Justice was not impressed by this argument: confirming its earlier approach it held that to dismiss a woman employed for an indefinite period simply because she would be temporarily prevented from working because of pregnancy was contrary to European law.[79] In particular the Court held that there could be no question of comparing a woman temporarily unable to work because of pregnancy with a man similarly incapable for medical or other reasons: pregnancy is not in any way comparable with a pathological condition and even less so with unavailability for work on non-medical grounds. Such a trenchant rejection of the distinction put forward in the House of Lords is refreshing in its emphasis that pregnancy discrimination is sex discrimination but it was met by immediate claims from employers' organisations that it would seriously disadvantage women by discouraging the employment of women of child-bearing age. It will take more than a ruling from the European Court to persuade employers that the pregnant worker is anything more than an expensive and troublesome deviation from the normal (male) pattern of employee.

If pregnancy is not to place women at a grave disadvantage in the employment market and make a mockery of the notion of equal opportunities something more positive is necessary. The policy adopted in the United Kingdom and in other European countries has been to grant pregnant workers certain additional legal rights. A note of caution has often been sounded about awarding women such rights:

> [I]f society recognizes pregnancy as requiring special solicitude, it is a slippery slope back to the 'protectionist' legislation that historically barred women from the workplace.[80]

This, however, misconceives the purpose of such rights. Rather than representing an admission of women's inability to cope, they are an acknowledgment of the need for society as a whole to share the burdens of reproduction. The bearing and rearing of children benefits society as a whole and therefore society must ensure that those who are most intimately involved in this process should not suffer as a consequence. The worrying feature of such rights is that they focus on pregnancy and therefore on women. It would be far more satisfactory if other rights, such as parental leave, were also available which would stress the responsibility of both men and women toward their children, rather than present this as solely a "woman's issue".[81] The UK offers a good example of how awarding pregnant workers special protection does not necessarily meet the needs of those women.

Almost twenty years ago the United Kingdom began to introduce legal rights for pregnant workers until ultimately there were four such rights. These were the right not to be unlawfully dismissed because of pregnancy; the right to return to the same job after the birth; the right to paid time off for ante-natal care and the right to Statutory Maternity Pay (SMP).[82] There was general agreement that this network of rights, though better than no protection, offered women less than that enjoyed by their counterparts in the European Union.[83] The Trade Union Reform and Employment Rights Act 1993 (the 1993 Act) modified these rights in order to comply with the Protection of Pregnant Workers Directive[84] which the United Kingdom, together with every other State in the Union, was required to implement by October 1994.

To appreciate the approach taken in the 1993 Act to the pregnant worker, a little needs to be said about the network of rights it replaced. If the State is serious in its commitment to equal opportunity, it should ensure that a woman is able to combine the demands of both motherhood and career. As originally conceived the rights offered women a way of tackling the unfair treatment too often associated with pregnancy and substantial numbers of women benefited from their existence.[85] They reinforced the view that when a woman becomes pregnant she may, quite legitimately, wish to remain in paid employment. The major weakness of the scheme, however, was that the network of maternity rights was part of the general scheme of employment rights. Access to employment rights required a worker to satisfy a qualifying threshold stated in terms of length of employment and the same thresholds were used to control access to maternity rights. Rather than being granted these rights automatically in order to protect her position in the labour market, a woman was forced to earn them and, inevitably, large numbers of women failed to do so and suffered the consequences. One study estimated that forty per cent of women employees failed to fulfil the criteria necessary for claiming maternity leave.[86] Inability to qualify was, however, not evenly spread throughout the population of working women and those engaged in semi-skilled and unskilled manual work were less likely to qualify than those holding professional or managerial positions.[87]

The other major disadvantages experienced with this network of rights was the excessive complexity associated with its day-to-day application, and its restrictive interpretation. Much of this seems to be attributable to a desire on the part of the courts, and indeed the legislators, not to burden employers with excessive demands. Courts referred to the need "to make industrial sense of an Act of Parliament relating to industrial relations and not industrial nonsense."[88] They saw it as their task to balance the competing interests of employers and employees. This perception was misplaced since the legislation was meant to safeguard the position of women in the labour force by attempting to ensure that pregnancy was not used as an excuse to deny women equal opportunities with men. As the House of Lords stated "it is often a considerable inconvenience to an employer to have to make the necessary arrangements to keep a woman's job open for her while she is absent from work in order to have a baby, but this is a price that has to be paid as part of the social and legal recognition of the equal status of women in the workplace."[89] All too often the legislation had the opposite effect. As one commentator pointed out:

> [t]he continuous service requirement has been criticised by those concerned to promote equal opportunities on the grounds that it reduces women's flexibility in the labour market - and hence may reduce their career opportunities - by making it possible that women of childbearing age may have to choose between maintaining their statutory entitlement and advancing their careers through changes of employer.[90]

The 1993 Act now approaches the treatment of pregnant workers as a matter of health and safety rather than an industrial relations issue and this gives a different emphasis to the perception of pregnant workers.[91] In the first place the 1993 Act provides that all pregnant workers, regardless of their length of service, are entitled to return to their previous employment after a fourteen week period of maternity leave.[92] The decision to abandon qualifying thresholds is logical if the desire is to ensure a woman's well-being during the period directly before and after the birth of her child. During that fourteen week period, all those rights to which a woman may be entitled under her contract of employment, with the exception of remuneration, continue to accrue.[93] This means, therefore, that benefits such as a woman's pension contributions and holiday entitlement will not be affected. Absences because of pregnancy are thus not allowed to have an adverse effect upon her employment situation, except for pay. The Pregnancy Directive provides that a pregnant worker is entitled to an allowance "at least equivalent to that which the worker concerned would receive in the event of a break in her activities on grounds connected with her state of health."[94] If, however, pregnant employees are already entitled to greater benefits than those contemplated in the Directive these must remain in being.

The need to pay a woman whilst on maternity leave is, on one level at least, a health and safety issue since if she does not receive any income whilst on leave the temptation is for her to return to work before this is advisable.[95]   There are, however, two major criticisms of the system of maternity benefit set out in the 1993 Act. First, the level of benefit paid to pregnant employees is very low, as compared to the rest of Europe. From October 1994 a woman who has been continuously employed in the same job for twenty-six weeks, provided she can satisfy this condition by the fifteenth week before the expected week of confinement, will be entitled to eighteen weeks SMP: six weeks at ninety per cent of her weekly earnings and the remaining twelve weeks at a rate of £52.50 per week. Women who fail to qualify for SMP may claim maternity allowance which is payable at the rate of £52.50 a week, provided the pregnant employee has paid twenty-six national insurance contributions in the sixty-six weeks before her baby is due.[96] These rules will inevitably mean that some women, particularly those below the minimum earnings threshold for national insurance contributions, will receive no maternity benefit whatsoever.[97] Even those eligible to claim will receive a far from generous payment. It is difficult to justify these low levels of benefit, particularly since, in its draft form, the Directive provided that pregnant workers should receive eighty per cent of their weekly salary for eighteen weeks. It was in the light of opposition from the United Kingdom that this was changed.

As the law now stands pregnant workers in general receive the same rates of benefit as employees who are absent from work because of illness. This appears still to equate pregnant workers with sick workers, though the Directive specifically refutes such a comparison.[98] Pregnancy is not an illness and there seems no reason not to pay benefits that reflect a woman's weekly earnings whilst she is absent on maternity leave. The United Kingdom government has, however, resolutely refused to do so. Its thinking reflects its approach to social security payments in general. The State provides a basic level of help either to those who contribute towards the social security system (via national insurance contributions) or to those who have no alternative resources (via means-tested benefits). In order to enjoy a more generous level of provision individuals are left to make their own arrangements. Employers may be persuaded to offer more realistic maternity benefits through the process of collective bargaining or employees must rely on their own resources. Indeed there may be the unspoken assumption in the case of pregnancy that a pregnant worker should have a man to support her whilst she is absent from work and hence should require no additional help from the State.

On the other hand, one positive benefit to emerge from the 1993 Act is the protection accorded a pregnant worker from dismissal during her pregnancy and immediately after the birth of her child. The Act takes the view that:

> a pregnant woman has the right to continue in employment until she takes her maternity leave. If she is incapable of work due to pregnancy, she should be treated as sick and eligible for sick pay where appropriate. If she is not permitted

> to do her job because of the dangers to her or the baby, she should be offered alternative work or suspended with pay. She should not be dismissed.[99]

This emphasises that pregnancy should not be used as an excuse for dismissal in order to avoid the problems, such as absences from work, that are sometimes associated with pregnancy. Once, however, a woman returns from maternity leave she no longer enjoys this protection. If she is forced to take time off because of long-term effects of her pregnancy or because her child is sick her employer may well be entitled to dismiss her.[100] After the birth she is again regarded first and foremost as a worker who is subject to the same laws as any other worker regarding absences from work. The special protection that she enjoyed whilst she was a pregnant worker was based on the health and safety considerations of being a worker who is *pregnant*. When no longer pregnant, her chance of enjoying equal opportunities with men is limited since there is no account taken of the fact that she is a *woman* worker with all the background disadvantages, such as caring responsibilities, that this involves. The only protection that she is offered as a *woman* worker is via the anti-discrimination legislation and that simply asks the question how her treatment compares with that accorded to a man.

There is, moreover, no guarantee that a woman's ability to combine motherhood and paid employment will be substantially improved as a consequence of the 1993 Act. There is general agreement that a fourteen week period of maternity leave is too short. Some women will be entitled to longer periods either because better terms have been agreed with their employer or because as a matter of law they are entitled to a forty week period of leave.[101] For those women who can claim only the legal minimum they may have to return to work within three weeks of their baby's birth. One of the factors that will be most influential in persuading a woman whether or not to return to work will be the availability of affordable, good quality child care and this is hard to find in the UK. Child care is not regarded as a work issue nor one that has to be tackled systematically if women are to enjoy equal opportunities. Instead it is regarded as a private matter in which government interference is inappropriate. Hence the public/private divide is manipulated to present this as a personal/family matter. This contrasts with how a pregnant woman is treated if she takes the personal/family decision to refuse a blood transfusion and risk the life of the foetus. The UK government has refused to recognise that the welfare of children is a matter of public concern and hence that the costs of child care should be borne by society at large rather than the individual. Without this institutional framework of child care and parental leave women will find their ability to function as workers severely restricted as compared with men.

CONCLUSION

The deficiencies in the law illustrated in this chapter result from its failure to address directly the idea of Pregnant Woman. The law approaches the question tangentially and much depends on which area of law is deemed most appropriate to handle a particular issue. In the public sphere the pregnant worker finds that her legal position is deemed to be most appropriately determined by employment law and health and safety regulations. The focus is on her status as a worker but one who happens to be pregnant and her interests must be balanced against those of her employer. In the private realm, her pregnancy means that she is identified no longer as Woman but as Pregnant Woman and her interests are balanced against those of the foetus.

Increasing numbers of women combine a career and motherhood and undoubtedly some have benefited from the law. The fact that women do succeed in their dual role is, however, a tribute to their determination and ingenuity rather than to the law. They have to pay a heavy price to continue in paid employment and American writers refer to women's double shift, that is their paid work outside and their unpaid work in the home.[102] For many women paid employment is their guarantee of financial independence, and they have recognised, though the law may not have done so, that a woman can no longer regard financial dependency on a man as acceptable. This chapter's final message is not that women are victims of the law but that they lack a voice in the decision-making process, both in the private and the public sphere and at the national and European level. Until their voice is heard the law will continue to fail to recognise the rights, the needs and the aspirations of Pregnant Woman.

NOTES

1.   *Turley v. Allders Department Store* [1980] I.C.R. 66, at p.70.

2.   See S.Sheldon, "The Law of Abortion and the Politics of Medicalisation" in this volume for the consequences of perceiving the foetus as a separate being in the abortion debate.

3.   For example, a man's occupation, if it exposes him to certain compounds, can threaten his partner's pregnancy or his ability to reproduce. See G.Chamberlain ed., *Pregnant Women at Work* (1984).

4.   C.Gilligan, *In a Different Voice* (1982) chapter 1.

5.   J.Halpern, L.Midge and J.Hickman, "Pregnancy as a source of bias in performance appraisals" (1993) 14 *Journal of Organizational Behaviour* 649; J.A.Scott, *Women and the Law* (1990) at pp.563-565.

6.   For example the majority of employees earning below the low pay threshold are women: Equal Opportunities Commission, *Women and Men in Britain 1993* (1993).

7.   H.Joshi, "The Cost of Caring" in *Women and Poverty in Britain the 1990s*, eds. C.Glendinning and J.Millar (1992) at p.114.

8.   J.Williams, "Gender Wars: Selfless Women in the Republic of Choice" (1991) 66 *New York University Law Review* 1559.

9.   See the results of the survey conducted by Susan McRae in *Maternity Rights in Britain* (1991).

10.   S.McRae, *ibid.*, chapter 6. Her findings indicate that the number of women forced to return to part-time work or faced with occupational downgrading may have declined.

11.   H.Joshi, *supra*, n.7, at p.116.

12.   H. Joshi, *ibid.*, at p.117.

13.   Pension rights normally accrue over a working lifetime. In the case of a state pension, a woman's absences from work in order to care for her children or, in certain circumstances an invalid, may not jeopardise her right to a pension. Home responsibilities protection permits years of home responsibility to be deducted from those years in which national insurance contributions for a pension should have been made. See R.Poynter and C.Martin, *Rights Guide to Non-Means-Tested Benefits*, (1993) at p.183. This is not the case with an occupational or a personal pension. When a woman is not working her occupational or personal pension will simply be frozen.

14.   The use of capitals for terms such as Pregnant Woman indicates a reference to the legal or social construction of those terms. A similar convention is used by other feminist writers. See, for example, C.Smart ed., *Regulating Womanhood: Historical Essays on Marriage, Motherhood and Sexuality* (1992).

15.   M.J.Frug, "A Postmodern Feminist Legal Manifesto (An Unfinished Draft)" (1992) 105 *Harvard Law Review* 1045, at p.1059.

16.   The Sex Discrimination Act 1986 and the Employment Act 1989 removed many of the restrictions on the hours when and the places where women might work.

17.   (1908) 208 U.S. 412.

18.   S.Kamerman, A.Kahn, and P.Kingston, *Maternity Policies and Working Women* (1983) at p.32.

19.   As a result of the Pregnancy Directive (Council Directive 92/85 on the introduction of measures to encourage improvements in the health and safety at work of pregnant workers and workers who have recently given birth or are breastfeeding), Member States of the European Union have harmonised their laws on the treatment of pregnant workers so as to provide a basic set of rights. These include protection from dismissal and a fourteen week period of paid maternity leave. In the USA the Pregnancy Discrimination Act 1978 expands the notion of sex discrimination to cover pregnancy discrimination. There is, however, no federal legislation on issues such as the need to provide paid maternity leave of a specified period.

20.   R.Dworkin, *Law's Empire* (1986).

21.   It is not coincidental that pregnant women are at once labelled mother (or at least mother-to-be).

22. See, for example, *C v. S* [1988] Q.B. 135; *Paton v. BPAS Trustees* [1979] Q.B. 276.
23. *Re F (in utero)* [1988] 2 All E.R. 193. See J.E.S.Fortin, "Can You Ward a Foetus?" (1988) 51 *M.L.R.* 768.
24. See, for example, *Tremblay v. Daigle* [1989] 2 S.C.R. 530, 62 D.L.R. (4th) 634 (Canadian Supreme Court); *Roe v. Wade* (1973) 410 U.S. 113 (U.S. Supreme Court) but see D.E.Johnsen, "The Creation of Fetal Rights: Conflicts with Women's Constitutional Rights to Liberty, Privacy and Equal Protection" (1986) 95 *Yale Law Journal* 599; and A.Diduck, "Legislating Ideologies of Motherhood" (1993) 2 *Social and Legal Studies* 461. For the position in a civil law system see, for example, M.Coester, "The protection of the embryo in German family law" (1993) 5 *Journal of Child Law* 88.
25. *Schloendorff v. Society of New York Hospital* (1914) 211 N.Y. 125.
26. *Bouvia v. Superior Court* (1986) 225 Cal. Rptr. 297 (Cal. C.A.) is a US example of a twenty-eight year-old quadriplegic with cerebral palsy and in continual pain from arthritis asserting her right in hospital to refuse food in order to die. In the UK the right to refuse life-sustaining treatment has been set out by the House of Lords in *Airedale NHS Trust v. Bland* [1993] 1 All E.R. 821.
27. (1990) 67 D.L.R. (4th) 321 (Ont C.A.).
28. *Ibid.*, at p.328 and p.330.
29. *Airedale NHS Trust v. Bland* [1993] 1 All E.R. 821.
30. *Ibid.*, at p.860.
31. *Re T (adult: refusal of medical treatment)* [1992] 4 All E.R. 649.
32. *Ibid.*, at p.653.
33. Also the prevention of suicide and the protection of the integrity of the medical profession: *In the Matter of Claire Conroy* (1985) 486 A. 2d 1209.
34. For further examples, see "Developments - Medical Technology and the Law, Section III: State Intervention During Pregnancy" (1990) 103 *Harvard Law Review* 1566. Figures cited there state that by mid-1987 fifteen court orders for caesarians had been sought in eleven States and thirteen had been granted.
35. (1987) 533 A. 2d 611 (D.C.).
36. (1990) 573 A. 2d 1235 (D.C., C.A.).
37. *Ibid.*, at p.1252.
38. [1992] 4 All E.R. 671. In "Two Patients Or One? Problems of Consent in Obstetrics" (1993) 1 *Medical Law International* 97, Dr Lisa Miller cites an example of a woman who refused an internal examination and who was held down, kicking and screaming by six people.
39. *Supra*, n.36, per Associate Judge Belson, at p.1256. See also *Baby R* [1988] 15 R.F.L. 3d 225, Ontario, (cited in Diduck, *op cit.*, n.24), in which a caesarian was ordered on the basis that the child was in need of protection; the doctor was authorised to do all that was necessary for the *child*, but was told that there was no consent to perform any procedure on the *mother*.
40. See, for example, *McFall v. Shimp* (1978) 10 Pa. D&C 3d 90, in which a US court refused to order a cousin to donate bone marrow even though the potential recipient would die without

it.

41.   *Ibid.*

42.   See, for example, L.Miller, *supra*, n.38.

43.   See especially N.Rhoden, "The Judge in the Delivery Room: The Emergency of Court-Ordered Caesarian" (1986) 74 Cal. L.R. 1951.   In the context of court ordered blood transfusions, see *Raleigh-Fitkin Paul Memorial Hospital v. Anderson* (1964) 201 A. 2d 537 (N.J.).

44.   Compare *D. v Berkshire C.C.* [1987] 1 All E.R. 20, where the House of Lords held that, in considering whether to remove a baby from her mother where she was born suffering drug withdrawal symptoms, it was correct to take into account the circumstances which existed prior to the baby's birth.

45.   (1986) *N.Y. Times*, 9 October, at A22, col.1.

46.   *State v. Johnson* (1989) (Fla. Cir. Ct., 13 July): sentence of fifteen years probation.

47.   See the examples given in D.Roberts, "Punishing Drug Addicts Who Have Babies: Women Of Color, Equality And The Right Of Privacy" (1991) 104 *Harvard Law Review* 1419.

48.   *U.S. v. Vaughn* (1988) D.C. Sup. Ct, cited in D.Roberts, *ibid.*, at p.1431.

49.   *Harvard Law Review, op. cit.*, n.34, at pp.1574-1577.   In the UK see *D v. Berkshire C.C.*, *supra*, n.44, but see now the Children Act 1989 and compare M.D.A.Freeman, "Care after 1991" in *Children and the Law*, ed. D.Freestone (1990), A.Bainham, "Care after 1991 - a reply" (1991) 3 *The Journal of Child Law* 99.   Under the Congenital Disabilities (Civil Liability) Act 1976, s.2, a child may not sue its mother for injury in utero unless it resulted from a car accident where the mother was driving.   In *Burton v. Islington Health Authority* [1992] 3 All E.R. 833, the Court of Appeal seems to accept the possibility that prior to the Act it would have been possible at common law for a child to sue its mother for pre-natal injury caused by alcohol or diet (per Dillon LJ at p.843).

50.   G.Chamberlain, *supra*, n.3.

51.   S.Lorber, "Legal Considerations of Reproductive Hazards in Industry in the United Kingdom" in G.Chamberlain, *ibid.*, 213, at p.214.

52.   Health and Safety at Work Act 1974, s.2.

53.   Control of Lead at Work Regulations 1980, S.I. 1980/1248, Regulation 6.

54.   *Edwards v. National Coal Board* [1949] 1 All E.R. 743.

55.   This was the case prior to 1993 amendments provided there was no suitable alternative work available (Employment Protection (Consolidation) Act 1978, s.60(1)).

56.   Council Directive 92/85, *supra* n.19.

57.   Management of Health and Safety at Work (Amendment) Regulations 1994 (in draft).

58.   *Ibid.*, Regulation 2.   See also the Employment Protection (Consolidation) Act 1978, ss.45-47, as amended.   The Pregnancy Directive improves the *employment* rights of pregnant workers but was passed as a *health and safety* measure under Article 118A of the Treaty of Rome which requires only a qualified majority vote.

59.   [1994] I.R.L.R. 364 (E.C.J.).

60.   L.Miller, *supra*, n.38, at p.99.

61. [1981] I.C.R. 299.

62. Employment Act 1989, s.3, amending the Sex Discrimination Act 1975, s.51.

63. (1991) U.S. 113 L. Ed. 2d 158; 111 S.Ct 1196; and see (1991) 37 *Equal Opportunities Review* at p. 26.

64. Bureau of National Affairs, *Pregnancy and Employment* (1987).

65. The Act provides that women affected by pregnancy, childbirth or related conditions are to be entitled to equal treatment with others who are similarly situated in their ability to work.

66. See, for example, S.Faludi, "Reproductive Rights under the Backlash" in *Backlash: The Undeclared War Against Women* (1992) at pp.475-476.

67. From chemicals, radiation or from infection such as rubella.

68. 886 F. 2d 871 (7th Cir), at p. 897.

69. For an account of the relevant case law, see A.Morris and S.M.Nott, "The Legal Response to Pregnancy" (1992) 12 *Legal Studies* 54.

70. Sex Discrimination Act 1975, s.1.

71. *Turley v. Allders Department Store* [1980] I.C.R. 66.

72. *Hayes v. Malleable Working Men's Club* [1985] I.R.L.R. 367.

73. A.Morris and S.M.Nott, *supra*, n.69, at pp.70-72.

74. For a discussion of the maleness of the standard used in tackling sex discrimination, see C.MacKinnon, *Toward a Feminist Theory of the State*, (1989) chapter 12.

75. *Geduldig v. Aiello* (1974) 417 U.S. 484 and *General Electric v. Gilbert* (1976) 429 U.S. 125.

76. Civil Rights Act 1964, Title VII, section 701, subsection (k).

77. *Dekker v. Stichting Vormingscentrum voor Jonge Volwassenen (VJV-Centrum)* [1991] I.R.L.R. 27, at p.29.

78. [1992] 4 All E.R. 929.

79. C-32/93 [1994] I.R.L.R. 482.

80. S.D.O'Connor, "Portia's Progress" (1991) 66 *New York University Law Review* 1546, at p.1554.

81. Some years ago the European Union attempted to agree a Directive on parental leave but the proposal was dropped because of opposition from the UK. See F.Rutherford, "The proposal for a European Directive on parental leave: some reasons why it failed" (1989) 17 *Policy and Politics* 301; "Paternity leave" (1994) 55 *Equal Opportunities Review* 14. In September 1994 the UK blocked planned legislation on paternity leave, using its right under the Maastricht Treaty to opt out of EU social policy. The remaining eleven Member States will proceed with the measure. See (1994) *The Independent*, 23 September and (1994) *The Times*, 23 September.

82. These rights were set out in ss.60,33,45 and 31A of the Employment Protection (Consolidation) Act 1978 and s.46 of the Social Security Act 1986. These have been amended to take account of Council Directive 92/85 on the protection of pregnant workers.

83. Women of Europe Supplement, *Childcare in the European Communities 1985-1990* (1990).

84. Council Directive 92/85, *supra*, n.19.

85. S.McRae, *supra*, n.9.

86.   *Ibid.*, at p.xxv and chapter 5.

87.   *Ibid.*

88.   *Grimsby Carpet Company v. Bedford* [1987] I.R.L.R. 438, at p.440.

89.   *Brown v. Stockton on Tees Borough Council* [1988] I.R.L.R. 263, at p.266.

90.   S.McRae, *supra*, n.9, at p.146.

91.   *Supra*, n.58.

92.   Trade Union Reform and Employment Rights Act 1993, s.23, adding new sections 33-37A to Part III, Employment Protection (Consolidation) Act 1978.

93.   *Ibid.*, s.23.

94.   Council Directive 92/85, article 11.

95.   In the case of the Pregnancy Directive, this was disputed by the UK government which argued that the Directive was really dealing with social security issues such as maternity pay.

96.   Social Security Terms and Conditions of Employment - The Maternity Allowance and Statutory Maternity Pay Regulations 1994, S.I. 1994/1230; Social Security Terms and Conditions of Employment - The Social Security Maternity Benefits and Statutory Sick Pay (Amendment) Regulations 1994, S.I. 1994/1367.

97.   It is estimated that twenty per cent of pregnant employees earn below the national insurance lower earnings threshold - currently £57 per week (figure quoted in (1994) 55 *Equal Opportunities Review* at p.38).

98.   Council Directive 92/85; Statement of the Council and the Commission concerning Article 11(3) of Directive 92/85/EEC, entered in the minutes of the 1608th meeting of the Council (Luxembourg, 19 October 1992).

99.   (1993) 50 *Equal Opportunities Review* at p.31.

100.   *Hertz v. Aldi Marked K/S* [1991] I.R.L.R. 31.

101.   Trade Union Reform and Employment Rights Act 1993, Schedule 2. The implementation of the Pregnancy Directive is not allowed to divest workers of rights that they already enjoyed if those rights guarantee workers more favourable treatment than is provided for in the Directive. Prior to the 1993 Act pregnant workers who could satisfy a qualifying threshold were entitled to up to forty weeks maternity leave. Schedule 2 preserves this right provided a worker satisfies the qualifying threshold.

102.   J.Williams, *supra*, n.8, at p.1595.

4 Making "social judgments that go beyond the purely medical": The Reproductive Revolution and Access to Fertility Treatment Services

SUSAN MILLNS

INTRODUCTION[1]

Over the past two decades what has come to be known as the "reproductive revolution" has gathered momentum fast. Some women, previously unable to have children, have realised their ambition to enter into motherhood with the aid of new reproductive technologies, such as in vitro fertilisation, embryo transfer and embryo freezing. The novelty of these reproductive technologies seems self-evident in that, for example, the use of in vitro fertilisation to create the first "test-tube" baby in 1978 marked a significant break away from the oldest route to conception, that is through heterosexual intercourse.

However, this is not to say that the originality of the new techniques of aided conception has escaped investigation. Renate Duelli Klein, in answer to the question, "[w]hat's 'new' about the 'new' reproductive technologies?" responds "[i]n one way - not much; in another - everything."[2] According to Klein, the newness of the technologies lies in the fact that it is now women's body parts which can be used in reproduction, rather than their bodies as a whole. Now "[w]omen are being dismembered - split into separate reproductive parts which can be reassembled, perhaps in a different order, perhaps using parts from different women."[3] It is not simply the female body which has become dis-integrated through use of the new technologies, but also the whole idea of what it means for a woman to have a child. Michelle Stanworth argues that through the new reproductive technologies the concept of motherhood is being deconstructed, so that "in place of 'mother', there will be ovarian mothers who supply eggs, uterine mothers who give birth to children and, presumably, social mothers who raise them."[4]

If the deconstruction of motherhood marks what is original about the new technologies, what is unoriginal? Klein argues that the lack of originality lies with the ideology which underpins their use. This, she argues, is not so very different from the ideology governing the use of "old" technologies such as contraception, sterilisation and abortion:

> Whether 'old' or 'new', these procedures have in common that they represent an artificial invasion of the human body - predominantly the female body. Increasingly more and more control is taken away from an individual's body and 'concentrated in the hands of 'experts' ... [A]ssessment of the 'old' as well as the 'new' reproductive technologies must recognize them as powerful socio-economic and political instruments of control.[5]

A similar view is expressed by Patricia Spallone, who argues that the new reproductive technologies "come from the same scientific approach to reproduction control which brought us 'old' reproductive technologies ..."[6]

In this respect the reproductive revolution has failed to live up to its name. A detour via the Oxford English Dictionary reveals that a revolution is a "complete overthrow of the established government in any country or State by those who were previously subject to it; a forcible substitution of a new ruler or form of government". It is apparent that the rulers of the new reproductive Republic are not so different from those of the old. Control of the technologies lies in the hands of "experts", in the hands of those who wield economic and political power, in the hands of those who define the nature and meaning of the scientific, in short, "pharmacrats" as Gena Corea describes them.[7]

Klein is right to acknowledge that such a concentration of power in the hands of experts may be growing, but this does not mean that prior to the new technologies those subject to the old regime, that is women, exercised greater control over their reproductive destinies. Women who have been refused abortions, who have been sterilised or been given contraception against their better judgment might argue that they were equally unable to determine their reproductive lives under the old regime as they are now. Women's reproductive choices have always been under the control of political, socio-economic and medical forces. The fact that they may be more so today, does not mean there is a new ruler, but merely more of the same.

Klein's argument leads her to caution against the use of reproductive technologies which she believes do not work in the interests of women. She is not alone in this attitude. Gena Corea argues that the new technologies have assimilated human reproduction to factory production.[8] The "Mother Machine" produces her commodity, the product of her labour, and a commodity which is increasingly subject to a form of quality control. Women seeking access to new reproductive technologies are persuaded by widely-publicised success stories which belie the reality that many women fail to conceive, and those who do have less chance of successfully carrying a foetus to term. The promise of a miracle, coupled with the desperate longing for a child, both encouraged by the introduction of the new technologies, it is argued, do not advantage women.

In the face of such a critique what strategies might be proposed to counter the increasing hold of experts over the reproductive process? Advocating an end to the use of the new reproductive techniques is probably not an option. As Derek Morgan and Robert Lee point out, "science has crossed a Rubicon for which there is no return ticket."[9] Even if it were an option it is uncertain whether the removal of the new technologies would substantially loosen the grip of experts over the reproductive process. Patricia Spallone, in the introduction to her critique of reproductive technologies states "I do not mean to imply that removing the technologies will automatically give back to women control over our own bodies."[10] She argues, using the example of Margaret Atwood's novel "The Handmaid's Tale", that women may find themselves submitted to reproductive control even in the absence of technology. Spallone need not have looked to such a futuristic example to illustrate her argument because the assumption that women ever had control, and therefore that there is something to be handed back to them, is open to challenge.

One strategy advocated by some feminists is that women, in order to counter the increasing intrusion of medicine on their reproductive lives, might begin to assert a role for themselves by learning and practising techniques such as self-examination, menstrual extraction and self-insemination.[11] A less tangible, but more visionary strategy, may be the advocacy of a woman-centred approach or "feminist ethic" within the context of the new technologies:

> A feminist ethic holds that the aims of reproductive health care and medical research must be focused on what will serve women best, not what will serve scientists best ...

> The starting point for reasserting a women-centred ethic is the reassertion that *women are our bodies* and *women are ourselves, autonomous.* Our Bodies, Ourselves is so obvious yet so revolutionary that it is a contemporary feminist statement.[12]

The purpose of this chapter is to examine the potential for this assertion of "Our Bodies, Ourselves" and claims for autonomous motherhood within the context of the new reproductive technologies. The aim is not to advocate disengagement with reproductive technology, but rather to investigate the orientation and direction of that technology, more specifically by challenging the ideology underpinning who is deemed a suitable recipient.

This investigation highlights another aspect of what is not new about the new technologies and what is not revolutionary about the reproductive revolution.

While it has been acknowledged that the new reproductive technologies have brought about fundamental change in the process of reproduction by the achievement of conception through deconstructed and dis-integrated female bodies, this radical breakup of the processes of conception, gestation and rearing of children, and the distribution of these functions amongst different women, is matched by the potential breakdown of the structure in which reproduction has traditionally been confined, that is, the heterosexual family unit. There is now the potential for women to determine how to achieve a pregnancy, at what time in their lives, and within what type of family unit. The new reproductive technologies might in one sense pave the way for extended family ties and a new formulation of parenting which goes beyond the model of the nuclear family.

It is not surprising, however, to find that this very potential has been perceived as one of the greatest dangers of the new technologies. The heated debate surrounding their use is fanned because, as Stanworth argues, the technologies "crystallize issues at the heart of contemporary controversies over sexuality, parenthood, reproduction and the family".[13] The crystallisation of these issues has concentrated upon traditional views of what sexuality, parenthood, reproduction and the family are to mean. Thus, while the techniques of assisted conception may themselves be original, at present the structures within which the techniques are made available have not been revolutionised.

It will be argued that the ideology which underpins access to reproductive technologies is one which seeks the reconstruction of the heterosexual family despite the widely-acknowledged breakdown of this institution, and despite the deconstruction of the female body in the new processes of reproduction. Those women deemed suitable for access to the technologies are precisely those who, prior to the reproductive revolution, would have been perceived as suitable mothers, that is those who will uphold and reinforce the crumbling model of heterosexual family life.

The result of this analysis is to argue for greater self-determination in relation to reproductive choices. This would necessitate an increase in availability of the technologies and involves a challenge to the selective basis on which they are currently offered. There are undoubtedly those who will view this as a form of collusion with male powers operating the technologies. In pointing out her own weakness in her previous defence of pornography, Corea states:

> I have acted in the past as the agent of male power. But I did not understand what I was doing. When others had helped me to understand - through their spoken words, their books, their actions - I ended my complicity.[14]

This appeal to false consciousness obscures the reality of the desires of those who want children. It matters little in terms of this reality that the desire for parenthood might be socially constructed. While it exists, it seems harsh to tell women seeking to conceive through use of the new technologies that they should fight their desire for the common good of all women; that they should understand that by their action they are perpetuating patriarchal control. It is equally harsh to tell Louise Brown, the first "test-tube" baby, that in the interests of all women she ought not to have been born. To do so, would be to concede the playing field of the new technologies to the very powers Corea and Klein so mistrust.

There are, however, those who argue that the relationship between women and male dominated scientific disciplines is so ambivalent that even the advocacy of "feminist scientists", who might steer the use of these technologies in a more woman-centred direction, would be of little value:

> Science, we believe mirrors the power relations in society, and to try to add on feminist values to its current structure could only result in a superficial, if any, change. Only in a feminist society would a truly feminist science develop.[15]

The realisation of a "feminist society", however such a term is construed, is difficult to contemplate without engagement with society's present structures and institutions. The scientific playing field may not be level, but to refuse even to set foot upon it leaves a wide open goal for those administering the technologies. Such an abdication of involvement is unhelpful and ultimately self-defeating, especially for lawyers who have to contend with the increasing willingness of legislators to entrust decisions relating to reproduction to the medical profession.[16] As with access to abortion, access to reproductive technology is restricted. Like abortion, which is lawful only in certain circumstances to be ascertained by two registered medical practitioners,[17] the use of reproductive technology to aid conception is subject to medical control.   The following section will outline the legal requirements in relation to access to the new technologies in the United Kingdom, with an emphasis on finding out who are deemed prime recipients. Several *causes célèbres* will then be examined in order to show how in practice the re-integration of traditional family values is being superimposed upon the use of the new reproductive technologies.

TO TREAT OR NOT TO TREAT

Before commencing upon an examination of the legal provisions relating to access to new reproductive technologies, it is worth making two points in relation to the resourcing of these technologies. First, regardless of other factors, access will often depend on being able to afford the technology. Although available through the National Health Service, waiting lists are long and the technologies over-subscribed. The financing of technologies is beyond the scope of this chapter,[18] but it is worth bearing in mind that, despite the commodification of babies being widely resisted, it is the case that those who can afford to pay will gain access to services faster and be allowed to undergo more treatment cycles at a private institution than those who cannot afford to attend such an institution.

Secondly, a more general point about the financing of these technologies might be made. There are some who would argue that, instead of being used in the selective treatment of some individuals' infertility, resources should be directed towards investigation of the *causes* of infertility. Infertility may be caused by physical abnormalities, such as blocked fallopian tubes in women or undescended testes in men. Also infertility may have its origin in social or environmental factors, such as diet, life-style or pollution, or might be medically induced through, for example, the effects of contraception, through badly-performed abortions, or through the lack of treatment of sexually transmitted diseases. Mrs Ann Winterton MP addressed this point in the parliamentary debate in the House of Commons on the White Paper later to become the Human Fertilisation and Embryology Act 1990:

> IVF is only an appropriate treatment for infertility in a minority of cases. Those who want a solution to the majority of cases of infertility would do well to heed this fact and to accept that it would be a far better use of resources, and would help a great many more women to bear children, if those resources were used to highlight the problems of promiscuous sexual activity and abortion so as to prevent the occurrence of infertility in the first place.[19]

Emphasis on the causes of infertility may, however, have adverse consequences. Rothman points out that one such consequence is "victim-blaming", that is blaming the victim for her own infertility.[20] The above argument made by Mrs Ann Winterton might easily lead on to a suggestion that if a woman has undergone an abortion or has had several sexual relationships and has subsequently become infertile, she should legitimately be refused access to reproductive technologies. An obvious and undesirable response is then to say that, if abortion and promiscuity cause infertility, women should not be permitted to indulge in these practices. This would detract from women's claims for sexual and reproductive autonomy and would fail to address important concerns about the safety of current methods of abortion, the effectiveness of contraceptives and the treatment of sexually transmitted diseases.

1. Reproductive rights

The law governing access to the new reproductive technologies in the United Kingdom, the Human Fertilisation and Embryology Act 1990, does not dwell upon the question of resources. Instead the focus is upon suitable parenting. Thus there is no automatic entitlement to the use of reproductive technologies. There is within the Act, as within the law generally, no recognition of a right to reproduce nor a corresponding right not to reproduce. The potential of an appeal to rights in reproductive matters has been well-documented elsewhere.[21] It is worth noting, however, that while the right to reproduce has been mooted by judges within the context of both the common law and international human rights law, it has not yet been discussed specifically in relation to new reproductive technologies.[22] In *Re D*,[23] in the context of the proposed sterilisation of a mentally handicapped minor, Justice Heilbron stated that:

> [t]he type of operation proposed is one which involves the deprivation of a basic human right, namely the right of a woman to reproduce, and therefore it would, if performed on a woman for non-therapeutic reasons and without her consent, be a violation of such right.[24]

The formulation of the right to reproduce as a basic human right is not apparent in existing international human rights conventions. If such a right were to be viewed within the context of an international declaration of rights it would have to be formulated within broader rights such as the right to private and family life, or the right to found a family. For example, Articles 8(1) and 12 of the European Convention on Human Rights, which guarantee that "[e]veryone has the right to respect for his private and family life, his home and his correspondence" and that "[m]en and women of marriageable age have the right to marry and to found a family ...", might arguably be construed as encompassing a right to reproduce. So far the European Commission of Human Rights has dealt with the foundation of families in the case of adoption,[25] but has never articulated a specific right to reproduce in this context.

One might envisage, however, a challenge made by a lesbian or an unmarried woman who had been refused access to reproductive technologies because of her sexual orientation or marital status. She might argue that there had been a violation of Articles 8 and 12[26] coupled with a violation of Article 14, which provides that:

> [t]he enjoyment of the rights and freedoms set forth in this Convention shall be secured without discrimination on any ground such as sex, race, colour, language, religion, political or other opinion, national or social origin, association with a national minority, property, birth or other status.

It could be argued that the phrase "or other status" at the end of Article 14 includes marital status or sexual orientation,[27] and that, were it to be accepted that access to reproductive technologies came within the ambit of either Article 8 or 12, then the criteria governing access might provoke discrimination in the enjoyment of the rights contained within these Articles and hence a violation of the Convention.

Of course, bringing reproductive technologies within the sphere of what might be protected by the right to family life or the right to found a family, does not mean that these rights would be protected absolutely. Van Dijk and van Hoof point out that in relation to adoption cases there is no "right to adopt" and that it is up to national authorities to decide the regulation of adoption in their Member States.[28] Presumably the same would be true of access to reproductive technologies. Access criteria might then be justified by reference to national law under Article 12 which states that the right to marry and found a family is to be guaranteed "according to the national laws governing the exercise of this right." Under Article 8(2) a violation of the right to family life might be justified in order to secure "the prevention of disorder ... [and] the protection of health or morals". Given the margin of appreciation accorded to Member States in matters such as sexuality,[29] the necessity to protect public morality and prevent disorder by denying lesbians and single women access to reproductive technologies, might be judged to outweigh any interference in their family life.

2. Access provision

Where there exists no absolute right to reproduce and where access to fertility treatments is limited to certain women, the thorny question of to whom, is far from easy to answer. Just as the desire for motherhood does not touch all women, those women who *do* desire motherhood are not necessarily those who fit the popular image of the desirable mother. Thus on the one hand there exists "a powerful ideology of motherhood - the belief that motherhood is the natural, desired and ultimate goal of all 'normal' women, and that women who deny their 'maternal instincts' are selfish, peculiar or disturbed."[30] On the other hand some women are criticised for giving way to their instincts because they are viewed as unsuitable mothers. According to Michelle Stanworth, "a belief in maternal instinct coexists with obstacles to autonomous motherhood - obstacles, that is, to motherhood for women who are not in a stable relationship to a man."[31] The requirement of a relationship between a woman and a man is, as will be shown in more detail below, only one factor in barring the way to autonomous motherhood. Furthermore, even those infertile women who exhibit the characteristics of the ideal mother are not permitted to be over-zealous in their quest for motherhood. If the treatment they receive is unsuccessful they are expected to come to terms with their state of childlessness and may be criticised for being unable to do so.

Those women who do decide to pursue their maternal instinct, and strike out on the route to motherhood via new reproductive technologies, will be subjected to screening by treatment centres to assess their suitability. The Human Fertilisation and Embryology Authority issues treatment licences to those centres which may carry out infertility treatments involving the use of donated gametes or donated embryos or the creation of embryos outside, or partly inside and partly outside, the body.[32] Screening for access to the treatments is then conducted in accordance with the Human Fertilisation and Embryology Act 1990. Section 13(5) of this Act provides that:

> [a] woman shall not be provided with treatment services unless account has been taken of the welfare of any child who may be born as a result of the treatment (including the need of that child for a father), and of any other child who may be affected by the birth.

In practice access to reproductive technologies is also governed by individual policies in operation at each clinic operating under the guidance of Ethics Committees.[33] Such policies are further put into operation by individual consultants. According to the Code of Practice introduced by the Human Fertilisation and Embryology Authority to govern the operation of the 1990 Act, "[t]he views of all those at the centre who have been involved with the prospective parents should be taken into account when deciding whether or not to offer treatment" and "[t]he decision to provide treatment should be taken in the light of all the available information."[34]

Section 13(5) itself is not very expansive. It has its origins in the Warnock Report on Human Fertilisation and Embryology issued in 1984 and is further amplified in the Code of Practice. Both these documents shed light on the criteria to be considered when a treatment centre is seeking to fulfil its obligations arising under s.13(5). The Committee of Inquiry into Human Fertilisation and Embryology, chaired by Dame Mary Warnock, was set up in 1982 to examine the implications of developments in the field of human assisted reproduction. After addressing the scarcity of resources the Report states:

> some individuals will have a more compelling case for treatment than others. In the circumstances, medical practitioners will, clearly, use their *clinical judgment* as to the priority of the individual case bearing in mind such considerations as the patient's age, the duration of infertility and the likelihood that treatment will be successful. *So far this is not contentious. ...*
>
> This question of eligibility for treatment is a very difficult one, and we believe that hard and fast rules are not applicable to its solution. We recognise that this will place a heavy burden of responsibility on the individual consultant who must make *social judgments that go beyond the purely medical* ...[35]

This issue, described here as "not contentious", merits the further scrutiny accorded it in the remainder of this chapter. Suffice to say at this stage that the presumption that medical practitioners will take the decision as to who to treat goes uncontested by Warnock. Thus the possibility of autonomous motherhood is not countenanced even at this early stage. Medical practitioners, it is stated, will use their "clinical" judgment when assessing the impact of age, duration of infertility and likelihood of successful treatment. However, beyond this, they are required to make judgments which "go beyond the purely medical", that is to say "social" judgments. The desirability of such judgments lying in the hands of the medical profession is very much open to challenge, especially where the need for "hard and fast rules" has been rejected and, consequently, there remains wide discretion in the decision-making process.

However, in order to create guide-lines, rather than hard and fast rules, further amplification of s.13(5) is given in the Code of Practice issued by the Human Fertilisation and Embryology Authority:

> [I]n deciding whether or not to offer treatment, centres should take account both of the wishes and needs of the people seeking treatment and of the needs of any children who may be involved. Neither consideration is paramount over the other, and the subject should be approached with great care and sensitivity. Centres should avoid adopting any policy or criteria which may appear arbitrary or discriminatory.[36]

Centres are cautioned, therefore, not against the adoption of discriminatory policies, but against the *appearance* of any such discrimination. The insistence is, therefore, on applying criteria fairly but not in preventing arbitrariness and discrimination in the selection of appropriate criteria. The Code of Practice goes on to outline what may be relevant in assessing whether to grant access to reproductive technologies:

a.   The commitment of the person seeking treatment and that of her husband or partner (if any) to have a child.

b.   Their age and medical history and the medical history of their families.

c.   The needs of any child who may be born, and the meeting of those needs by the prospective parent(s).

d.   Any risk of harm to the child such as that resulting from inherited disorders, problems during pregnancy or from neglect or abuse.

e.   The effect on any existing children in the family.[37]

Section 13(5), as amplified by the Code of Practice, seeks, therefore, to strike a balance. Morgan and Lee say of the 1990 Act generally that "[i]t seeks to balance what are the sometimes conflicting interests of the involuntary childless and the children of the reproduction revolution."[38] This is exemplified in s.13(5). But what if in carrying out this balancing exercise a medical practitioner is thought to have tipped the scales in the wrong direction? Can a challenge be mounted against the decision to refuse access to reproductive technologies? The possibility of a case being brought to the European Court of Human Rights has been discussed above. Such a drastic step may not be wholly unnecessary given that neither the 1990 Act, nor the Code of Practice, provide a review mechanism against a decision not to treat.

The Code of Practice states simply that, before the decision to treat is made, clients are to be given "a fair opportunity to state their views ... and to meet any objections raised to providing them with treatment."[39] Once the decision is made, the centre should explain to those it is refusing to treat the reasons for this refusal and the factors which may induce it to change its decision.[40] An application for judicial review of the decision to refuse access to the new technologies is not out of the question where it might be shown that a treatment centre had failed to exercise its discretion in considering the criteria set out in the 1990 Act and the Code of Practice, or had exercised this discretion incorrectly. A case brought by a former prostitute challenging the refusal to treat her, prior to the implementation of the Human Fertilisation and Embryology Act 1990, and discussed in more detail below, provides support for the reviewability of the decision to refuse treatment, although it may offer little in the way of comfort to those non-conformist mothers seeking such treatment.[41] In practice, rather than pursuing a legal solution to this problem, a more obvious strategy for those with the resources is simply to go elsewhere, and to shop around amongst treatment centres, either at home or abroad,[42] until a willing centre is found. While a solution for some, this does not clarify the criteria for access to reproductive technologies and exposes the lack of accountability in the decision-making process surrounding the provision of the new reproductive technologies. By taking specific examples, and looking at the component parts of s.13(5), the following section will examine the making of clinical and social judgments in the granting of the use of reproductive technologies to some women and the refusal to grant access to others.

"SOCIAL JUDGMENTS THAT GO BEYOND THE PURELY MEDICAL"

Section 13(5), in providing that "[a] woman shall not be provided with treatment services unless account has been taken of the welfare of any child who may be born as a result of the treatment ...", requires initial consideration to be given to the nature of what is offered by treatment centres which goes some way towards explaining to whom access to new reproductive technologies is granted. The description of the new technologies as "treatment services" raises a question about how infertility itself should be viewed. One possibility is that it is seen as an illness necessitating treatment. Another is that reproductive technologies service the desire for motherhood of those women not wanting to conceive through heterosexual intercourse. The tension between the terms "treatment" and "service" in the description of new reproductive technologies replicates the tension between "clinical" and "social" decision-making by the medical profession.

If the "treatment" aspect of reproductive treatment services is stressed, this implies that infertility is a disease and all those patients who find themselves suffering from it might expect to be treated. The clinical discretion of the medical practitioner would be called for in deciding on a medical basis, and given limited resources, which of those suffering from the disease had the best chance of receiving successful treatment. On the other hand, if viewed as a "service", screening clients on the basis of social as well as medical criteria may be more justifiable, as clients would not be in a position to expect access to the service simply because of their infertility. Ultimately, medical criteria might be dispensed with altogether and clients granted access simply on the basis of having sufficient financial resources to purchase the service.

Some feminists have resisted the description of new reproductive technologies as treatments. They argue that control over women, perpetuated through use of the technologies, is disguised by the rhetoric of therapy and the cure of disease and illness. Corea argues the language exists to describe reproductive technologies in terms of therapy, but not in terms of "social control or political rule".[43] So talk of treatment obscures the reality of who is performing or offering that treatment. The implications of using the language of treatment and service is illustrated in a somewhat macabre fashion by the Code of Practice adopted by the Human Fertilisation and Embryology Authority. The Code describes the woman seeking treatment services as a "client". The point at which the client becomes a "patient" is when treatment without consent is contemplated, that is "where the procedure is necessary to save the patient's life, cannot be postponed, and she is unconscious and cannot indicate her wishes."[44] The patient receiving medical treatment in this scenario, unconscious and oblivious, is clearly subject to medical, if not social and political, control.

Others have argued that infertility may be viewed as "disability".[45] But that, even so, to talk of the "cure" of this disability may be misleading. Cure does not necessarily lie in the use of test-tube technology, which is merely one way of dealing with the *effect* of infertility. Rothman points out that fertile women may undergo treatment where it is their male partner who is infertile, for example where he has a low sperm count. In this instance the infertility becomes that of the couple, rather than the man, and the woman is subjected to treatment in order to secure genetic paternity.[46]

It is apparent, however, that in terms of gaining access to reproductive technology, there is an implicit presumption that the treatment service is sought for the treatment of infertility. This raises an important point in relation to voluntarily childless women, for example those lesbians and single women who, although not infertile, seek access to the technologies rather than trying to conceive via heterosexual intercourse or self-insemination. The reasons for wanting to use a treatment centre rather than an informal arrangement to bring about conception are varied.[47] A suitable and healthy donor does not have to be tracked down as sperm is readily available at the treatment centre. The donor will remain anonymous and the legal status of the child resulting from the aided conception will be different. Where an unmarried woman receives donor insemination at a treatment centre, without an accompanying male partner, the child is presumed to be fatherless.[48] Where a woman inseminates herself privately this arrangement falls outside the ambit of the 1990 Act. Conception via self-insemination is dealt with in the same way as conception via intercourse so that the sperm donor is the child's legal father. The implications of this distinction have become highly visible with the passage of the Child Support Act 1991. In requiring a woman claiming social security benefits to name the father of her child in order to secure maintenance from him, this Act has the effect of tying a woman, whose aim was autonomous motherhood, to a man with whom she may have had no contact.[49] For example, in June 1994, for the first time ever, two lesbians were granted joint parental rights over their child. However, this development was countered by the news that the woman who gave birth to the child, and who became impregnated after having intercourse with a male friend, had fallen foul of the Child Support Act. The child's biological father was pursued by the Child Support Agency which demanded maintenance for the child, despite an agreement drawn up between the parties stating that the father would not be involved in raising the child.[50]

The paramount consideration given to infertility in deciding whether to offer treatment services, may mean that biologically fertile women fall at the first hurdle of clinical judgment before arriving at the hurdles of social criteria. Once infertility is established, though, other factors come into play under s.13(5) before a woman is allowed to proceed along the route to motherhood. These factors revolve around two main concepts which the subsection interrelates. First, the welfare of the child to be born through the use of technologies and that of any other children, and second the need of a child for a father.

1. Child welfare and the bodily unfit: a clinical judgment?

The issue of child welfare is one which may be a factor in the making of a medical assessment of the woman requesting treatment services, where her body is so constituted as to raise questions about her being physically fit to carry and raise a child. Of those deemed bodily unfit for access to treatment services, the most obvious example is the older woman. On 25 December 1993 a fifty-nine year-old British woman gave birth to twins after having been refused access to treatment services in the United Kingdom and subsequently obtaining them in Italy.[51] In cases such as this, concern is expressed on two grounds. The first is that the physical implications of child-bearing cannot be borne so well by older women. Such implications include the increased possibility of multiple births through the use of fertility drugs, high blood pressure, the pains of childbirth or, alternatively, the increased need for a caesarian, and the difficulty of producing breast milk. The second ground is that older women are unable to cope with the stress of rearing a child. The older woman is, therefore, deemed literally physically unfit for child-bearing and child-rearing.

Under the Human Fertilisation and Embryology Authority's Code of Practice no upper age limit is set for receiving treatment services. There is merely an upper age limit imposed for the donation of semen (age fifty-five) and for the donation of eggs (age thirty-five).[52] Some consultants have expressed the view that the matter is one between the woman and her doctor and that every case must be considered individually.[53] Such individual consideration should involve a distinction being drawn between child-bearing and child-rearing. A woman who wants to receive treatment services because her menopause has been unusually early, may be physically incapable of bearing a child, but is not thereby incapable of rearing one. Similarly an older woman, with a wealth of life-experience and time to devote to bringing up a child, is not necessarily incapable of doing so simply because of her age.

The case of the physically unfit mother is revealing of the absence of discussion of an unfit aged father. While it appears that it is only the woman's attributes which are being put under the spot-light, questions might legitimately be asked about men fathering children at a late stage in life. While virile older men are congratulated for still having it in them, a woman's "shrivelled old uterus", as one male doctor describes it,[54] is seen as past it and incapable of fulfilling any further useful function. Just because it is biologically possible for older men to father children, this is irrelevant in terms of their suitability for child-rearing. If one aim of restricting access to treatment services is to provide a child with two parents until that child's middle-age, then, all things being equal, more emphasis should be placed on the age of the father.[55]

A woman's physical signs of ageing may have less to do with the refusal to allow her access to reproductive technologies, than the fact that by doing so she is being reprimanded for her failure to bear children earlier in life. Where a woman has decided to postpone having children while pursuing a successful career, some might argue that she should be prepared to live with the consequences of her decision. It was reported that the fifty-nine year-old woman, cited above, had a successful career and was a millionaire business woman. Had she really wanted to be a mother, why was she not prepared to sacrifice her career for this? This question, of course, presupposes that there exists a real possibility of choice for women to pursue a successful career or to choose to start a family, and says nothing about the circumstances which make it extremely difficult for women, and not men, to do both.[56]

There is, further, something which appears subversive about the pregnancy of an older woman. Her pregnancy serves as a reminder of her sexuality, something which is widely ignored or dismissed as nonexistent. This is not unlike the lack of discussion of the sexuality of women with disabilities whose sexual needs often go unrecognised.[57] In the field of reproductive technologies it is quite probable that under the auspices of s.13(5), and the making of a clinical judgment, a woman with a physical disability might similarly be refused access to treatment services on the basis that to do so would not be in the interests of any resulting child.

At the level of discrimination against older people and disabled people, it is also appropriate to consider the implications of racial discrimination in the use of reproductive technologies. While it is recognised that such discrimination may not operate at the stage of making a medical judgment about physical suitability to enter parenthood, it is at this juncture that the liaison between clinical and social decision-making criteria becomes apparent. Women of colour may not be physically unsuitable recipients of reproductive technologies, but their colour may be a factor in determining whether to grant access. Notably this might be the case where the woman seeking access does not want to be implanted with an egg or embryo of her own ethnic background.

In "The Mother Machine" Gena Corea prophesied:

> Since we live in a society where white people are valued more highly than those of color, these technologies will not affect all women equally. There will be no great demand for the eggs of a black woman. But there may well be a demand for her womb - a womb which could gestate the embryo of a white woman and man.[58]

Corea goes on to refer to her work on surrogacy. But this statement has implications for recent developments in access to fertility treatments. It was reported in January 1994 that in Italy a black woman in a partnership with a white man had been implanted with the egg of a white woman and had subsequently given birth to a white baby.[59] The Human Fertilisation and Embryology Authority was keen to point out initially that such treatment would not have been permissible in the United Kingdom and responded by saying that such moves would be banned.[60] However, the Bourn Hall Clinic in Cambridge subsequently took the decision to implant a black woman, married to a husband of mixed race, with a white donor's egg.[61] This was due to the lack of availability of coloured donor eggs, the couple having been waiting for four years, and because the resulting child would have been of mixed race whichever egg was chosen.

These examples raise important questions about the reasons why a woman of colour would wish to have a white child and why clinics would be unhappy to provide a white donor egg to this end. The woman in the Italian example cited above had chosen to have a white child because she feared a child of mixed-race may suffer discrimination. Her choice in this matter was based on purely social criteria. In the British example, although undoubtedly there would be similar repercussions in terms of societal prejudice, the decision to offer treatment services was justified by reference to the physical impediment of a lack of coloured donor eggs.

The "designer baby" debate, which has been played out in the media over the issue of choice of skin colour, has obscured the similarities in relation to choice of other characteristics. The Human Fertilisation and Embryology Authority's Code of Practice, states that:

> when selecting donated gametes for treatment, centres should take into account each prospective parent's preferences in relation to the general physical characteristics of the donor which can be matched in accordance with good clinical practice. ...[62]

Is not skin colour a physical characteristic which might be expected to be considered in the selection of the donated egg? Is it so radically different from the expression of a preference for eye or hair colour? Furthermore, in all cases of egg donation, the child is not related genetically to its mother. This would be the case whether the woman had expressed a preference for a black or white donor, or a blue-eyed or brown-eyed donor. Of course, the obvious difference is that people are not discriminated against on the basis of their eye colour, while they are on the basis of the colour of their skin. Similarly, if one draws an analogy with sex selection, it is societal prejudice directed against the resulting child, be it female or coloured, which provokes a reaction against this particular specification of the designer baby. A strict application of the child welfare principle, which would logically suggest that it is in the best interests of the child that it should suffer as little discrimination as possible and therefore that it would be better off if white and male, is offensively eugenic and goes no way towards tackling societal discrimination and prejudice.

The justification of the decision to implant a black woman with a white donor's egg on the basis of the unavailability of black donor eggs shows the fluidity between decision-making on clinical and social grounds. It highlights the social implications of any decision to offer treatment services which cannot necessarily be divorced from medical and physical criteria. However, regardless of the physical characteristics of the woman seeking access to reproductive technologies, it is still possible for medical practitioners to go beyond the exercise of their clinical discretion and to base their decision to offer or to refuse treatment services on purely social grounds.

2. The need of a child for a father: marriage, death and single parenting: a social judgment?

Section 13(5), in requiring consideration to be given to the welfare of the child born as a result of reproductive technologies, explicitly provides that consideration be given to the needs of a child for a father. This means that some women may legitimately be refused access to treatments on the basis of having an insufficient or inappropriate relationship with a man. It is precisely this aspect of s.13(5) which seeks to re-integrate the heterosexual family unit, in the face of its dis-integration, through the use of the new technologies. This criterion refocuses ideologies familiar in other policies on parenting, such as adoption and fostering, and in this sense represents all that is not revolutionary about the reproductive revolution. It seeks to approximate as far as possible the criterion necessary for biological natural conception, that is the union of a man and a woman. Thus the artificiality of artificial conception is merely that it occurs without the act of intercourse.

(a) *Is marriage a necessity?* First, it is appropriate to speculate upon the meaning of the phrase "the need of a child for a father" in the context of marital and non-marital relations. As Stanworth argues "[t]o those who see sex, marriage and parenthood as an indissoluble triad, the conceptive technologies offer another dangerous precedent; they separate parenthood from 'the sexual act', and do not ensure that parenthood will be confined to marriage."[63] Some, therefore, might argue that conception without sexual intercourse through the use of donor gametes is immoral, and that it constitutes a form of adultery. In law, this has been held not to be the case because:

> [f]or adultery to be committed there must be the two parties physically present and engaging in the sexual act at the same time ... Just as artificial insemination extracts procreation entirely from the nexus of human relationships in or outside of marriage, so does the extraction of the nexus of human relationship from the act of procreation remove artificial insemination from the classification of sexual intercourse.[64]

Section 13(5) does not demand the "nexus of human relationships" of the woman seeking fertility treatments to be that of marriage. This is in accordance with the view expressed in the Warnock Report, that "we are not prepared to recommend that access to treatment should be based exclusively on the legal status of marriage."[65]

However, this should not be taken to mean that the woman need not be involved in a relationship with a man, far from it:

> To judge from the evidence many believe that the interests of the child dictate that it should be born into a home where there is a loving, stable, heterosexual relationship and that, therefore the *deliberate* creation of a child for a woman who 'is not a partner in such a relationship is morally wrong. ...

> [W]e believe that as a general rule it is better for children to be born into a two-parent family, with both father and mother, although we recognise that it is impossible to predict with any certainty how lasting such a relationship will be.[66]

The instability of such a relationship is recognised, yet is prioritised over the lack of a relationship, or the relationship between two people of the same sex.[67] The need of a child for a father for however short a period is prioritised over the welfare of the child in terms of stability.

The popular response to single parenting was highlighted in May 1993 when the birth of sextuplets to Jean Gibbins and her partner Jan Vince was announced.[68] Unmarried, and living apart, Ms Gibbins and Mr Vince had been in a relationship for six years. Mr Vince had an ex-wife and three children by her, whom he had not seen for seven years, and the couple also had one child together already. In this case treatment had been given to increase ovulation, (which does not require a licence from the Human Fertilisation and Embryology Authority) and was widely censured after the event by the press and members of the government for the imposition on tax-payers of a one parent family of seven children.

This British example makes interesting reading when placed alongside the French case *Consorts Parpalaix c/ le Centre d'Etude et de Conservation du Sperme (CECOS) et autre*[69] in which the creation of a one-parent family was explicitly sanctioned, the father in this case being dead. Alain Parpalaix, who had been living with his girlfriend Corinne, had cancer of the testicles. He was warned by his doctor of the risk of sterility which his treatment for the cancer could bring about and, in 1981, gave sperm to CECOS, the national body which oversees fertility treatments and stores gametes. Alain died on 25 December 1983 having married Corinne two days previously. Corinne asked CECOS for the sperm with a view to using it for artificial insemination but CECOS refused. The *tribunal de grande instance de Créteil* decided, however, that this refusal was unlawful on the basis that this was a matter of contract law, and the contract between Alain and CECOS contained the obligation to conserve and to give back the sperm either to Alain or to a third party. This obligation resulted from the fact that, during his illness, Alain had expressed on several occasions, including to CECOS, his wish to preserve his chances of procreating. CECOS had never made known to Alain its opposition to the release of sperm after the death of the client,[70] and was therefore bound to fulfil Alain's wishes.

The difficulty with addressing this issue as a matter of French private law, was that all contracts must have an object which is lawful and within the commercial domain[71] and sperm, being part of the human body, is not within that domain. The question arose, therefore, of the licit nature of the agreement. It is at this point that the relationship between Alain and Corinne became important as the court stressed the value of the marriage of the parties, emphasising that both a religious and civil ceremony had taken place. The contract was not, therefore, illicit or contrary to natural law because one of the aims of marriage is procreation and artificial insemination would bring about this aim. Thus in this case the fact of marriage overrode any consideration of the creation of a one parent family, and any consideration of the effect on the child of finding out that one of its parents was dead at the time of conception.

The *Parpalaix* case has been heavily criticised[72] and in a more recent case, *Pirès*, the opposite view was taken.[73] Madame Pirès had had six attempts at in vitro fertilisation. The seventh time was successful and one embryo was implanted and two further embryos frozen. She and her husband signed a document to the effect that the embryos should be destroyed if the couple were no longer to stay together. However, while on his way to visit his wife who had miscarried two months into her pregnancy, Monsieur Pirès was killed in a car accident. At first instance the *tribunal de grande instance de Toulouse* refused to give the embryos over to Madame Pirès. Similarly, on appeal, the *cour d'appel de Toulouse* decided that the two frozen embryos should be destroyed.

In the United Kingdom, the Human Fertilisation and Embryology Act 1990, schedule 3, s.2(2)(b), provides that where storage of gametes or embryos is consented to, those consenting must state what will happen to them in the event of death. However, the Warnock Report had voiced concern about the use of the gametes of a dead man stating that "[t]he use by a widow of her dead husband's semen for AIH is a practice which we feel should be actively discouraged."[74] With regard to embryos, the Report recommended that:

> when one of a couple dies the right to use or dispose or [sic] any embryo stored by that couple should pass to the survivor. We make this recommendation notwithstanding our reservations about the possibility of posthumous pregnancies.[75]

The absence of an express prohibition on posthumous pregnancy[76] reveals the priorities of those assessing where the welfare of the child lies. It appears that the spectre of a dead father figure is more readily acceptable than no father figure at all, or than a living parent who is in a same-sex relationship with the woman seeking treatment services.

The death of the male sperm donor and Warnock's reluctance to allow the use of his sperm thereafter, can be compared with examples of pregnant women who are kept alive on life-support machines until they "give birth".[77] The use of women's bodies after their deaths while the products of male bodies are treated more circumspectly raises questions about the roles of men and women in the reproductive and parenting process. Arguably it makes a difference that an embryo is implanted already in the case of the dead female incubator, but not in the case of the dead male sperm donor. Alternatively it might appear that an absent mother is thought rather less important than an absent father. Furthermore, in the light of the Human Fertilisation and Embryology Authority's response to its public consultation document on "Donated Ovarian Tissue in Embryo Research and Assisted Conception" the recommendation that ovarian tissue from foetuses and cadavers be used for research purposes shows the use to which the female body may now be put on death or even before life.[78]

(b) *Is marriage enough?* It may be asked finally whether a heterosexual partnership in itself is enough to secure access to the new reproductive technologies. It has already been noted that the stability or longevity of that partnership does not seem to be highly rated. But again it appears that ideologies of suitable behaviour by women may prevail in determining access to treatment. The case of *R v. Ethical Committee of St Mary's Hospital (Manchester), Ex parte Harriott*,[79] although decided prior to the passage of the Human Fertilisation and Embryology Act 1990, specifically deals with a challenge to the decision not to offer reproductive technologies and therefore provides a useful indicator of judicial attitudes towards the provision of the technologies. Ms Harriott, a married woman, had been refused in vitro fertilisation treatment at her regional IVF Unit. The decision not to treat was taken by a consultant who decided that Harriott's name should be removed from the IVF waiting list after discovering that she had been refused the possibility of adoption, due to her convictions for soliciting and the running of a brothel, and because she allegedly had a poor understanding of the role of a foster-parent.

Harriott was told of the decision to remove her from the waiting list, but not the true reason for it at this stage, as Justice Schiemann said "perhaps, out of a sense of delicacy".[80] Subsequently The Infertility Service Ethical Committee at the hospital considered the decision in Harriott's case at one of its meetings, although it was not minuted, and decided that the decision was one for the medical team to make. It was only then that Harriott was told the real reason for the refusal to treat. She applied unsuccessfully for judicial review to quash the advice of the committee and the decision of the medical team.

The advice given by the Ethical Committee in this case was not of a nature to be subject to review, because the committee had merely advised that the consultant make up her own mind. This advice was "unobjectionable" in the opinion of the judge.[81] However, this was not to say that the Ethical Committee's decision would never be subject to review. Justice Schiemann stated:

> [i]f the committee had advised, for instance, that the IVF unit should in principle refuse all such treatment to anyone who was a Jew or coloured, then I think the courts might well grant a declaration that such a policy was illegal.[82]

As far as the role of the consultant was concerned, Harriott argued that she was under a duty to act fairly when considering whether to remove a woman from the IVF list. Here the judge admitted that the doctor/patient relationship is within the ambit of administrative law, and therefore reviewable, but said the consultant had acted reasonably in this case. Furthermore, it was perfectly legitimate to have recourse to the rules governing the placing of children in adoption cases, when deciding access to fertility treatment.

It is clear that in this case Harriott's sexual past was one of the reasons for the refusal to treat her. The ideology about suitable parenthood evidenced through adoption policy was taken as offering guidance in the availability of fertility treatments. Harriott's sexual history was too dangerous for her to be deemed a suitable recipient. This was despite the fact that she was now married, and that there was no implication that her present liaison with her husband was in any way suspect or that he would not fulfil the requirements of fatherhood.

Subsequent to the *Harriott* case, the Human Fertilisation and Embryology Authority's Code of Practice states that treatment centres should approach the client's GP to inquire whether there are any circumstances why the client may not be suitable for treatment,[83] one example of such unsuitability being given as "evidence of a previous relevant conviction".[84] While presumably "relevant" convictions would include those for offences such as sexual assault and violence, it is by no means beyond the realm of possibility that a conviction for prostitution would also be deemed relevant for the purpose of refusing access to reproductive technologies.

CONCLUSION

The reproductive revolution is not all it may first appear. While Gena Corea argues that "[t]o describe what we are now witnessing, 'revolution' is too small a word",[85] in terms of the ideologics underpinning the use of new reproductive technologies very little has changed. If anything, the emphasis on heterosexual parenting has been strengthened.

However, for the resourceful, the restrictions legitimated by s.13(5) do not necessarily mean life-long childlessness. While the United Kingdom has been at the forefront of both the technology and therefore also legal developments, the availability of new reproductive technologies in places such as Italy, where regulation is less developed, means that the crossing of national borders to search for treatment is one way of circumventing the application of the criteria in s.13(5).

It is unlikely, however, that this state of affairs will persist.[86]   Other European countries are taking steps to introduce legislation in this area to restrict access to reproductive technologies. In Italy the National Committee for Bioethics reported in June 1994 that the availability of reproductive technologies should be limited. This Committee recommended that reproductive technologies should not be available to older women, lesbians and single women, or women seeking babies of a certain colour because of racial prejudice. It also recommended that surrogacy be criminalised.[87]

The French parliament also in June 1994 approved legislation on bioethics which had been before it since November 1992.[88]   The *Sénat*, the upper house, had sought to limit the availability of reproductive technologies to those who had been married for two years or could prove they had been in a stable relationship for a similar period.   It was largely successful in that the final text requires that the new technologies be made available only to couples (defined as a man and a woman) who must be alive (thus consolidating the jurisprudence in the *Pirès* case), of an age to procreate and be able to prove that they have led a communal life for at least two years.[89]   This legislation subsequently survived an unsuccessful challenge to its constitutionality before the Constitutional Council. It had been alleged that the proposed law violated the right to individual liberty (including the right to do as one chooses with one's own body). The Constitutional Council, however, preferred the view that the law was constitutional because it assured respect for human dignity (and by extension respect for the human body), a concept which is vaguely alluded to in the Preamble to the Constitution of 1946, but which had never before been articulated as a constitutional principle.[90]

In the light of such proposals and legislation it appears that on a European scale the question of access to reproductive technologies is to be limited to those deemed the most suitable couples, suitability being determined by conformity to existing ideals of heterosexual family life. The real revolution, the overturning of such conditions in favour of autonomous motherhood and self-determination for women of their reproductive lives, has yet to come.

NOTES

1. The citation in the title of this chapter is taken from M.Warnock, *A Question of Life: The Warnock Report on Human Fertilisation and Embryology* (1984) at para. 2.13.
2. R.D.Klein, "What's 'New' about the 'New' Reproductive Technologies" in *Man-Made Women: How New Reproductive Technologies Affect Women*, ed. G.Corea et al. (1985) 64, at p.64.
3. R.D.Klein, *ibid.,* at p.66.
4. M.Stanworth, "The Deconstruction of Motherhood" in *Reproductive Technologies: Gender, Motherhood and Medicine*, ed. M. Stanworth (1987) 10, at p.16.
5. R.D.Klein, *supra*, n.2, at p.65.
6. P.Spallone, *Beyond Conception: The New Politics of Reproduction* (1989) at p.14.
7. G.Corea, *The Mother Machine: Reproductive Technologies from Artificial Insemination to Artificial Wombs* (1988) at p.2.
8. G.Corea, *ibid.*, at p.16.
9. D.Morgan and R.G.Lee, *Blackstone's Guide to the Human Fertilisation and Embryology Act 1990* (1991) at p.3.
10. P.Spallone, *supra*, n.6, at p.4.
11. See for example, F.Hornstein, "Children by Donor Insemination: A New Choice for Lesbians", R.D.Klein "Doing It Ourselves: Self Insemination" and C.Downer "Through the Speculum" in *Test-Tube Women: What Future For Motherhood?*, eds. R.Arditti et al. (1984) 373, 382, 419; R.Chalker and C.Downer, *A Woman's Book of Choices: Abortion, Menstrual Extraction, RU-486* (1992).
12. P.Spallone, *supra*, n.6, at pp.31-32.
13. M.Stanworth, *supra,* n.4, at p.18.
14. G.Corea, *supra*, n.7, at p.4.
15. R.Arditti et al., "Introduction" in *Test-Tube Women: What Future For Motherhood?*, *supra*, n.11, 1, at p.4.
16. See S.Sheldon, "The Law of Abortion and the Politics of Medicalisation" in this volume.
17. These circumstances are outlined in S.Sheldon, *ibid.*
18. See further D.Morgan and R.G.Lee, *supra*, n.9, at pp.12-14, and G.Douglas, *Law, Fertility and Reproduction* (1991) at pp.115-116.
19. A.Winterton, 126 *H.C. Debs.* col.1240 (4 February 1988).
20. B.K.Rothman, *Recreating Motherhood* (1989) at p.146.
21. E.Kingdom, *What's Wrong With Rights?* (1991); C.Smart, *Feminism and the Power of Law* (1989) chapter 7; G.Douglas, *supra*, n.18, chapter 2; E.Kingdom "Body Politics and Rights" and F.Beveridge and S.Mullally, "Human Rights and Body Politics" in this volume.
22. The implications of such a discussion are analysed by A.Liu, *Artificial Reproduction and Reproductive Rights* (1991) chapter 3.
23. *Re D (a minor) (wardship: sterilisation)* [1976] 1 All E.R. 326.
24. *Ibid.*, at p. 332. In the subsequent case of *Re B (a minor) (wardship: sterilisation)* [1987] 2

All E.R. 206, at p.213, Lord Hailsham stated that Justice Heilbron was correct to refer to the deprivation of a basic human right of a woman to reproduce but that "this right is only such when reproduction is the result of informed choice" of which the ward in this case, a seventeen year-old mentally handicapped woman, was incapable.

25. Appl. 7229/75 *X and Y v. United Kingdom* (1978) 12 D. & R. 32. See P.van Dijk and G.J.H.van Hoof, *Theory and Practice of the European Convention on Human Rights* (1990) at p.448.

26. P.van Dijk and G.J.H.van Hoof, *ibid.*, suggest that, while originally designed to go hand in hand, given social change and the increasing numbers of unmarried cohabiting couples, the right to marry and the right to found a family contained in Article 12 might be uncoupled. Therefore the right to found a family might be violated despite the victim not being married.

27. S.Millns, "Homosexual Rights and Wrongs under the European Convention on Human Rights: A Question of Privacy or Equality?" in *Legal Visions of the New Europe*, eds. B.S.Jackson and D.McGoldrick (1993) 225.

28. P.van Dijk and G.J.H.van Hoof, *supra*, n.25, at pp.448-449.

29. For example, British transsexuals have been unsuccessful in their attempts to convince the European Court of Human Rights that the failure to alter the sex on their birth certificate is a violation of the right to private life. This is because the margin of appreciation is wide enough to encompass the distinct system of birth registration in the United Kingdom. See *Cossey v. United Kingdom* (1990) 13 E.H.R.R. 622; *Rees v. United Kingdom* (1986) 9 E.H.R.R. 56.

30. M.Stanworth, *supra*, n.4, at p.15.

31. M.Stanworth, *ibid.*.

32. See further D.Morgan and R.G.Lee, *supra*, n.9, at p.27.

33. Practices, therefore, differ between institutions. For example, it is reported that Hammersmith clinic will treat single women and lesbians, while St Mary's Hospital in Manchester will only treat childless couples in heterosexual relationships who have been cohabiting for at least three years; (1993) *The Independent*, 25 May.

34. Human Fertilisation and Embryology Authority, *Code of Practice* (June 1993) at paras. 3.26, 3.28.

35. M.Warnock, *supra*, n.1, at paras. 2.12, 2.13, my emphasis.

36. Human Fertilisation and Embryology Authority, *supra*, n.34, at para. 3.3.

37. Human Fertilisation and Embryology Authority, *ibid.*, at para. 3.16.

38. D.Morgan and R.G.Lee, *supra*, n.9, at p.26.

39. Human Fertilisation and Embryology Authority, *supra*, n.34, at para. 3.26.

40. Human Fertilisation and Embryology Authority, *ibid.*, at para. 3.29.

41. *R v. Ethical Committee of St Mary's Hospital (Manchester) Ex parte Harriott* [1988] 1 F.L.R. 512. On 17 October 1994, however, a thirty-seven year-old woman was refused leave to seek judicial review of Sheffield Health Authority's decision to deny her IVF treatment on the grounds of her age. The application of an age criterion was held to be lawful because shortage of resources meant treatment should be limited to those whom it would most benefit

((1994) *The Times*, 18 October, (1994) *The Independent*, 18 October).

42. The implications of a form of "procreative tourism" are examined by L.Nielson, "Procreative Tourism, Genetic Testing and the Law" (1994) ISFL Conference, Cardiff.
43. G.Corea, *supra*, n.7, at p.2.
44. Human Fertilisation and Embryology Authority, *supra*, n.34, at para. 5.4.
45. B.K.Rothman, *supra*, n.20, at pp.143-151.
46. B.K.Rothman, *ibid.*, at pp.149-50.
47. See L.Doyal, "Managing Conception: Self-insemination and the Limits of Réproductive Freedom" (1994) 22 *Policy and Politics* 89.
48. This occurs by default. Section 28 of the Human Fertilisation and Embryology Act 1990 explains the meaning of the term "father": the husband of a married woman who receives embryo transfer, gamete or zygote intra-fallopian transfer, or artificial insemination is the child's legal father (s.28(2)), as is the male partner of an unmarried woman who undergoes treatment as part of a couple (s.28(3)). The consenting donor of gametes is not to be treated as the child's legal father (s.28(6)(a)).
49. L.Doyal, *supra*, n.47, at p.92.
50. (1994) *The Independent*, 30 June.
51. (1993) *The Times*, 28 December.
52. Human Fertilisation and Embryology Authority, *supra*, n.34, at para.3.33.
53. (1993) *The Independent*, 28 December; (1993) *The Times*, 28 December.
54. Dr T.Stuttaford in *The Times*, *ibid.*
55. In the case of the fifty-nine year-old woman cited the woman's partner was fourteen years younger than herself. However, in a more recent case a sixty-two year-old Italian woman, whose husband was aged sixty-four, gave birth having also received treatment in Italy; (1994) *The Independent*, 19 July; (1994) *The Times*, 19 July.
56. See A.Morris and S.Nott, "The Law's Engagement with Pregnancy" in this volume.
57. See A.Finger, "Claiming *all* of our Bodies: Reproductive Rights and Disabilities" and M.Saxton, "Born and Unborn: The Implications of Reproductive Technologies for People with Disabilities" in R.Arditti et al. eds. *supra*, n.11, 281, 298; K.Keywood, "Sterilising the Woman with Learning Difficulties - In Her Best Interests?" in this volume.
58. G.Corea, *supra*, n.7, at p.2.
59. (1994) *The Independent*, 2 January.
60. *Ibid.*
61. (1994) *The Independent*, 3 January.
62. Human Fertilisation and Embryology Authority, *supra*, n.34, at para. 3.20.
63. M.Stanworth, *supra*, n.4, at p.23.
64. *Maclennan v. Maclennan* [1958] S.C. 105, per Lord Wheatly at p.113.
65. M.Warnock, *supra*, n.1, at para. 2.5.
66. M.Warnock, *ibid.*, at paras. 2.9, 2.11.
67. D.Morgan and R.G.Lee, *supra*, n.9, at p.12.
68. (1993) *The Independent*, 24 and 25 May.

69.   *Consorts Parpalaix c/ le Centre d'Etude et de Conservation du Sperme (CECOS) et autre* (1984) 1 August; (1984) *Gazette du Palais* 16-18 September, 11.

70.   CECOS only started warning donors of its attitude to posthumous insemination about two years after Alain gave his sperm.

71.   This obligation results from a combination of Articles 6, 1108, 1126 and 1128 of the French Civil Code.

72.   A.Sériaux, "Droit naturel et procréation artificielle: quelle jurisprudence?" (1985) *Recueil 'Dalloz-Sirey* (chronique) 53.

73.   (1994) *Le Monde*, 13 May.

74.   M.Warnock, *supra*, n.1, at para. 10.9.

75.   M.Warnock, *ibid.*, at para. 10.12.

76.   This is a matter of discretion for the medical practitioner, as the surviving partner has no right to insist on the stored gametes or embryos being given over to her (Human Fertilisation and Embryology Act 1990 ss.14(1)(b) and 4(1)(b)). See D.Morgan and R.G.Lee, *supra*, n.9. at pp.138-139.

77.   In 1986 Deborah Bell, twenty-four weeks into her pregnancy, suffered a brain haemorrhage and, after being placed on a ventilator for five weeks, was delivered of a baby girl. A more recent German case is that of Marion Ploch, aged eighteen, who, at thirteen weeks pregnant was involved in a serious car accident, declared brain dead, and incubated her foetus while on a ventilator; (1992) *The Independent*, 1 November.

78.   Human Fertilisation and Embryology Authority, *Donated Ovarian Tissue in Embryo Research and Assisted Conception Report* (July 1994) at para. 5.

79.   *Supra*, n.41.

80.   *Ibid.*, at p.517.

81.   *Ibid.*, at p.519.

82.   *Ibid.*, at pp.518-519.

83.   Human Fertilisation and Embryology Authority, *supra*, n.34, at para. 3.22.

84.   Human Fertilisation and Embryology Authority, *ibid.*, at para. 3.24.

85.   G.Corea, *supra*, n.7, at p.293, prefers the term "metarevolution".

86.   See D.Morgan and L.Nielson, "Dangerous Liaisons? Law, Technology, Reproduction and European Ethics" in *Law, Health and Medical Regulation*, eds. S.McVeigh and S.Wheeler (1992) 52.

87.   (1994) *La Repubblica*, 29 June.

88.   Laws nos.94.653, 94.654, of 29 July 1994 ((1994) *Journal Officiel de la République Française*, 30 July, 11056). See (1994) *Le Monde*, 13 June and 14 July.

89.   Article 8 of Law no.94.654 inserts Art. L.152-2 into the Public Health Code to this effect.

90.   Decision of the Constitutional Council of 27 July 1994 ((1994) *Journal Officiel de la République Française* 29 July, 11024). See (1994) *Le Monde*, 29 July.

5 The Law of Abortion and the Politics of Medicalisation

SALLY SHELDON

> Political technologies advance by taking what is essentially a political problem removing it from the realm of political discourse, and recasting it in the neutral language of science. Once this is accomplished the problems become technical ones for specialists to debate.[1]

Whilst abortion remains a focal point for conflict and contestation in Britain, the past decades have witnessed the emergence of a seemingly consensual medical framework which has structured discussion of it. In this sense, the focal point of the political debate has shifted from a religious/moral to a medico/moral one.[2] This has fundamentally influenced both the law and the strategies of the political players in that debate who, in their efforts either to achieve legal reform or to protect the status quo, deploy more and more sophisticated medical arguments and knowledges. In this paper, I wish to examine the importance of this shift from the perspective of a feminist lawyer. I will give a broad overview of the development of the medicalisation of abortion as (re)constructed in statute law during the past thirty years, and the implications this has for a feminist politics aiming to ensure women's access to safe, legal terminations. I will concentrate primarily on two important legal landmarks: the 1967 Abortion Act and the amendments made to it by the 1990 Human Fertilisation and Embryology Act, pausing briefly along the way to look at one of the most important of the numerous Private Members' Bills which have challenged the 1967 Act.

The argument which I wish to make is not that it is "wrong" to view abortion as a medical phenomenon, but rather that to do so is problematic for two reasons. First, to focus a debate is always and inevitably to narrow it: the pre-eminence of the medical framework has led to the marginalisation and exclusion of other accounts of abortion, notably those of women facing unwanted pregnancy. Secondly, the acceptance of abortion as an area for expert, medical knowledges cannot but serve to entrench medical control, and such control lies at the root of many of the problems facing women seeking abortion in Britain today. In historical terms, the medicalisation of abortion is integrally connected with the extension and entrenchment of medical control over it. Medicalisation has been crucial both to the extension of women's freedom to terminate their pregnancies, and to the limitation of this freedom.

THE ABORTION ACT 1967

Legal abortion in Britain is governed by the 1967 Abortion Act which provides a series of exceptions to the blanket ban on the offences of the "procurement of miscarriage" and the supply and procurement of instruments, poisons or other noxious things for such a purpose, which are contained in ss.58 and 59 of the Offences Against the Person Act 1861.[3] Section 1(1) of the Abortion Act provides that an abortion will be lawful if performed by a registered medical practitioner, after two registered medical practitioners have formed an opinion in good faith as to the existence of certain circumstances. Since 1990, these are as follows:

a)   that the pregnancy has not exceeded its twenty-fourth week and that the continuance of the pregnancy would involve risk, greater than if the pregnancy were terminated, of injury to the physical or mental health of the pregnant woman or any existing children of her family; or

b)   that the termination is necessary to prevent grave permanent injury to the physical or mental health of the pregnant woman; or

c)   that the continuance of the pregnancy would involve risk to the life of the pregnant woman, greater than if the pregnancy were terminated; or

d)   that there is a substantial risk that if the child were born it would suffer from such physical or mental abnormalities as to be seriously handicapped.

In comparison with other Western abortion statutes, the British Abortion Act is notable for two reasons: first for its relatively high, "liberal" upper time limit, and secondly for its "illiberal" failure to accord the woman more autonomy in the early weeks of pregnancy. A woman seeking an abortion must always obtain the signatures of two doctors: she is never legally entitled to authorise the termination of her pregnancy herself. The apparent paradox presented by the fact that the British legislation is simultaneously amongst the most and least liberal of Western abortion laws, can be untangled by a re-reading of the Abortion Act in the light of the parliamentary debates which preceded its enactment. The (re)codification of abortion as a medical event, serves to ground an abdication of control and the granting of a large area of discretion to doctors. The Act allows terminations late into the course of a pregnancy but resists any challenge to medical control on the basis of claims of female reproductive autonomy.

The Abortion Act is an important landmark in the legal recognition of abortion as a medical phenomenon. It substitutes a medicalised regulatory framework of control over abortion for the previous system of criminal prohibition. This in many ways was a statutory recognition of the existing state of medical practice and judicial tolerance towards it. Doctors were already performing terminations on the basis of the 1938 decision in *R v. Bourne*, which permitted them to terminate pregnancies where, in their opinion, carrying them to term would leave the woman a physical or mental wreck.[4] The reform eventually accepted in 1967 was also the result of years of campaigning by the Abortion Law Reform Association, and a popular feeling of sympathy for the situation of women facing unwanted pregnancies. However, I would argue that the Act was less influenced by a desire to extend women's reproductive autonomy than by the pressure applied by a medical profession anxious to tighten its monopoly of control over female reproduction, and the need for the State to reassert its authority over the existing law.[5] In this sense, the medicalisation of abortion contributed to its partial legalisation, but is historically closely linked to the entrenchment and extension of a network of medical control. Here I wish to highlight three factors which were important in leading to partial decriminalisation, and which also marked the form taken by the legislation.

1. Abortion and the State: taking control of a situation of widespread illegality

By the late 1960s, the situation of widespread de facto female resistance to the law had revealed ss.58 and 59 of the Offences Against the Person Act to be wholly inadequate for dealing with the problem of abortion. A combination of juries' sympathies for the defendants, police reluctance to prosecute and public obstruction of their enquiries resulted in a situation whereby in 1966, at a time when an estimated 10,000 to 250,000 illegal abortions per year were taking place, there were only sixty-two prosecutions for illegal abortions, just twenty-eight of which resulted in prison sentences.[6] Moreover, abortions of dubious legality were already widely available in the private sector for those women who had enough money to pay for them.[7] It was believed that partial decriminalisation would serve both to clarify the law and to ease the worries of doctors regarding possible prosecution. More importantly, it would serve to bring unwanted pregnancy and abortion within the ambit of a regulatory medical framework, where it might be more effectively monitored and controlled by the State. As Roy Jenkins, then Home Secretary, summarised the arguments in favour of reform:

> the existing law on abortion is uncertain and is also, and perhaps more importantly, harsh and archaic and ... is in urgent need of reform ... How can anyone believe otherwise when perhaps as many as 100,000 illegal operations per year take place, that the present law has shown itself quite unable to deal with the problem? ... [T]he law is consistently flouted by those who have the means to do so ... it causes many otherwise thoroughly law-abiding citizens to act on the fringe, or perhaps on the wrong side of the law. As the Minister responsible for law enforcement, I believe that to be a thoroughly bad thing.[8]

Underlying the reform, then, was the need for the State to reassert itself, for abortion to be rendered visible and to be brought within a more effective network of control. Henceforward abortions would be performed only in hospitals or specially licensed premises[9] and would be subject to a strict regime of notification which would allow for their monitoring.[10]

2. Abortion and doctors: protecting the medical monopoly

The model of law adopted was also underpinned by the demands of various medical groups,[11] and the Act serves to protect medical autonomy and discretion rather than to grant substantive rights to the woman, even where she finds herself in the most extreme circumstances envisaged by the reformers. The regulation introduced offers the qualified doctor (and derivatively his/her patient) a valid defence against the Offences Against the Person Act for a termination which was medically authorised and performed.[12] The crucial point here is that the law operates to grant a woman and doctor together some rights against the State, but provides no safeguards to protect the woman's privacy or autonomy vis-à-vis her doctor.[13]

The clear desire to avoid giving any substantive rights to women is most clearly illustrated by the parliamentary debates on the issue of whether the Abortion Act should carry a "social clause" (whereby the need for abortion might be established with regard to socio-economic factors), and a clause allowing abortion in case of rape or incest. The Bill originally introduced by David Steel did carry such clauses, clause 1(c) allowing doctors to authorise abortion where: "the pregnant woman's capacity as a mother will be severely overstrained by the care of a child or of another child as the case may be" and clause 1(d) where "the pregnant woman is a defective or became pregnant while under the age of sixteen or became pregnant as a result of rape". These clauses were, however, opposed by all of the major medical bodies, who felt that women might interpret them to mean they had a *right* to demand abortions where the circumstances outlined were met.[14] For example, the Royal Medico-Psychological Association warned that:

[s]pelling out in detail when a doctor should or should not have the right to induce abortion, even if the legislation is cast in permissive terms, would have the effect of introducing an element of coercion in the sense that in each defined situation the patient might reasonably expect the doctor to acquiesce and the role of the surgeon or gynaecologist would be reduced to that of a technician carrying out an objectionable task.[15]

Following pressure from medical groups, the two clauses were subsequently removed. It was asserted that in case of rape or incest, abortion would already be available under other provisions, notably the risk to the woman's mental health. Further, to remove the rape clause, it was argued, would mean that women would not feel they had an automatic right to termination in these circumstances, and would therefore minimise the risk of their fabricating stories of rape in order to qualify for abortion.[16] As Hindell and Simms comment:

David Steel, the medical profession, and the Government were propounding the view that the law must not be made too clear lest the public read it and began to demand their rights. Much better to leave it vague and fuzzy so that doctors would have total discretion in the matter of abortion and so that patients would be unable to argue.[17]

The social clause was likewise removed, to be replaced by a form of wording which, whilst allowing social and economic factors to be taken into account, makes it absolutely clear that the decision remains with the doctor. Thus, under s.1(2), the doctor is authorised in determining whether the continuance of pregnancy would involve such risks to life or to mental and physical health as are specified in s.1(1), to take account "of the pregnant woman's actual or reasonably foreseeable environment".[18] This ensures that socio-economic factors are assessed only in so far as they are subject to evaluation by a doctor and that he/she, rather than the woman herself, remains the ultimate judge even in relation to the woman's own environment.

3. The woman seeking abortion: a focus on desperate and extreme cases

The shift from a model of criminal prohibition to one of a decentralised network of medical control was equally grounded on a particular construction of the woman seeking to terminate a pregnancy, which supported the choice of the doctor as the obvious expert to take control of abortion.[19] The woman was seen as irrational and emotionally unstable - in need of the support and control which could be provided by the doctor. A good illustration of the various kinds of women who the reformers envisaged helping was given by Lord Silkin when introducing his (1966) Bill to the

Commons:

> There are women who suffer from illnesses, which ... will ... make [them] less able
> to bear the burdens of motherhood ... There is the case of the woman who is in
> prison, serving a long term commencing between the beginning of the pregnancy
> and the time at which she will give birth. Obviously that woman is inadequate to
> be a mother of a child. There is the persistent offender, or the shop-lifter, and there
> is the mother who has in the past been found guilty of neglecting or ill-treatment of
> her existing children. These are some of the cases I have in mind. There is the
> drug taker or the alcoholic. I am sure the right reverend Prelate (the Bishop of
> Exeter) would not suggest that such a mother is a fit person to be in charge of
> children. There is the woman who already has a large family, perhaps six or seven
> children ... There is the question of the woman who loses her husband during
> pregnancy and has to go out to work, and obviously cannot bear the strain of doing
> a full day's work, and looking after a child. There is the woman whose husband is
> a drunkard or a ne'er-do-well, or is in prison serving a long term, and she has to go
> to work. These are the cases I have in mind.[20]

The picture drawn of the aborting woman contrasts strongly with the representation
of the doctor who stands for calm and rational judgment, high ethical standards and
responsible control.[21]   The possibility of legal abortion, it was argued, would
encourage women to approach their GPs who could then take control of the
situation. Indeed, it was hoped that mere contact with this mature, responsible and
reassuringly male figure might dissuade the woman from seeking to terminate a
pregnancy - the need for an abortion often being posited here as a direct
consequence of her hysteria and derangement, rather than a decision which might
reflect an informed and reasoned assessment of her concrete situation. This point is
made repeatedly both in parliamentary debates and in the academic literature:

> If we allow abortion to become lawful under certain conditions, a woman will go to
> her doctor and discuss with him the problems which arise ... he may well be able to
> offer that support which is necessary for her to continue to full term and
> successfully to have a child.[22]

> An important medical result of legalizing abortion would be that it would enable
> the patient to take proper professional advice. It is, of course, always open to a
> doctor to dissuade his patient from the operation by pointing out any harmful
> effects that he thinks it may have.[23]

> It does not follow that because women desire termination it will automatically be
> carried out. If we manage to get a girl such as that into the hands of the medical

profession, the Bill is succeeding in its objective. ... If the Bill encourages that kind of climate, it will have been worthwhile.[24]

David Steel, the Bill's sponsor, made the same point again in 1990 where he related that doctors had told him that they now have the chance to see women before they abort and to discourage them from doing so. One told him that:

[o]ne of the effects of the 1967 legislation has been that people will come to his surgery and discuss abortion with him, whereas pre-1967 they would not have done so and he would have lost control of what was happening and the patient might have ended up with a back-street abortion or going into a private clinic.[25]

To sum up, the Abortion Act serves to recognise abortion as a problem which can be better dealt with by medical regulation than by criminal prohibition. The partial decriminalisation of abortion entrenched the doctors' control of abortion and marked the recognition in law of the era of the doctor as the "parallel judge" who could administer and exercise power more quickly and effectively than a state-centred apparatus.[26] The very "nature" of the woman seeking an abortion made this model of control particularly suitable. Abortion is (re)defined as a matter for expert medical knowledge.

MEDICAL PRACTICE AND THE REGULATION OF ABORTION SINCE 1967

The recognition of abortion as a medical, rather than criminal, matter has had tremendous benefits for women in terms of improving access to safe, legal abortion services. Moreover, the medicalised statute adopted was no doubt the only one which it would have been possible to steer through Parliament at that time. In the years following the Abortion Act's entry into force, doctors have gradually become more liberal in the provision of abortion, which has thus become more freely available. The field of medical discretion has been zealously protected by the judiciary and doctors have thus been safe from threat of prosecution should they choose to take a liberal interpretation of the Act. According to Baker P:

Not only would it be a bold and brave judge who would seek to interfere with the discretion of doctors acting under the [Abortion] Act, but I think he would really be a foolish judge who would attempt to do any such thing, unless possibly, there is clear bad faith and an obvious attempt to perpetrate a criminal offence. Even then, of course, the question is whether that is a matter which should be left to the Director of Public Prosecutions and the Attorney-General.[27]

Further, even in those areas where senior obstetricians/gynaecologists remain hostile to abortion and NHS abortions are difficult to obtain, non-NHS clinics have been established to offer inexpensive terminations.

From a feminist perspective, however, the medical model embodied in the Abortion Act has clear and enduring shortcomings. The decision of whether a termination is appropriate for a particular woman remains that of two doctors rather than the woman herself. Medical professionals are hence legally recognised as more trustworthy and more capable of taking important reproductive decisions than women are, even though the doctor will inevitably have less knowledge of our concrete situations, our needs and aspirations. Secondly, the fact that this decision rests with a doctor can also have negative implications on the very concrete level of access to abortion services. A woman seeking abortion has a choice - she can either approach her GP (and have the possibility of NHS funding for her termination) or she can go to one of the non-NHS abortion clinics. If she takes the former option, she has no way of knowing beforehand the doctor's views on abortion. Where the doctor is hostile to abortion, she may have to endure moralising lectures and judgmental treatment in order to be granted (or indeed refused) authorisation for a termination. Women's accounts of being subjected to such treatment are not uncommon.[28] In 1990 a proposed amendment suggesting that doctors who are conscientious objectors under s.4 of the Abortion Act should register on a list, which would then be available for public consultation, was rejected. A woman still has no way of knowing, therefore, if her GP is hostile to abortion before approaching him/her. Moreover, there is no obligation for an anti-choice doctor to refer a woman to another doctor who is of a different moral opinion.

Problems also arise with regard to funding. If a woman chooses to go to a non-NHS clinic she will normally have to pay for her own abortion. The law leaves control over which terminations shall be performed in the hands of the doctors who control NHS facilities - in this case the senior hospital gynaecologists and obstetricians. This results in the anomalous situation whereby in 1992, ninety-three per cent of women in North Tyneside had their pregnancies terminated within the NHS, as compared to just one per cent of women in Coventry and Dudley District Health Authorities (where the hospitals are controlled by anti-choice doctors).[29] The two authorisations necessary to secure an abortion stand as obstacles in women's way and have contributed to delay in the provision of abortion. This may create particular problems for younger and older women, who (for different reasons) may delay in consulting their doctors. Women have also reported that they are reluctant to request a NHS termination, because they fear hostile treatment, bureaucracy and delay.[30]

Thus, although the very broad discretion accorded to doctors under the 1967 Act has greatly extended women's access to safe, legal terminations, it also remains at the root of many of the limitations on that access. Medicalisation (re)casts abortion as a technical problem, to be determined by experts. This has, to a certain extent, contributed to an apparent depoliticisation and served to shield women's access to abortion from outside attacks. However, it has entrenched that access firmly in the sphere of medical discretion. The Abortion Act works in terms of protecting the medical relationship from outside interference, and does not foresee the need to protect women within that relationship.

THE ALTON BILL (1988)

In recent years it seems that the pre-eminence of the medical framework has become increasingly accepted in political discourse (both inside and outside of Parliament). The Alton Bill was one of the most recent of a long series of Private Members' Bills which attempted to restrict the application of the Abortion Act. It was introduced into Parliament in October 1987 by the Liberal MP for Mossley Hill (Liverpool), David Alton, and received its second reading in the House of Commons on 22 January 1988, where it was passed by a majority of 296 to 251. The main provision of the Bill was a reduction in the upper time-limit for legal abortion to eighteen weeks, with exemptions allowing abortion until twenty-eight weeks only where termination was necessary to save the life of the woman or where the child was likely to be born dead or with physical abnormalities so serious that its life could not be independently sustained. A further exemption for women under eighteen years old who had suffered incest or rape was introduced at committee stage. After vigorous campaigning by both pro- and anti-choice supporters, the Bill ran out of time at the report stage which follows the committee stage and thus failed without being put to a final vote.

Although the Alton Bill was defeated, one group of feminist writers has highlighted the powerful legacy which it left behind. They assert that the terms in which abortion was considered were constructed in such a way that little space was left for women's needs or interests or for exploring reproduction as a social, rather than technological, biological or individual issue.[31] One member of this group, Deborah Steinberg, argued that although the Alton Bill ultimately failed in that it did not pass into law, it was successful in several respects in shifting the terrain of the meaning of abortion, and establishing or further entrenching certain assumptions in the public consciousness. Amongst the legacies of the Alton campaign listed by Steinberg is the increasing degree of reliance on medical/scientific knowledges to define abortion.[32] The perceived importance of such knowledges was fostered in media coverage which established a seemingly "consensual" framework for discussion which took the form of a "medico-moral rhetoric" drawing upon a fusion of Christian dogma and state-of-the-art medical technological knowledge and inviting "objective" decision-making and "rational" dialogue.[33] These writers conclude that:

> the debate focused on fetal viability and the established role of medical expertise in
> the adjudications surrounding abortion in Britain. In addition, the enhanced role of
> medical expertise went hand-in-hand with the harnessing of abortion rights to the
> technological capacities of modern medicine and an unquestioning faith in
> scientific progress. Prenatal diagnosis, technological systems for sustaining
> infants born prematurely and the technology which produces photo-images of
> fetuses were all invoked frequently during the Alton abortion controversy. In such
> circumstances, medical judgments and technical possibilities or limitations, not
> women's needs or lives, set the parameters of debate.[34]

The Alton Bill forms the background for the amendments which were introduced to
the Abortion Act in 1990.

THE HUMAN FERTILISATION AND EMBRYOLOGY ACT 1990

In 1990, s.37 of the Human Fertilisation and Embryology Act made the first
amendments to the Abortion Act since its introduction. Although the inclusion of a
clause dealing with abortion into a Bill intended to regulate embryo research and
fertility treatment was bitterly opposed by pro-choice activists, the actual reforms
achieved were widely greeted as a victory. Anne Kane, coordinator of the pro-
choice Stop the Amendment Campaign, wrote triumphantly that:

> [t]he outcome of voting on the abortion amendments to the government sponsored
> Embryology Bill was a massive defeat for the anti-abortionists, which poses a new
> stage in women's struggle for reproductive control. It decisively confirms the
> impact of the underlying trends in the position of women, and the political
> developments these make possible. Success in this most difficult abortion battle
> rested more than ever before on the tactical choices made by the Pro Choice
> movement. It is crucial that the left and the whole movement learn the lessons of
> these tactics and how the campaign was waged and won.[35]

Whilst the 1990 reforms entrenched a comparatively high upper time-limit into the
law, however, they cannot be seen as an unmitigated victory. First, the adoption of
a medical framework for political debate served to exclude broader social
considerations - in this light the adoption of viability as a cut off point is in itself
problematic. Secondly, the opportunity for a move towards liberalisation of the law
was missed, the medicalisation of the debates making it difficult to challenge
medical control over access to abortion. Finally, the parliamentary debates also

highlighted a worrying use of medical knowledges to support a construction of the foetus as a separate individual.

1. The limits of viability

The most important change made to the Abortion Act by the 1990 legislation was to insert a fixed upper time-limit of twenty-four weeks. Exceptions to this limit allow terminations until term where abortion is necessary to prevent grave permanent injury to the physical or mental health of the woman, or where continuance of the pregnancy threatens the life of the woman, or where there is a substantial risk that if the child is born it would suffer from such physical or mental abnormalities as to be seriously handicapped.[36] The limit adopted is that recommended by the Royal College of Obstetricians and Gynaecologists - twenty-four weeks is the point when the foetus is deemed to become "viable" or capable of sustaining independent life outside the womb. David Steel, recommending the adoption of this limit, told the House of Commons that:

> [i]t would be a great mistake for the House to set aside the opinion of established medical bodies ... We are not entitled to cast aside all these opinions as though they did not matter, or to pluck out of the air a figure that we think might be better.[37]

The choice is here presented as between the acceptance of medical judgment or complete arbitrariness: it seems that there are no valid considerations other than medical ones.

Anti-choice MPs opposed this time-limit not with their traditional religious-moral arguments of foetal humanity, but rather with medical "facts" and a reliance on scientific knowledges. In particular, they emphasised the need to "legislate for the future" as:

> medical techniques are advancing so rapidly that, long before 20 years is up, we shall regard a termination within 20 weeks as ludicrous ... By that time, medical techniques will be so good that a foetus will be viable much earlier than that.[38]

Once again, the medical framework for debate was clearly marked in press coverage. For example, on 23 April 1990, the day before the MPs voted on the proposed amendments, *The Guardian* ran an article which was described as "an attempt to summarise the arguments". It was entitled: "Most doctors opt for twenty-four-week limit" and began with the words: "[t]here are few supporters for retaining the present 28-week limit, as the medical consensus is that babies are viable from twenty-four weeks, given the intensive care and technology of modern premature baby units." Thus the perceived framework within which the issue of abortion should be decided was essentially structured by medical knowledges, broader social issues being obscured.[39]

The adoption of viability as the cut-off point for abortions was heralded as a victory for pro-choice campaigners, as it currently ensures an upper limit which is high in comparison to other Western abortion laws. However, the effect of the 1990 debates has been to entrench in the public - and parliamentary - consciousness that abortion is permissible prior to viability, but should be forbidden after this point. This is a notion which future campaigns may find hard to dislodge. One letter to *The Times* goes so far as to argue that the destruction of the handicapped viable foetus is no longer a matter of abortion, but rather of euthanasia.[40] Whilst the present state of medical science makes it impossible to sustain neo-natal life at much less than twenty-four weeks of gestational development for reasons of lung development, it is surely not inconceivable that this limit will be gradually pushed downwards.[41] If this happens, pro-choice groups will face a particularly bitter struggle to try and separate out the legitimacy of abortion from the notion of viability.

More immediately, the concentration on viability as the decisive factor obscures other considerations. As McNeil writes, the adoption of viability as a dividing line shifts the focus of decision-making away from women who make complex evaluations of their particular circumstances and of the *social* sustainability of new life. Such decisions have little to do with what medical science can sustain technologically:

> saying that it is theoretically possible to plug a 24-week-old foetus into life support apparatuses is very different from saying that you personally will take primary responsibility for supporting - in every sense - a child through to adulthood.[42]

2. The entrenchment of medical control

Another cause for concern at the medicalisation of public and parliamentary debate is that this can only further serve to entrench medical control of abortion.[43] The more abortion becomes viewed as primarily a medical phenomenon, the more it seems inevitable that it must fall into the sphere of authority of doctors who should maintain both their technical control over it *and* the power to decide who should have access to abortion services. The medical control of abortion is accepted within the 1990 debates, when even pro-choice MPs emphasise that the decision to terminate a pregnancy should be made in conjunction with a doctor.[44] In 1990, two amendments which addressed the medical control of abortion were tabled. The first, which sought to allow abortion on request within the first twelve weeks of pregnancy, was not selected for vote. The second, which sought to allow abortions during the same period with the approval of only one doctor, was defeated by 228 to 200 votes. Thus, Parliament sees it as more acceptable to allow the abortion of handicapped foetuses until birth than it does to allow this step towards female reproductive autonomy. The failure to pass either of these proposals through Parliament is a missed opportunity as it is unlikely abortion will be put to the vote again in the near future.

3. Foetal separation

The other worrying trend, highlighted during the debates on the Human Fertilisation and Embryology Bill, is the use of medical knowledges to support the construction of the foetus as a separate individual. Whilst anti-choice supporters have long made such assertions, these have been phrased in a religious-moral rhetoric. Now such claims have been recoded in a form which exploits the prevalence of an assumption of foetal separation in medical discourse.[45] During the 1990 parliamentary debates, the Society for the Protection of Unborn Children (SPUC) sent each MP a plastic replica of a foetus at twenty weeks of gestation. Although various MPs expressed their distaste at this strategy as "obscene"[46] and "a gross act of bad taste",[47] not one commented on what I would see as the most worrying aspect of this tactic: that the foetus is represented in total abstraction from the body of the woman that carried it. It emphasises everything that is "babylike" about a foetus whilst hiding the essential difference from a baby - that whilst the baby is separate and can exist independently of its mother (where there is someone else to care for it), the foetus is not and cannot exist without the body of the pregnant woman which actively nourishes and supports it. Its representation as a free-floating and separate entity embodies a fundamental deceit, and one which has not been adequately contested. An anti-choice sympathiser in Parliament commented:

> [w]hen I opened my parcel I found a legitimate and graphic piece of campaigning, because nobody disputes that that is what a 20-week old foetus looks like. If somebody had been able to produce medical evidence that this was a grotesque mock-up that was totally inaccurate and grossly misleading, it would have been the most obscene piece of campaigning that anyone could indulge in. However nobody has suggested that. When I was in the Post Office yesterday an hon. Member came in, took his parcel, opened it, and threw it in the bin. I could not help thinking that this is what happens to many foetuses.[48]

Worryingly, no one in the House of Commons challenged Cormack to suggest that this abstraction of the foetus from the body of the woman, this "graphic piece of campaigning" was indeed a "grotesque mock-up" and "totally inaccurate and grossly misleading" and that indeed it should not only be *medical* evidence which has the authority to challenge it. The failure to note this essential deceit in SPUC's representation of the issue reflects an unconscious acceptance of the construction of abortion as revolving essentially around this free-floating foetus and what status is to be attributed to it.   Once the woman is abstracted from the equation in this way then SPUC are already half-way to proving their argument and a central claim: that there is a negligible difference between a foetus in the last stages of gestational development and the newborn baby.   Such an assertion is made by Anne Widdecombe:

> At the moment, a child in an incubator can be kept alive, loved and cherished with all the resources of medical science being devoted to saving it, while a child of identical age and identical gestation in the womb has no rights and can be destroyed. There is something wrong with the law which allows that degree of inequity between *two individuals who are exactly the same except that we can see one and we cannot see the other* ... we must bring about a situation in which there is at least equality. At present, we have a law which states that *a child who is seen is protected but that a child at an identical stage who is not seen is not protected.*[49]

In this argument, Widdecombe completely obscures the presence of the woman whose body is sustaining the pregnancy.   She is challenged by Emma Nicholson who notes that:

> [t]he hon. Member for Maidstone (Miss Widdecombe) talked of identical babies whose only difference at 20 weeks was that one was visible and the other invisible to the naked eye. That is not true because the baby invisible to the naked eye may be hideously deformed and if born and brought to life, may face a future of unimaginable suffering. It may be visible to the naked eye through modern machinery and perhaps it can be kept alive, despite its wretched existence for many years.[50]

Having implicitly accepted the central importance of the foetus and ignoring the occlusion of the pregnant woman, Nicholson adopts the terrain set out by Widdecombe and uses an essentially eugenicist argument to oppose her.

In practice, the medicalisation of public and parliamentary debate, the representations suggesting foetal separation and the perceived logicality of medical control are integrally related and mutually supporting.   As medical knowledges become more important, the issue of the (medically determined) status of foetal life becomes increasingly central and the place of medical knowledges and the authority of medical experts becomes ever more entrenched.   Moreover, developments in other areas of medicine - such as obstetrics, the management of childbirth and in utero surgery - have equally led to the construction of the foetus as a separate patient, with the doctor the person best placed to represent its interests.[51]   This conceptualisation of the medical role equally serves to reinforce a sense of the doctor as the "foetal protector", and the right authority to take control in cases involving a request for an abortion.

CONCLUSIONS

I have argued above that the recasting of abortion as a narrow technical issue, its (re)construction as essentially a matter for the expert knowledge and control of doctors and medical science has had very positive effects in paving the way for women's access to the provision of safe, legal terminations. Medicalisation has also played a central role in the apparent depoliticisation of abortion in Britain. Moreover, it seems that medical knowledges, and the protection of medical discretion, have in many instances benefited pro-choice positions. This was crucial in the partial decriminalisation of abortion in 1967. A model of law which had sought to give more control directly to women and which had not commanded the support of the medical profession could never have succeeded. It has also been important in protecting the Abortion Act from repeated attacks over the years and likewise in entrenching a comparatively high upper time limit in the law in 1990.

But medicalisation also has serious shortcomings. It has entrenched a medical model of control which leaves women dependent on medical goodwill. As Brazier notes: "[b]y making doctors the 'gatekeepers' for the [Abortion] Act, abortion in England is a privilege granted or withheld at the doctors' discretion".[52] The law has constructed women seeking abortion as supplicants, who must go cap in hand to request permission to terminate their pregnancies. Refusals may result in women carrying unwanted pregnancies to term; they will certainly result in later terminations and women having to find the money to fund their own abortions. Moreover, it seems that women's awareness of the possibility of encountering refusal, hostile treatment and unnecessary bureaucracy in the public sector results in many going straight to private clinics.[53] Such an impression of the situation in the minds of the general public may also be implicated in the continuing occurrence of illegal abortions within certain minority groups.[54] Medical control has also resulted in severe regional inequality as regards NHS funding, as the hospital consultants who control the allocation of resources are perfectly within their rights should they choose to refuse to allow abortions within "their" hospitals. Thus, women's access to funded abortion in England and Wales is dependent on geographical chance and our access to sympathetic services within the NHS is dependent on luck. The English legal model is one of abdication of control to doctors: doctors are free to be as liberal - or as illiberal - as they choose.

For those who believe women should have the right to control their own fertility, medicalisation has thus been both the greatest strength and the greatest weakness of the British legislation. It has left access to abortion well protected against outside challenge, yet entirely dependent on medical goodwill. Moreover, the medicalisation of abortion has now become so grounded in our understanding of it that it becomes difficult even to imagine an alternative legal context.[55] What worries me is that it seems that the most effective way of protecting and entrenching women's access to abortion services has been (and may continue to be) to work within this medical framework, deploying medical knowledges and arguments. However, it is difficult to see how this can be done without reinforcing the idea that abortion is essentially a medical phenomenon, and thus to accept that control should rest in medical hands.

Diane Munday, an early and active member of the Abortion Law Reform Association, in an interview commemorating twenty-five years of the Abortion Act, expressed her regret that:

> Britain, which pioneered abortion legislation, now lags behind the rest of Europe where abortion on request in the first three months of pregnancy is available in 13 countries. Here, 'rigid' legal requirements remain in place, which led to many abortions being carried out much later in pregnancy than necessary.[56]

Various factors have contributed to the lack of progress over these years, including the existence of an active and well-organised anti-choice movement. The medicalised model adopted by British abortion law which I have discussed here is also implicated. It remains to ask whether it would be recommendable (or indeed politically feasible) to try to go beyond this medical framework, and to place more emphasis on broader considerations of women's needs or circumstances in the political debate concerning abortion.[57] To challenge medicalisation is undoubtedly dangerous. It risks alienating the medical groups which have such influence at the parliamentary and judicial level. Further, attempts to challenge the definition of abortion as a medical matter, may also be read as an implicit challenge to the claim that it is the Secretary of State's duty under the National Health Service Act 1977 to provide for it. However, to challenge the hegemonic medical control of abortion would also seem to be a necessary step in the development of a more pro-active pro-choice campaign. If the law regarding abortion is to be improved - in the sense of being made more sensitive to women's needs and circumstances, and in giving greater reproductive autonomy to women - it is essential for the feminist movement to take a more pro-active stance and to make its voice heard, so that access to abortion may be protected not merely on doctors' terms, but also on women's. An essential part of a pro-active strategy is to challenge the basic assumptions underlying the current regulation of abortion: the medicalisation, the perceived need for medical control and the constructions of women seeking abortion which underpin it.

ACKNOWLEDGMENTS

This chapter is drawn from doctoral research carried out at the European University Institute in Florence. I would like to thank my co-supervisors, Peter Fitzpatrick and Gunther Teubner for their help and support, and Eugene MacNamee, Julia Sohrab and Michael Thomson for their comments on an earlier version.

NOTES

1.   H.Dreyfus and P.Rabinow, *Michel Foucault: Beyond Structuralism and Hermeneutics* (1982) at p.196.

2.   W. Fyfe, "Abortion Acts: 1803 to 1967" in *Off-Centre: Feminism and Cultural Studies*, eds. S.Franklin et al. (1991) 160, at p.161.

3.   The 1967 Act was never extended to Northern Ireland where abortion is still illegal unless continuance of pregnancy would be such as to make the woman a mental or physical wreck: *R v. Bourne* [1938] 3 All E.R. 612.

4.   *R v. Bourne* [1938] 3 All E.R. 612.

5.   This argument is developed more fully in S.Sheldon, "The British Abortion Act (1967) - A Permissive Reform?" in *European University Institute Working Papers, Law No. 94/2* (1994).

6.   J.K.Mason, *Medico-Legal Aspects of Reproduction and Parenthood* (1990) at p.105.

7.   P.Ferris, *The Nameless* (1966); A.Jenkins, *Law for the Rich* (1960); K.Hindell and M.Simms, *Abortion Law Reformed* (1971); B.Dickens, *Abortion and the Law* (1966); V.Greenwood and J.Young, *Abortion in Demand* (1976).

8.   R.Jenkins, 732 *H.C. Debs.*, cols.1141-2 (22 July 1966).

9.   Section 1(3). Section 1(4) provides that this restriction shall not apply when a registered medical practitioner is of the opinion, formed in good faith, that termination is immediately necessary to save the life, or to prevent grave, permanent injury to the physical or mental health of the pregnant woman. Section 1(3) was amended in 1990 to allow the relevant authorities to approve simultaneously a "class of places" for the performance of terminations by way of specified abortifacient drugs.

10.   Under s.2 there is a duty for the Minister of Health (or the Secretary of State for Scotland) to ensure that any practitioner who terminates a pregnancy must provide to the Ministry of Health (or Scottish Home and Health Department) "such notice of the termination and such other information relating to the termination as may be so prescribed". Under s.4(1) of the Abortion Regulations, S.I. 1968/390, the operating practitioner is required to notify the abortion to the Chief Medical Officer within seven days.

11.   See especially J.Keown, *Abortion, Doctors and the Law: Some Aspects of the Legal Regulation of Abortion in England from 1803 to 1982* (1988).

12.   Thus, s.1(1) provides that "a person shall not be guilty of an offence under the law relating to

abortion when a pregnancy is terminated by a registered medical practitioner if two registered medical practitioners are of the opinion formed in good faith ..." [that certain conditions are fulfilled].

13.   This is to be contrasted with legislation in France, Denmark, Italy, the Netherlands, Norway, Sweden, the USA (and soon maybe also in Spain) which allows for elective early terminations.

14.   J.Keown, *supra*, n.11, at p.87.

15.   J.Keown, *ibid.*, at p.89. See Keown for the same objections from all other major medical bodies.

16.   The idea that women might fabricate charges is put forward several times in the parliamentary debates. See S.Sheldon, "'Who is the Mother to Make the Judgment?': the Constructions of Women in English Abortion Law" (1993) 1 *Feminist Legal Studies* 3.

17.   K.Hindell and M.Simms, *supra*, n.7, at p.185.

18.   Compare this to the formula put forward by the Royal College of Obstetricians and Gynaecologists (RCOG) which suggested that the law might provide that the practitioner could take into account such circumstances, whether past, present or prospective as were in the doctor's opinion relevant to the physical or mental health of the woman or of the child if born. See also the joint report of the RCOG and British Medical Association which argued for a subclause which had virtually identical wording to that of the Act. See J.Keown, *supra*, n.11, at p.92 and p.97.

19.   See S.Sheldon, *supra*, n.16.

20.   In K.Hindell and M.Simms, *supra*, n.7. The Bill was later dropped to allow the reformers to concentrate on advancing the Steel Bill. See S.Sheldon, *supra*, n.16, for a more thorough exposition of the constructions of the woman seeking abortion which underpin the Abortion Act.

21.   For example, Steel, 732 *H.C. Debs.*, col.1076 (22 July 1966); 750 *H.C. Debs.*, col.1348 (13 July 1967); Owen, 732 *H.C. Debs.*, col.1116 (22 July 1966); Dunwoody, 732 *H.C. Debs.*, col.1096 (22 July 1966). See S.Sheldon, *supra*, n.16.

22.   732 *H.C. Debs.*, col.1116 (22 July 1966). See also D.Steel, 732 *H.C. Debs.*, col.1076 (22 July 1955). Bernard Dickens puts forward the same point as an argument for reform (see B.Dickens, *supra*, n.7, at p.133).

23.   G.Williams, *The Sanctity of Life and the Criminal Law* (1958).

24.   D.Steel, 750 *H.C. Debs.*, col.1349 (13 July 1967).

25.   D.Steel, 171 *H.C. Debs.*, col.210 (24 April 1990).

26.   M.Foucault, *Discipline and Punish: The Birth of the Prison* (1977).

27.   *Paton v. Trustees of BPAS* [1978] 2 All E.R. 987, at p.992. Cited approvingly by Lord Donaldson MR in *C v. S* [1987] 1 All E.R. 1230, at p.1243.

28.   In particular, see V.Davies, *Abortion and Afterwards* (1991); D.Winn, *Experiences of Abortion* (1988); A.Neustatter and G.Newson, *Mixed Feelings: the Experience of Abortion* (1986); D.Cossey, *Abortion and Conscientious Objection* (1982).

29.   Office of Population Censuses and Surveys statistics for 1992. These figures exclude NHS

funded agency abortions which account for between seven and eight per cent of abortions performed in England and Wales.

30. (1993) 50 *Abortion Review*; C.Francome, *Abortion Practice in Britain and the United States* (1986) at p.53.

31. Science and Technology Sub-Group (Centre for Cultural Studies, University of Birmingham), "Feminism and Abortion: Pasts, Presents and Futures" in *Off-Centre: Feminism and Cultural Studies*, ed. S.Franklin et al. (1991) 214, at p.215.

32. D.L.Steinberg, "Adversarial Politics: the Legal Construction of Abortion" in *Off-Centre Feminism and Cultural Studies*, eds. S.Franklin et al. (1991).

33. T.Randles, "The Alton Bill and the Media's Consensual Position" in *Off-Centre Feminism and Cultural Studies*, eds. S.Franklin et al. (1991) 207. See also M.McNeil, "Putting the Alton Bill in Context" in the same collection, on press panics during the period of debate over the Alton Bill, which reinforced the perceived centrality of the foetus.

34. Science and Technology Sub Group, *supra*, n.31, at p.214.

35. A.Kane, "Anti-Abortionists Defeated" (1990) 7 *Socialist Action* 18.

36. Section 1(1)(b) to (d).

37. D.Steel, 171 *H.C. Debs.*, col.204 (24 April 1990). See also D.Steel, 171 *H.C. Debs.*, cols.206-7 (24 April 1990); H.Harman, 171 *H.C. Debs.*, col.262 (24 April 1990).

38. Kellett-Bowman, 171 *H.C. Debs.*, col.241 (24 April 1990). See also Smyth, 171 *H.C. Debs.*, col.241 (24 April 1990); K.Clarke, 171 *H.C. Debs.*, cols.264, 267 (24 April 1990); Amess, 171 *H.C. Debs.*, col.255 (24 April 1990); B.Braine, 171 *H.C. Debs.*, cols.215, 216 (24 April 1990); Alton, 171 *H.C. Debs.*, col.223 (24 April 1990).

39. S.Franklin, "Fetal Fascinations: New Dimensions to the Medical-Scientific Constructions of Fetal Personhood" in *Off-Centre: Feminism and Cultural Studies*, eds. S.Franklin et al. (1991) 190, at p.200; and M.McNeil, *supra*, n.33, 154.

40. Letter from Nigel de S. Cameron, editor of "Ethics and Medicine", (1990) *The Times*, 2 May: "do our legislators truly intend the unborn to be destroyed well beyond viability, for any other cause than to save the life of the mother? The answer may, of course, be 'yes'; and - if so - we will have moved from the discussion of abortion to that on euthanasia."

41. N.K.Rhoden, "Late Abortions and Technological Advances in Fetal Viability: Some Legal Considerations" (1985) 17 *Family Planning Perspectives* 160.

42. M. McNeil, *supra*, n.33. at p.156.

43. The entrenchment of medical control is also apparent in relation to other provisions of the Human Fertilisation and Embryology Act 1990. See S.Millns, "Making 'social judgments that go beyond the purely medical': The Reproductive Revolution and Access to Fertility Treatment Services" in this volume.

44. T.Gorman, 171 *H.C. Debs.*, col.232 (24 April 1990); D.Primarolo, 171 *H.C. Debs.*, col.248 (24 April 1990); E.Nicholson, 171 *H.C. Debs.*, col.250 (24 April 1990).

45. For the presence of such assumptions in medical discourse, see the work of, inter alia, A.Oakley, *The Captured Womb: A History of the Medical Care of Pregnant Women* (1984); R.Petchesky, "Foetal Images: The Power of Visual Culture in the Politics of Reproduction"

in *Reproductive Technologies: Gender, Motherhood and Medicine*, ed. M.Stanworth (1987); S.Franklin, *supra*, n.39.

46.   Doran, 171 *H.C. Debs.*, col.213 (24 April 1990).

47.   MacKay, 171 *H.C. Debs.*, col.243 (24 April 1990).

48.   Cormack, 171 *H.C. Debs.*, col.208 (24 April 1990).

49.   A.Widdecome, 171 *H.C. Debs.*, col.192 (24 April 1990), my emphasis.

50.   E.Nicholson, 171 *H.C. Debs.*, col.249 (24 April 1990).

51.   S.Franklin, *supra*, n.39; W.Arney, *Power and the Profession of Obstetrics* (1982) at p.135; R.Petchesky, *supra*, n.45, at p.57; D.Callahan, "How Technology is Reframing the Abortion Debate" in *Hastings Center Report* (1986) 33.

52.   M.Brazier, *Medicine, Patients and the Law* (1992) at p.292.

53.   *Abortion Review* and C.Francome, *supra*, n.30.

54.   See S.Daud, "Abortion, Contraception and Ethnic Minorities" in *Progress Postponed: Abortion in the 1990s*, ed. K.Newman (1993).

55.   L.Gordon, "Review of James Mohr's Abortion in America: The Origins and Evolutions of National Policy" (1980) 13 *J. Social Pol.* 515.

56.   L.Hunt, "Stigma and Secrecy that Marked a Different World" (1993) *The Independent*, 27 April.

57.   See R.Petchesky, *Abortion and Woman's Choice: The State, Sexuality, and Reproductive Freedom* (1986); E.Kingdom, "Problems With Rights", *Conference: The Rights of Women* (1992) European University Institute, Florence.

6   Sterilising the Woman with Learning Difficulties – In Her Best Interests?

KIRSTY KEYWOOD

INTRODUCTION

Consent to medical treatment has been described as "the legal and ethical expression of the human right to respect for autonomy and self determination."[1] Respect for the right to autonomy, it is said, is contingent upon the capacity of the right-holder to give valid consent, upon that consent being given voluntarily and the patient being appropriately informed.[2] In order for consent to be recognised and respected at law, patients aged sixteen years and over[3] must be able to understand in broad terms the nature and purpose of the proposed treatment.[4] Persons under sixteen may also be deemed legally competent to consent to treatment if they can show that they too understand the implications of the treatment in question.[5] But what of the person whose learning difficulties are such that she is not capable of giving legally valid consent to medical treatment? In such cases, it is suggested that respect for the wishes of the patient should be balanced against the need to guarantee the patient's welfare.[6] Few would advocate that persons with learning difficulties should have *all* their treatment preferences respected, particularly if those preferences will result in harm to the patient.[7] But the effect of such a paternalistic approach is that persons with learning difficulties who fail to reach the requisite level of understanding will be deprived of their autonomy. Adequate safeguards must therefore be installed to ensure the right balance is struck between autonomy and paternalism if the incompetent patient is not to be abused.

This chapter will argue that the sterilisation of women with learning difficulties is one area in which the balance between autonomy and paternalism is currently struck in favour of paternalism. I shall also attempt to demonstrate that the sterilisation debate does not simply raise issues about the autonomy-paternalism conflict, but also raises wider moral, social and political questions, many of which have been ignored. The first section examines the legal problems surrounding the sterilisation question and considers to what extent paternalism has triumphed over autonomy. Many of the arguments raised in this section have been commonly cited by other academics and I do not therefore propose to recite all of them.[8]   The remaining sections deal with the wider issues surrounding the sterilisation of women with learning difficulties, many of which have received insufficient consideration by parties to the sterilisation debate.   Sections two and three consider the extent to which learning difficulty and sexuality are socially constructed, and how myths surrounding the sexuality of women with learning difficulties have been perpetuated by the medical profession and judiciary. A consideration of both the social construction of learning disability and of female sexuality will, it is hoped, provide an explanation as to why it is women and not men with learning difficulties who are sterilised under the present legal system.   Section four considers the political dimension to the sterilisation question, examining the effect of the government's financial commitment to community care and its impact on women with learning difficulties. Section five seeks to resolve the sterilisation debate by considering whether there exists a theoretical justification for the continuance or prohibition of compulsory sterilisation programmes and further whether any such justification can be translated into an effective strategy which will provide adequate support for women with learning difficulties.

LEGAL PERSPECTIVES: THE BEST INTERESTS TEST - IN WHOSE INTERESTS?

The sterilisation of women under the age of eighteen is permitted under the welfare principle, that is, if the procedure is in the woman's best interests.[9] A woman with learning difficulties who does not understand the nature and purpose of the procedure is incapable of consenting to the sterilisation and is thus dependent upon others to consent to medical procedures on her behalf. Power to consent to procedures which are in the minor's best interests is usually vested with parents, the local authority if the girl is in care, or with the court if she is made a ward. In cases involving sterilisation the power to consent is usually vested in the court as a result of wardship proceedings,[10] although there is no legal obligation on parents or local authorities to have the minor made a ward of court.[11]   Wardship enables the judiciary to undertake an independent scrutiny as to whether sterilisation is justified as being in the woman's best interests. Such a procedure also guarantees that the medical staff performing the sterilisation will not incur legal liability for trespass to the person.

The situation for women over eighteen is more problematic, however, as the power to consent on behalf of minors expires upon the patient reaching the age of eighteen. Despite some initial speculation as to the survival of the Crown's inherent parens patriae jurisdiction into adulthood,[12] the House of Lords has confirmed that the jurisdiction ceased to have effect when the power to consent to treatment on behalf of persons of unsound mind was transferred to the guardianship provisions of the Mental Health Act 1959.[13]   These guardianship powers were greatly diminished under the 1983 Mental Health Act,[14] leaving a lacuna in the law with regard to consent to medical treatment on behalf of the mentally disordered. Since there is no person or authority legally empowered to consent to the sterilisation of the woman with learning difficulties, recourse is made to the common law doctrine of necessity. The doctrine permits doctors to carry out medical treatment on the incompetent person, provided that the treatment is in her best interests,[15] notwithstanding her inability to consent to treatment. Such treatment will be in the patient's best interests *only* if it is carried out in order to save the life of the patient or to ensure improvement or prevent deterioration in the patient's physical or mental health.[16] The doctrine is not confined to situations of emergency where the patient is temporarily incompetent but extends to those who are unable to consent by reason of permanent incompetence, such as persons with learning difficulties.[17]

Whatever the age of the woman, the crucial factor to be determined is whether sterilisation is in her best interests. Given that sterilisation involves the deprivation of the capacity to reproduce, it is important to consider whether the best interests test provides adequate protection to women with learning difficulties. The test has been criticised for failing to provide a principled approach to the problem of sterilisation.[18] Under the best interest test every case turns on its own facts without appearing to be based on any explicit legal principles or providing general guidance as to which factors are relevant to the question of sterilisation. Such an approach offers little or no guidance to carers and health care workers contemplating sterilisation for their female charges and leaves the adjudication of sterilisation cases to the unfettered discretion of the judiciary. This is not to say that the decisions of the judiciary in sterilisation cases are completely devoid of any systematic reasoning, but rather that reasoning has been kept hidden from public scrutiny. As Kennedy rightly remarks: "[the best interests test] is a somewhat crude conclusion of social policy. It allows lawyers and courts to persuade themselves and others that theirs is a principled approach to law. ... In fact, of course, there is general principle (or principles) but the court is not telling."[19]

There may be nothing intrinsically wrong in having a legal test like the best interests test that is devoid of any explicit legal principles. Indeed many legal tests are based purely on implicit legal principles, for example the "duty of care" concept in tort law. Provided that these implicit legal principles can be deduced and scrutinised, there is little cause for complaint. The difficulty arises, however, when the implicit principles upon which the legal concept is based are wholly inappropriate and take into account irrelevant considerations. This is the case with the best interests test, when applied to the question of sterilisation of women with learning difficulties. Analysis of the case-law reveals that the factors taken into account and the principles followed by the court are cause for concern for mentally handicapped women and their carers. Implicit principles that can be deduced from the cases demonstrate the unwarranted deference to medical opinion in determining whether sterilisation for contraceptive purposes is in the woman's best interests; the perpetuation of myths surrounding the sexuality of women with learning difficulties; and the courts' attempts to solve a social problem by surgical means. The above principles are not only injurious to the individual women who are the subjects of sterilisation cases, but the consideration of such factors misrepresents the social reality of the lives of all women with learning difficulties.

For a long time there has existed a rather special relationship between the medical profession and the judiciary. The courts, conscious to respect the clinical freedom of doctors, have frequently declined to undertake an extensive scrutiny into matters of diagnosis and treatment, believing these to be matters to be regulated by the medical profession itself.[20] Only in cases of clear abuse of duty, where diagnosis or treatment of a patient is not supported by a responsible body of medical opinion, will the doctor be found liable in negligence.[21]

In cases of sterilisation, the views of the medical profession by and large have been accepted without challenge. In many cases there has been no medical objection to the proposed sterilisation, and the court has simply been called in to confirm the legality of the decision to sterilise. This appears to have been little more than a process of rubber-stamping the doctor's decision without undertaking any independent scrutiny. In *Re M*[22] Justice Bush, in authorising the sterilisation, simply confirmed that there was complete agreement among the doctors that sterilisation was the only effective means of contraception available to the seventeen year-old. Only in the case of *Re D*[23] has the court taken an active role in challenging the clinical freedom of the doctors involved in the decision to sterilise. In that case Justice Heilbron declared that the decision to sterilise a seventeen year-old woman for contraceptive reasons (rather than for the purposes of curing disease or disorder) does not lie within the doctor's sole clinical judgment. In recognising that the woman's intellectual capacity might improve in future years, the judge refused to authorise the sterilisation as being in her best interests.

In the case of mentally handicapped adults, the proposed sterilisation will be in the patient's best interests if the decision to sterilise is supported by a responsible body of medical opinion.[24] This strategy by and large precludes the judge from challenging medical opinions as to the desirability of sterilisation. Although in theory the judiciary retains the right to override a body of medical opinion if the views of that body are irresponsible or unreasonable,[25] in practice the judge will accept the opinions of clinicians.[26] Indeed, it has been argued that the application of the *Bolam* test to the question of treating patients who are unable to give valid consent, "does little more than protect [women with learning difficulties] from the complete maverick whom none of his colleagues would back in his decision to sterilise."[27] The Bolam test, the purpose of which is said to balance the interests of the doctor (clinical freedom) against the interests of the patient (to receive satisfactory medical treatment),[28] cannot be applied to the question of sterilisation. The latter requires that the court ascertains the best interests of the woman with learning difficulties and makes no reference to the interests of the medical practitioners involved. Others have pointed out that the standard of care in negligence cannot be resorted to when dealing with the very limited exception to the consent principle.[29] To recognise that a responsible body of medical opinion approves of sterilisation does not provide a guarantee that the best interests of the woman with learning difficulties will be served. One only has to look to cases like *Re D* to recognise that medical practitioners can and do get it wrong.[30]

The failure of the judiciary to challenge the assertions of the medical profession can only prove detrimental to the woman for whom sterilisation is suggested. Case-law has shown that if there is no disagreement among medical practitioners as to the proposed sterilisation, the judiciary will treat the opinions of these professionals as statements of fact. The cases of *Re B*[31] and *F v. West Berkshire*[32] both demonstrate that in considering alternative contraceptive measures, the court does not question why the fitting of an inter-uterine device would not be a preferable alternative to sterilisation. The fitting of such a device gives rise to a slight risk of infection but does not bring with it the psychological trauma of a surgical operation and the loss of reproductive capacities. The courts seem ready to accept the views of medical practitioners as to the potential side-effects of contraception, but do not bother to consult these same experts on the possible side-effects attached to sterilisation.[33] If there exists any disagreement between practitioners as to the desirability of sterilisation, the judge simply justifies his decision to approve sterilisation by hiding behind the *Bolam* principle in the case of adult women.[34] In the case of the proposed sterilisation of a minor, the judiciary provides no explanation for its preference of one body of medical opinion over another.[35] If the woman with learning difficulties is to have her best interests determined by others, it is imperative that the court undertakes a thorough examination of all evidence relating to the proposed sterilisation. To defer to the medical profession is to leave the woman with learning difficulties at the mercy of those who seek to have her sterilised. It is in this way that the best interests of the patient become the best interests of medical practitioners.

THE CONSTRUCTION OF LEARNING DIFFICULTY

A closer examination of the judgments in sterilisation cases reveals the emphasis placed by the court and medical profession on the pathology of learning difficulties. The women who are the subject of sterilisation cases are frequently referred to in terms of their pathology, that is, what is wrong or abnormal about them. The most common example of this is the description of women in terms of their intellectual capacity, usually by reference to their mental age.[36] To equate women with small children is to deny the years of practical experience of these women and the extent of their behavioural skills which cannot be measured by intelligence testing. By labelling persons intellectually abnormal, the medical and "psy" professions explain the difference in treatment between "them" and "us" as arising from *their* abnormalities rather than *our* responses to these differences.   This clinical explanation of mental handicap thus views learning difficulty as a medical problem requiring a medical (or rather a surgical) solution. It has been rightly argued that the medical profession has overstepped its authority and has not stopped at providing medical care for the mentally disabled. In focusing on the psychological abnormalities of the person with learning difficulties, it has created a way of thinking that justifies the exclusion of persons with learning difficulties from enjoyment of society on the same terms as the non-disabled.[37] In sterilisation cases the courts have paid little attention to the behavioural skills of the woman with learning difficulties, relying essentially on medical testimony as to her mental condition and intellectual ability. As Carson rightly notes, parenting is a skill which can be measured by reference to behavioural ability rather than intelligence.[38]

Analysis of sterilisation cases reveals that reference to the psychological disfunction of women with learning difficulties has been used as a justification to sterilise women without examining the environmental influences on learning ability, such as the conditions the women live in or the quality of care they receive. In the case of *Re B*[39] the court took note of the fact that the seventeen year-old woman was unable to comprehend the link between intercourse and pregnancy. What was not considered, however, was the quality of sex education the woman had been given.   If the link between intercourse and pregnancy had never been explained to her, or had been explained in purely clinical terms which she could not be expected to understand, it should hardly come as a surprise to hear that her understanding of the consequences of intercourse was rather vague. In the case of *Re P*[40] the judge, prior to authorising sterilisation on a seventeen year-old woman, heard evidence that the woman's perception of sexual intercourse as painful would protect her from unwanted sexual advances.[41] This again clearly raises concern about the quality of the sex education provided which is not questioned by the judge. The vulnerability of the woman with learning difficulties has been taken into account by the court when determining her best interests. In *Re P* the seventeen year-old woman's vulnerability to sexual exploitation was remarked upon by a psychiatrist who commented that "girls like T are readily seduced". This statement was not challenged by the court as suggesting that her present environment was in any way unsatisfactory.[42] The concern that such women might be seduced, due to their trusting nature and dependence on others, ignores the extent to which their dependence has been fostered by an environment which prevents them from making choices and having those choices respected by others.

The courts' reliance on the medical explanation of learning difficulty ignores the extent to which it is a social construct. The courts are trying to answer the question, "how should society react to the sexuality of persons with learning difficulties?" by reference to a medical ideology which has no place in the treatment of persons with learning difficulties in society. The question should be answered by analysing society's response to learning difficulty, rather than perceiving learning difficulty as the inherent cause of the problem.

THE CONSTRUCTION OF SEXUALITY

The sterilisation of women with learning difficulties provides an insight into the social construction of sexuality. By attaching social and cultural values to certain sexual practices such as homosexuality, and to particular sexual partners, for example those with learning difficulties, the dominant social groups are able to define what is acceptable sexual behaviour and consequently what is deviant. Once certain practices and partners have been constructed as deviant, there exists some justification for prohibiting or regulating them. The cultural norms which are presently attached to the sexuality of women with learning difficulties are based upon myths which deny the reality of their sexuality and justify their sterilisation. It is necessary therefore to deconstruct their sexuality and provide a more realistic account of their sexual needs: a realistic appraisal of the sexuality of women with learning difficulties would not justify non-consensual sterilisation procedures for contraceptive purposes.

The present construction of the sexuality of women with learning difficulties is based not only on myths surrounding the sexuality of mentally handicapped persons, but also on myths relating to female sexuality. In sterilisation cases, the myths are restated and compounded by the courts and it becomes apparent that women with learning difficulties are being sterilised not only on the grounds of their intellectual subnormality but also because of their gender. Despite the growing recognition of the sexual needs of persons with learning difficulties,[43] the belief that these people have uncontrollable sexual desires, thus rendering them a threat to the rest of the population, has been accepted for many years and still persists. Citing Barr,[44] Craft notes that: "[t]he sexual desires [in mental defectives] are exaggerated in proportion to the animal over the physic forces."[45] This assumption, that people with learning difficulties pose a sexual threat, has also been made in sterilisation cases. In *Re B*[46] Lord Hailsham noted that the woman, who was showing signs of sexual awareness, would become a danger to others.

A contrasting, but equally relevant, myth pertaining to mental handicap is that people with learning difficulties are child-like and have no sexual desires. As Craft notes, this belief stems from the myth that children are asexual until puberty: "[w]hatever their actual age, individuals with mental handicaps remain forever children. Children are not sexual, therefore those who have a mental handicap cannot be sexual."[47] This view of the sexual immaturity of persons with learning difficulties has been compounded by some of the judges in sterilisation cases, who, as was noted earlier, constantly refer to the women about to be sterilised in terms of their mental age. In the case of *Re P* Justice Eastham noted that the seventeen year-old woman "although she looks perfectly normal, her intellectual development is that of a child of 6 years."[48] This may well explain the judiciary's reluctance to acknowledge the sexual needs of people with learning difficulties, focusing rather on their vulnerability and need for protection.

The courts' concern for the vulnerability of women with learning difficulties is well-founded, as many women run the risk of sexual exploitation. It is disappointing to note, however, that the judiciary are only concerned with preventing the physical manifestations of that exploitation (i.e. pregnancy), rather than putting an end to any sexual abuse that may be taking place. In the case of *Re W*,[49] Justice Hollis commented that a twenty year-old woman could not be taught to protect herself from unwanted sexual advances and that consequently there was a risk that someone might take advantage of her. In confirming that sterilisation was in the woman's best interests, the judge did not address the woman's need to be protected from sexual abuse. Even after a sterilisation operation, the woman would still be at risk of sexual exploitation through physical and emotional abuse and sexually transmitted diseases. The only way to effectively combat such exploitation is the development of programmes which aim to foster independence and confidence. Craft outlines the situations in which abuse may take place. At no point does she state that persons with learning difficulties are inherently vulnerable due to their intellectual impairment. Instead she identifies the vulnerability as stemming from the person's environment, in the form of institutional hierarchies, unscrupulous carers and inadequate support services.[50] The solution to the problem of vulnerability of persons with learning difficulties lies in the development of socio-sexual education programmes and the encouragement of decision-making and assertive behaviour. A surgical strategy solves nothing.

It is also unfortunate to note that the courts' somewhat misplaced concern for the woman's vulnerability seems to be at the expense of recognition of her sexual needs and desires. Morgan has rightly noted that the courts in the case of *F v. West Berkshire*[51] failed to ascertain F's precise sexual needs and wants, commenting only that she described her physical involvement with her partner as "nice".[52] In failing to ascertain whether F enjoyed penetrative heterosexual intercourse,[53] more or less than other forms of physical contact, or more or less than contact with members of the same sex, the courts have remained indifferent to her sexuality. This may be because the courts feel that persons with learning difficulties, like children, should not be encouraged or allowed to explore their sexuality. Instead they must simply be protected from some of its consequences. The courts perception of women with learning difficulties as asexual creatures, requiring protection from unwanted sexual advances provides them with a justification to approve sterilisation operations. Their reasoning, however, is ill-founded and ignores the reality of the experiences of women with learning difficulties.

A further erroneous assumption lies in the belief that mentally handicapped persons will in turn give birth to children with learning difficulties, thus resulting in the decline of the nation's intelligence. This belief was the main justification for the implementation of the eugenic policies of the early twentieth century,[54] and was echoed by the American judiciary in the famous case of *Buck v. Bell*, which, in upholding the legality of compulsory sterilisation legislation, claimed that "three generations of imbeciles are enough."[55] The view that parents with learning difficulties give birth to children with similar conditions has been discredited by studies which show that incidence of mental retardation through organic causes (i.e. biological accidents) among the offspring of parents with learning difficulties is equal to the rest of the population.[56] There is some evidence to suggest, however, that parents with low IQs which cannot be explained by any organic pathology are more likely to have children with low IQs.[57] This may be explained, however, on the grounds that persons with learning difficulties are likely to live in impoverished circumstances and it is impossible to say whether the learning difficulties of children are a result of living in poverty, or a consequence of being raised by parents with learning difficulties.

The fear of intellectual decline, though explicitly stated to have no relevance to UK sterilisation cases,[58] clearly has some import on a judge's decision to approve sterilisation. The fact that a woman with learning difficulties might give birth to a handicapped child has been cited as a relevant factor in determining the woman's best interests. In the case of *Re M*[59] Justice Bush was keen to stress that sterilisations on women with learning difficulties should not be carried out "merely because they are severely handicapped or weak, or likely to give birth to children who may equally be so."[60] It is somewhat surprising to note that he then went on to authorise the sterilisation of the seventeen year-old ward on the ground that if she became pregnant, there was a fifty per cent chance of her disability being passed on to the foetus. In such an eventuality, the judge assumed that the foetus would have to be aborted. Such an assumption clearly smacks of eugenic ideology. The abortion of a foetus on the sole ground that it would be intellectually impaired if allowed to be born, adds to the myth that people with learning difficulties are less desirable members of society.

Thus we see how the myths surrounding the sexuality of people with mental handicap have found their way into court judgments. The reliance of the court on these myths provide justification for sterilisation procedures on people with learning difficulties. What these myths do not explain, however, is why it is only women who are sterilised. If the court were guided solely by myths surrounding mental handicap, one would expect to see both men and women subject to applications to approve the legality of sterilisation. It is no accident that the only people to be the subject of court proceedings to confirm the legality of sterilisation are women. Many legal commentators have acknowledged the apparent discrepancy in the application of the law to women with learning difficulties, but few have considered in detail why this discrepancy exists. Feminist commentators warn us that we should not view the law as a neutral tool, which by chance provides apparently different consequences for men and women.[61] Indeed we should look beyond the effects of the law and examine precisely *why* the law operates differently for men and women.

For centuries the sexuality of women has been perceived as dangerous and capricious. Women have always been associated with the natural rather than the cerebral and, being closer to nature, they have been viewed as less rational and controlled by their emotions and their desires. This aspect of female sexuality has been highlighted historically in many areas of the law, particularly in rape trials, the prohibition of prostitution and the application to women of the defence of insanity.[62] More recently the notion that female sexuality is somehow irresponsible has been reflected in the Warnock *Report of the Committee of Inquiry into Human Fertilisation and Embryology*[63] on the subject of surrogacy arrangements, where, as Smart points out, the woman who offers her body to carry someone else's child, is perceived as pathological; a woman who does not know what she is doing and who must be protected from herself.[64] A similar attitude can be found in sterilisation cases, where the woman with learning difficulties is viewed as someone who needs protecting from the effects of her sexuality. It may be that the courts have failed to consider the woman's sexual needs because the judiciary feel that it would be impossible to ascertain them. However, the assumption in sterilisation cases is that if a woman is engaging in some form of sexual contact, it will inevitably lead to penetrative intercourse and thus give rise to a risk of pregnancy. In the case of *Re B*,[65] Lord Oliver noted that the young woman was showing signs of sexual awareness and had started touching her genitals and making advances toward members of staff and residents. From this he concluded that there was an obvious risk of pregnancy but did not ascertain whether the woman was in fact having penetrative intercourse or indeed whether she wanted to have it.[66] Other judgments highlight the assumption that women with learning difficulties are promiscuous. The House of Lords case of *F v. West Berkshire*[67] heard evidence that the woman in question was involved in a sexual relationship with a man, P. Despite the clinical advantages of vasectomy over sterilisation, the court declined to consider whether it would be preferable to operate on P, or even to educate him in the use of condoms. The assumption that has been drawn from the court's decision is that even if P were sterilised, F would remain at risk of pregnancy.[68] If F is having a sexual relationship with one man, the assumption is that she is probably having sex with others.

A further cause for concern lies in the fact that the courts' preoccupation with women with learning difficulties is to protect them from pregnancy. They do not address the more serious risks of sexual exploitation or sexually transmitted diseases. As previously mentioned, the courts are aware that exploitation is a real risk for women with learning difficulties, but it is clearly not a risk the judiciary are prepared to eliminate. As for sexually transmitted diseases, Carson rightly notes that "there can be few contra-indications to the use of condoms! And yet, without the use of condoms or only having one partner, safe sex cannot be practised."[69] Given that the sexuality of women is perceived as irrational, the courts cannot ascertain what women want and, by implication, what they do not want.[70] It is therefore impossible to protect women from abuse as they do not know what they enjoy. The best the judiciary can do is to guard against one physical result of their (presumed) sexuality, that is, pregnancy.

In short, the courts' failure to recognise the potential contraceptive responsibilities of male partners; the assumption that women will be promiscuous; the failure to consider the risk of pregnancy in isolation from risks of sexual abuse and sexually transmitted diseases, suggest that the courts are seeking not to protect women from unwanted sexual advances from male residents, relatives or staff, but rather to protect women from the consequences of their own capricious sexuality.

STERILISATION AND RESOURCE ALLOCATION

In ascertaining that mental handicap and sexuality are both socially constructed phenomena, it becomes easy to see that the reaction to the sexuality of persons with learning difficulties is a social problem, rather than a medical one. Ryan and Thomas rightly state that the clinical diagnosis by the medical profession of mental handicap does not in itself justify the exclusion of mentally handicapped persons from society by placing them in institutions,[71] nor does it justify removal of their reproductive capacities. In defining persons with learning difficulties in terms of their pathology, however, the medical profession has endorsed a way of thinking about persons who are intellectually less advanced which justifies their subordinate treatment in society. Viewing the issue of the sexuality of persons with learning difficulties purely from a medical perspective ignores the extent to which society is to blame for creating the problem. At present society is prepared to acknowledge that women with learning difficulties should live in the community as opposed to institutions, and should also be allowed to express themselves sexually, provided that expression does not lead to pregnancy. This recognition of the (limited) status of the person with learning difficulties is reflected in current government policy on mental handicap. Influenced by principles of normalisation, the government's community care policy advocates that persons with learning difficulties are better off living in the community rather than long-stay hospitals. The extent to which the State is prepared to accept the sexual desires of the mentally handicapped is a question which has so far received no explicit answer. Like normalisation principles, the government's policy on accommodating the sexual needs of persons with learning difficulties is vague. This is a matter which has been left to the judges. The response from the judiciary is that women with learning difficulties may be sexual, but their sexual freedom is conditional on contraceptive measures being taken. Parenting is an aspect of the sexuality of women with learning difficulties which society is not yet prepared to accept.

It is important to consider why the courts have taken such a stance in determining the best interests of women with learning difficulties, particularly since other jurisdictions have refused to authorise sterilisation operations, warning that courts should be reluctant to solve a social problem like this through surgery.[72] The answer may lie in the government's under-funding of community care, a policy which seeks to provide persons with learning difficulties with a more "normal" environment by transferring the responsibility of care for persons with learning difficulties from hospitals to local authorities. Unfortunately a transfer of funds from hospitals to local authorities to meet the needs of persons now living in the community has not ensued, with NHS authorities using the funds to meet their own budgetary demands.[73] The consequence for women with learning difficulties, many of whom are living in the community whether in hostels or with family members, is that they are deprived of adequate support services to meet their needs.

This may well explain why the courts consider that women with learning difficulties who live in the community will be vulnerable to unwanted sexual advances. In the case of *Re P*[74], the judge noted that P's future care was vague, it being uncertain whether she would obtain a place at a residential unit and added "[w]e do not really know where she will end up." To provide some protection against her vulnerability, Justice Eastham concluded that sterilisation was in her best interests. The judge failed to consider how local support services might be utilised to prevent the exploitation of her vulnerability in the first place. A similar point has been made by Lee and Morgan regarding community-based training centres and hostels. They ask "[w]hy are these centres so underfunded and understaffed that they cannot adequately protect women vulnerable to sexual abuse?"[75] The solution to the risk of sexual exploitation in such circumstances surely cannot be sterilisation for the victims, for this will only eliminate the physical symptoms of such abuse. The only way to combat exploitation in hostels and day-centres is to provide adequate staffing levels to ensure that good client-staff relationships are maintained, and further, as has already been suggested, that sufficient resources are allocated to assertiveness training classes and sex-education programmes. For those women who are not resident in community-based projects, there must be opportunity for training programmes and the establishment of a local support network to ensure that women living alone are physically and emotionally secure in the community.

The government's under-funding of community care also means that women with learning difficulties will not be given adequate training in parenting skills and parental responsibilities. In many of the sterilisation cases, the judiciary view the issue as involving a trade off between sexual freedom on the one hand and personal freedom on the other.[76] It is the belief of the judiciary that if the woman with learning difficulties is to enjoy as full a life in the community as possible, it is imperative that she does not become pregnant. Since the authorities cannot guarantee that the woman with learning difficulties will not conceive, the only solution is to sterilise her. The assumption throughout the judgments is that if the woman were to have a child, it would be taken away from her. In the case of *Re P*[77] Justice Eastham noted that any child born to P would have to be removed from her. This he claimed would have a particularly devastating effect on her as she had some maternal feelings. Noting also that P's future care in the community was uncertain, he assumed that P's interests would be best served by sterilisation.[78] Indeed he may be correct in his assumption that sterilisation was in her best interests, given that P would receive little support from the authorities as a parent with learning difficulties in the community. Nevertheless research suggests that, although women with learning difficulties may not have adequate parenting skills, they can still be trained to be good parents.[79]

Women with learning difficulties may not make good parents if they are deprived of social support services, but they may be no worse than the teenage single parent or the parent addicted to drugs or alcohol. In the latter instances, the authorities are prepared to take all reasonable steps to ensure that mother and child stay together. In the former, the possibility of assisting the mother-child relationship is rejected. To deny women with learning difficulties the opportunity to keep their children and develop their parenting skills, simply because society cannot afford the financial expenditure, sends out a grim message to *all* persons with learning difficulties; namely that sterilisation is the appropriate course of action, as they do not deserve to be parents. It may well be then that, given financial constraints, the judiciary are trying to adopt the most pragmatic strategy for the woman with learning difficulties. As Josephine Shaw comments, "it is in the mentally handicapped person's best interests that she gets the best out of underfunded care; it is not irrational, although it may be unfair, to argue that this is best achieved through sterilisation."[80] The consequences of this approach are, however, worrying. If the judges continue to view the question of sterilisation as a need to make life for the woman with learning difficulties as comfortable as possible in the present economic climate, they will fail to resolve the underlying problems associated with sterilisation. Lee and Morgan stress that the judiciary "have no effective means by which to effect a cure even if they had been prepared to recognise the symptoms. The cure which they proposed however, seems to be a striking example of iatrogenic disease."[81]   The sterilisation debate cannot take place without an examination of questions of resource allocation. Only after consideration of the wider political questions of the funding of community care can we hope to truly ascertain whether sterilisation is in the best interests of women with learning difficulties.

AN ALTERNATIVE STRATEGY

The courts, in reaching a pragmatic solution, have ignored the fundamental issues attached to sterilisation. By failing to address fully the wider question "is it *ever* justifiable to sterilise a woman with learning difficulties?" the courts have reached an unsatisfactory solution.[82] The following section will consider the theoretical arguments advanced for and against the sterilisation of women with learning difficulties, and it is hoped, will resolve some of the underlying disputes relating to sterilisation. Scroggie maintains that we need not undertake such a daunting task as there will be always some moral remainder in sterilisation cases.[83] This is not, however, an adequate position. Unless some attempt is made, whether by academics, legal practitioners or philosophers, to provide a theoretical justification for the continuance/prohibition of the sterilisation of women with learning difficulties, the controversy will persist.[84]

1. Sterilisation - a violation of the right to reproduce?
    The sterilisation of women with learning difficulties for contraceptive purposes has been condemned as a violation of the human right to reproduce. Kennedy asserts that the right to reproduce is a prima facie right which can be "trumped" on certain grounds, one of which is sterilisation for therapeutic purposes. As for sterilisation as a means of contraception, Kennedy argues that the right to reproduce is violated as the harm (actual and symbolic) done to the woman is greater than any harm that may have been avoided.[85] In the case of *Re D*, Justice Heilbron stated

that sterilisation involves the deprivation of the basic human right to reproduce and if performed on a woman for non-therapeutic grounds without her consent would constitute a violation of that right.[86]   Rights talk is therefore an attractive and powerful means of argument for those opposed to the sterilisation of women with learning difficulties for contraceptive reasons.[87]   It must be seriously questioned, however, whether recourse to rights discourse in general and the right to reproduce in particular will provide a helpful strategy in resolving the sterilisation argument. It will become apparent in this section that the right to reproduce has been pitted against the right to sterilisation, thus creating a clash of rights.   Once a clash of rights is established, we are left in a situation of stalemate.   Others, including academics and members of the judiciary, have rejected rights discourse in this field, arguing that persons with learning difficulties are incapable of possessing rights. In addition, feminists have warned against the use of rights talk to protect the interests of women under the law for many reasons, and many of their arguments will be relevant to the sterilisation question.   These factors will next be analysed to demonstrate why a right-based approach to the sterilisation of women with learning difficulties will fail to provide a morally sound and unproblematic justification for the prohibition of such a practice.

The right to reproduce, it has been argued,[88] is merely a facet of the wider right to privacy which also incorporates the right to *choose* sterilisation as a means of contraception. Struble argues that the woman with learning difficulties should not be denied the exercise of the right *not* to procreate, simply because of her legal incompetence. Citing *Re Grady*[89] Struble claims that the courts' power to consent on behalf of an incompetent woman produces a more compassionate result than denying the woman any chance of exercising her right to sterilisation.[90]   If we are to accept that there is such a thing as a right to reproduce, it is difficult to see how we can deny the existence of a corresponding right not to reproduce. The claims of opponents of sterilisation that the procedure violates the right to reproduce, will be met by the counter-claim that to prohibit the sterilisation of women with learning difficulties constitutes a violation of the right to sterilisation. Indeed, in North America, we are now witnessing a backlash against the prohibition of sterilisation, precisely on these grounds.[91]

Some commentators have sought to resolve the clash of rights and uphold the right to reproduce by contrasting the circumstances surrounding recourse to sterilisation by competent women and women with learning difficulties.[92] Competent women usually elect sterilisation as a mode of contraception after having a desired number of children to complete their family. Women with learning difficulties, however, are sterilised under quite different circumstances, usually before having given birth to any children and even when they are not involved in sexual relationships. This fact alone, however, cannot serve to justify the denial of the right of the mentally incompetent to choose sterilisation, for it simply tells us of the circumstances in which the right is exercised. Opponents of current sterilisation practices would be simply objecting to the circumstances in which the right to sterilisation is presently exercised, rather than its exercise per se. On such an analysis, if women with learning difficulties were in future permitted to keep their offspring and develop a family life, there could in theory be little objection to the exercise of the right to choose sterilisation.

Rights have also been used to pit the interests of one group against another. This is clearly seen in the abortion debate, where the right of the mother to self-determination, (the right to choose) has been pitted against the right to life of the foetus. This very same approach can be discerned in the sterilisation debate, where the right of the woman to reproduce has been perceived as conflicting with the right of the child to an adequate upbringing.[93]   A more controversial aspect of the rights debate is the argument that persons with learning difficulties do not possess legal rights, and therefore any objection to the sterilisation of women with learning difficulties as a violation of the right to reproduce is ill-founded.   In rejecting natural right theories, Feldman insists that rights are a description of social relationships.   A right cannot be said to belong to someone, unless that person is capable of acknowledging his/her social responsibilities: "asserting a right against individuals involves ... reciprocal responsibilities towards the state and society."[94] Feldman notes that in order to discharge this responsibility, and consequently exercise a particular right, the person in question must have a conception of the self and her position in the social group and also have the capacity to make a choice.[95] Applying this reasoning to sterilisation cases, Feldman argues that a woman who is unable to make a choice whether or not to reproduce, cannot claim to possess the right in the first place.   This is a view clearly shared by the Law Lords in the case of *Re B*,[96] who were unimpressed with the invocation of rights discourse. Disagreeing with Justice Heilbron's assertion in *Re D* that sterilisation involves the deprivation of a woman's fundamental right to reproduce,[97] Lord Oliver stated that the right to reproduce was valueless if unaccompanied by the ability to exercise a choice in the matter.[98] Lord Hailsham added that it was quite unrealistic to talk of the right to reproduce, when claimed by a person who is incapable of understanding the causal connection between intercourse and pregnancy, and its consequences.

Feldman also notes that certain responsibilities attach to specific rights. When talking of the right to do something, such as the right to reproduce, there exists a corresponding obligation to take responsibility for the consequences of the deed.[99] In sterilisation cases, the judiciary have frequently made reference to the woman's inability to care for any children she may conceive when considering her best interests.[100] According to Feldman, such a consideration is morally justified as it further demonstrates that the women in question are unable to fulfil their social responsibilities:

"If people want such a right, they must be willing and able to take responsibility for bringing up their offspring. If they are not, the right to reproduce is no more than a right to impose unquantified burdens on other members of society, present and future, for the sake of personal gratification."[101]

Feldman's theory of rights is certainly not accepted by all commentators on the sterilisation debate. Justice Heilbron clearly understood the right to reproduce as belonging to all persons by virtue of their humanity and irrespective of intellectual capacity.[102] Lee and Morgan also adopt a "natural rights" approach and warn of the dangers of reserving rights for the intellectually "normal". They assert that limiting the enjoyment of the right to reproduce to those of a certain mental capacity ignores the status of reproduction as a fundamental human right and places the rights of persons with learning difficulties on a slippery slope.[103] Such an approach can lead to the dangerous practice of according rights only to those who have attributes that society considers desirable, thus enabling the dominant (male) group to control the freedom and behaviour of the less powerful notwithstanding their common humanity.

There are further problems to be encountered if one is to view the question of sterilisation from a rights-based perspective, which are unrelated to the theoretical foundations of rights. Further objections are based on the practical implications of a rights-based approach, many of which have been raised by feminists. Kingdom has argued that any appeal to rights will prevent the formulation of effective, detailed policies.[104] This may well be true in the case of sterilisation, as any appeal to rights may give the impression that a simple, effective solution to the problem has been found. The prohibition of sterilisation of women with learning difficulties may be said to be justified on the ground that it violates the woman's right to reproduce. But if sterilisation were then to be prohibited, would the fate of women with learning difficulties be any better? It may well be that women would be spared the trauma of sterilisation, but may be deprived of their personal freedom to come and go as they please, for fear that they will be seduced or otherwise engage in sexual activity. Although the practice of sterilisation would have ceased, the underlying negative attitudes to the sexuality of women with learning difficulties persist. Policy-makers may continue to view the situation of the woman with learning difficulties as involving a trade-off between her physical and her sexual freedom. If a woman's sexual freedom is to be granted, then it may be at the expense of her personal liberty. Alternatively, the prohibition of sterilisations in the name of protecting the right to reproduce may in practice mean nothing more than that women with learning difficulties will be able to give birth to children who will automatically be taken into care. Again, on the surface it may appear that a victory has been won but, in reality, the women concerned are in no better position.

Ryan and Thomas are wary of an appeal to rights to solve the current problems facing persons with learning difficulties generally, and focus on the dangers attached to appeals to the right to "normality".[105] They argue that rights to equal treatment often overlook material, cultural and psychological inequalities. Unless these too are resolved, any claim that a victory has been struck for persons with learning difficulties, will have a hollow ring to it. The prohibition of sterilisations in the name of the right to reproduce would not solve the problems faced by women with learning difficulties, or their carers, nor would it address the wider social, moral and political issues involved.

A further objection to a rights-based approach which is particularly relevant to sterilisation is the fact that rights claims can be framed in terms of a general right and subsequently commandeered for purposes which are detrimental to women. In sterilisation cases, the right to reproduce has been invoked on both sides of the sterilisation debate. It is not inconceivable, given that we are still living in the shadows of the eugenic policies of the 1920s, that sterilisation could be performed for eugenic purposes;[106] a suggestion which the judiciary is keen to deny.[107] An appeal to rights to safeguard the interests of women with learning difficulties will at best prove problematic and at worst morally untenable. It is advisable therefore to consider an alternative strategy to ascertain whether the sterilisation of women with learning difficulties is justifiable.

2. Sterilisation falling within a special category of medical treatment?

One way of resolving the theoretical dilemmas associated with the sterilisation of women with learning difficulties is to view sterilisation as a special form of medical treatment requiring extraordinary safeguards. Sterilisation would thus be placed in the same category as psychosurgery[108] and hormone implants[109] which, due to their potential to fundamentally alter a patient's personality,[110] cannot be undertaken without the prior consent of the patient.[111] The justifications advanced for viewing sterilisation as a special form of treatment have been accepted by the Canadian judiciary, which recognised the serious intrusion on a person's rights, resulting from an irreversible operation of this nature.[112] The English judiciary has also gone some way to recognising that sterilisation should be distinguished from other medical procedures which can be carried out despite the patient's inability to consent. In the case of *F v. West Berkshire* Lord Brandon acknowledged the special features of sterilisation, in particular its generally irreversible nature and the resultant deprivation of a woman's capacity to reproduce, but subsequently declined to afford women with learning difficulties any additional safeguards.[113]

There has been some support for the acknowledgment of the special status of sterilisation operations among academics, although there remains disagreement as to the extent of the safeguards provided. Fortin advocates the performance of sterilisation operations on women with learning difficulties following approval by an independent second opinion, notwithstanding the patient's inability to consent.[114]   Kennedy on the other hand argues that sterilisation operations for contraceptive purposes should only be carried out if the woman concerned has the capacity to consent to the procedure.[115]   If one admits that there is something special about sterilisation operations which means that they should be treated differently from most other medical procedures, the only way to acknowledge this difference, in my view, is to adopt the position supported by Kennedy. Fortin's proposal simply suggests that the current judicial and medical practice does not truly ascertain the best interests of the woman with learning difficulties who is about to be sterilised - it says nothing about the special nature of sterilisations per se. Kennedy justifies his conclusion that sterilisations performed on women with learning difficulties without their (valid) consent are unjustifiable on the grounds that the harm avoided through sterilisation (such as the trauma of pregnancy or possible abortions) can never be greater than the harm inflicted.[116]   Harm is interpreted as both actual and symbolic. Not only does he consider the impact on the woman of having her reproductive organs tampered with but also the symbolic message that this practice sends out to the rest of society, that women with learning difficulties are less worthy of our time, resources and respect:

> [N]on-consensual non-therapeutic sterilisation involves the destruction of an essential feature of a person's identity, of that which at a very basic level represents a sense of self. A woman may be mentally handicapped. She may have a mental age of four or five years. But if she is 25 she has many of the qualities of a 25-year old. In particular, she has 25 years of experience and has seen how women and men are treated and how they react and behave. Some sense that women are different and that the difference lies in the fact that they are women will have been acquired, rudimentary as it may be. Womanness is inextricably identified with reproductive capacity, although this may not be its only feature. To destroy irrevocably this reproductive capacity is, on this analysis, to destroy a fundamental, perhaps the only remaining, element of a sense of self. Institutionalised and ignored, the woman is now to be sterilised.[117]

If we are to recognise that sterilisation has special consequences which are not ordinarily present in most other procedures, it is imperative that this special status is reflected in the way we deal with sterilisation cases. Some would argue that sterilisation is not in the same category as psychosurgery as sterilisation nowadays can be reversed in many cases.[118] This is true, although it does not deal with the objections to non-consensual sterilisations outlined above. To account for the fact that some sterilisations can be reversed, it may be sufficient to require legally valid consent by the patient without additional safeguards such as the approval of an independent second opinion, as is required in cases of psychosurgery and hormone implants.[119]

The above approach provides a sound theoretical basis for a response to the issue of non-consensual sterilisation. It does however raise one problematic question relating to the law's reliance on tests of intelligence as a means of ascertaining capacity to consent. It has been noted that the court's obsession with intelligence testing has the effect of reserving certain activities and choices, such as sexual intercourse, parenting and medical treatment, for the intellectually "normal".[120] It could be argued that to prohibit the sterilisation of women with learning difficulties who are not able to give valid consent at law, is merely an extension of this pernicious practice. This argument raises wider questions about consent tests generally and the circumstances in which persons with learning difficulties make choices (in under-staffed, under-resourced institutions where a relationship of dependency is fostered), which cannot be addressed without consideration of questions of resource allocation. To counteract any possible objection to my proposed strategy, a re-evaluation of tests of capacity is required.[121] In order that capacity to consent is correctly evaluated, it is important to consider the circumstances in which the choices of women with learning difficulties are made. If, for example, a woman is resident in an environment which does not allow her to make her own decisions, or to have those decisions respected, it should come as no surprise to note that she does not understand the consequences of her choices. It is inappropriate to conclude that a woman who does not understand the link between intercourse and pregnancy, as was the case in *Re B*,[122] is incapable of ever consenting to a sterilisation operation. Women with learning difficulties must be given every opportunity to develop their decision-making skills. This may well result in many of those presently deemed unable to give valid consent to sterilisation becoming legally empowered to choose sterilisation as a suitable contraceptive regime. If consent tests are to reflect the skills and abilities of persons with learning difficulties, it is essential that every attempt has been made to ensure that these skills are fully developed. For women with learning difficulties this requires an environment which encourages them to develop decision-making skills to their maximum potential, and that adequate resources are available to facilitate this aim. It is only in this context that the validity of consent to sterilisation can truly be ascertained.

CONCLUSION

In considering the wider social, moral and political issues surrounding the sterilisation of women with learning difficulties, I have attempted to show that the present legal position is untenable on a number of grounds. Many academics have already alluded to the legal problems associated with the practice of sterilisations, but have not considered in sufficient detail the further dimensions to the sterilisation question. Unless we are prepared to look beyond the present legal difficulties, the underlying controversy of the sterilisation of women with learning difficulties will persist. It is imperative that we address the question whether or not it is ever justifiable to sterilise women with learning difficulties and consider furthermore how we should respond to the social and political aspects of sterilisation. The strategy I have proposed touches upon these aspects. Indeed, my proposal for the prohibition of non-consensual sterilisations, together with the re-evaluation of consent tests may seem wholly unrealistic in the present economic climate. It is imperative, however, that we begin to acknowledge the social and political realities of sterilisation if we are to be certain that our response to the issue will be satisfactory.

NOTES

1. I.Kennedy, "Patients, Doctors and Human Rights" in *Human Rights for the 1990's,* eds. R.Blackburn and J.Taylor (1991) at p.84.

2. I.Kennedy, *ibid.*

3. Family Law Reform Act 1969, s.8(1).

4. *Chatterton v. Gerson* [1981] Q.B. 432.

5. *Gillick v. West Norfolk and Wisbech Area Health Authority and another* [1985] 3 All E.R. 402.

6. P.Fennel, "Inscribing Paternalism in the Law: Consent to Treatment and Mental Disorder" (1990) 17 *Jo. Law & Soc.* 29.

7. For example, Ian Kennedy argues that respecting the wishes of an incompetent patient does not guarantee respect for patient autonomy; *supra*, n.1, at p.85.

8. For a fuller discussion of the legal problems surrounding the sterilisation of women with learning difficulties, see A.Bainham, "Wardship: effect and uses - medical treatment" (1987) 137 *N.L.J.* 518; S.P.De Cruz, "Sterilization, Wardship and Human Rights" (1988) 18 *Fam. Law* 6; A.Grubb and D.Pearl, "Sterilisation and the Courts" (1987) 46 *C.L.J.* 439; M.Shone, "Mental Health - Sterilization of Mentally Retarded Persons - Parens Patriae Power: Re Eve" (1987) 66 *Can. Bar Rev* 635.

9. Children Act 1989, s.1(1).

10. For example, *Re D (a minor) (wardship: sterilisation)* [1976] 1 All E.R. 326.

11. Neither Lord Templeman's dicta in *Re B (a minor) (wardship: sterilisation)* [1987] 2 All E.R. 206, nor the Official Solicitor's Practice Note [1993] 2 F.L.R. 222, both of which state that applications for sterilisations will require the prior authorisation of the High Court, are legally binding. Note also that the court can confirm whether sterilisation is in a minor's best interests following an application for a specific issue order (*Re HG (Specific Issue Order: Sterilisation)* [1993] 1 F.L.R. 587).

12. *Re B (a minor) (wardship: sterilisation)* [1987] 2 All E.R. 206, per Lord Oliver.

13.   *F v. West Berkshire Health Authority and another (Mental Health Act Commission Intervening)* [1989] 2 All E.R. 545, per Lord Brandon at p.552.

14.   Mental Health Act 1983, s.8(1).

15.   *Supra*, n.13, per Lord Brandon at p.551.

16.   *Ibid.*

17.   *Ibid.*

18.   I.Kennedy, *supra*, n.1, at p.90.

19.   I.Kennedy, *ibid.*, at p.90.

20.   Note, for example, the failure of doctors to warn patients of inherent risks in medical procedures. Such a failure to warn will not render the consent invalid and will not therefore constitute a trespass to the person; *Sidaway v. Bethlem Royal Hospital Governors and others* [1985] 1 All E.R. 643. Note also the deference of the judiciary to decisions by doctors to perform abortions; S.Sheldon, "The Law of Abortion and the Politics of Medicalisation" in this volume.

21.   *Bolam v. Friern HMC* [1957] 2 All E.R. 118.

22.   *Re M (A Minor) (Wardship: Sterilisation)* [1988] 2 F.L.R. 497.

23.   *Supra*, n.10.

24.   *Supra*, n.13, per Lord Griffiths at p.560, applying the Bolam test.

25.   *Supra*, n.20, per Lords Bridge and Keith.

26.   Note Lord Goff's admission that there is a "high degree of likelihood that [the opinions of the doctors] will be accepted", *supra*, n.13, at p.569.

27.   M.Brazier, "Down the Slippery Slope" (1990) 6 *Prof. Neg.* 25.

28.   D.Morgan, "F v. West Berkshire Health Authority" (1990) *Jo. Law & Soc.* 204, at p.208.

29.   J.Shaw, "Sterilisation of Mentally Handicapped People: Judges Rule OK?" (1990) 53 *M.L.R.* 91, at p.104.

30.   Note Justice Heilbron's remark that " [the doctor], whose sincerity cannot be challenged, was persuaded by his emotional involvement with Mrs B's considerable problems and anxieties, and his strong personal views on sterilisation...", *supra*, n.10, at p.331.

31.   *Supra*, n.11.

32.   *Supra*, n.13.

33.   Note that in the case of *Re B* the House of Lords considered sterilisation to be in the seventeen year-old woman's best interests as, should she become pregnant, she would pick at the scar left following caesarian delivery. What the same court did not consider, however, is that sterilisation by occlusion of the fallopian tubes or hysterectomy both require surgical incisions and would also have given rise to the possibility of the woman picking at her scars; *supra*, n.12, per Lord Oliver at p.217.

34.   See, for example, *Re W (Mental Patient) (Sterilisation)* [1993] 1 F.L.R. 381.

35.   See, for example, *Re P (A Minor) (Wardship: Sterilisation)* [1989] 1 F.L.R. 182, at p.192.

36.   See, for example, *F v.West Berkshire*, where a thirty-six year-old woman was described as having the mental capacity of a five year-old child; *supra*, n.13, per Lord Brandon at p.549.

37.   J.Ryan and F.Thomas, *The Politics of Mental Handicap* (1987) at p.15.

38.   D.Carson, "The Sexuality of People with Learning Difficulties" [1989] 6 *J.S.W.L.* 354.

39.   *Supra*, n.12, per Lord Oliver at p.216.

40.   *Supra*, n.35.

41.   *Ibid.*

42.   *Ibid.*

43.   See, for example, J.Ware, "The Development of a Morals and Ethics Curriculum for Students with Severe Learning Difficulties" and Robinson, "Experiences of Sex Education Programmes for Adults who are Intellectually Handicapped" both in *Mental Handicap and Sexuality: Issues and Perspectives*, ed. A.Craft (1987).

44.   M.W.Barr and E.F.Maloney, *Types of Mental Defectives* (1921).

45.   A.Craft, *supra*, n.43, at p.14.

46.   *Supra*, n.12, per Lord Hailsham at p.213.

47.   A.Craft, *supra*, n.43, at p.13.

48.   *Supra*, n.35, at p.183.

49.   *Supra*, n.34, at pp.382-3.

50.   A.Craft, *supra*, n.43, at p.24.

51.   *Supra*, n.13.

52.   D.Morgan, *supra*, n.28, at p.210.

53.   Note also that the House of Lords did not even manage to ascertain whether F was indeed having penetrative sex, commenting only that "[t]he relationship is of a sexual nature and probably involves sexual intercourse, or something close to it, about twice a month"; *supra*, n.13, per Lord Brandon at p.549.

54.   For a discussion of the implementation of eugenic ideology into social policy, see J.Radford, "Sterilization versus Segregation: Control of the 'Feebleminded', 1900 - 1938" (1991) 33 *Social Science & Medicine* 448.

55.   *Buck v. Bell* (1927) 274 U.S. 200, Sup Ct, per Justice Holmes.

56.   Laxova et al., "An etiological study of 53 female patients from a subnormality hospital and their offspring" (1973) 17 *J. Ment. Defic. Research* 193, cited in L.Andron and A.Tymchuk, "Parents who are Mentally Retarded" in A.Craft *supra*, n.43, at p.238.

57.   E.Reed and S.Reed, *Mental Retardation: a family study* (1965) cited in L.Andron and A.Tymchuk, *ibid*, at p.241.

58.   *Supra*, n.12, per Lord Oliver at p.214.

59.   *Supra*, n.22.

60.   *Ibid.*, at p.499.

61.   For example, M.J.Mossman, "Feminism and Legal Method: the Difference it Makes" cited in C.Smart, *Feminism and the Power of Law* (1989) at p.22.

62.   For an overview of the construction of female sexuality in these areas, see C.Smart, *ibid.*, at p.94.

63.   HMSO Cmnd 9314.

64.   C.Smart, *supra*, n.61, at p.107.

65.   *Supra*, n.12.

66. *Ibid.*, at p.216.

67. *Supra*, n.13, per Lord Brandon at p.549.

68. D.Carson, *supra*, n.38, at p.366.

69. D.Carson, *ibid.*, at p.364.

70. An identical approach to female sexuality is discernible in rape trials. See C.Smart, *supra*, n.61, at p.29.

71. J.Ryan and F.Thomas, *supra*, n.37, at p.15.

72. For example, La Forest J in *Re Eve* (1986) 31 D.L.R. (4th) 1, Supreme Court of Canada.

73. J.Ryan and F.Thomas point out that the funds from the closure and sale of mental hospitals have not been channelled into community based projects, *supra*, n.37, at p.156. R.G.Lee and D.Morgan note the Audit Commission's observation that health authorities have absorbed half of the £1 billion resources ploughed into mental handicap services, despite caring for only twenty-five per cent of service users ("Sterilisation and Mental Handicap: Sapping the Strength of the State?" (1988) 15 *Jo. Law & Soc.* 242).

74. *Supra*, n.35, at p.184.

75. R.G.Lee and D.Morgan, *supra*, n.73 at p.239.

76. See, for example, *Re B*, *supra*, n.12 per Dillon LJ at p.209; *Re M*, *supra*, n.22, at p.498.

77. *Supra*, n.35, at p.194.

78. *Ibid.*

79. L.Andron and A.Tymchuck, *supra*, n.56.

80. J.Shaw, *supra*, n.29, at p.99.

81. R.G.Lee and D.Morgan, *supra*, n.73, at p.242.

82. Although the courts have made some attempt to address the moral claim that sterilisation violates the fundamental right to reproduce; see below at n.86 et seq.

83. F.Scroggie, "Why do parents want their children sterilised? A broader approach to sterilisation requests" (1990) 2 *J.C.L.* 35, at p.37.

84. See, for example, the controversy surrounding compulsory sterilisation programmes in the US during the early 1900s and current population control policies in the US; discussed in T.M.Shapiro, *Population Control Politics: Women, Sterilization and Reproductive Choice* (1985).

85. I.Kennedy, *supra*, n.1, at p.105.

86. *Supra*, n.10, at p.333.

87. For a discussion of the utility of claiming rights, see E.Kingdom, "Body Politics and Rights" in this volume. In the context of rights claims made by women seeking access to reproductive technologies, see S.Millns, "Making 'social judgments that go beyond the purely medical': The Reproductive Revolution and Access to Fertility Treatment Services" in this volume.

88. For example, C.Struble, "Protection of the Mentally Retarded Individual's Right to Choose Sterilization: The Effect of the Clear and Convincing Evidence Standard" (1983) 12 *Capital University Law Review* 413, at p.418.

89. (1981) 85 N.J. 235, 426 A. 2d 467.

90. C.Struble, *supra*, n.88, at p.420.

91. For example, M.Shone, *supra*, n.8; C.Struble, *supra*, n.88.

92. R.G.Lee and D.Morgan, *supra*, n.73, at p.233.

93. A.Thomas, "For Her Own Good - A Reply" (1987) 84 *L.S.G.* 1196.

94. D.Feldman, "Rights, Capacity and Social Responsibility" (1987) 16 *Anglo-Am. L. Rev.* 97, at p.102.

95. D.Feldman, *ibid.*, at p.105.

96. *Supra*, n.12.

97. *Supra*, n.10, at p.332.

98. *Supra*, n.12, at p.219.

99. D.Feldman, *supra*, n.94, at p.113.

100. For example, *Re M*, *supra*, n.22, at p.498; *Re P*, *supra*, n.35, at p.183.

101. D.Feldman, *supra*, n.94 at p.113.

102. *Supra*, n.10, at p.332.

103. R.G.Lee and D.Morgan, *supra*, n.73, at p.233.

104. E.Kingdom, "The Sexual Politics of Sterilisation" in *What's Wrong With Rights?* (1991) at p.72.

105. J.Ryan and F.Thomas, *supra*, n.37, at   p.132.

106. Indeed, it may be that this is already happening under the present law. See *Re M*, *supra*, n.22 where Bush J approved sterilisation bearing in mind that any foetus conceived by M would have to be terminated, there being a fifty per cent chance of mental retardation.

107. *Supra*, n.12, per Lord Oliver at p.219.

108. Mental Health Act 1983, s.57.

109. The Mental Health (Hospital, Guardianship and Consent to Treatment) Regulations 1983, S.I. 1983/893, Regulation 16.

110. J.Fortin, "Sterilization, the Mentally Ill and Consent to Treatment" (1988) *M.L.R.* 634, at p.642.

111. Note that psychosurgery and hormone implants also require a second opinion before treatment can go ahead (Mental Health Act 1983, s.57).

112. *Supra*, n.72, per La Forest J at p.32.

113. *Supra*, n.13, at p.552.

114. J.Fortin, *supra*, n.110, at p.642.

115. I.Kennedy, *supra*, n.1, at p.104.

116. I.Kennedy, *ibid.*, at p.105.

117. I.Kennedy, *ibid.*

118. See, for example, *Re M*, *supra*, n.22, at p.497, where Bush J noted expert testimony claiming that sterilisations performed by occlusion of the fallopian tubes can be reversed in fifty to seventy-five per cent of cases.

119. Mental Health Act 1983, s.57.

120. D.Carson, *supra*, n.38 at p.367 et seq.

121. See D.Carson, *ibid.*

122.   *Supra*, n.12.

7 Female Circumcision: Mutilation or Modification?

LOIS S. BIBBINGS

The collection of practices which are referred to as female circumcision (FC) or female genital mutilation (FGM) have been a subject of frequent discussion in recent years. This chapter will refer to some of these debates; cataloguing the range of responses to FC/FGM by writers, campaigners, governments and the international human rights system. The aim of the chapter is, initially, to use these reactions as an aid to conceptualise the various perceptions of the practices and, subsequently, to reconceptualise FC/FGM in the context of other body modification techniques.

FEMALE CIRCUMCISION OR FEMALE GENITAL MUTILATION

1. What is female circumcision?

The practices under discussion tend to be referred to as FC or FGM. Whereas the terms essentially refer to the same collection of practices, the main distinction is the conception of FC/FGM which they portray. The major justification for using the latter phrase is semantically to convey a sense of horror and disgust at such "mutilation". The resultant terminology is thus value-loaded. The use of the phrase FGM also serves to distinguish the many different forms of FC/FGM from male circumcision which is less varied, less controversial[1] and does not involve the same degree of tissue removal and/or infibulation as is common in most forms of FC/FGM. In fact it is argued that only one form of FC/FGM is comparable to male circumcision.[2]

However, there is another, more general, objection to using either FC or FGM. The use of these terms is misleading as they imply that the "practice" described represents a unitary whole. However, it is clear from the definitions given below that this is not the case. In addition, such categorisations are limiting as they fail to encompass all forms of non-essential genital operations.[3] Thus it would, as I will argue, be more pertinent to consider each of the procedures which are commonly referred to as FC/FGM alongside other forms of non-essential body modification performed in Western and Third World countries. Indeed, in the section below on body modification this is the approach adopted. It is not, however, the approach of the majority of commentators on FC/FGM,[4] and therefore, within the sections prior to that on body modification, the conventional terminology is used.

   It is necessary at the outset of this chapter to offer some definitions of the genital operations commonly referred to as FC/FGM, where they occur and why they are practised. Definitions of the different procedures vary within texts which address the subject,[5] but, nevertheless, it is possible to give a brief description of some general categories of FC/FGM:[6]

(a) *Ritual Circumcision* This is the least severe form of FC/FGM. It entails the pricking of the clitoral hood prepuce to release a drop of blood.[7]

(b) *Sunna* This term, which means "tradition" in Arabic, is used by Muslims to denote the cutting away of the prepuce or hood of the clitoris. However, practices referred to as sunna circumcision can reportedly involve the removal of the clitoris or the excision of parts of the labia minora.

(c) *Clitoridectomy* The excision of the clitoris.

(d) *Infibulation* Infibulation involves the excision of all or part of the mons veneris, the labia majora, the labia minora and the clitoris; the raw wounds having been sewn together to leave only a small aperture for the urinary and menstrual flows. This is often referred to as Pharonic circumcision because it is rumoured to originate in Egypt.   Ironically in Egypt it has been referred to as Sudanese circumcision.[8]

(e) *Deinfibulation* This procedure involves cutting apart the healed wound which is necessary for childbirth. Partial deinfibulation is also often necessary for sexual penetration to be possible.

(f) *Reinfibulation* This involves re-closing the wound and is sometimes carried out after childbirth.[9]

(g) *Excision* Excision can refer to any form of female circumcision but can also refer to the cutting of labial tissue. (The word is used as a generic term within this chapter.)

(h) *Introcision* This involves cutting into the vagina and/or the splitting of the perineum and has reportedly been practised amongst Australian aborigines.[10]

2. Age

The age at which such procedures are performed varies in different cultures. Operations are carried out soon after birth, at seven years of age, during adolescence (often as an initiation rite), or upon young or older women.[11] Most commonly these procedures are performed on girls aged between three and ten.[12]

3. Consequences[13]

There are a number of potential health risks, immediate and long-term, physical and psychological, which can result from some forms of FC/FGM. The consequences depend, not only upon the type of procedure which is performed, but also upon the circumstances in which it is conducted. For example, if the circumciser practises in sterile conditions, both realising and heeding the dangers of cutting into the pudendal artery or the dorsal artery of the clitoris, the risks of harmful consequences are lessened. However, where this is not the case, the operation often proves to be dangerous and sometimes fatal. Many girls bleed to death as a result of clumsy or inexperienced operators. In addition, unsterilised instruments and surroundings can lead to infection, tetanus, or septicaemia and can encourage the spread of HIV and AIDS. The use of traditional compounds, such as powdered dung, to stop bleeding can also increase the risk of infection. In addition, newly circumcised females may develop urinary infections as a result of a failure to urinate fearing, justifiably, increased pain.

Once the procedure has been performed the circumcised female may suffer post-operative shock. If hospital treatment is either not sought or not available death may result. Also after the operation in some instances scar tissue can become so enlarged that it affects movement. For infibulated women and girls the flow of urine and menstrual blood can be prevented or greatly slowed possibly resulting in the accumulation of these substances. FC/FGM can also cause loss of sexual sensitivity and can make orgasm less likely or even (perhaps) impossible, depending on the form of procedure performed.[14]

In addition, infibulation in particular can cause difficulties in relation to sexual intercourse and childbirth. As a result, partial or full deinfibulation is often necessary and this, of course, carries similar risks to the initial procedure. This is the same for reinfibulation where it is practised.

4. Origins and occurrences of FC/FGM

The fragmented nature of the practices referred to as FC or FGM is further complicated by the uncertain origins of the practices and the disparate cultures in which they are, or have been, performed. Whilst it is widely acknowledged that

FC/FGM predates both Christianity and Islam, it is unclear where or when such practices began; or indeed whether they were the invention of a single culture and proceeded to spread to others. The practices are estimated to be nearly 2,500 years old. Some writers have claimed that they originated in Egypt or amongst the Hamito-Semitic inhabitants of the shores of the Red Sea, whilst others dispute the existence of a common source.[15] Despite this uncertainty, it is evident that such practices exist, and have existed, in many different cultures and religious and ethnic groups throughout the world: in Asia, Australia (amongst aborigines), Europe (including Britain and Russia), Latin America (Peru, Brazil and some parts of Mexico), the USA, the Roman Empire and amongst Oriental and African Jews, Christians and Muslims. In addition, the practices are arguably more varied than those already described above.[16] For instance, the use of chastity belts could be cited as comparable to the practices which are commonly referred to as FC or FGM. In many cases these contraptions enclosed the anus and urinary opening along with the vaginal opening, perhaps allowing only some limited holes or flaps for urination and defecation. Although these devices were removable, they could be locked in place for substantial periods of time. Indeed they most probably caused side effects similar to infibulation, particularly as a result of the build up of bodily waste and discharges.[17] In addition, the Romans used (removable) metal labia rings which pierced the skin and held the two sides of the labia minora together to ensure the chastity or celibacy of their female slaves. Similar devices were also sometimes used for male slaves where the foreskin would be pierced in such a way as to prevent erection. This presumably represented a less severe and less permanent option to castration.[18]

In more modern times in the West clitoridectomies have been used as a treatment in medical science. In nineteenth century Britain and early twentieth century North America this procedure was used by some doctors as a cure for masturbation and various mental conditions.[19] There is, however, at least one more recent example. In the 1980s Dr James C. Burt faced charges from the Ohio State Medical Board in relation to procedures which he had performed on 170 female patients. The surgery was performed to significantly redesign the external and internal female genitals as he believed that "women are structurally inadequate for intercourse". The operations, it was argued (by Burt), cured frigidity; instead his patients suffered sexual disfunction, scarring and infections, and required corrective surgery.[20] In addition some cosmetic procedures practiced in the West today are similar, if not identical, to forms of FC/FGM; although, as is discussed below, they tend not to be viewed as such.

Today the practices which are grouped together as FC/FGM are becoming a more direct issue within countries which could be described as traditionally non-practising. This is largely the result of immigration. Populations which originate from cultures where FC/FGM is traditional perpetuate this custom. This has occurred within the UK and has sparked a legislative response. Female circumcision has been identified as an unsupportable practice and is consequentially criminalised in the Prohibition of Female Circumcision Act 1985.

5. Justifications for FC/FGM

Just as the practices known collectively as FC/FGM are varied, so are the justifications or reasons given by practising societies for performing these operations.[21] An awareness of the range of justifications is important as a preamble to any discussion or analysis of contemporary responses to such practices.

Many cultures invoke a combination of reasons for the practices. The idea of clitoridectomy as treatment has already been mentioned, however, other cultures similarly stress the idea of curing or, perhaps more precisely, controlling what are perceived to be "problems" associated with females and female sexuality.

The idea of controlling or eradicating the uncontrollable, is a common thread in many practising cultures. Frequently female sexual desire is viewed as being beyond the individual female's control and hence some strategy must be conceived by society to remedy this. Another explanation is the importance in many cultures of ensuring that paternity can be established so that economic interests in land and other forms of property are certain. Also, particularly in societies which practise infibulation, there is a tendency for virginity to be an absolute prerequisite for marriage. Infibulation is viewed as a means of ensuring this although it is, of course, not infallible.[22] In such cultures women who have not been operated upon are considered unmarriageable both because of their uncertain virginity and their unconventional physical appearance.[23] The latter view is common; uncut genitals are considered ugly, animalistic, or unnatural. Thus beauty has come to be associated with the excised form in some cultures. For example, one of the words which is used to describe their form of FC/FGM by the Maures of Mauritania, "tizian", means "to make more beautiful".[24]

Another justification is that the clitoris is believed to be a dangerous part of the body which could prevent conception, kill a baby at birth or harm a husband.[25] Elsewhere it is a commonly held belief that uncut genitals will grow to hang down between the legs hindering movement and mimicking the male member.[26]

Studies which have examined the justifications for the various forms of traditional excision have found that religious requirements or traditions are one of the most commonly cited.[27] Some believe that the Islamic faith requires female genitals to be excised although it has recently been argued that such procedures are merely customary or preferable but not essential.[28]

Today another commonly expressed reason for perpetuating these practices is the continuation of tradition in an increasingly changing world as a means of preserving and reaffirming one's cultural identity. Indeed Myers et al., writing about the practice in Southern Nigeria, argue that this was the only reason given.[29]

The force of culture and cultural pressures should therefore not be underestimated.[30]

RESPONSES TO FC/FGM

The collection of practices which are referred to as FC/FGM have become a relatively frequent subject of discussion and media campaigns (including both television documentaries and broadsheets), amongst women and within feminist, human rights and/or academic circles.[31] Such debates now take place in countries which have no long-term and on-going tradition of excision (predominantly States in the West), within those where FC/FGM has been practised for hundreds or thousands of years (most often Third World States) and at an international level.

Those contributions which emanate from within non-practising countries are relatively recent in origin. Until the late 1970s the only discussions tended to be within anthropological, sociological and psychological accounts of "primitive" or "native" practices and these do not represent attempts to alter or eradicate the practices.[32] However, the earliest attempts to end FC/FGM were instigated by British colonial governments and Christian missionaries. Not surprisingly such efforts were largely unsuccessful. For instance, attempts in the 1940s by the British government in Sudan to outlaw infibulation took no account of local culture. As a result such procedures were merely driven underground and their continuance became a symbol of resistance to foreign influences. Thus such episodes arguably incited resistance to change.[33]

In countries within which forms of FC/FGM are traditionally practised some have also spoken out against the practices. African women began to publicise their concerns during the late 1970s.[34] By the early 1980s a sizable opposition to FC/FGM had developed in Africa.[35]

Notwithstanding the comparative youth of the debates, many of the reactions have been vehement.[36] However, commentators and campaigners have not been united in their responses. Indeed various splits have emerged between, for example, Western and Third World feminists, and between those who argue for FGM to be recognised as an abuse of human (or more specifically women's) rights and those who maintain that some respect for different cultures must, at the very least, be iterated if not maintained. These various positions are, of course, not mutually exclusive.

Many from practising States have spoken out against FC/FGM practices. For example, Egyptian Nawal El Saadawi has condemned such procedures.[37] Asmal El Dareer, who was circumcised at the age of eleven, has examined the incidence of FC/FGM and assessed the possibility of eradicating these practices within the Sudan. Her book, *Woman, Why do you Weep? Circumcision and its Consequences*, is based upon material from a four year research project on the subject.[38] Raqiya Haji Dualeh Abdalla undertook a similar piece of research in Somalia and has called for wide-ranging government action in a strategy aimed at ending the tradition.[39]

Some writers from practising States welcome Westerners to condemn the practices, whereas others, like Edda Gachukia of Kenya, reject Western involvement as outside interference and seek locally-based initiatives.[40] Nevertheless, even Gachukia recognises the value of international organisations and genuinely interested individuals supporting local expertise and effort.[41] This resistance to Western campaigns, which has in part been triggered by the Western approaches themselves, is a focal point in discussions about FC/FGM at an international level. Therefore before considering this conflict it is necessary to look at some of these Western reactions.

Westerners from traditionally non-practising States have tended to be highly critical of FC/FGM, viewing it as a violation of rights or, for some feminists, as an example of patriarchal oppression. Western feminists in particular have tended to attack such customs and call for their eradication. Mary Daly, for example, identifies the practices as an "'unmentionable' manifestation of the atrocity which is phallocracy".[42] Hers is an extreme view which maintains that no female could truly choose to be mutilated in such a way or to perform such procedures upon others. Thus Daly views the arguments of a young Egyptian woman doctor, who stated that if she had a daughter she would circumcise her herself, as the result of phallocentric ideologies perpetrated by patriarchy.[43]

Alison Slack also considers whether the choice to be circumcised can ever be truly voluntary.[44] In discussing the position of adults she recognises that actions are influenced by available information and by social, economic and cultural pressures. Thus, she argues that false, inaccurate or limited information as to the nature and consequences of an action and/or the presence of severe pressures to conform may render an act involuntary or less voluntary than it would otherwise be. So whilst in some circumstances an action might be deemed to be (comparatively) freely chosen (an informed choice), in others the same action may be viewed as an abuse of human rights.

Westerners have also attacked FC/FGM from a human rights perspective describing the practices as savage or barbaric.[45] For example, Ben Whitaker, a UK member of the UN Sub-Commission on the Prevention of Discrimination and the Protection of Minorities, which investigated FC/FGM, has made strong statements condemning the practice and describing it as a violation of human rights which is analogous to slavery.[46] Other similar responses occurred during the UN Decade of Women (1975-85) when Western feminists attempted to expose FGM as oppressive and barbaric.[47]

Such overtly critical comments by Westerners are one reason for Third World objections to Western involvement in the development and implementation of policy in relation to FC/FGM. Those from cultures which have a tradition of genital alteration view outsiders who condemn such procedures as standing in judgment upon their culture and their people.[48] In addition, practising societies reject the imposition of Western norms upon their very different cultures. Thus the universality of human rights is questioned and the issue of cultural relativism is raised.

Cultural relativists argue that there is infinite cultural diversity and that all cultural practices are equally valid. Therefore any attempt to devise a cross-cultural standard (like human rights) by which to judge practices or behaviour will itself be culturally specific.[49] Thus it has been suggested that the rights focused upon within the international human rights system, with their emphasis upon individualism, are ideologically Western: the international human rights system "provides only one particular interpretation of human rights, and ... this Western notion may not be successfully applicable to non-Western areas".[50] In this analysis the application of human rights world-wide would be a form of cultural imperialism. Some within practising cultures clearly adhere to this view. Jomo Kenyatta, former president of Kenya, has stated that:

> [t]he overwhelming majority of [those from cultures which have a tradition of genital alteration] believe that it is the secret aim of those who attack this centuries-old custom to disintegrate their social order and thereby hasten their Europeanisation.[51]

Thus *any* Western intervention risks being viewed as quasi-colonialist or even racist. However, even attacks upon FC/FGM from within a practising State can cause resistance. When Kenyatta's successor, President Daniel Arap Moi issued a decree against FC/FGM the measure was greeted with accusations that he was attempting to suppress the culture of tribes to which he did not belong.[52]

Some African governments have used similar cultural relativist arguments to resist pressure for action against FC/FGM, effectively arguing that the continuation of the practices amounts to a cultural right. This argument has, in the past, reportedly deflected the WHO from the issue.[53] The issue of cultural rights in relation to FC/FGM has recently been raised in Britain by Poline Nyaga, of Brent London Borough Council, who has called for the legalisation of female circumcision.[54]

Similarly, some Third World critics of Western feminism have, despite their own rejection of such practices, challenged the latter's attitudes to FC/FGM. For example, Marie Angelique Savane, President of the Association of African Women, published an article criticising the cultural insensitivity of Westerners.[55] Such objections are, in part, one facet of a wider debate which centres around calls for Western feminists to reconsider their conceptions of women, women's oppression and women's needs in the light of cultural difference. The suggestion here is that both feminism as a discourse and women-centred approaches are culturally specific. Thus Third World women wish to deny the monolithic and essentialist view of women which many Western feminists perpetuate.[56] Daly in particular has been criticised for her portrayal of women as a homogeneous group and as victims of male power.[57]

Vehement Western feminist anti-FC/FGM statements also tend to anger those from the Third World because sometimes they are viewed as being patronising and as revealing latent racism.[58] There is particular resentment of those who refer to customs as "barbaric".[59]

Those who respond either to Western rights-based or feminist arguments tend to stress that Third World women (and men) have very different conceptions not only of rights but also of exploitation, oppression and needs. Thus it has been argued that calls for the abolition of the various forms of excision are less important than basic economic and material requirements including sufficient supplies of food and clean water.[60] In addition, the Western focus upon FC/FGM means that the role of multinational corporations, (often Western in origin), and their exploitation of labour, is either ignored or granted a lower priority.[61]

More specifically, there has been criticism of some Western feminists' tendency to sexualise issues; to use sexualism as a "lens" by which to measure women in other cultures.[62] In relation to FC/FGM this has involved a tendency to focus upon the clitoris and clitoridectomy whilst marginalising historical and political aspects of the practice. Chandra Talpade Mohanty has noted that Fran Hosken, in writing about human rights and FGM, bases her whole discussion upon the premise that the purpose of the practice is to mutilate the sexual pleasure and satisfaction of women,[63] and T. Patterson observed at the 1982 African Studies Association meeting that many objected to Hosken's focus upon clitoridectomy as the major form of women's oppression in Africa and the Middle East.[64]

Thus several common factors are discernible in many of the Western approaches to FC/FGM. Generally, non-practising States look down from above upon (practising) Third World peoples and their cultures and attempt to argue or imply that the Western way is best. Angela Gilliam has noted this in relation to the work of Fran Hosken who is now considered an expert on the subject of FC/FGM.[65] Such responses also frequently objectify women from practising cultures rather than recognising them as subjects. Thus, for example, some feminist approaches to FC/FGM have either ignored or dismissed Third World women's arguments supporting the practices (by implication as a form of "false consciousness") or have offered maternalistically to change the mind of what Karen Engle has described as the "Exotic Other Female". Engle concludes that both human and women's rights-based approaches tend (albeit to varying degrees) to imagine, rather than engage, the "Exotic Other Female".[66]

The result of such clashes or differences between Westerners and those from practising States (most of whom wish to eradicate FC/FGM) can clearly be divisive. In particular, not only is Western support rejected or treated with suspicion but also heavy-handed statements and actions against the practices have tended to drive them underground.   In consequence operations are performed in secret and increasingly upon younger girls.   The latter trend could also be viewed as an attempt to avoid resistance from older girls.[67]

Third World reactions to Western criticisms of FC/FGM have, however, had a clear effect upon Western and international responses and initiatives. The perceived cultural sensitivity of the discussion of FC/FGM as a human rights issue arguably led the WHO to delay consideration of the practices.[68] Also there has been some recognition that a new approach must be adopted if international initiatives are to be successful in their attempts to lessen the frequency of, or eradicate, FC/FGM.[69] Thus Westerners have tended to step back and allow those from practising cultures to formulate policy and guide actions. For example, Western members of the UN Sub-Commission on the Prevention of Discrimination and the Protection of Minorities which considered FC/FGM did not, for the most part, participate in discussions (Ben Whitaker, mentioned above, being the exception).[70] Thus, more recently, Western and international efforts tend to take a supporting role and Westerners are generally more aware of cultural issues. However, it should not be supposed that resistance to the eradication of FC/FGM emanates only from practising States: UNICEF has apparently found it difficult to gain unified support against FC/FGM from its own personnel.[71]

FEMALE GENITAL ALTERATION AND OTHER BODY MODIFICATION PRACTICES

From the definitions given at the beginning of this chapter it is clear that FC/FGM is by no means a unitary practice. The terms are used to describe a variety of very different procedures which are (or have been) performed within many cultures for a variety of reasons. Yet those who condemn these practices usually assume that all of these procedures are sufficiently similar to be linked. In addition, the practices grouped together as FC/FGM often fail to include all forms of non-essential female genital operation, instead focusing upon those traditional forms most associated with the Third World. As a result these practices are isolated from the context of other permanent body modification techniques. This is symptomatic of a general tendency to conceal, over simplify or generalise when considering issues related to FC/FGM. For example, it has been shown that assumptions are made about Third World women, Third World culture and the universality of human rights. Reconceptualising FC/FGM practices as fragmented forms of body modification allows for a more accurate and less culturally specific view to be adopted. This will allow parallels to be drawn between the ways in which FC/FGM, cosmetic surgery and other forms of permanent body modification are perceived.

Body modification can be defined as either the permanent (irreversible) or temporary alteration or adornment of the body. Such procedures are often described as being *elective* as they are operations which are performed for aesthetic reasons or are non-essential. Those which can be described as permanent include cosmetic surgery, body and facial piercings (any loose flesh on any part of the body can potentially be pierced, including the ears, nose, tongue, cheeks, lip, eyebrows, nipples, navels and male and female genitals), scarification (the making of marks on the flesh by burning or cutting) and tattoos. Some of these procedures, like ear piercing and tattooing, are reasonably acceptable (although not uncontroversial) in the West whilst others can be described as being nonmainstream.[72] James Myers, who studied Western body modifiers (those who have these procedures performed upon their bodies) in the USA, describes such phenomena as being as old as "the genus Homo [sic]" and reaffirms Thevos's observation that the "self retouching impulse" distinguishes humans from other animals.[73] If this is true it should be expected that forms of body modification are present in every culture. It is therefore important to consider the body altering techniques which are practised in the West, to compare them with Third World practices, to consider why they are performed and to assess how they are viewed by Western feminists and advocates of human rights. This facilitates a comparison with the practices known as FC/FGM.

Cosmetic surgery is becoming increasingly popular in the West amongst women and men. Whilst some proponents of human rights have not perceived cosmetic surgery as a major concern, the practice has not gone unchallenged. Feminist commentators on women's cosmetic surgery often perceive it as an example of body fascism; as a facet of patriarchal oppression which portrays the female form as imperfect and perpetuates norms of feminine beauty and the need for conformity.[74] Thus the "choice" to be operated upon is often dismissed as the result of "false consciousness". There are clear parallels here to the manner in which some feminist or rights-based critics of traditional practices have denied the validity of the Exotic Other Female's choice to be "mutilated". In such accounts of FC/FGM and cosmetic surgery the women who choose to undergo the procedures themselves, perform them on others or cause them to be performed on others, are frequently undermined and belittled. Kathy Davis presents a challenge to the conventional feminist view of cosmetic surgery.[75] She argues that "[c]osmetic surgery may be, first and foremost, about being ordinary, taking one's life in one's hands, and determining how much suffering is fair" and that a woman who chooses cosmetic surgery may have realistically balanced the suffering caused by her present situation against that which the solution offered by cosmetic surgery would entail.[76] "When viewed against this backdrop, the decision could conceivably become a moment of triumph - a moment when a women turns the tables and does something to help herself."[77]   Thus, in this model, the decision to be operated upon could itself conceivably be perceived as being liberating or empowering.   In addition, Davis has noted that feminist arguments which are based upon the notion of false consciousness tend only to pin this label upon those who "choose" to act in a manner of which they (the feminists) disapprove.   Thus, whereas the level or accuracy of available information about a particular course of action may be viewed as having some effect upon a person's ability to make a valid or fully informed choice, it is arbitrary to suggest that actions which are thought to be barbaric or mutilating cannot be a matter for valid consent.[78]

Similarly advocates of the various forms of body alteration in the West have argued that body modification can be viewed as a means of empowerment which allows an individual to redefine or recreate her/himself.   This argument is particularly common amongst those who practice forms of nonmainstream body modification in the West.   For example, women in particular view such practices as empowering or as a means of reclaiming their bodies after breast-feeding or even sexual abuse.[79]   Such alterations can also serve as a form of initiation into a group or subculture.   Alternatively modifications may be chosen for aesthetic reasons and viewed as a means of beautification (by making a person's body conform to a conventional image of beauty or making their appearance more distinctive and individual).   Similarly in some parts of Africa FC/FGM is considered equally fashionable.[80]   In this view body modification is a means of bodily self-determination.   Thus, here again, there are parallels with the justifications for FC/FGM.

Some modifiers see their alterations as a form of art or of bodily self expression. Indeed this is the basic premise of *Body Art*, a periodical which examines forms of human physical expression including tattooing, piercing, body painting, and bodybuilding which in this context tends to be referred to as "body sculpture".   An extreme example of such expression is that of French performance artist, Orlan, who has undergone a series of major cosmetic operations as part of her performance.[81]

The majority of nonmainstream practices (which often have Third World or "tribal" origins) are viewed as primitive, deviant, repulsive or barbaric by Westerners when practised in the West.   Myers noted this in relation to his study of such practices in the USA when he described, and refuted, "the general public's assessment that people so involved are psychological misfits bent on disfigurement and self-mutilation".[82]   This popular conception again mirrors some of the more vehement reactions to FC/FGM discussed above.   It would, perhaps, be interesting to learn the response of Third World populations upon discovering that in the West some women have fat sucked from their bodies (lyposuction), lumps of silicon placed in their breasts, their skin stretched or chemically scraped and their tummies tucked for aesthetic reasons, suffering considerable pain and discomfort in the process and risking unforeseen health complications or indeed the complete lack of success of the operation.[83]

Rhoda E. Howard has noted this inconsistency suggesting that Westerners should not be so shocked by FC/FGM, given Western forms of "self mutilation" like plastic surgery and incessant dieting. Similarly Ruth Rosen has described breast implant surgery as "barbaric" and similar to other "mutilations" which are viewed as violations of human rights.[84] Body modifiers have also noted the inconsistent attitudes towards different forms of alteration:

> What's really shocking is that you can go to a doctor and pay large sums of money so they can cut open your body and rearrange you. Breast jobs, nose jobs, bicep implants are all expensive alterations to conform to some norm and they turn round and call us freaks![85]

In the context of other forms of body modification FC/FGM practices become examples of non-essential genital operations. In the West a variety of such alterations are performed by cosmetic surgeons. Some of these procedures are identical to forms of FC/FGM although they are performed within hospitals or sterile conditions (and thus the risk of infection and accidents is lower). For example, the removal of excess labial tissue is most often performed for aesthetic reasons although some women reportedly suffer physical discomfort from enlarged labia.[86] The removal of the clitoral hood or prepuce is reported an operation which some women now request in the USA. The procedure is claimed to increase sexual pleasure by exposing a larger proportion of the clitoris.[87] Indeed Dr L. Wollman has defined "female circumcision" as a surgical procedure used in some cases of frigidity which involves the removal of a small amount of the tissue which covers the clitoris itself.[88] Female genital piercings of the labia minora, labia majora and clitoris are also said to enhance sexual experience.[89] Such views contrast sharply with Daly's conception of all forms of FC/FGM as "mutilation" and as a means of controlling and limiting female sexual potential.

It is by no means the case that critics of FC/FGM fail to consider other forms of body modification. For example, Daly refers to FGM and Chinese footbinding alongside other practices which she identifies as facets of the global oppression of women.[90] However, where these comparisons are made they are either brief or they tend to merely list other forms of body alteration (in the West and Third World) as being additional examples of mutilation.[91]

The above comparisons are undoubtedly useful as they allow FC/FGM to be considered in a wider cross-cultural perspective than that which is most often adopted. However, there are various major differences between FC/FGM as practised within traditional cultures and some other forms of body alteration. It is arguable that there exists in some cultures greater social, economic and cultural pressures to be excised than there are, for example, amongst Westerners to have cosmetic surgery. In addition, the health risks associated with FC/FGM are most often significantly greater than those incurred in relation to similar procedures in the West where it is usually trained medical personnel who perform alterations. However, the most significant distinction is the fact that in most cases FC/FGM is performed upon young children at the request of family members. In the West most body altering procedures tend to be performed upon adults at their behest.[92] Indeed some practices are deemed illegal if performed upon those under the age of majority. For example, in Britain it is actually illegal to tattoo anyone under the age of eighteen.[93] This raises the issue of parental consent. Slack considers this arguing that, whilst an educated and fully informed woman *may* (in some circumstances) be deemed capable of "voluntarily" deciding to be excised, such a non-essential, life altering operation should not be performed upon a child without her understanding and consent.[94] Slack maintains that in the latter situation the performance of an operation would amount to a violation of human rights. Thus she argues that ideally such a decision "is better postponed until the individual can decide for herself - until the time she has reached adulthood".[95] However, Slack's analysis is limited. She fails to consider at what age adulthood might be deemed to have begun (cultural conceptions of childhood vary), nor does she suggest at what point an adult decision would be deemed sufficiently voluntary. This approach ostensibly represents a compromise between cultural relativism and human rights made for the protection of children (and those adults not deemed to possess sufficient knowledge or freewill). Nevertheless it entails the negation of culture by (implicitly) proposing that, in order to avoid potential violations of human rights, practising societies should postpone operations *traditionally* performed upon the young until adulthood.

CONCLUSION

Considering and comparing the various forms of body alteration, Western and Third World in origin, involves a recognition of cultural diversity both globally, and *within* Western (the modifiers in Myers' USA study were part of an American subculture) and Third World States. This perspective also helps to reverse the tendency for critics of FC/FGM to focus upon Third World traditional practices, whilst marginalising or dismissing comparable or identical procedures in the West. Much can also be learned from the Western body modifiers and their stated reasons for altering or decorating their bodies. In many instances they are remarkably similar to those given in relation to FC/FGM. Such justifications from Westerners are no more nor less credible than those emanating from "non-Western" cultures.

ACKNOWLEDGMENTS

An earlier draft of this chapter was presented as part of the University of Liverpool Faculty of Law's staff seminar programme in 1994. Thanks go to those attending for their comments.

NOTES

1. Although recently some have spoken out against the practice. See, for example, "Circumcision is rarely necessary" (1994) *The Times*, 24 February; "Mother wins injury award for son's circumcision" (1994) *The Independent on Sunday*, 22 May.

2. Removal of the clitoral hood or prepuce, a procedure often referred to as "sunna", has been described as being truly comparable to male circumcision. Dr Ahmed Abu-El-Futuh Shandall has argued this. However, his definition of sunna seems to include the excision of some of the labia minora in addition to the prepuce. See A.Shandall, "Circumcision and Infibulation of Females" (1967) 5 *Sudan Medical Journal* 179.

3. I use the word "operation" to cover the various contexts in which FC practices are performed. Whilst this would include those performed in sanitary conditions by medically qualified personnel, it would also cover those performed by local barbers, or traditional practitioners who may well have no, or limited, knowledge of anatomy or of the importance of sterile conditions.

4. A.T.Slack, "Female Circumcision: A Critical Appraisal" (1988) 10 *Human Rights Quarterly* 437, considers the possibility that some forms of the collection of procedures known as FC could, in some circumstances, be viewed differently from others.

5. See, for example, A.Shandall, *supra*, n. 2.

6. For more detailed discussion of these procedures see L.P.Sanderson, *Against the Mutilation of Women: The Struggle to End Unnecessary Suffering* (1981) chapter 2; A.T.Slack, *supra*, n.4, at pp.440-443; *Report of the Working Group on Traditional Practices Affecting the Health of Women and Children*, (1986) U.N. Doc. E/CN.4/1986/42. For clear diagrammatic illustrations of the vulva and of an infibulated vulva see E.Dorkenoo and S.Elworthy, *Female Genital Mutilation: Proposals for Change*, (1992 2nd ed.) at p.6.

7. "Female Circumcision: A Norm in Africa" (1985) *International Herald Tribune*, 29 July.

8. L.P.Sanderson, *supra*, n.6, at p.14.

9. For description and discussion of the consequences of deinfibulation and reinfibulation see A.El Dareer, *Women, Why Do You Weep? Circumcision and Its Consequences* (1982) chapter 3.

10. In the past this was reported to be a practice of the Ditta Pitta tribe of Australia. See L.P.Sanderson, *supra*, n.6, at p.16.

11. See E.Dorkenoo and S.Elworthy, *supra*, n.6, at p.7 and A.T.Slack, *supra*, n.4, at pp.442-3.

12. A.T.Slack, *ibid.*, at p.443.

13.   For fuller consideration of possible consequences see E.Dorkenoo and S.Elworthy, *supra*, n.6, at pp.8-10; A.El Dareer, *supra*, n.9, chapter 2.

14.   This is not wholly clear, but some have argued that infibulation or other operations which involve clitoridectomy would end the possibility of reaching sexual climax (see E.Dorkenoo and S.Elworthy, *ibid.*, at p.9). Certainly, it is arguable that the potential trauma associated with such a genital operation may lead to severe sexual problems.

15.   For a more detailed discussion of the history and geography of FC/FGM see L.P.Sanderson, *supra*, n.6, chapter 2.

16.   For further variations see M.Daly, *Gyn/Ecology: The Metaethics of Radical Feminism* (1991 - new introduction) at p.155; R.H.D.Abdalla, *Sisters in Affliction: Circumcision and Infibulation of Women in Africa* (1982) chapter 3; see also the section in this chapter on body modification.

17.   See M.Daly, *ibid.*, at p.155.

18.   J.Myers, "Nonmainstream Body Modification" (1992) 21 *Journal of Contemporary Ethnography* 267, at p.301.

19.   E.Showalter, *Sexual Anarchy: Gender and Culture at the Fin de Siècle* (1991) at p.130. See also R.H.D.Abdalla, *supra*, n.16, at pp.74-75.

20.   "Charges against Doctor Bring Ire and Questions" (1988) *New York Times*, 11 December, and "Physician Charged Over 'Love Surgery' Surrenders License" (1989) *New York Times*, 26 January, cited in E. Showalter, *ibid.*, at pp.141-142.

21.   For consideration of the various reasons see A.T.Slack, *supra*, n.4, at pp.445-450; E.Dorkenoo and S.Elworthy, *supra*, n.6, at pp.13-15; S.Armstrong, "Female Circumcision: fighting a cruel tradition" (1991) *New Scientist*, 2 February, 42, at pp.44-45.

22.   A.Shandall, *supra*, n.2.

23.   Elizabeth Oram makes this point in relation to the Maures of Mauritania (E.Oram, "Zainaba" in *Opening the Gates: A Century of Arab Feminist Writing*, eds. M.Badran and M.Cook (1990) 64).

24.   E.Oram *ibid.*, at p.71, n.1.

25.   E.Dorkenoo and S.Elworthy, *supra*, n.6, at p.13.

26.   E.Dorkenoo and S.Elworthy, *ibid.*.

27.   See, for example, A.El Dareer, *supra*, n.9, at p.71.

28.   See E.Dorkenoo and S.Elworthy, *supra*, n.6, at pp.13-14 and R.H.D.Abdalla, *supra*, n.16, at pp.82-84.

29.   R.A.Myers et al., "Circumcision: Its Nature and Practice Among Some Ethnic Groups in Southern Nigeria" (1985) 21 *Social Science and Medicine* 581, at p.583.

30.   Some families who wish to end circumcision still continue the practices because, they claim, of the pressure to maintain customs (N.Atiya, *Five Egyptian Women Tell Their Stories* (1982), at p.11). Similar attitudes have been found to exist in relation to male circumcision in the USA (C.C.Harris, "The Cultural Decision-Making Model: Focus Circumcision" (1985) 6 *Health Care for Women International* 27).

31.   Television documentaries include: *Female Circumcision,* Forty Minutes, BBC2, (1983) 3

March; *A Cruel Ritual,* Forty Minutes, BBC2, (1991) 21 February; *Warrior Marks,* Channel 4, (1993) 14 October (also published as a book: A.Walker and P.Parmar, *Warrior Marks: Female Genital Mutilation and the Sexual Binding of Women* (1993)) which was presented by American novelist Alice Walker, whose novel *Possessing The Secret of Joy* (1992) explores the life of Tashi, a woman who chose to follow tradition and be circumcised.

32.   R.Howard, "Women's Rights in English Speaking Sub-Saharan Africa" in *Human Rights and Development in Africa,* eds. C.Welch and R.Meltzer (1984), at p.66. See also B.Bettelheim, *Symbolic Wounds: Puberty Rights and the Envious Male* (1962, 2nd ed.).

33.   K.Brennan, "The Influence of Cultural Relativism on International Human Rights Law: Female Circumcision as a Case Study" (1989) 7 *Law and Inequality: A Journal of Theory and Practice* 367, at pp.396-7. A similar response was evident in Kenya (S.Armstrong, *supra,* n.21, at p.45).

34.   See L.P.Sanderson, *supra,* n.6, at p.9.

35.   L.P.Sanderson, *ibid.;* K.Brennan, *supra,* n.33, at p.379. For examples see A.Gevins, "Tackling Tradition: African Women Speak Out Against Female Circumcision" in *Third World: Second Sex,* ed. M.Davis (1983) vol.1, at p.244; N.El Saadawi, *The Hidden Face of Eve: Women in the Arab World* (1980) chapters 1,6; M.Badran and M.Cook, *supra,* n.23, at pp.63-83 and pp.168-173.

36.   Arguably the two most well-known early critical accounts of FC/FGM are those by F.Hosken, *The Hosken Report: Genital and Sexual Mutilation of Females* (1982) and M.Daly, *supra,* n.16, chapter 5.

37.   See generally N.El Saadawi, *supra,* n.35.

38.   A.El Dareer, *supra,* n.9.

39.   R.H.D.Abdalla, *supra,* n.16.

40.   See A.Gilliam, "Women's Equality and National Liberation" in *Third World Women and the Politics of Feminism,* eds. C.T.Mohanty et al., (1991) 218.

41.   A.Gilliam, *ibid..*

42.   M.Daly, *supra,* n.16, at p.157.

43.   M.Daly, *ibid.,* at p.165.

44.   A.T.Slack, *supra,* n.4, at pp.470-472.

45.   Those who adopt a human rights approach tend to consider FC/FGM in terms of various rights guaranteed within international human rights declarations, covenants or conventions. For example, such procedures may be judged to violate Article 5 of the UN Declaration of Human Rights 1948 which states that "[n]o one shall be subjected to torture or to cruel, inhuman or degrading treatment or punishment". For examples of this approach, which Karen Engle has termed "doctrinalist" ("Female Subjects of Public International Law: Human Rights and the Exotic Other Female" (1992) 26 *New England Law Review* 1509, at pp.1513-1515), see A.T.Slack, *ibid.,* at pp.464-468; E.Dorkenoo and S.Elworthy, *supra,* n.6, at pp.4,16; S.Armstrong *supra,* n.21, at p.45.

46.   Summary Record of the 909th Meeting (1981) UN Doc. E/CN4/Sub.2/SR909, at pp.2-3.

47.   A.Gilliam *supra,* n.40, at p.218; S.Armstrong, *supra,* n.21, at p.45.

48.   C.Ramazanoglu, *Feminism and the Contradictions of Oppression* (1989) at p.143.

49.   For further discussion of cultural relativism see A.Pollis and P.Schwab, "Human Rights: A Western Construct with Limited Application" in *Human Rights: Cultural and Ideological Perspectives*, eds. A.Pollis and P.Schwab (1979) 1; C.Murphy, "Objections to Western Conceptions of Human Rights" (1981) 9 *Hofstra Law Review* 433; A.Renteln, "The Unanswered Challenge of Relativism and the Consequences for Human Rights" (1984) 7 *Human Rights Quarterly* 514.

50.   'A.Pollis and P.Schwab, *ibid.*, at p.1.

51.   J.Kenyatta, *Facing Mt Kenya: The Tribal Life of the Kikuyu* (1953) at p.135.

52.   S.Armstrong, *supra*, n.21, at p.45. Arap Moi's tribe is the Luo which has no tradition of performing any FC/FGM procedures.

53.   S.Armstrong, *ibid.*.

54.   See (1993) *The Guardian*, 8 February; (1992) *The Observer*, 14 February.

55.   M.A.Savane, "Why We Are Against the International Campaign" (1979) 40 *International Child Welfare Review* 38.

56.   C.Ramazanoglu, *supra*, n.48, at pp.138-170; see in particular pp.141-146.

57.   See, for example, C.T.Mohanty et al., *supra*, n.40, at p.76, n.7; C.Ramazanoglu, *ibid.*, at p.143, n.3.

58.   See, for example, A.Gilliam, *supra*, n.40, at p.218.

59.   See M.A.Savane, *supra*, n.55, at pp.38-39.

60.   See, for example, *ibid.*.

61.   See A.Gilliam, *supra*, n.40, at p.218.

62.   A. Gilliam, *ibid.*, at pp.218-219.

63.   C.T.Mohanty, "Under Western Eyes: Feminist Scholarship and Colonial Discourses" in C.T.Mohanty et al., *supra*, n.40, 51, at p.57.

64.   T.Patterson, "Out of Egypt: A Talk with Nawal El Saadawi" (1983) *Freedomways*, Special Middle East Issue, Pt.2, 2313.

65.   A. Gilliam, *supra*, n.40, at p.219.

66.   See K.Engle, *supra*, n.45, in particular pp.1509-1513 and pp.1523-1526.

67.   E.Dorkenoo and S.Elworthy, *supra*, n.6, at pp.7,12. The criminalisation of FC/FGM practices can cause such procedures to be done in secret. For example, in the UK, s.1(1)(a) of the Prohibition of Female Circumcision Act 1985 makes it an offence to "excise, infibulate or otherwise mutilate the whole or any part of the labia majora or labia minora or clitoris of another person". Yet such procedures are secretly performed by private doctors or by circumcisers. Alternatively, children are sent abroad, ostensibly to visit relatives, and return excised. See R.Hedley and E.Dorkenno, *Child Protection and Female Genital Mutilation: Advice for Health, Education, and Social Work Professionals* (1992) at p.8.

68.   See E.Dorkenoo and S.Elworthy, *ibid.*, at p.17.

69.   Strategies against FC/FGM vary greatly. They emanate from the international human rights system, national governments and non-governmental organisations. Some aim to eradicate all forms of FC/FGM and others to reduce the incidence of, or eradicate, the more severe

practices like infibulation. Strategies include: education programmes (for children, parents, medical staff, midwives, and traditional circumcisers); criminalising the operations; exposing myths or misunderstandings about the female body and female sexuality; persuading religious leaders to confirm that the practice is not required by Islam; medicalisation (allowing such procedures to be performed in hospitals or teaching circumcisers basic anatomy and the importance of hygiene). For more detailed descriptions see S.Armstrong, *supra*, n.21, at pp.45-47; E.Dorkenoo and S.Elworthy, *ibid.*, at pp.17-12,27,30-32,34; E.Oram, *supra*, n.23, at pp.63-71.

70.   See K.Brennan, *supra*, n.33, at pp.382-383.

71.   See E.Dorkenoo and S.Elworthy, *supra*, n.6, at p.19.

72.   J.Myers, *supra*, n.18.

73.   J.Myers, *ibid.*, at p.267. See M.Thevos, *The Painted Body* (1984) at p.3.

74.   See, for example, N.Wolf, *The Beauty Myth* (1990); W.Chapkis, *Beauty Secrets* (1986).

75.   K.Davis, "Remaking the She-Devil: A Critical look at Feminist Approaches to Beauty" (1991) 6 *Hypatia* 21.

76.   K.Davis, *ibid.*, at p.21.

77.   K.Davis, *ibid.*, at p.23.

78.   K.Davis, *ibid.*, at p.22.

79.   "Our Bodies, Our Piercings: Women Talk Piercing" 17 *Body Art* (1992) 7.

80.   See E.Dorkenoo and S.Elworthy, *supra*, n.6, at p.12.

81.   See (1994) *The Observer, Life Magazine*, 17 April, at pp.38-42.

82.   J.Myers, *supra*, n.18, at p.268.

83.   K.Davis, *supra*, n.75, at pp.23-24.

84.   Cited in K.Engle, *supra*, n.45, at p.1511. See R.E.Howard, "Health and the Social Degradation of Dishonoured Groups", paper presented at the *Conference on Human Rights in the 21st Century* (Banff, Alberta, Canada, 24 October 1990 (on file with the *New England Law Review*)); R.Rosen, "Perspective on Women's Health: Draw the Line at the Knife" (1991) *L.A. Times*, 17 November.

85.   T.Coleman, "Body Manipulations" (1992) 17 *Body Art* 32, at p.33.

86.   *Elle* (1993) December, 174. The Healthwise Medical Group in North London offer advice to those seeking genital alterations.

87.   See, for example, "Letters" 1 *Links* 4 (published by FORWARD, Foundation for Women's Health): "My own partner has enjoyed unimaginable pleasure after the removal of an excessive clitoral hood in 1976".

88.   L.Wollman, "Female Circumcision" (1973) 20 *Journal of the American Society of Psychosomatic Dentistry and Medicine* 4.

89.   "Our Bodies, Our Piercings: Women Talk Piercing" *supra*, n.79.

90.   See M.Daly, *supra*, n.16, at pp.107-312.

91.   For further examples see *Report of the Working Group on Traditional Practices Affecting the Health of Women and Children*, *supra*, n.6, which referred to various traditional practices including FC/FGM, force-feeding of women and facial scarification; A.T.Slack, *supra*, n.4,

at pp.462-464.

92.   Whilst it is true that some forms of body alteration are performed upon children (like ear-piercing) this is very different from FC/FGM practices in other cultures where the operation is always, or normally, performed upon the very young.

93.   Tattooing of Minors Act 1969. For a discussion of the legality in Britain of the various forms of body alteration, see L.Bibbings and P.Alldridge, "Sexual Expression, Body Alteration, and the Defence of Consent" (1993) 20 *Journal of Law and Society* 356.

94.   A.T.Slack, *supra*, n.4, at pp.468-472.

95.   A.T.Slack, *ibid.*, at p.470.

8   Legal Responses to Battered Women Who Kill

MARIE FOX

INTRODUCTION

Christina Lyon's essay in this collection addresses the issue of domestic violence -
overwhelmingly violence perpetrated by men on women or children. This chapter
shifts the inquiry to a very specific focus on the actions of female survivors of such
violence who strike back with lethal force against their abusive partners, although I
conclude that their actions should always be located within the broader context
which Lyon outlines. My essay examines the adequacy of the response of the
criminal justice system to battered women who kill.[1] Defences in the criminal law
are a paradigm illustration of the manner in which law has been constructed from a
male perspective, according to male standards, so that it either excludes, devalues or
distorts women's experiences and motivations.[2]   Historically designed to
accommodate entirely different situations, not only do such defences exclude
female perspectives, they also fail to highlight the abuse the woman has suffered,
and function so that blame for the man's death is attributed solely to the woman or
her impaired mental responsibility, often resulting either in a murder conviction or
one of manslaughter by reason of diminished responsibility. However, the failures
of the legal process to accord justice to battered women are manifold, extending
beyond the manner in which substantive defences are framed, to the way in which
testimony is filtered and shaped by the rules of evidence through to the application
of the law by judge and jury.[3] Hence the battered woman is caught in a double bind
- the legal system not only trivialises the violence to her body in labelling it
"domestic"; it also fails to accommodate her behaviour if she transcends the
parameters of traditional womanhood by fighting back.
   At the heart of this essay is the issue whether we can do justice to the battered
woman who kills without either pathologising her or treating her as a victim. Also,

keeping in view the broader issue of justice for women generally, we must be aware that focusing exclusively on the actions of the woman who resorts to deadly force so that we can frame a defence to accommodate her action, risks trivialising and underplaying the violence which has been done to her body by the deceased. A focus on extreme cases also helps disguise the violence suffered by other women who do not resort to lethal force. We need to be careful not to exclude them from the category of domestic violence, or to leave outwith new or reconstituted defences those women who may not appear so cowed by what they have endured. Much of the current debate reveals a tension between those who are most concerned with attaining justice for the specific hard case of the battered woman who kills, and those who aim at securing justice for women as a gender and feel concern about the stigmatising effect of gender-specific defences. An issue to address is whether it is possible to do justice for all. I would argue that to do so we must challenge the assumptions on which the debate is presently premised. We must contest implicit assumptions in that debate which pit the battered woman against other women, constructing her as different and exceptional in opposition to them. Instead we should seek to explore the continuities between her situation and those of power and control in all heterosexual relationships.[4] The growing volume of feminist literature focusing on the particular situation of the battered woman who kills may cause us to lose sight of the endemic nature of violence against women in our society if it portrays cases of battered women who kill as exceptional and different rather than the tip of an iceberg of violence.

To achieve justice for battered women who kill, we must select a different focus which shifts attention to their abusers. These men may require treatment, but we should resist the urge to pathologise the individual male and recognise how our society is structured in a way which implicitly condones male violence. Martha Mahoney has exposed the irony that the most complete description of women's suffering from domestic violence to enter legal discourse is the point at which violence against women finally results in harm to a man.[5] It seems that the law is more concerned with seeking ways to punish or treat women who have done violence to the body of a man than in ensuring the safety and autonomy of the many women who are left exposed to potentially lethal male violence in the home. In throwing the net wider to encompass the abuser we can avoid becoming completely enmeshed in legalistic discussion about the nature of defences and scrutiny of the battered woman who strikes back, and instead foreground the abuse which she has suffered. I would contend that doing so is the way to produce significant legal changes. Notwithstanding feminist scholarship and much public concern, little has been achieved in this jurisdiction by way of concrete improvement in the law to reflect the dilemma of the battered woman who strikes back.[6] I would question whether it is possible to incorporate different perspectives into law, or effect meaningful law reform until there is greater societal understanding of the experiences of battered women, and argue that law as currently constructed obscures that reality. At the moment we run the danger of over-focusing on law, which in turn has focused on and reinforced the pathology of battered women. Meanwhile in the United States a backlash is already emerging against defences for battered women, partly because these wider questions were not addressed.[7]

CURRENT DEFENCES IN BRITISH CRIMINAL LAW - RECONSTRUCTION OR ABOLITION?

Much debate on securing justice for women who kill has focused on the issue of whether it is possible to reform existing defences in the criminal law so that they incorporate the experiences of battered women, or whether it is necessary to construct gender-specific defences to fit their particular situation. This debate reflects the dilemma outlined above between doing justice in individual hard cases, while avoiding stigmatising women as weaker or more vulnerable or irrational than men. Three criminal law defences might be utilised by the battered woman who kills.[8] I wish to focus on provocation, since in this jurisdiction much academic and popular criticism has been levelled at that defence, and efforts at law reform have mainly concentrated on it, largely due to the focus of the appellate level courts in *R v. Thornton*[9] and *R v. Ahluwalia*[10]. Also, many feminist criticisms of it apply equally to other defences. Provocation is designed to deal with the situation where the prudent, rational "man of law"[11] loses his reason and acts with brute force, and allows the judge a virtually unfettered discretion as to sentence, unlike a murder conviction which carries a mandatory life sentence. Although this common law defence has been modified since being legislatively defined in s.3 of the Homicide Act 1957,[12] it is still best summarised in the classic direction to the jury delivered by Devlin J in *R v. Duffy*:

> Provocation is some act or series of acts, done by the dead man to the accused, which would cause in any reasonable person, and actually causes in the accused, a sudden and temporary loss of self-control, rendering the accused so subject to passion as to make him or her for the moment not master of his mind.[13]

Thus, the defence of provocation involves a dual subjective/objective test. To successfully avail of it, the accused must demonstrate that she was actually provoked to lose her self-control (a test which clearly relates to what she actually experienced); and then it is left to the jury to decide whether a reasonable person would have lost self-control and acted thus when subjected to such provocation.[14] Although the objective limb of the test was significantly modified in *R v. Camplin*[15] where the House of Lords ruled that the reasonable person was to be endowed with fixed characteristics of the accused, such as age and sex,[16] it is debatable whether this has improved women's chances of successfully using the defence, given judicial perceptions of typical female responses to provocative events.

Certainly, an examination of British case-law produces numerous dicta to support the view that judges think in terms which are paradigmatically male. In at least four separate ways they have demonstrated their incomprehension of the battered woman's situation. The first misunderstanding relates to the general physical differences in female and male bodies. This is exemplified by the cases of *Thornton* and *Ahluwalia*. In waiting until their violent husbands were asleep and employing weapons against them, their cases fitted a pattern of domestic killings by women who have been subjected to cumulative violence. However, rather than acknowledging this, the courts abstracted each woman from her social situation and construed her actions as deliberate and premeditated. Thus, the individualisation introduced by *Camplin* does not avail women like Sara Thornton or Kiranjit Ahluwalia whose reactions were not the instantaneous and hot-blooded ones of some males. In *Thornton* the trial judge quoted with approval the direction of Devlin J (approved by the Court of Appeal) in *Duffy* which explicitly ruled out the possibility of locating the woman's act in the context of the violent relationship:

> Circumstances which merely predispose to a violent act are not enough ... Indeed circumstances which induce a desire for revenge are inconsistent with provocation, since the conscious formulation of a desire for revenge means that a person had time to think, to reflect, *and that would negative a sudden temporary loss of self-control which is of the essence of provocation* ... most acts of provocation are cases of sudden quarrels, sudden blows inflicted with an instrument already in the hand, perhaps being used, or being picked up, where there has been no time for reflection ... Fists might be answered with fists, but not with a deadly weapon ...[17]

From this it is clear that the paradigmatic case of provocation for a judge is a sudden fight between two males of approximately equal strength - a model which effectively excludes most women from the ambit of the defence. Similar assumptions underpin comparable dicta in cases like *R v. Phillips*[18] and *R v. Mancini*.[19] These betray a failure to recognise the relative disparity in physical strength between women and men which deny most women the opportunity of striking a simple blow, which would only be likely to precipitate greater wrath. For as long as judges fail to take on board such considerations female reactions to male violence will be classified as revenge and thus murder.

In this way, since the biology of the reasonable person is implicitly male, female defendants continue to be judged against a male referent, even though *Camplin* speaks of a "reasonable woman" test. Huge assumptions are built into the supposedly neutral objective test.[20] As Hilary Allen points out:

> [t]he now commonplace use of the term "reasonable person" keeps alive the "illusion" of a universal and unitary subject of the law, but having been pushed on the matter, legal discourse has found itself unable to sustain such a construct. And what has been asserted instead is a standard that is anything but universal or ungendered or androgynous: on the contrary it is variable, differentiated, and very firmly gendered.[21]

Recognition of the gendered nature of reasonableness prompted Madame Justice Bertha Wilson to argue, in a Canadian case, that since the "ordinary man" does not typically find himself in the situation of a battered spouse, the "definition of what is reasonable must be adapted to circumstances which are, by and large, foreign to the world inhabited by the hypothetical 'reasonable man'."[22] However, British judges have resisted attempts to redefine reasonableness, and the formidable obstacles to doing so have been articulated by Schneider, who concedes that early work on battered women underestimated the psychological barriers to perceiving women as reasonable, and suggests that the "enormous credibility problems that women face as complainants and witnesses ... seem almost insurmountable."[23]

Secondly, judges take an unduly restrictive view of what constitutes a provocative event, limiting this to certain situations and incidents - those to which men are particularly likely to react violently.[24] As Taylor contends, what law really deems provocative is women who assert their sexual independence.[25] Thus, women who refuse sex with their partners, leave or threaten to leave them, or commit adultery will be characterised as having provoked their partners to understandable violence.[26] To effect meaningful reform for women the judiciary must recognise that women respond in different ways and situations from men - usually resorting to violence, not in the case of infidelity, but where their personal safety or that of their children is at stake.[27] Thus, as currently constituted, law appears to place a greater premium on a man's sexual pride than on a woman's personal safety. Furthermore, the statutory definition of provocation which extends the defence to cover verbal abuse appears to equate such abuse with violent physical assault.[28] Again this entails that men are more likely to benefit from the defence, given their propensity to react to weaker stimuli than women.

Thirdly, judges also fail to grasp the complexity and diversity of possible emotional responses to which those circumstances give rise. Although they acknowledge the *rage* resulting in loss of self-control which men feel in provocative situations; the *fear* or *despair* which cumulative violence may engender in women is not so readily accepted by the judiciary as causing female defendants to use weapons in order to retaliate or defend themselves. As Douzinas and Warrington have proposed: "[i]n the idiom of cognition, fear is either reasonable and can be understood by the judge or is unreasonable and therefore non-existent."[29] Moreover, where a woman displays anger (and her response is likely to be a complex amalgam of the two emotions), she is characterised as "unfeminine" and threatening. By definition an angry woman who breaks the law commits a double transgression - she is seen as offending both the tenets of the criminal law and the dictates of nature.[30] Whereas for men violence per se is not unacceptable - it becomes so only when they go too far - for women displays of violence are always deemed unacceptable and unnatural.

Judges also fail to appreciate the effect on a woman of living with the constant threat of abuse.[31] In stressing that juries should focus upon the blameworthy conduct of the defendant, and not that of the victim,[32] law colludes in downplaying the violence to which the woman's body has been subjected. Yet, the essence of provocation entails blameworthy conduct by the victim, and as Edwards argues, "[w]hen a male defendant stands trial ... all too frequently the blame attaching to the dead woman becomes a crucial part of the defence of provocation ...".[33] To fully assess the responsibility of a woman for her actions we surely need to have available a broader picture of the context of her actions which will include the assessment of responsibility for the final violent act.[34]

Fourthly, judges have demonstrated a wholly unrealistic appreciation of the options available to battered women. This is perhaps best exemplified by the trial judge's comment in *Thornton* that she had "other alternatives available, like walking out or going upstairs".[35] More generally, judges lack awareness of the effect of cultural conditioning on women not to react aggressively, even in situations where they are under threat.[36] They are denied the opportunities open to boys to learn how to defend themselves in threatening situations. This entails that they are typically no match for men in hand-to-hand combat and can only repel a male assailant by resorting to deadly weapons.[37]

In North America, by contrast, battered women usually plead self-defence rather than provocation. In constituting a complete defence and justification for the woman's actions it has obvious advantages over provocation. Arguably it may also better reflect the woman's own testimony as to events.[38] In Britain and other Commonwealth countries there appears to have been a reluctance to plead the defence partly because a contested trial will always ensue. However, failure to plead it may cause some women to be convicted of manslaughter who ought to be acquitted on the grounds that they acted in justifiable self-defence. For example, Easteal points out that at least some of the ten women in her sample of Australian offenders who had killed sexual intimates would probably have been acquitted in the United States on the basis of self-defence.[39] Undoubtedly this is also true in Britain.[40]

However, it should be noted that even in North America acquittals on this basis are rare. Schuller and Vidmar blame this low acquittal rate on two factors - the legal doctrine of self-defence and the presumed beliefs that people harbour about the consequences and effects of male violence against women in intimate relationships.[41] As far as the legal doctrine is concerned, the problems women encounter in successfully pleading the defence stem from how it incorporates definitions and standards which are broadly similar to those of provocation. In her perusal of the North American literature on self-defence Holly Maguigan identifies four common feminist criticisms of the self-defence doctrine.[42] First, as it assesses the defendant on an objective basis, the standards for measuring the reasonableness of the defendant's actions incorporate the same male bias evident in provocation.[43] In deciding what is reasonable, law has traditionally taken the "ordinary man" as its reference point. Secondly, the requirement that the danger facing the defendant must be imminent[44] functions in much the same way as the requirement of suddenness in provocation. If there is any delay in the defendant's reaction to the abuse she has suffered she may be excluded from the ambit of both defences. Thirdly, self-defence is traditionally premised on a single confrontational encounter and ill-fits the position of the battered woman who, having become familiar with the pattern of violence, may strike at her abuser in anticipation of an attack.[45] The paradigm self-defence case is the "bar room brawl" situation,[46] where the combatants are roughly equal in strength and do not have a history of violence with one another. Once again the requirement that the force used to meet threatened harm be proportional conflicts with the physical resources and socialisation of women.[47] Fourthly, although British law, in contrast to some North American jurisdictions, imposes no duty to retreat,[48] it is a factor to be taken into account in assessing the reasonableness of the defendant's response. As Christine Boyle has argued, there is a huge question mark hanging over the issue of when retreat is reasonable - "[i]f retreat is reasonable when it is safe, then it would appear that in functional terms there is a duty to retreat, and it simply makes the law more obscure to deny this".[49] The implicit requirement of a duty to retreat poses immense problems for battered women given the extreme danger which they face in their homes.[50] This is compounded by the fact that such danger occurs in the context of an ideology of family life which emphasises non-violence. More generally, Boyle has suggested that the whole defence may be premised on masculinist norms and valorise particular notions of male virtue.[51]

Having canvassed their arguments, Maguigan questions many of the assumptions made by these feminist scholars, in particular their widespread belief that cases involving battered women are very different from the norm of self-defence cases. In particular, she attacks the assumption that most killings by battered women occur in non-confrontational situations. She argues that the existing standards are sufficiently flexible to accommodate the actions of the battered woman and do not require re-definition. However, Maguigan does concede that how law operates in practice is more important than doctrinal definitions - "to say that existing definitions can accommodate the self defense claims of battered women and can provide for their evaluation in the relevant social context is not to say that trial courts apply those definitions when the defendants are battered women".[52] Moreover, although she may be right in contending that feminists have exaggerated the different situation of battered women, a perusal of the cases does indicate that many women do wait until their partner is incapacitated through drink or sleep before attacking him[53] - a factor which does significantly distinguish her case from that of the traditional model of self-defence.

A similar argument to Maguigan's has been made in a British context by Aileen McColgan who argues that the doctrine of self-defence as applied in the United Kingdom is even more amenable to an interpretation favourable to the battered woman who kills. She contends that what is required is not an alteration or extension of the defence but "a rethinking of the way in which the requirement that the defendant's use of force be reasonable is applied to cases other than those involving the traditional model of a one-off adversarial meeting between strangers".[54] It remains, however, unclear how such a paradigm shift in judicial thinking can be effected in a British context. One way might be to look to the influential American case of *State v. Wanrow*.[55] Although the case did not concern a battered woman, its recognition that additional characteristics are present where a woman is faced with a male attacker has great significance for battered woman cases. As Eber argues, what was crucial in the court's analysis was its recognition that the success of a self-defence plea is dependent on the presentation of an overall picture of the woman's situation to the jury.[56] It is Eber's belief that expert testimony as to the existence of battered woman syndrome is the best way of presenting such a complete picture to the jury. Since McColgan rejects the necessity for such testimony,[57] she may need to present more concrete alternative proposals on reshaping judicial and jury attitudes. Moreover, even in the States it is unclear how far *Wanrow* has availed battered women. As Kasian et al. argue, although *Wanrow* helped to alter the legal conception of reasonable force, most juries are still likely to view the means used by many female domestic homicide victims as excessive.[58]

Given how self-defence and provocation are rigidly defined and structured to reflect male standards of behaviour and experiences, it may appear that the best strategy for battered women who kill, and wish to avoid a life sentence, is to plead diminished responsibility. It is more amorphous and less rigidly defined against the standards of the reasonable person, so that it does not so closely correspond to purely male experiences. Due to its less rigid structure it permits the woman more opportunity to construct her own narrative of events. According to s.2 of the Homicide Act 1957[59] this partial defence comprises two elements - firstly that the accused was suffering from an *abnormality of mind* (caused by arrested development or inherent causes or disease or injury), and secondly that this abnormality of mind *substantially impaired* her mental responsibility. Commentators have argued that it is the defence best equipped to deal with those who act out of despair as battered women often do,[60] and certainly in practical terms diminished responsibility has often been a legal mechanism to reach an acceptable result in cases involving women.[61] Moreover, as prosecutors and judges generally accept pleas of guilty to manslaughter on the basis of diminished responsibility[62] it may avoid the necessity of the defendant undergoing a public trial.[63]

However, diminished responsibility is a problematic concept. It attracts criticism because of its indefinable boundaries which largely result from embodying a confused quasi-legal quasi-medical formula.[64] It is not surprising that judges and prosecutors are so keen to accept "diminished" pleas given that it effectively enables them to duck the question of whether the woman was really responsible, without unsettling the fixed standards and definitions of the other defences. Perhaps the best example of this is provided by *R v. Ahluwalia* where the court, in its readiness to return a verdict of manslaughter by reason of diminished responsibility, abandoned the strictness of its usual rules on new evidence.[65] Thus, though it is easier for women who kill to avail of this defence than those of self-defence and provocation,[66] feminists have reacted ambivalently to the defence. Partly this is because the crucial factor in a successful plea of diminished responsibility seems to be engagement of jury sympathy. It thus leaves those women who do not secure the sympathy of the jury very vulnerable. In particular, this defence seemingly fails to account for the actions of women who are assertive, intelligent and sexually liberated, like Sara Thornton.[67] A further risk with feminist endorsement of this defence is that the broad terms in which it is framed affords a defence to many men who kill their partners, usually in response to their assertions of independence.[68] Moreover, defence reliance on diminished responsibility pleas and judicial willingness to accept them may further reinforce perceptions of women as unreasonable which compound their difficulties in pleading the other male-oriented defences.[69] It also perpetuates a mind/body dualism by its exclusive focus on the mental state of the battered woman who kills, thereby again underplaying the physical violence to her body which is frequently the catalyst for the violence which she perpetrates on the body of the man.

LAW REFORM?

Given the unsatisfactory nature of defences in the criminal law it is clear that the quality of justice currently experienced by battered women who kill is unacceptably haphazard.[70] The best she can wish for is to avoid engaging with substantive law in hope that there will be a decision not to prosecute, or that the prosecution and judge will accept a plea of not guilty by reason of diminished responsibility. But the unacceptable uncertainty in relying on such discretion is best illustrated by the life-sentence which Sara Thornton and others are currently serving.

In recognition of these problems there have been a number of attempts since December 1991, through the introduction of Private Members' Bills,[71] to change the law on provocation along the lines of a New South Wales model.[72] Their aim was to reform the defence by removing the requirement that a provoked loss of self-control must be *sudden*; and expressly stipulating that the effect of cumulative violence should be taken into account by the jury. This would no doubt be significant for women like Thornton and Ahluwalia - as Donna Martinson has argued, the suddenness requirement can prevent the context of the woman's actions from being fully considered.[73] However, given the much greater incidence of lethal force perpetrated against women by their male partners, this is another reform which could prove double-edged by allowing an even greater number of men a defence to killing their partners. It must be questioned whether provocation could ever be reformed in such a way as to benefit some women without putting the lives of yet more at risk, and begs the more fundamental question of whether we can any longer justify a defence of provocation - one which appears to be premised on the acceptability of losing control. Martinson cites a Canadian text which queries why the single exculpatory human emotion accommodated by law is murderous patriarchal rage and links recent developments of the defence in North America to "the validation of patriarchal attitudes and reactions."[74] A consideration of such issues has led Horder to advocate that the defence be abolished on the grounds that it reinforces perceptions of men being the natural aggressors of women.[75] Easteal's research points to a similar conclusion as her sample indicates that, where a man pleaded provocation on a charge of killing his partner, for some judges and jurors his jealousy and inability to accept the end of the relationship was perceived as a sufficient basis for losing his self-control.[76] The amorphous nature of diminished responsibility, and its extremely loose interpretation by the courts renders it equally difficult to reform in a way that would be meaningful for women. Thus, of the traditional defences available to battered women who kill, self-defence does seem the most amenable to reform, and efforts to reform that defence would at least have the merit of accommodating women within a traditional legal framework, without suggesting that they are inherently different from men. However I think it is questionable how far this defence can really provide a voice to battered women who kill, due to prevailing judicial attitudes.[77] Indeed given the deeply embedded masculinist attitudes of judges in this jurisdiction it must be questionable how far it will be possible to apply feminist-inspired law reform to the benefit of women. One way of changing judicial perception of the law on self-defence is Ewing's suggestion of a new concept of "psychological self-defence" which would explicitly take into account the psychological harm to the battered woman, but this has been subjected to considerable criticism.[78] My pessimism about the possibility of meaningful reform to existing defences to incorporate the perspectives of women leads to the question of whether it is possible to formulate alternative defences which do reflect a woman's perspective.

GENDER SPECIFIC DEFENCES OR EXPERT TESTIMONY ON BATTERED WOMEN?

One alternative to reformulating existing defences would be to introduce new gender specific defences designed by feminist practitioners expressly to incorporate the experiences and perceptions of women. However such attempts are fraught with danger as the existing defence of infanticide shows.[79] In recognition of the dangers of developing a new defence limited to women, most commentators and judges have sought instead to use expert testimony as an avenue for incorporating women's experience into the doctrinal evolution of some other defence.[80] In North America it has been incorporated into a plea of self-defence through reliance on testimony directed at explaining the woman's responses to the jury and demonstrating that she reasonably believed that deadly force was necessary to protect herself.[81] As Kasian et al. note, the function of such testimony is to convince a jury that the woman held a reasonable belief that her life was in imminent danger and consequently that her behaviour should be viewed as reasonable.[82] Expert testimony on battered women has focused on evidence of "battered woman syndrome" - a theory posited by Dr Leonore Walker who suggests that violent relationships typically follow a cyclical pattern. This battering cycle is characterised by an initial phase of minor, tension-building incidents, followed by an acute battering incident, and a tender loving phase or "honeymoon period", which persuades the woman of the possibility that the relationship can be reformed.[83] Eventually repetition of this three-stage cycle leads to a state of psychological paralysis known as "learned helplessness", which is what causes the woman to remain in the battering relationship. In *Lavallee v. R* Wilson J stressed the need for expert evidence:

> Expert evidence on the psychological effect of battering on wives and common law partners must be both relevant and necessary ... How can the mental state of the appellant be appreciated without it? The average member of the public can be forgiven for asking why would a woman put up with this form of treatment ... why does she not cut loose and make a new form of life for herself? Such is the reaction of the average person confronted with the so-called 'battered wife syndrome'. We need help to understand it and help is available from trained professionals.[84]

Such testimony thus operates to enable the jury to understand what the accused woman reasonably perceived, given *her* situation and experiences. The original aim of introducing battered woman syndrome evidence was thus to challenge the generic concept of reasonableness which operates in our criminal law by forcing it to include the perspectives of women.[85] Battered woman syndrome was expressly designed to operate differently from infanticide and pre-menstrual syndrome. Whereas they remain rooted in the psychology or pathology of the woman herself, rather than the circumstances in which she finds herself,[86] battered woman syndrome seeks to combine psychological evidence with evidence as to social and economic conditions. Indeed, as Schuller and Vidmar note "[d]espite the label *syndrome*, battered woman syndrome is not a diagnosable mental disorder, but is rather a descriptive term that refers to the *effects* of abuse on a woman".[87]

Mahoney points to the main advantages of battered woman syndrome, which are that it collects and summarises what do appear to be the experiences and perceptions of many battered women, and presents them to the court through the medium of an expert which renders them more accessible.[88] However, as she cautions, much depends on the lens through which expert testimony is filtered and how it is interpreted.[89] A major problem with the way in which battered woman syndrome evidence has emerged in court has been its reliance on the theory of "learned helplessness" and resultant focus on the issue of why the woman stayed in the abusive relationship, rather than why she killed - a focus exemplified in the quotation cited above from Madame Justice Wilson. Legal interpretation of the syndrome has made the woman appear helpless and dysfunctional,[90] thus affecting how she is perceived in court and by the broader public. It is argued that the concept of learned helplessness is too reductionist to encompass the variety of responses which women exhibit in their attempts to end abuse, omitting many other social, economic and emotional reasons which may dictate that a woman remain with an abusive partner.[91] Mihjalovich contends that, when expert testimony about learned helplessness is introduced at trial, the jury is asked to ignore the ways a woman is competent and efficient due to her highly developed survival skills, and to focus instead on the totality of her learned helplessness.[92]

As well as being reductionist, there is also a discernible tendency towards over-generalising which Walker cautioned against in her early work.[93] Courts may have been receptive to such evidence because in presenting all abused women as passive victims it matches societal perceptions of women in general. Schneider now contends that the legal strategy which led to the introduction of expert testimony on battered woman syndrome has been subverted by the tenacity of such sex stereotyping. Thus, rather than presenting her actions as reasonable, "[w]hen battered woman syndrome is presented or heard in a way that sounds like passivity or incapacity, it does not address the basic fact of the woman's action and contradicts a presentation of reasonableness."[94]

The fact that there is a necessity for expert witnesses to convey the woman's story to the court may itself reinforce the idea of her as incompetent. This is especially so since much of the evidence which the expert gives is purely historical or biographical recitation - there is no reason why it could not be given by the woman herself.[95] More crucially, by filtering the woman's experience through psychiatric evidence, the result may be to exclude her stories, or distort them by abstracting and reinterpreting them. As Isobel Grant argues, "[c]ontext is removed. The experience is made to fit the small repertoire of stories of the expert which are further reshaped by the frames of the legal system".[96] This leads to the further problem that a woman who reacts with lethal force may simply be forced to conform to another stereotype - that of the "reasonable battered woman". This may be an even more disabling stereotype for women than that of the gendered "reasonable person" given that the images which learned helplessness convey are of powerlessness, passivity and submissiveness. Thus, expert testimony, which was designed to displace stereotypes, has come to embody new ones. As Mahoney notes, such testimony is marked by a profound irony:

> Domestic violence is beyond the layman's ken (even though we know it is fairly common) because some jurors will interpret their *own* experience through cultural perceptions that distort understanding and make it difficult for all of us to talk about the subject, and because cultural stereotypes will shape the vision of battered women by jurors who have *no* personal experience of such violence as well ... Therefore, one result of the highly publicized legal focus on battered woman syndrome and learned helplessness has been to inappropriately increase cultural attention to the battered woman's psychological makeup.[97]

The admissibility of battered woman syndrome testimony fits in with a disturbing trend towards developing diagnostic categories that apply only to women.[98] The major problem, once again, is that while the evidence of "battered woman syndrome" may help the individual women escape a murder conviction, it does so only by again labelling *her* rather than her abuser as the problem. And in being viewed as evidence of incapacity battered woman syndrome reinforces the link between women and irrationality. The reality of gender oppression is obscured as the battered woman becomes "the abnormal actor, the one whose conduct must be explained by an expert."[99] Thus, when we rely on battered woman syndrome we are affecting a closure - the defendant must be diagnosed in terms of symptoms, predisposing factors and so on, and attention is directed away from broader social problems.[100] Moreover, it is not even clear that expert testimony as to battered woman syndrome actually does produce leniency for women. Although the few existing empirical studies are difficult to reconcile, jury simulation exercises have found that the introduction of such expert testimony does not seem to significantly affect the outcome of cases.[101]

Anne Coughlin would go further and argue that the problem does not simply lie with how battered woman syndrome has been interpreted in practice. Rather, "the fundamental premise of the defense [sic] is that women lack the psychological capacity to choose lawful means to extricate themselves from abusive males."[102] Coughlin finds it significant that the emergence of this syndrome in the late 1970s coincided with the effective death of the marital coercion doctrine. She argues that both "defences" reinforce perceptions of women as irresponsible and suggests that, even if the "scientific bases for our understanding of woman's submissive nature ... have changed ... the underlying understanding endures".[103]

The admission of battered woman syndrome evidence in British courts would even more strongly reinforce this association between women and irrationality, as it would probably be used in support of a plea of provocation or diminished responsibility rather than self-defence. Nigel Eastman has argued that since battered woman syndrome is not a disease in international classificatory terms, it would "almost certainly [fail] to be regarded as one of the types of abnormality of mind within the parenthetic clause of s.2 of the Homicide Act". Hence in his view, in Britain evidence of the syndrome could only be admitted in relation to a provocation defence, although he does point out that the necessity of a medical report would lend some support to an alternative plea of diminished responsibility.[104] However, the result of *Ahluwalia*, where the Court of Appeal did indeed indicate that they may admit evidence of battered woman syndrome in relation to a defence of provocation, but only if it was medically documented, and where the Lord Chief Justice clearly favoured pleas of diminished responsibility over provocation, suggests, as McColgan contends, that the future defence of many more battered women will be argued on the basis of diminished responsibility.[105] Thus there is a clear link between the law's denial to women of the defences of self-defence and provocation, and its receptivity to pleas of diminished responsibility and perhaps increasingly to the introduction of battered woman's syndrome - both strategies are premised on a model which allows the woman more scope to tell her story but only through the intervention of experts who pathologise her actions and downplay their social context. In resisting male violence and transcending the law the battered woman must be deemed mentally incapacitated and not fully responsible for her acts. Again this sits particularly ill with the image of a woman like Sara Thornton. Crucially it does not seem to account for the tension inherent in the testimony of why a supposedly helpless woman may resort to such a transgressive and violent act. As Mahoney points out, battered woman syndrome [and diminished responsibility evidence] creates "a double bind in which women must prove helplessness in court after they have killed an abusive partner and therefore do not appear helpless as the term is ordinarily understood."[106] Similarly, O'Donovan has contended:

battered women can be understood as temporarily abnormal under diminished responsibility or semi-permanently abnormal under battered woman syndrome. But the language of ordinariness is not open to women, unless they kill under circumstances permitted by the traditional common law paradigms of defence.[107]

Perhaps there is some scope for utilising this syndrome in the cause of battered woman defendants but only if it moves away from its current tendency to generalise - assimilating the experiences of all battered women and marking them off as different from the experiences of all other women. Given the difficulties all lay persons experience appearing in court, the battered woman may need help to convey her story, but it should not be filtered through medical testimony. Instead, evidence locating her actions in external circumstances could be given by women working in refuges for battered women.[108] The current paradigm needs more radical alteration than the simple admission of expert testimony on battered woman syndrome would provide.

PROBLEMS IN THE CURRENT PARADIGM

So far this essay has focused on the problematic and male-biased nature of substantive defences in the criminal law. However the criminal process is much broader than this,[109] and we need to consider also the way in which this process frames the issues to be addressed. As Maguigan points out, academic lawyers are too prone to confine their discussion to doctrinal law, without considering how purely legal definitions work within the context of the system as a whole, and whether they will effect a difference in practice - "[t]he predictors of not-guilty verdicts are many and varied. Few are susceptible to change through legal re-definition".[110] This consideration makes it necessary to focus on how events outside of doctrinal criminal law shape the way in which facts have been constructed and how people and situations are labelled. For instance, the strategy adopted by defence counsel and the attitude of the prosecution will be crucial - once the case reaches the trial judge it will already have been packaged in a particular way and it is only then that legal doctrine comes into play. Certainly the inconsistencies in how victims of cumulative violence are treated in practice bears this out. In fact, the causes for concern really arise only in that minority of cases, albeit the most visible ones, where the doctrinal law *is* strictly applied. This in itself illustrates the limited utility of doctrinal reforms. Indeed, even posing questions in such terms may be indicative of how difficult it is to move beyond the parameters of debate as currently constructed. However we must do so if we are ever to succeed in doing justice to battered women. It seems to me that the fundamental problem with discussing the criminal justice system's response to women who kill is that it leads to a preoccupation with individuals who act in an atypical manner and obscures the fact that these are the most extreme cases, which only enter the courts due to the total breakdown of wider societal structures.

The exclusive focus on the most dramatic cases where women react with lethal violence may be partly explained in terms of media coverage. In this sense, highlighting of cases like Thornton and Ahluwalia has been used in order to obscure more basic issues. Martha Minow has documented the "dynamic of brief public fascination with individual horror stories followed by extended public quiescence about the more widespread problem".[111] We need to be careful not to replicate the concerns of the media in their focus on hard cases when we posit law reform aimed at dealing with highly visible individual hard cases. Phyllis Chesler has castigated North American feminists for allowing their agenda to be dictated by the media,[112] and given the fact that it can lead to this cycle of outrage and quiescence, we need to avoid the same thing happening here. We need to resist the temptation to get bogged down in questions which are enmeshed in the existing media and legal paradigms, such as how the penal system should deal with women who have transgressed its laws. The more fundamental issues which need to be faced are how and why so many women in our society become involved with men who have a propensity for violence, and finding themselves in such situations why they lack the control and options to leave.

A related question concerns the attitudes of juries and how much attention they pay to slotting cases into categories of defence as opposed to dispensing justice as they see it. Clearly jury sympathy is crucial for a successful plea of diminished responsibility, but equally this may be a factor in self-defence or provocation cases. Why for example have so many juries convicted women who kill in these circumstances of murder? Obviously convictions result partly from the dualistic way in which legal method frames the either/or question - is this woman guilty of murder or not? Nonetheless, the juries in *Thornton*, *Ahluwalia* and a host of other cases clearly thought these women had done something deserving of censure - a view which does not seem to accord with that of feminist lawyers and others who aim to shape public opinion on this issue. Jurors' views may be to do with what Wilson J identifies as a "popular mythology about domestic violence" - "[e]ither she was not as badly beaten as she claims or she would have left the man long ago. Or, if she was battered that severely, she must have stayed out of some masochistic enjoyment of it."[113] There is a failure to identify with the battered woman, even amongst women jurors,[114] which again results partly from the legal images of battered women found in court room discourses where the extent, frequency and severity of the violence may be exaggerated. Jurors' failure to identify with or even recognise the experiences of the battered woman stems from the fact that the legal system constructs the battered women as other to them, and thus they do not recognise themselves or their friends in the stigmatised picture of the battered woman which emerges in court. Mahoney's research found that "women often emphasize that they do not fit their own stereotypes of battered women".[115] This appears to account for the irony that many jurors appear to need expert testimony on a phenomenon which features in the lives of many of them.

Another problem relates to the sentencing stage. There has been much talk of late about the desirability of abolishing the mandatory life-sentence for murder.[116] Although this would entail the abolition of provocation and diminished responsibility, it must be questioned whether such a reform would improve the situation, given how our judges continue to resist the imposition of scrutiny over the sentencing stage.[117] Once again, sentencing in such cases is an issue which had attracted little empirical research, but Easteal's research demonstrates the lack of consistency in sentencing females and males who have killed their partners.[118]

CONCLUSION

As the debate is currently constructed, it seems that the media, academic lawyers and the legal system are colluding in avoiding the tougher question of how, and indeed whether it is possible, to do justice to the individual battered woman without cost to women as a class. To act justly we must broaden the issue beyond what happens in the trial court, where the law is applied, or at appellate level where it may be reformed. Although I continue to believe that reform of criminal law is important, I think that its role in securing justice for women is limited. To effect the changes necessary to do justice to battered women we need to adopt a position outside of law.

What this might entail in practice, at a minimum, is to require that society devote adequate resources to the funding of refuges, to advertising their existence, and to emphasising the widespread nature of domestic violence, thus decreasing the stigma which still attaches to it. The necessity for such measures is illustrated by the case-law. Both Thornton and Ahluwalia had approached numerous groups and agencies for help to no avail.[119] As we have seen judges (and probably juries) tend to assume wrongly that other options are available. We cannot rest content with pointing out the lack of such options (and turning again to law reform); but must insist that resources be made available to enable women to leave violent relationships.[120] However, inevitably such measures are an exercise in damage limitation. Moreover, it is important to address the fact that the dependency of many women upon violent men is emotional as well as physical, economic and social, which makes the problem much more intractable.[121] Although feelings of emotional dependency may actually stem from a culturally created lack of self-esteem, this does not make them any less real, and women have encountered problems because courts, even when they do perceive fear as a reason for not leaving the relationship, do not regard love as an equally valid reason.[122] Change therefore will require more than simply providing resources which would help empower women to leave.[123]

In the longer term, more intractable problems need to be tackled such as that of sex-stereotyping. Dealing with this issue requires knowledge of attitudes held by actual and potential jurors. The many murder convictions of battered women who have killed suggest a lack of understanding of their plight. If empirical research were to confirm this, it would be necessary to formulate strategies to combat this (including perhaps a revised form of expert testimony to convey the reality of the battered woman's situation to the court) although again there is a need for empirical study to assess the impact of such testimony.[124] Certainly, many commentators see the function of expert testimony as being primarily educative,[125] although it is questionable whether this is the most effective educational strategy. It may be better if actual and potential jurors were to be educated about domestic violence through media coverage of the issue which could not only reach a broader audience but may be more susceptible to feminist influence.[126] Even more crucially, at an earlier stage we need to consider how the education system as well as the media has a role to play in combatting sex-stereotyping. One practical way of reducing this would be to empower young girls by educating them in self-defence tactics. Not only would this enable them to physically defend themselves, it would also subvert the perceptions of their male peers that they are weak and passive. However, although one goal must certainly be to increase knowledge, there is the further major question as to whether knowledge of an issue translates into sensitivity in handling it at the trial stage.[127]

Another practical, albeit more difficult, way of effecting meaningful change would be to articulate a language to enable battered women to convey their experiences to society. This raises a general problem of *whose* truth gets to count - that of the lawyer or layperson.[128] Minow has argued that there may be more fundamental problems than legal or evidential ones when it comes to a woman articulating her experience of violence, as the words simply do not exist to enable her to convey the reality of her life. She identifies the need for a different language which reflects the experiences of those abused by domestic violence and which does not trivialise or distance us from the horrific reality of it as much judicial discourse does.[129] Thus, language has a vital part to play in rendering domestic violence visible and helping us re-shape our perceptions of battered women. We have to use language to promote a new understanding of violence against women which recognises the power and control at play in violent relationships. Only when women can articulate their experiences and render visible to society and juries the extreme physical and emotional abuse to women's bodies which the oxymoronic term "domestic violence" obscures, can we begin to formulate a more effective strategy for legal intervention which really protects women and prevents men from inflicting such violence.

Mahoney agrees that we have lacked the explanatory language and litigative strategies to expose the batterer's quest for power and control - the link between the conduct of the batterer and the experience of the woman.[130] She has suggested that a way forward would be to coin the term "separation assault" to convey the particularity of violence provoked by the woman's actual or threatened separation from the man. Her suggestion supplies a valuable starting point for further discussion. There is certainly a need to allow women to name their experience, and to shift the emphasis to the batterer's behaviour. The concept of separation assault may also heighten awareness of the difficulties and obstacles in the way of leaving a violent relationship and cause separation to be perceived as victory, rather than failure to leave being perceived as defeat.

However, Mahoney's suggestion is also problematic. In the first place, it may be questioned whether the phrase "separation assault" is sufficiently powerful and condemnatory to express societal revulsion at the behaviour of violent men. Moreover, whilst encompassing the actions of her abuser, it continues to focus on her behaviour in leaving or staying, rather than his in battering her. Schneider pertinently suggests "[i]nstead of asking 'why doesn't the woman leave' we should ask 'why does the man batter' or perhaps, more significantly, 'why does society tolerate men who batter?'"[131] Such tolerance is pervasive. As Minow points out, "[s]ociety is organized to permit violence in the home - it is organized through images in the mass media and through broadly based social attitudes that condone violence."[132] These images, which are replicated in the law, must be contested.

However, the task is an enormous and perhaps ultimately a utopian one. Law is implicated in the current plight of battered women especially if they kill their abusers. It can be used to effect change but its role is inevitably limited. While we should continue to strive for ways to ameliorate the position of the battered woman who kills, by seeking to educate judges and jurors, and questioning the existence of defences like provocation, law can most effectively be used in an attempt to prevent the situation ever arising where the woman feels compelled to fight back with lethal force.[133] Before that point it must intervene to remove the male perpetrator of abuse. As Eber contends, given the ineffectiveness of the available legislation and remedies, the legal system has thus far evaded its responsibility to treat this critical problem as a crime against society.[134] Various options have been canvassed, such as criminal statutes to deal specifically with domestic violence,[135] although, as Eber argues, there is a need for very clear definitions in any proposed statutes, as well as an awareness that they could lead to such violence being deemed of a different, and less serious order, than "real" violence occurring in the public sphere. Whatever measures are taken to deal with domestic violence must reflect its gravity and criminality.[136] Such interventions are also essentially short-term, and limited to curtailing the extreme manifestations of woman abuse. In the longer term our concern must be to prevent such violence from ever occurring. This will involve locating the particularity of the battered woman's experience in the context of the generality of inequality and power imbalance that currently seems integral to intimate relationships[137] and seeking to change that inequality.

ACKNOWLEDGMENTS

Many people read and commented on earlier drafts of this paper. My thanks are especially due to Andrew Ashworth, Sean Doran, John Jackson and Simon Lee.

NOTES

1.   In using the term "battered woman" I am conscious both of the stigma which attaches to it and of its reductionist nature. As Elizabeth Schneider has argued, it has a restrictive meaning which defines the woman exclusively in terms of her battering experience as well as a tendency to treat the experiences of all battered women as though they are alike. See E.Schneider, "Particularity and Generality: Challenges of Feminist Theory and Practice in Work on Woman-Abuse" (1992) 67 *New York University Law Review* 520, at p.530. Also, Martha Mahoney suggests that the label's focus on the woman creates a tendency to perceive her, rather than the abusive man or relationship, as the problem (M.Mahoney, "Legal Images of Battered Women: Redefining the Issue of Separation" (1991) 90 *Michigan Law Review* 1, at p.24). However, I am persuaded by the advantages of retaining the term. Initially it was coined to establish the "battered woman" as a social and legal concept and to highlight the problems she faces (E.Schneider, pp.567-8). Given that the legal claims of such women remain tenuous, I agree with Mahoney (at pp.25-6) that, instead of jettisoning the construct we should seek to contest the stigma which attaches to it, since no other term conveys as clearly the gendered nature of domestic violence and the sense of harm and danger which the woman endures.

2.   See, for example, C.Boyle et al., *A Feminist Review of Criminal Law* (1985) at pp.38-47; L.Taylor, "Provoked Reason in Men and Women: Heat-of-Passion Manslaughter and Imperfect Self-Defense" (1986) 33 *U.C.L.A. Law Review* 1679; C.Wells, "Domestic Violence and Self-Defence" (1990) 140 *New Law Journal* 1380; K.O'Donovan, "Defences for Battered Women Who Kill" (1991) 18 *Journal of Law and Society* 219; S.Yeo, "Resolving Gender Bias in Criminal Defences" (1993) 19 *Monash University Law Review* 104.

3.   Indeed Maguigan argues that it is how law is applied in practice, rather than how it is defined, which is problematic for battered women (H.Maguigan, "Battered Women and Self-Defense: Myths and Misconceptions in Current Reform Proposals" (1991) 140 *University of Pennsylvania Law Review* 379).

4. Of course battering is not confined to heterosexual relationships, although it has been even more hidden in gay relationships. However, within those relationships, issues of power and control may differ significantly; as may ways of analysing such battering. See E.Schneider, *supra*, n.1, at pp.539-545; M.Mahoney, *supra*, n.1, at pp.49-53.

5. M.Mahoney, *ibid.*, at p.35. We also know more of the stresses and strains under which defendant battered women have lived than we do of the battered woman who continues to endure the violent relationship.

6. Though there has been judicial acknowledgement of the need for legislative reform as well as attempts to effect such change (see n.71 and n.72 *infra*).

7. P.Chesler, "A Woman's Right to Self-defense: the Case of Aileen Carol Wuornos" (1993) 66 *St John's Law Review* 933, at p.967. Ironically feminist efforts to extend the concept of battering to reveal that it forms part of a continuum of violence against partners or other intimates may weaken the claims of battered women who kill as they emerge as not being so very different from other women who do not react as they did. See E.Schneider, *supra*, n.1, at p.539-48.

8. For convenience I will refer to provocation, diminished responsibility and self-defence as "defences" although the first two are partial defences which reduce a murder conviction to one of manslaughter thus avoiding a mandatory life sentence and allowing the judge discretion as to sentence; while self-defence may be more accurately characterised as negativing the element of unlawfulness. See J.C.Smith and B.Hogan, *Criminal Law* (1992, 7th ed.), at pp.88-89.

9. [1992] 1 All E.R. 306.

10. [1992] 4 All E.R. 889.

11. Ngaire Naffine has demonstrated how the man of law is "a middle-class man whose masculinity assumes a middle-class form" (N.Naffine, *Law and the Sexes: Explorations in Feminist Jurisprudence* (1990) at p.115). Thus, where law does incorporate male experiences and standards they are not necessarily those of all men. The maleness enshrined in law is a particular variant of masculinity, "a high-brow, cultivated form of masculinity, which depends upon an ability to think and act intelligently, not with brute force" (N.Naffine, at p.116).

12. S.3(1) "Where on a charge of murder there is evidence on which the jury can find that the person charged was provoked (whether by things done or by things said or by both together) to lose his self-control, the question whether the provocation was enough to make a reasonable man do as he did shall be left to be determined by the jury; and in determining that question the jury shall take into account everything both done and said according to the effect which, in their opinion, it would have on a reasonable man."

13. Cited by Lord Goddard CJ in *R v. Duffy* [1949] 1 All E.R. 932, at p.932.

14. In practice it is relatively easy for the defence to persuade the judge to put provocation in issue provided there is sufficient evidence to raise a doubt in the minds of the jury (see S.Doran, "Alternative Defences: the 'invisible burden' on the trial judge" [1991] *Criminal Law Review* 878). The more interesting issue is why juries do not accept the plea.

15.   [1978] 2 All E.R. 168.

16.   *Ibid.*, at p.174. See S.Edwards, "Battered Women who Kill" (1990) 140 *New Law Journal* 1380, who argues, at p.1380, that notwithstanding *Camplin*, "[t]he mythical 'reasonable man' ... remains resolute and recalcitrant in refusing to acknowledge, let alone embrace, the battered woman".

17.   *R v. Duffy, supra*, n.13, at pp.932-3, my emphasis. The requirement of suddenness was approved by the Court of Appeal in both *Thornton* and *Ahluwalia*. But see J.Horder, '"Provocation and Loss of Self Control" (1992) 108 *Law Quarterly Review* 191 who argues that this interpretation of the law is historically wrong.

18.   [1969] A.C. 130, at p.137.

19.   [1942] A.C. 1, at p.9.

20.   See R.Collins, "Language, History and the Legal Process: A Profile of the Reasonable Man" (1977) 8 *Rutgers-Camden Law Journal* 311.

21.   H.Allen, "One Law for All Reasonable Persons?" (1988) 16 *International Journal of the Sociology of Law* 419, at p.424. See also L.Taylor, *supra*, n.2, at p.1691: "rather than developing a separate standard for women, criminal law has held and continues to hold female defendants to a male standard of reasonableness".

22.   *R v. Lavallee* [1990] 1 S.C.R. 852 at p.874.

23.   E.Schneider, *supra*, n.1, at p.566.

24.   See K.O'Donovan, *supra*, n.2, at p.224.

25.   See L.Taylor, *supra*, n.2, at pp.1692-1697.

26.   For example, adultery has always been regarded as the paradigm example of provocative conduct. As Ashworth points out, law's preoccupation with the situation of the defendant who kills his adulterous wife or her lover is indicative of the subjective, class, gender and race-specific nature of the supposedly "objective" standard of provocation (A.Ashworth, "The Doctrine of Provocation" (1976) 35 *Cambridge Law Journal* 292). For almost three centuries judges assumed that women did not act in such a hot-blooded manner. Although the defence is now available to women, this, as Taylor argues, is a shallow concession to equality given that women rarely react with lethal force in the event of a partner's infidelity (see L.Taylor, *ibid.*, at p.1697). Thus, if the only concession to equality is to extend to women the categories of provocative event which apply to men, the situation has actually disimproved for women. The law continues to disadvantage them, but more insidiously, because such discrimination operates under the cover of a standard which appears gender-neutral.

27.   L.Taylor, *ibid.*, at p.1719. Significantly, in *Camplin* the Law Lords, overlooking the real threat posed by violent men, could explicitly envisage only one situation where the reasonable woman might react differently from the reasonable man - "if words of 'grievous insult' reflecting on her chastity or way of life were addressed to her" (per Lord Morris at p.177. See also Lord Simon at p.180). As K.O'Donovan remarks, "a woman's chastity may be of more concern to her male partner than it is to her" (*supra*, n.2, at pp.226-7).

28.   See S.Bandalli, "Battered Wives and Provocation" (1992) *New Law Journal* 212.

29. C.Douzinas and R.Warrington, "'A Well-Founded Fear of Justice': Law and Ethics in Post-Modernity" (1991) 2 *Law and Critique* 115, at pp.130-1 (writing in the context of immigrants' fears of persecution in their homeland). Horder makes the further point that "the defence of provocation [focused on anger] is ... poorly equipped to deal with those who are driven to act as they do out of despair" (J.Horder, *Provocation and Responsibility* (1992) at p.91).

30. See B.Campbell, "Foreword" in A.Jones, *Women Who Kill* (1991) at p.xi; A.Lloyd, "Villains or victims?" (1991) *The Guardian*, 12 March.

31. For a personal account of this reality see M.Callery, "In the Best Interest of the Children" (1990) 13 *Harvard Women's Law Journal* 383.

32. For example, in *R v. Duffy* Devlin J instructed the jury "... you are not concerned with blame here - the blame attaching to the dead man" (*supra*, n.13, at p.932).

33. S.Edwards, "Provoking Her Own Demise: From Common Assault to Homicide" in *Women, Violence and Social Control*, eds. J.Hanmer and M.Maynard (1987) 152 at p.162. This contention certainly seems borne out by cases where men kill their partners. See, for example, *R v. McQueen* (1990) *Belfast Telegraph*, 9 May, where the "constant nagging" of the defendant's wife was deemed to be provocation and a three year sentence was imposed by the Lord Chief Justice; *R v. McGrail* (1991) *The Independent*, 6 August, where Mr Justice Popplewell, imposing a two year suspended sentence commented that living with the defendant's wife "would have tried the patience of a saint"; *R v. Singh* (1992) *The Times*, 30 January, where an eighteen month suspended sentence was received by a man who had strangled his "nagging", "domineering" wife.

34. Of course the victim's blameworthy actions will be relevant and amount to cumulative provocation providing it culminates in a sudden explosion, and in those circumstances the cumulative effect of the provocation will be taken into account in assessing its gravity. See M.Wasik, "Cumulative Provocation and Domestic Killing" [1982] *Criminal Law Review* 29 and J.Horder, *supra*, n.29, at p.189. Thus the crucial element of delay, characterised as pre-meditation or desire for revenge in the cases of *Thornton* and *Ahluwalia* operated to deny them the defence and remove from the jury the role of considering the extent to which their husbands had precipitated their own deaths. Contrast this with the much broader time frame adopted in some self-defence cases: *Attorney General for Northern Ireland's Reference* [1977] A.C. 105; *Attorney General's Reference (No 2 of 1983)* [1984] Q.B. 456. For an argument that we need to broaden our notion of criminal responsibility to encompass the actions of battered women see A.Coughlin, "Excusing Women" (1994) *University of California Law Review* 1. See also M.Kelman, "Interpretive Construction in the Substantive Criminal Law" (1981) 33 *Stanford Law Review* 591.

35. *R v. Thornton*, *supra*, n.9, at p.312. See also the cases discussed in S.Edwards, "Gender 'Justice'? Defending Defendants and Mitigating Sentence" in *Gender, Sex and the Law*, ed. S.Edwards (1985) 129, at pp.140-143.

36. Indeed, the criminal justice system itself, through its treatment of women who have experienced rape or violence, reinforces the notion that women should be passive and

acquiesce in their assigned gender role.

37.   See Wilson J in *Lavallee v. R*, *supra*, n.22, at p.883.

38.   See D.Nicolson and R.Sanghiv, "Battered Women and Provocation: The Implications of *R v. Ahluwalia*" [1993] *Criminal Law Review* 728, at p.738; C.Wells, "Domestic Violence and Self-Defence" (1990) 140 *New Law Journal* 1380.

39.   P.Easteal, "Sentencing Those Who Kill Their Sexual Intimates: An Australian Study" (1993) 21 *International Journal of the Sociology of Law* 189, at p.213.

40.   See, for example, *R v. Oatridge* [1992] *Criminal Law Review* 205, where the Court of Appeal conceded that there was a possible case of self-defence where a woman knifed her drunken and violent lover to death; and over-turned her manslaughter conviction on the grounds that the trial judge should have put to the jury that she honestly believed she was in imminent danger of being killed by him. See also A.McColgan, "In Defence of Battered Women who Kill" (1993) 12 *Oxford Journal of Legal Studies* 508, at p.515: "[e]ven where women kill in the course of a violent attack upon them, defence lawyers and the courts are apparently blind to the possibilities of a self-defence plea."

41.   R.Schuller and N.Vidmar, "Battered Women Syndrome Evidence in the Court Room: A Review of the Literature" (1992) 16 *Law and Human Behaviour* 273 at p.275.

42.   H.Maguigan, *supra*, n.3, at p.385.

43.   Although in the case of self-defence the reasonableness of the defendant's actions are judged in the circumstances as she honestly believed them to be. See *Beckford v. R* [1988] A.C. 130.

44.   In Britain it seems that imminence of the expected attack is merely a factor to be taken into account in determining whether the defendant's use of force was necessary. See *Palmer v. R* [1971] A.C. 814, and discussion in A.McColgan, *supra*, n.40, at pp.517-8.

45.   See M.Mihjalovich, "Does Plight Make Right: The Battered Woman Syndrome, Expert Testimony and the Law of Self-Defense" (1987) 62 *Indiana Law Journal* 1253, at p.1257.

46.   See Wilson J in *Lavallee v. R*, *supra*, n.22 at p.876.

47.   See M.MacCrimmon, "The Social Construction of Reality and the Rules of Evidence" in D.Martinson et al., "A Forum on *Lavallee v. R*: Women and Self-Defence" (1991) 25 *University of British Columbia Law Review* 23, at p.42. Although, as Maguigan points out, the proportionality requirement does not necessarily rule out the use of weapons against an unarmed assailant (*supra*, n.3, at p.386).

48.   *R v. McInnes* [1971] 3 All E.R. 295.

49.   C.Boyle, "A Duty to Retreat?" in D.Martinson et al., *supra*, n.47, at p.62, n.174. See also A.McColgan, *supra*, n.40 at p.517.

50.   This may be exacerbated in the case of some women, such as those who suffer disabilities or learning difficulties, those who are members of tightly knit communities or immigrants whose legal status is uncertain (see C.Boyle, *ibid.*, at p.65), or those who have children.

51.   C.Boyle, *ibid.*, at p.63.

52.   H.Maguigan, *supra*, n.3, at p.386.

53.   For example, the cases of *Thornton*, *supra*, n.9; *Ahluwalia*, *supra*, n.10; *Lavallee v. R*, *supra*,

n.22; and *State v. Stewart* 243 Kan. 639, 763 P. 2d 572 (1988) all fit this pattern. Moreover, in his study Ewing found that in two thirds of the one hundred cases he reviewed the woman had killed outside of a direct confrontation (C.P.Ewing, *Battered Women Who Kill: Psychological Self-Defense as Legal Justification* (1987)). See also S.Edwards, *supra*, n.35, at p.142.

54.   A.McColgan, *supra*, n.40 at p.527.

55.   88 Wash. 2d 221, 559 P. 2d 548 (1977).

56.   L.P.Eber, "The Battered Wife's Dilemma: To Kill or To Be Killed" (1981) 32 *The Hastings Law Journal* 895, at p.920. In *Wanrow*, Yvonne Wanrow killed a man named Wesler who came up behind her in her friend's house when her children were present. Whereas Wesler was 6'2", Yvonne Wanrow was 5'4" and dependent upon a crutch. Wanrow knew that Wesler was a convicted child molester who had recently pulled her son of his bicycle and dragged him into a house. The Washington Supreme Court reversed Wanrow's conviction for second-degree murder and first-degree assault, stating that on a self-defence plea: "[i]t is clear that the jury is entitled to consider *all* of the circumstances surrounding the incident in determining whether [the] defendant had reasonable grounds to believe grievous bodily harm was about to be inflicted" (*ibid.*, at p.236). See further Elizabeth Kingdom "Body Politics and Rights" in this volume, n.50 and accompanying text.

57.   See A.McColgan, *supra*, n.40, at p.526.

58.   M.Kasian et al., "Battered Women Who Kill: Jury Simulation and Legal Defenses" (1993) *Law and Human Behaviour* 289, at p.290.

59.   S.2(1) "Where a person kills or is party to the killing of another, he shall not be convicted of murder if he was suffering from such abnormality of mind (whether arising from a condition of arrested or retarded development of mind or any inherent causes or induced by disease or injury) as substantially impaired his mental responsibility for his acts and omissions in doing or being a party to the killing ... (3) ... [he] shall be liable instead to be convicted of manslaughter."

60.   See, for example, J.Horder, *supra*, n.29, at pp.191-2; M.Mihjalovich, *supra*, n.45, at p.1278.

61.   For example, *R v. Ahluwalia*, *supra*, n.10; *R v. Sainsbury* (1991) *The Independent*, 14 December; *R v. Scotland* (1992) *The Guardian*, 24 March. See the discussion of these cases in H.Kennedy, *Eve Was Framed: Women and British Justice* (1992) at pp.190-221 and A.Kirsta, *Deadlier Than the Male: Violence and Aggression in Women* (1994) at pp.178-226. Rocco Cipparone's arguments as to why battered women in the United States should plead temporary insanity for strategic reasons, because it allows in all kinds of evidence which might otherwise be deemed irrelevant, and shows how the woman either viewed her options from a distorted perspective or was driven to breaking point, seem to apply equally to diminished responsibility (R.Cipparone, "The Defense of Battered Women Who Kill" (1985) 135 *University of Pennsylvania Law Review* 427).

62.   Suzanne Dell's research suggests this happens in eighty per cent of cases (S.Dell, "Diminished Responsibility Reconsidered" [1982] *Criminal Law Review* 809, at p.811).

63.   See H.Kennedy, *supra*, n.61, at p.207.

64. See C.Bell and M.Fox, "'A Tragedy of Two Women': Contextualising the Dynamics of Woman-Killing" (1994) unpublished paper.

65. See D.Nicolson and R.Sanghiv, *supra*, n.38, at p.736: "This willingness to accept evidence of diminished responsibility suggests that battered women are more likely to evoke a favourable judicial response if they confine themselves to medical-type excuses rather than the partial justification of provocation."

66. See H.Allen, *Justice Unbalanced: Gender, Psychiatry and Judicial Decisions* (1987). Though see L.Radford, "Pleading for Time: Justice for Battered Women Who Kill" in *Moving Targets: Women, Murder and Representation*, ed. H.Birch (1993) 172. On the difficulty in drawing conclusions from Home Office statistics on the relative success or failure rates of provocation as a partial defence when pleaded by women as opposed to men, see S.Bandalli, "Provocation from the Home Office" [1992] *Criminal Law Review* 716.

67. See J.Nadel, *Sara Thornton: The Story of a Woman who Killed* (1993).

68. See C.Bell and M.Fox, *supra*, n.64; L.Radford, *supra*, n.66, at p.183.

69. As O'Donovan argues, *(supra*, n.2, at p.230), "[i]nstead of proposing herself as a legal subject responsible for her actions, she denies this and proposes abnormality of mind ... [T]he focus is on her mental state at the time of what is acknowledged as a crime. Her personality, characteristics and problems are on trial." See also K.O'Donovan, "Law's Knowledge: The Judge, The Expert, The Battered Woman and Her Syndrome" (1993) 20 *Journal of Law and Society* 427, at p.432.

70. See A.McColgan, *supra*, n.40, at p.509.

71. The first such bill was introduced by Jack Ashley MP in December 1991.

72. The New South Wales Crimes Act 1900 was amended in 1982 following the recommendations of a Parliamentary Committee on domestic violence. Section 20(2) now states that the provocative conduct of the deceased is relevant regardless of whether such conduct "occurred immediately before the act or omission causing death or at any previous time". For discussion, see S.Yeo, "Provocation Down Under" (1991) 141 *New Law Journal* 1200. In *R v.Ahluwalia*, *supra*, n.10, at p.896, the Lord Chief Justice pointed to the need for legislative reform of the British law on provocation.

73. D.Martinson, "Implications of *Lavallee v. R* for Other Criminal Law Doctrines" in D.Martinson et al., *supra*, n.47, at pp.31-2.

74. D.Martinson, *ibid.*, at p.26, citing T.Pickard and P.Goldman, *Dimensions of Criminal Law* Vol. II (1989) at E-6.

75. J.Horder, *supra*, n.29, at p.192.

76. P.Easteal, *supra*, n.39 at p.201. She further notes, at p.214, how the biggest determining factor in length of sentence imposed is "the nature of the victim and her degree of compatibility with societal norms ... Leaving one's husband, having an affair, not taking care of the children, nagging one's husband, lack of appreciation for the husband's work on behalf of the family are all *not* manifested by the 'ideal' woman".

77. Even A.McColgan, who favours the use of this defence, identifies judicial resistance to acquitting battered women who kill (*supra*, n.40, at p.521).

78. See C.P.Ewing, *supra*, n.53, and discussion in K.O'Donovan, *supra*, n.2, and D.Faigman, "Discerning Justice When Battered Women Kill" (1987) 39 *Hastings Law Journal* 207.

79. See K.O'Donovan, "The Medicalisation of Infanticide" [1984] *Criminal Law Review* 259. Though compare C.Maier-Katkin and R.Ogle, "A Rationale for Infanticide Laws" [1993] *Criminal Law Review* 902.

80. See Wilson J in *Lavallee v. R*, supra, n.22, at p.873.

81. See I.Grant, "The 'Syndromization' of Women's Experience" in D.Martinson et al., *supra*, n.47, at p.55. Indeed, Mihjalovich, *supra*, n.45, at pp.1259-60, notes that it effectively amounts to a judicially-created sub-category of self-defence for battered women.

82. M.Kasian et al., *supra*, n.58, at p.291.

83. L.Walker, *The Battered Woman* (1979) at pp.55-70. See also *The Battered Woman Syndrome* (1984) and *Terrifying Love* (1989).

84. *R v. Lavallee*, *supra*, n.22, at pp.871-2.

85. See E.Schneider, *supra*, n.1, at p.562. See also, E.Schneider, "Equal Rights to Trial for Women: Sex Bias in the Law of Self-Defense" (1980) 15 *Harvard Civil Rights - Civil Liberties Law Review* 623.

86. On the contested nature of these defences amongst feminist scholars see n.79, *infra*; L.Luckhaus, "A Plea for PMT in the Criminal Law" in *Gender, Sex and the Law*, ed. S.Edwards (1985) 160; S.Edwards, "Mad, bad or pre-menstrual" (1988) 140 *New Law Journal* 456; K.MCarthur, "'Through Her Looking Glass': Premenstrual Syndrome on Trial" (1989) 47 *University of Toronto Faculty of Law Review* 825; H.Allen, "At the Mercy of her Hormones: Premenstrual Tension and the Law" in *The Woman in Question*, eds. P.Adams and E.Cowie (1990) 200; B.McSherry, "The Return of the Raging Hormones Theory: Premenstrual Syndrome, Postpartum Disorders and Criminal Responsibility" (1993) 15 *Sydney Law Review* 292.

87. R.Schuller and N.Vidmar, *supra*, n.41, at p.281.

88. M.Mahoney, *supra*, n.1, at p.42.

89. M.Mahoney, *ibid.*, at p.4.

90. M.Mahoney, *ibid.*, at p.3.

91. See R.Schuller and N.Vidmar, *supra*, n.41 at p.280. Also see A.Browne, *When Battered Women Kill* (1987) at pp.75-87; R.E.Dobash and R.P.Dobash, *Women, Violence & Social Change* (1992) at pp.213-250 and R.J.Gelles and C.P.Cornell, *Intimate Violence in Families* (1990).

92. M.Mihjalovich, *supra*, n.45, at p.1268.

93. L.Walker, *supra*, n.83, at p.40.

94. E.Schneider, *supra*, n.1, at pp.561-2.

95. I.Grant, in D.Martinson et al., *supra*, n.47, at p.51, n.135.

96. I.Grant, *ibid.*, at pp.46-7. See also A.Coughlin, *supra*, n.34, for a trenchant critique of Walker's theory. At p.72, she suggests that "experts" like Walker do not describe the woman's own perspective in their testimony, nor give a feminist account of violence because their "testimony is based on research informed by the same cognitive patriarchal categories

that structure [law and psychiatry]". See also D.Faigman, *supra*, n.78 at pp.213-217.

97.   M.Mahoney, *supra*, n.1 at pp.42-43. See M.Mihjalovich, *supra*, n.45, at p.1265, who also questions whether domestic violence is beyond the understanding of a lay person, and calls for more empirical studies on jury attitudes, since the scant studies currently existing have reached conflicting conclusions on the beliefs actually held by jurors.

98.   See I.Grant, in D.Martinson et al., *supra*, n.47, at p.56. Alternatively, however, battered woman syndrome may be categorised as a sub-category of post-traumatic stress disorder which may apply to both women and men.

99.   I.Grant, *ibid.*, at pp.51-2.

100.   I.Grant, *ibid.*, at pp.53-4.

101.   See M.Kasian et al., *supra*, n.58 at p.298.

102.   A.Coughlin, *supra*, n.34, at p.7. See also M.Mihjalovich, *supra*, n.45, at p.1269, who notes the inherent inconsistency of permitting expert testimony describing a battered woman's unhealthy mental state to establish the reasonableness of her act of self-preservation.

103.   A.Coughlin, *ibid.*, at p.62.

104.   N.Eastman, "Abused Woman and Legal Excuses" (1992) *New Law Journal* 1549.

105.   A.McColgan, *supra*, n.40, at p.513. See also S.Edwards, "Battered Woman Syndrome" (1992) 142 *New Law Journal* 1350. Discussion of the evidential difficulties posed by battered woman syndrome is beyond the scope of this essay, but for an indication of the admissibility problem see A.Thar, "The Admissibility of Expert Testimony on Battered Wife Syndrome: An Evidentiary Analysis" (1982) 71 *Northwestern University Law Review* 348. Such problems may have been compounded by the recent Supreme Court decision in *Daubert* v. *Merrell Dow Pharmaceuticals* 113 S.Ct. 2786 (1993).

106.   M.Mahoney, *supra*, n.1, at p.40. See also D.Faigman, *supra*, n.78, at p.215.

107.   K.O'Donovan, *supra*, n.69, at p.432.

108.   K.O'Donovan, *ibid.*, at p.431, citing the Australian practice of calling on non-medical experts, such as criminologists, and suggestions that have been made there for the use of social workers as well as refuge workers. See also E.Sheehy, J.Stubbs and T.Tolmie, "Defending Battered Women on Trial: The Battered Woman Syndrome and its Limitations" (1992) 16 *Criminal Law Journal* 369, at p.393.

109.   See H.Packer, *The Limits of the Criminal Sanction* (1968).

110.   H.Maguigan, *supra*, n.3, at p.406. See also D.Nelken, "Critical Criminal Law" (1987) 14 *Journal of Law and Society* 105; (also published in *Critical Legal Studies*, eds. P.Fitzpatrick and A.Hunt (1987) 105).

111.   M.Minow, "Words and the Door to the Land of Change: Law, Language and Family Violence" (1990) 43 *Vanderbilt Law Review* 1665, at p.1683.

112.   P.Chesler, *supra*, n.7 at p.794.

113.   Wilson J in *Lavallee v. R, supra*, n.22, at pp.873.

114.   At Sara Thornton's trial, four of the twelve jurors were women (J.Nadel, *supra*, n.67 at p.110), although in Kiranjit Ahluwalia's case all of the jurors were white men (S.Lonsdale and P.Ghazi, "Women beaten by law" (1991) *The Observer*, 4 August).

115. M.Mahoney, *supra*, n.1, at p.8.

116. See Lord Justice Taylor, in an exclusive interview with *The Times* newspaper (1994) 27 June; A.Ashworth, "Reforming the Law of Murder" [1990] *Criminal Law Review* 75; A leader in *The Guardian* (1991) 27 August.

117. See, for example, N.Lacey, "Government as Manager, Citizen as Consumer: The Case of the Criminal Justice Act 1991" (1994) 57 *Modern Law Review* 534.

118. P.Easteal, *supra*, n.39, at pp.193,210,214.

119. See M.Mahoney, *supra*, n.1, at p.61, who demonstrates how typical this lack of provision is.

120. See M.Minow, *supra*, n.111, at p.1683.

121. See, for example, K.O'Donovan, *supra*, n.2, at p.235, n.116, citing a letter to her from Sara Thornton in which she wrote "I loved him. Sober, he was a warm, funny caring man who never hit me. I did not realise how much his drinking made him hate me." As O'Donovan comments, courts must take on board the fact that, for women, *connection* is important, and value women's view of relationships equally with men's.

122. See C.Littleton, "Women's Experience and the Problem of Transition: Perspectives on Male Battering of Women" (1989) *University of Chicago Legal Forum* 23; C.Boyle, in D.Martinson et al., *supra*, n.47, at pp.45,52; and A.Coughlin, *supra*, n.34, at pp.60-1. No value is placed by the courts on remaining in the relationship, nor is any credence given to a belief that the man may reform.

123. R.Langer, "Battered Women and the Criminal Injuries Compensation Board: *Re A.C.*" (1991) 55 *Saskatchewan Law Review* 453.

124. Of course in Britain, as a result of the Contempt of Court Act 1981, which forbids questioning of jurors, this would have to be achieved through jury simulation exercises.

125. See, for example, M.Bringer Cross, "The Expert as Educator: A Proposed Approach to the Use of Battered Woman Syndrome Expert Testimony" (1982) 35 *Vanderbilt Law Review* 741.

126. Of course, like the legal system, the media is also reactionary and gendered, but feminist campaigns around the cases of Thornton and Ahluwalia do seem to have had an impact at least in the broadsheet press as well as on television. See C.Bell and M.Fox, *supra*, n.64.

127. See R.Schuller and N.Vidmar, *supra*, n.41, at p.283-4.

128. See J.Jackson, "Law's Truth, Lay Truth and Lawyers' Truth: The Representation of Evidence in Adversary Trials" (1992) 3 *Law and Critique* 29.

129. M.Minow, *supra*, n.111, at pp.1672-5.

130. M.Mahoney, *supra*, n.1, at p.43.

131. E.Schneider, *supra*, n.1, at p.558. See also C.Littleton, *supra*, n.122, at p.29.

132. M.Minow, *supra*, n.111, at p.1671.

133. See C.M.Lyon, "Working Together - An Analysis of Collaborative Inter-Agency Responses to 'The Problem of Domestic Violence'" in this volume.

134. L.P.Eber, *supra*, n.56 at p.867.

135. See, for example, the discussion of Californian legislation in L.P.Eber, *ibid.*

136. See P.Easteal, *supra*, n.39,, at p.215: "If the aim of the justice system is to deter others from

engaging in the same criminal activity and stopping the person from reoffending, [a] plethora of lenient sentences would not be a strong deterrent. Judges are not existing in isolation. They are both agents of change and recipients of social attitudes. Thus, in that light, it is critically important that they hold and illustrate an opinion of the criminality and seriousness of domestic violence and homicide." As L.P.Eber argues, *supra*, n.56, at p.917, the inadequacy of the remedies available to battered women must be considered as integral to her perception of the danger inherent in her situation.

137.   'See E.Schneider, *supra*, n.1, at pp.558-9.

9 Working Together – An Analysis of Collaborative Inter-Agency Responses to "The Problem of Domestic Violence"

CHRISTINA M. LYON

INTRODUCTION[1]

Marie Fox's chapter[2] in this collection focuses from a feminist perspective on the flawed response of the criminal law and criminal justice system to battered women who kill. The focus of this chapter is an analysis of a continuing attempt by personnel working within both the civil and criminal justice systems to improve the responsiveness of the law to battered women who seek to invoke either the civil[3] or the criminal[4] law as a means of protection. The proponents of this continuing process are all representatives of a variety of different groups, serving on a Domestic Violence Forum which was created by the City Council[5] to promote and strengthen inter-agency co-operation and co-ordination.

BACKGROUND REASONS FOR ESTABLISHING THE DOMESTIC VIOLENCE FORUM

The City's Community Care Plan for 1992/3 referred to growing awareness of the issues relating to domestic violence with particular emphasis on the needs of women. This was highlighted in the City's Community Care Plan as an area of work where inter-agency co-operation and co-ordination needed to be strengthened. Although local authorities have no specific powers to provide services to people subject to domestic violence, the City Council approved the creation of a Domestic Violence Forum. The membership of the Forum was to include representation from social services, housing providers, health services, black women's welfare groups, black women's rights groups, the probation service, the police, voluntary organisations, the Crown Prosecution Service, the education directorate, the

Benefits Agency, the Child Support Agency and community health councils. Early on in its deliberations the Forum identified the fact that the issue of abuse of children was very clearly under the remit of Area Child Protection Committees and that a great deal had been done through legislation such as the Children Act 1989 and the concentration of social service resources on problems associated with child abuse. In consequence, the Forum felt it appropriate to concentrate its energies initially on partner violence whilst recognising that other key areas would need to be explored, such as the abuse of older people and other vulnerable adults. The Forum has been running for some two years and now describes itself as including people from all agencies involved with domestic violence trying to co-ordinate the services that are offered to *women* who have been subject to such violence. It cannot be claimed that formal agency interventions can be solely responsible for a cessation of violence against women,[6] but nevertheless a consideration of the variety of assistance which may be successful has in the United States of America pointed to the need for greater co-ordination amongst community services.[7] As well as consideration being given to the issue of greater collaboration with the various agencies who might be expected to offer assistance or protection to battered women, there clearly needed to be much closer collaboration and exploration with the courts as to how both criminal and civil court processes could be made more responsive to the needs of such women. In order to take so many issues forward the Domestic Violence Forum began to form sub-committees drafting in new people with particular experience in different areas to serve on the working groups. After some two years, the Domestic Violence Forum could be said to consist of the Chairs of the various working groups who represent the membership of those groups on the Forum but also it continues to include representatives from all the agencies involved with domestic violence.

THE WORKING GROUPS OF THE DOMESTIC VIOLENCE FORUM

The working groups which have so far been formed include: a Housing Working Group; a Victim Support Working Group; A Black Women's Working Group; a Civil and Criminal Working Group; a Children's Working Group; and a Perpetrators Working Group. It had previously been suggested that there should be an Education Working Group and a recent meeting of the Domestic Violence Forum noted that such a group had not yet been formed but that there was an intention to try to take this forward in the near future. Again at a recent meeting, concern was expressed that attendance at the Forum from representatives from health, the black women's group and the black women issues group had been sparse or non-existent. Attempts to remedy the problems over health were discussed and a letter written to the City's Health Authority and the Family Health Service

Authority for the area, encouraging much greater participation by the health service in the Forum. A Health Working Group is now in the course of being established. Further encouragement to attend the main Forum meetings was to be given to the representatives from the black women's groups as it was felt to be crucial that the Forum was informed of their views.

THE WORK OF THE WORKING GROUPS

The work done by each of the working groups differed enormously and clearly depended very much on the commitment demonstrated by the various constituent members. Some groups had difficulty getting members of their working groups to attend or to get the same members to attend consecutive meetings. Some groups were far more pro-active than others in seeking out information, leaflets distributed by other agencies in other parts of the country and in identifying areas of good practice or projects which could provide lessons for the work of the particular working group or the Domestic Violence Forum generally. It is proposed here to set out very briefly the progress which each of the working groups have made within the context of the reformulated description of the Forum which was issued in the latter part of the second year of its existence. To some extent, the aims set out in the description of the Forum which circulated at that stage, form the Forum's mission statement and it is interesting to measure the extent to which the working groups and in turn the whole Domestic Violence Forum measured up to the four identified aims. As formulated it was stated that the Forum is a multi-disciplinary group which will:

i.   strengthen inter-agency co-operation

ii.   maximise the choices and services available to women subject to domestic violence within their relationships

iii.   seek to reduce the level of domestic violence by changing public awareness and attitudes to programmes of public education

iv.   advise statutory and voluntary bodies on the future development and evaluation of services.

Looking at the various working groups reporting to the main Forum it became apparent that probably the one meeting most frequently and which had determined it would produce a working paper for action was that looking at the civil and criminal processes. It is worthwhile, however, to consider the feedback from the various working groups.

The Housing Working Group has had two meetings which were attended by only two people, so the Chair of this group reported that it had been rather difficult to get it going. The group had however looked at issues associated with housing, focusing particularly on the policies of various housing associations. The Chair of this working group felt that there should be more involvement of people from the Local Authority Housing Department so that there was an input from "mainstream" housing as well as a desirable involvement by members of the Local Authority's Homelessness Unit, who would deal with homelessness arising from domestic violence as an issue of priority need under the provisions of the Housing Act 1985. Since the patriarchal model of woman battering finds the source of such violence in society and how it is organised then both our legislative response to domestic violence through the assistance which is given in the housing legislation and the extremely narrow and restrictive way in which such guidance is interpreted must give rise to further questioning on the part of this particular working group.[8]

The work of the Victim Support Group is also at a very early stage and the members have agreed that there is a need for access to national help lines, and for the publication of leaflets with contact numbers and resources which might be available to victims of domestic violence. In the Forum's mission statement the term victim is stated to be appropriate for use at some times whilst at others the term survivor might be appropriate. The reason for this is an acknowledgement that women may be either at different times in their lives. Many women who experience domestic violence are said to resent the term "victim" and also resent the conceptualisation of their position as "battered woman syndrome". Much of this characterisation of course stems from early research on wife abuse by Lenore Walker[9] who also propounded the notion that women who are battered suffer from "learned helplessness". Both the notion of battered woman syndrome and learned helplessness are important elements of the "battered woman defence" discussed by Marie Fox in her chapter.[10] As Gelles points out[11] there are a number of questions about whether such a syndrome really exists, whether battered women do suffer from "learned helplessness" and whether such conceptualisations paint an inaccurate picture of helpless women. Gelles and Strauss found that the vast majority of women who were subjected to violence by their husbands left their homes for at least some period of time.[12] As Gelles notes:

> [t]he typical battered wife is hardly passive; she actively seeks to prevent further victimisation and is handicapped not by her own psychological limitations but by the lack of concrete and effective remedies available from agencies of social control and other social institutions.[13]

Much therefore needs to be done in the shaping of the objectives of the Victim

Support Group so that a much more rigorous and "supportive" network of support can be established through the workings of the various Victim Support Groups operating within the area.

The Children's Group had had a number of meetings in the course of which they identified the objectives of the group and the need for the criminal justice system to be made more accessible to carers. Their plan of action involved drawing up a list of people to contact in order to further their aims. Clearly, further development work was needed in this group and it might be anticipated that as further developments occur in relation to Child Support, the relevance of issues affecting this group will in turn be seen to be more relevant to the other groups.

As far as the Perpetrators Group was concerned, their single meeting had comprised a familiarisation session during the course of which they identified that the main area of work was with a court mandated scheme. This group was in the course of considering whether they should try to do something on their own and there was also some concern as to how their group related to the mission statement of the Forum.

The work of the Civil and Criminal Working Group was the most extensive of all the work done by any of the groups. It is now proposed to examine the working of this sub-group and its various recommendations principally with regard to the criminal processes and the criminal law's response to the issue of domestic violence.

THE CIVIL AND CRIMINAL WORKING GROUP

1. Background

The Civil and Criminal Working Group had met on a monthly basis since approximately two-thirds of the way through the first year of the establishment of the Forum. The group consisted of senior probation officers, two women members of the local police force's Dedicated Domestic Violence Unit and a male and female member of the Crown Prosecution Service. Other occasional attenders included male and female court clerks from the local City Magistrates' Court and a male magistrate from the same City Magistrates' Court. The group had been convened to review how cases involving domestic violence were processed principally through the criminal justice system and to identify ways in which the system might be improved. This involved working through the sequence of events, from the initial report to the police to the final disposal of the case. Issues such as the selection of the appropriate charge, bail, retraction by the complainant, support for the victim/survivor, and the avoidance of delay occupied the group for a very considerable period of time.

As a result of all its work, this group came up with a list of thirty-two recommendations which were put into writing by the senior probation officer and the senior crown prosecutor. The senior probation officer concerned was male and the senior crown prosecutor concerned was female.[5] These recommendations were subsequently discussed at a meeting arranged with senior officers in the police, the probation service, court clerks, social services and various voluntary organisations. One magistrate attended that meeting but this was in her capacity as a representative of a voluntary agency. Although invited, no magistrates attended nor did any member of the local judiciary. It was apparent both from the work of the working group and also from the recommendations which followed that the issue of delay was a major one and so special consideration was given to that topic. The role of the respective agencies - the police, the probation service, the Crown Prosecution Service, court clerks and magistrates - was continually under discussion with the primary objective being to improve all aspects of services which impacted upon victims/survivors.

Given the length of time in which domestic violence has been recognised as a serious problem within the world of social theorists and legal researchers, it was still quite staggering to realise that one of the main issues facing the group was that domestic violence was still not necessarily viewed throughout the legal processes as a "serious matter". Given the attention focused on this issue in England during the 1970s it appeared strange to see many of the issues which one had assumed had been accepted back then were still issues in the 1990s. Thus the notion of "its only a domestic" was described as still being common within all levels of the criminal justice system. Although the group noted that the idea was gradually being eroded as more became known of the true nature and extent of domestic violence, there was a clear view coming out of the group's reports that this erosion was far too slow.

Encouragingly, however, the meetings did reveal a very strong commitment from the City's police, probation service and the Crown Prosecution Service towards cases involving domestic violence. It was reported by this group that the probation service and Crown Prosecution Service had both formulated policy documents on the subject whilst the police had one Dedicated Domestic Violence Unit. However it became clear to the group that more was urgently required and indeed, that was one of the recommendations of this working group. In its introduction to the discussion of court processes, the reporters for the group note that "it is heartening to be able to meet and discuss the difficulties in this area; not so long ago the subject of domestic violence would not have been deemed to be one which necessitated this".

2. Consideration of the court process by the Civil and Criminal Working Group

The working group's report goes on to identify five features of the court process which demand fuller consideration and attention.

(a) *The Issue of Delay* This issue was discussed on many occasions and was identified as the major problem as far as successful prosecutions for domestic violence were concerned. The group observed, as had many earlier research studies, that the resolve of complainants to pursue a prosecution may become progressively weaker over time as a result of pressures arising from the domestic situation in which the perpetrator may still be around the home or as a result of worsening financial circumstances due to a withdrawal of monetary support in response to the pursuance of the prosecution.

(b) *Psychological Pressure through "The Process"* That the victim/survivor may appear to weaken in her resolve to keep the prosecution going was identified as being well known both to the perpetrator and to his lawyers. It was further recognised that both defendants and defence solicitors sometimes tried to exploit this to their advantage. The reporters of the working group noted that very often there was little that could be done if a part oral committal or trial was requested and all the parties knew that the whole purpose of such proceedings was merely "to see if she turns up". Again, in an effort to recognise the psychological pressure being placed on the victim/survivor, the group had succeeded in encouraging the minimisation of delay by the police, the Crown Prosecution Service and the courts and the working group was further discussing other ideas with a view to an improvement in this area of the process.

(c) *The Courts' Charter* The reporters for the working group noted that the government had sought to assist those who were called as witnesses through the publication of the Courts' Charter. This states "that a witness should not have to wait more than two hours before being called. Clearly this is of assistance when a case is actually before the court and all witnesses should be treated courteously, with the reason for any delay being explained to them as soon as practicable." The greatest delays were not however in the actual process once the case got to court and thus the group again identified that the major problem was getting the case into court.

(d) *Inter-Agency Collaboration* The working group identified that from the outset of the case, delay could be minimised by the police placing all defendants charged with offences involving domestic violence before the first available court. The police, it was said, should ensure that all relevant documents were processed and delivered to the Crown Prosecution Service in time for this first appearance. The Crown Prosecution Service would then be able to apply for conditional bail or custody - conditional bail at least would be appropriate in nearly all cases of domestic violence, primarily to prevent contact between the parties. It was then noted that the matter would usually be adjourned at this stage so that the file could be vetted and advance disclosure provided to the defence. The group noted that time guide-lines have been formulated in accordance with pre-trial issues to govern the length of adjournments at the magistrates' courts. They were, however, only guide-lines and the group noted that they were not adhered to at all times.

(e) *The Crown Prosecution Service Statement of Policy on Domestic Violence*
The reporters of the group noted that this statement of policy indicates that prosecutors should keep delays to a minimum, and should endeavour to ensure that domestic violence cases are not adjourned unnecessarily. It further notes that if an adjournment is required, for example in the event of a retraction, it should be for as short a time as is practicable to make the relevant enquiries.

These five points outlined the main observations which the reporters of the group identified as necessary to set out before going on to make their long list of recommendations. As is obvious, a great deal of attention focused on the adverse effects on women victims/survivors of domestic violence of delays and other difficulties in the court processes. The deliberations of the group here focused particularly on seeing prosecution as an important signalling process, not only to women victims/survivors but also to the male perpetrators. This of course clearly raises the issue of why so much attention should be focused on the criminal justice process. Is there any evidence to suggest that the attitude displayed by the courts will really have any major impact on the whole issue of domestic violence?

   Linked to this, another area of work engaged in by the group had been to look at the responses of police officers and the first four recommendations concentrated on the issues of police attitudes and experience of domestic violence. Trying to get the police to react more seriously to complaints about family violence in the United States resulted in recommendations issuing from the Attorney-General's Task Force on Family Violence in 1984.[14] In Law Enforcement Recommendation 2, the report states that, "consistent with State Law, the Chief Executive of every Law Enforcement Agency should establish arrest as the preferred response in cases of family violence."[15] Relying mainly on the results of field experiments conducted by Lawrence Sherman and Richard Berk,[16] the Attorney-General's report required police departments and criminal justice agencies henceforth to recognise domestic assaults as criminal activities and to respond accordingly. Although the Attorney-General's position on this was supported by the case of *Thurman v. City of Torrington*,[17] where a woman who, in June 1983, had been severely battered and left permanently injured whilst police officers stood by and watched, subsequently successfully settled her case for $1.9 million, more recent evidence from the United States would tend to suggest that a response of arrest evidencing a serious attitude by the police may in some cases be counter-productive.[18] It may be, therefore, that the working group would benefit from rather more analysis of the available research, particularly in the United States of America, which might tend to suggest that in certain circumstances more assertive police responses may lead to further negative effects on the female victims/survivors.

Many more recommendations follow which focus on far more restrictive approaches to the perpetrators of domestic violence with regard to restrictions on bail and the imposition of conditions as well as the whole issue of speed in the process. A number of recommendations focused on the issue of the support of the witness/victim with regard to court facilities, providing a safe and supportive environment and encouraging voluntary organisations to assist and support victims at all stages of the process and particularly at court. It is suggested that the Crown Prosecution Service should only instruct barristers who are "aware of, and sympathetic to" the issues surrounding domestic violence. A number of issues currently surfacing for debate within the criminal justice system in England generally also appear in the form of recommendations made by the working group. Thus it is suggested that the Crown Prosecution Service should not accept a binding over without considering the wishes of victims and that compensation appears to be of little relevance or assistance in cases of domestic violence.

The group itself, however, identified as most important its recommendation that the local City Magistrates' Court should establish a monthly domestic violence court.[19] Further, the group emphasised their recommendation that the Domestic Violence Court should be staffed by clerks, prosecutors and ushers who are familiar with, and sympathetic to, issues surrounding domestic violence.[20] This relates well to the broad mission statement of the Domestic Violence Forum and, given the extreme difficulties experienced by women victims/survivors in the whole court process, is to be welcomed. Most women experience the criminal court process as intimidating, alienating and totally unsympathetic to their position. Clearly, the work of this working group and the major changes in attitudes and approaches to female victims/survivors is to be welcomed.

The prevailing view amongst women who had to experience the criminal justice system as victims/survivors is that it is a very male dominated process. This too can inhibit women from pursuing their actions through the criminal courts. In the particular city under scrutiny, the police force had only one Dedicated Domestic Violence Unit with specially trained female police officers. As has already been identified, the Forum was calling for more of such units to be provided. Nevertheless for many women their first source of help, having been subjected to male violence, is to be at the receiving end of a response from a male police officer. Male police officers generally tend to be sent in to respond to "domestics" because they may have to cope with physical assault themselves. The violence of the whole situation is thus reinforced and may lead to further violence.[21] There are still many more male than female solicitors in private practice and women victims/survivors may not feel that their male solicitors really take their cases as seriously as they might if they were the subject of stranger assaults. The court system is slow to respond to arguments for change and the predominance of male judges and male magistrates may present further problems for the victims/survivors. One notable omission from the recommendations of the working group is that the staff of the proposed new Domestic Violence Court should, as far as possible, be women and there is not even a suggestion that the bench of magistrates might perhaps be altered to include two women and one man, rather than three men or occasionally, two men and one woman. This is doubtless because the ratio of female to male magistrates on the adult panel is nothing like sufficient to produce the desired heavily female ratio. Whilst, however, the sorts of judicial attitudes evidenced by Marie Fox in her chapter continue to hit the headlines from time to time,[22] women will continue to have little faith in the capacity of judges and magistrates to respond in the appropriate way to the problems of victims/survivors of domestic violence.

CONCLUSION

The Domestic Violence Forum and the report of the working group on the criminal court process are clearly at early stages in their development. Nevertheless, the awareness across the whole of the Domestic Violence Forum and the enthusiasm and commitment demonstrated by the Forum and its various working groups are a major step forward. Similar groups elsewhere should be fostered and encouraged. Clearly, much work remains to be done,[23] not least in the area of seeking to reduce the level of domestic violence by changing public awareness and attitudes through programmes of public education. The Domestic Violence Forum in the city concerned has yet to establish its Education Working Group and yet, fundamentally, this must be seen as one of the most important areas of development. It is only by extensive education programmes aimed at the youngest of children as well as older children and adults, that we will achieve the eradication of this age old persecution of women by men.

NOTES

1.   The title of this chapter is of course intended to remind readers of the Department of Health Guidance on Inter-Agency Collaboration in the field of child protection entitled *Working Together* (1991).

2.   See M.Fox, "Legal Responses to Battered Women Who Kill" in this volume.

3.   By resorting to the inadequate remedies provided by the Domestic Violence and Matrimonial Proceedings Act 1976, ss.16-18 of the Domestic Proceedings Magistrates' Courts Act 1978, and the Matrimonial Homes Act 1987. It should of course be pointed out that the civil law

relating to domestic violence has been subject to considerable scrutiny and various proposals for reform identified. See, inter alia, J.Barron, *Not Worth the Paper...? The Effectiveness of Legal Protection for Women and Children Experiencing Domestic Violence* (1990); Victim Support/National Inter-Agency Working Party Report, *Domestic Violence* (1992); Law Commission Report No.207, *Domestic Violence and Occupation of the Family Home* (1992); The Home Affairs Committee, *Report on Domestic Violence: Minutes of Evidence* (1992).

4.   Through reporting offences to the police which may range in severity from breach of the peace through common assault, unlawful wounding under s.20 of the Offences Against the Person Act 1861, to wounding with intent under s.18 of the 1861 Act.

5.   The City Council concerned is Liverpool. This chapter is a tribute to the hard work, dedication and commitment demonstrated by all the members of the Liverpool Domestic Violence Forum and their Working Groups and particularly to the Reporters of the Civil and Criminal Working Group, Sharon Thompson, Senior Prosecutor with the Crown Prosecution Service, and Gerry H. White, Senior Probation Officer with Merseyside Probation Service. Acknowledgment must also be given to Ann Gegg, Divisional Service Manager with Liverpool Social Services, whose vision and enthusiasm has been a driving force for the Forum, and to Vic Citarella, Director of Social Services in Liverpool, for his support. The chapter is based on the work of the Forum mainly up to June 1994.

6.   See L.Bowker, *Beating Wife Beating* (1983).

7.   See M.P.Brygger and J.L.Edleson, "The Domestic Abuse Project: A Multi Systems Intervention in Woman Battering" 2 *Journal of Interpersonal Violence* 324.

8.   For explanations of the patriarchal model of family violence, see R.E.Dobash and R.Dobash, *Violence against Wives* (1979); M.Paglow, *Family Violence* (1984); K.Yllo, "Political and Methodological Debates in Wife Abuse Research" in *Feminist Perspectives on Wife Abuse*, eds. K.Yllo and M.Bograd (1988) 28.

9.   See L.E.Walker, *The Battered Woman* (1979).

10. M. Fox, *supra*, n.2.

11. R.J.Gelles, "Family Violence" in *Family Violence Prevention and Treatment*, eds. R.L.Hampton et al. (1993) 1.

12. R.J.Gelles and M.A.Strauss, *Intimate Violence* (1988).

13. R.J.Gelles, *supra*, n.11, at pp.17-18.

14. Attorney General's Task Force on Family Violence Final Report (1984). For a broadly comparable development in England and Wales see Home Office Circular (60/90), *Domestic Violence* (July 1990) which sets down guide-lines for the police to deal with domestic violence in the same way as violence between strangers. Chief Officers of Police were asked to ensure that all police officers involved in the investigation of cases of domestic violence regard as their overriding priority "the protection of the victim and the apprehension of the offender". To this end they were to be "made fully aware of their responsibility to respond as law enforcement officers to requests from victims for help and of their powers to take action in cases of violence." As to how little, in reality, this circular did effect a change in attitude at least amongst more senior and older police officers, it is interesting to note the comments

of Mr Pacey, the Chief Constable of Gloucestershire, giving evidence to the Home Affairs Committee on behalf of ACPO, when he contrasted domestic violence with "serious crimes like burglaries" (The Home Affairs Committee, *supra*, n.3, at p.9).

15.   Attorney General's Task Force, *ibid.*, at p.22.

16.   L.W.Sherman and R.A.Berk, "The Specific Deterrent Effects of Arrest for Domestic Assault" (1984) 49 *American Sociological Review* 261.

17.   *Thurman v City of Torrington* (1985) 595 F. Supp. 1521.

18.   See, for example, R.A.Berk et al., "The Deterrent Effect of Arrest: A Bayesian Analysis of Four Field Experiments" (1992) 57 *American Sociological Review* 698; L.W.Sherman and D.Smith, "Crime, Punishment and Stake in Conformity: Milwaukee and Omaha Experiments" (1992) 57 *American Sociological Review* 680.

19.   Recommendation No.28.

20.   Recommendation No.29.

21.   For a more detailed analysis of the difficulties, see J.Hanmer, "Women and Policing in Britain" in *Women, Policing and Male Violence: International Perspectives*, eds. J.Hanmer et al. (1989) 90; T.Faragher, "The Police Response to Violence against Women in the Home" in *Private Violence and Public Policy*, ed. J.Paul (1985) 121.

22.   M. Fox, *supra*, n.2.

23.   Further work is also necessary on aspects of domestic violence not addressed in this chapter. For example, given the author's own particular parallel subject interest, it is necessary to consider that the male abuser has often been an abused child himself. As Alice Miller points out "people whose integrity has not been damaged in childhood ... will feel no need to harm another person or themselves" (A.Miller, *For your Own Good - The Roots of Violence in Child Rearing* (1987)).

10 Images of Women: Sentencing in Sexual Assault Cases in Scotland

SUSAN R. MOODY

On Wednesday, two of those unfortunate women who have abandoned all principle, industry, and shame, and two rather decent-looking men were charged with being drunk, disorderly, and disturbing the audience in the theatre on the preceding evening. One of the women kept down her veil, and seemed to feel some compunctious visitings of feeling; but the other ... dashed her veil aside, giggled, rolled her 'gooseberry eyes' and brazened out the whole trial with 'matchless intrepidity of face'. The young men admitted they had acted imprudently, and threw themselves on the lenity of the court ... both females were ordered to be detained till they found security to the amount of £5 for their future good behaviour.[1]

This image of women is a familiar one to students of criminology, depicting behaviour which represents a radical departure from the demeanour expected of women, both in public and before the court. The newspaper account echoes the disgust and revulsion that all right thinking people should feel when members of the female sex disgrace their womanhood. This attitude is not one which is purely of historical interest nor is it confined to women who commit crimes.

The last twenty-five years have seen the issue of gender emerge from the shadows and command a key position in the study of criminology and criminal justice. The pioneering work of Heidensohn[2] and Smart[3] in the United Kingdom, Chesney-Lind[4] and Klein[5] in the United States and Scutt[6] in Australia alerted criminologists to this previously neglected area. Feminist critiques of law revealed courts as "reflexive institutions in the active reaffirmation and reproduction of sexual division".[7] Empirical studies by, for instance, Carlen,[8] Eaton[9] and Worrall,[10] have provided detailed evidence not only that female offenders are treated differently from males but also that stereotyping of "good" and "bad" women by police, prosecutors, lawyers and magistrates is commonplace. "Bad" women have both transgressed the criminal law and abjured the feminine virtues of maternalism, submissiveness and self-effacement.

Research on sentencing of female offenders[11] shows that certain factors influence sentences in the case of women which do not affect the sentences given to men.[12] While this may lead to more lenient sentences overall[13] it can also result in greater severity where female offenders do not conform to the judiciary's image of respectable women.[14] "Alongside the witch the whore is the most potent image of female deviance."[15]   The key factor appears to be whether female offenders are "good" wives and mothers.   Donzelot's studies of the family demonstrate how the role of "mother" is the key socialising and controlling agent employed by the State to impose discipline.[16]   Any departure from this social ordering is therefore dangerous since "womanliness must never be out of mind, if masculine rule is to be kept intact."[17]   This is particularly important within the criminal justice process where law seeks to punish disorder.

Studies of rape and sexual assault cases[18] illustrate that the same stereotype of witch/whore is applied to the conduct of the victim before and during the trial, in spite of legislative provisions designed to prevent the admission of evidence about the complainer's previous sexual history.[19]   David Weisstub vividly describes the "legal mythos" surrounding the female victim, who is both the victim of others and the victim of her own weakwilled, hysterical and easily tempted nature, which lacks the essentially male virtue of rationality to control it.   In recognising her as a victim of crime we are also acknowledging her as a "criminal" victim who must be protected above all from herself.   The result is:

> to victimize her doubly, to pity her and to protect her from her tempestuous and irrational persona. Beguiling Eve is the mainstay of our Western psyche.[20]

It is not surprising, therefore, that, according to one writer, "the rape trial distils all of the problems that feminists have identified in relation to law".[21]

It hardly seems necessary to repeat such well-established conclusions about female stereotyping within the criminal justice system.   However, for the purpose of this chapter it is important to do so because of the striking contrast between the image of woman which colours the progress and outcome of sexual assaults before conviction and the female stereotypes which appear to be significant at the stage of sentencing in such cases.   Unlike the earlier part of the proceedings, where the complainer is often the only corroborating witness and therefore provides a central focus both for the prosecution and the defence case, at the sentencing stage she becomes the "absent" woman. This may be ascribed to a general sentencing policy in which the victim's role is unrecognised[22] but it is particularly stark in sexual assault cases involving women.

However, it would be wrong to conclude that judges do not have powerful female icons which are invoked when sentencing offenders in sexual assault cases. The wronged woman, the wounded woman, the weak woman and the wifely woman all feature in the images of women which people the case reports. This chapter is concerned with a description and analysis of these images, based on a sample of Scottish appeal cases[23] and newspaper reports.[24] My aim in this research is to examine images of women as they are revealed in sentencing in sexual assault cases.

SEXUAL ASSAULT: PRELIMINARY ISSUES

The definition of sexual assault in Scots law is important both because it sets the parameters for this study and because it anticipates some of the judicial assumptions about sexual assault which are likely to be reflected in sentencing. The official classification of crimes in Scotland categorises sexual offences under a separate category of "crimes of indecency", and defines sexual assault as rape, assault with intent to rape and indecent assault. In Scotland rape and assault with intent to rape[25] can only be committed by a male person on a female although a woman can be charged with indecent assault as can one man on another.[26] The phallocentric nature of these crimes is even more marked in the description of the crime of rape which must include penetration of the vagina by the penis. The unique nature of rape is intimately bound up with the regulation of reproduction and the control of female sexuality[27] so that special significance is given to penetration of the female body which may result in pregnancy. Rape in Scots law is "predicated uniquely on a social interpretation of physical capability".[28]

Undoubtedly there is merit in recognising that rape represents a particularly stark example of the exploitation of women by men and should not be gender neutralised. However, a broader definition of the crime of rape may be helpful in avoiding the danger of over-concentration on the mode of committing the offence rather than its meaning and impact.[29] For a woman the method by which such intrusion is achieved may not be the determining factor either in her interpretation of the act or its effects. A wider interpretation of assault would also provide a better reflection of the reality of sexual assault for women. A recent commentator on sexual offences in Scotland considers the problems in the current definition of rape and points to the need for change in defining this crime. He defines sexual assaults as "the actual or intended violation of the victim's sexual integrity".[30] Liz Kelly adds the important element of meaning in her definition:

> any physical, visual, verbal or sexual act that is experienced by the woman or girl, at the time or later, as a threat, invasion or assault, that has the effect of degrading or hurting her and/or takes away her ability to control intimate contact.[31]

Although Scots law adopts a fairly restrictive definition of rape, the narrative of charges in a sexual assault case may be very detailed, lending itself to amendment and deletion through plea-negotiation. A complainer may allege rape, an accused may be charged with rape, the indictment may contain specific reference to the elements required to prove rape but the conviction may be for an indecent assault, not infrequently one which is relatively minor.

Apart from the key issue of gender, which, in contrast to other crimes, is an integral element in the definition of sexual assaults against women, the other significant feature of such cases is the medicalisation of sexual offenders. Whereas in other areas of criminality it would be thought ridiculous to focus solely on individual pathology as the impetus for crime (and this would certainly be the case in the vast majority of non-sexual assaults) the legacy of Freud and positivist theories of crime causation continue to have a significant effect on judicial attitudes to sexual assaults.[32] In spite of the fact that the overwhelming body of research on sex offenders suggests that the majority are not suffering from mental abnormality the myth persists.[33] One psycho-analytical textbook confidently states that:

> rape and sexual assault are committed because the urge cannot be resisted - they are compulsive acts, arising from an unconscious autonomous complex. The act itself is not always spontaneous and unpremeditated but the urge comes up spontaneously and cannot be assuaged.[34]

The pathologising of the offender in such cases has the double bind of excusing his behaviour, with such diagnoses as "uncontrollable sexual urges" "hormone imbalance producing abnormal sexual drive", and putting the spotlight on the woman and her body. By reducing women to their sexual parts a spurious legal and medical neutrality is invoked masking the fact that:

> [t]he rape trial is a quintessential moment in which law provides a specific meaning to women's bodies, reproducing cultural beliefs about female sexuality, but also constructing its own legal lexicon of the female body and rehearsing its own very powerful mode of disqualification.[35]

THE PROCESSING OF SEXUAL ASSAULT CASES

Women provide not only the occasion of sin but also the justification for it. The result for the processing of sexual assaults involving attacks by men against women is that a large number of cases are never reported. It is estimated that no more than one in ten sexual assaults are reported to the police and that rape has the lowest reporting rate of any serious crime.[36] Women fear the secondary victimisation which so often appears to accompany the reporting of sexual assaults. In Scotland Rape Crisis Centres have documented that the majority of women who approach them have not reported the matter to the police.[37] Efforts have been made to encourage more women to report such cases. For instance, all but one of the eight Scottish Police Forces have established Female and Child Units to deal inter alia with complainers in sexual assaults. The police officers staffing these units receive special training and most have developed good working relationships with local Rape Crisis Centres and Victim Support Schemes, something which would have been unthinkable ten years ago.[38] However, though there is a marked upward trend in the number of cases reported to the police, from 823 in 1972 to 1604 in 1992, this is in fact lower than the increase in recorded crime generally which over the same twenty year period almost trebled.[39] Victim surveys consistently show that reported rapes represent a tiny minority of the real rate of serious sexual assaults on women.[40]

Once sexual assaults are reported they enjoy the dubious reputation of having the highest attrition rate of any crime. The research conducted by Chambers and Millar in 1981, which for the first time in the United Kingdom followed through a sample of sexual assault cases from initial reporting to final outcome, documents the drop-out rate between reporting and conviction.[41] Of 196 cases of rape and assault with intent to ravish reported to the police between 1980 and 1981, less than half, eighty-seven, were proceeded against and fifty-seven of those trials resulted in a conviction. The main reasons for the high attrition rate, according to Chambers and Millar, were "no-criming" by the police, the prosecutor's decision not to proceed, the abandonment of proceedings during the course of the trial or acquittal. In 1981 a well-documented case highlighted the stringent tests applied by prosecutors to sexual assault cases in Scotland.[42] A combination of alleged lack of corroborating evidence, concern about consent and a desire to "protect" the complainer led the prosecution authorities to abandon the prosecution.[43]

Since that time improvements have been made by police forces and the prosecution services in the processing of sexual assault cases and an important legislative change has been introduced into Scottish criminal procedure with the intention of benefiting the complainer in sexual assault cases. This provision bars the use of sexual character or sexual history evidence which was so frequently prayed in aid by the defence to impugn the chief prosecution witness, the complainer.[44] These provisions are similar though not identical to the Sexual Offences (Amendment) Act 1976, governing England and Wales. However, research into the effectiveness of this prohibition has shown that it has enjoyed limited success only.[45] It appears that such evidence is either introduced by asking the court to waive the prohibition as permitted under the open-ended and highly discretionary exceptions set down in the legislation (including, for instance, that great catch-all "in the interests of justice") or the defence manage to by-pass the statutory requirements and bring in previous sexual history in defiance of parliament's intention.

The Crown is likely to experience other difficulties in prosecuting sexual assaults. Corroboration is a requirement for establishing guilt in all criminal cases in Scotland unless specifically excluded by statute. This bites particularly deeply in sexual assaults where it is unlikely that, for example, other witnesses will be present. The reaction of many women is to eradicate material evidence, such as semen or blood, and there may be little or no evidence of force. The absence of consent is also crucial to a successful prosecution for any sexual assault. In Scotland the charge of rape is framed according to the rather quaint nineteenth century formulation "overcoming her will" and the Crown is required to prove this. Scots law appears now to be in line with the position in England and Wales following *Morgan*[46] so that the accused's belief in the complainer's consent, even though unreasonable, may result in an acquittal, provided that his belief was genuine.[47]

It is not surprising, given these difficulties, that the likelihood of a conviction in a case of sexual assault is significantly lower than for other crimes. According to Scottish Office statistics in 1992 about one in eight sexual assaults reported to the police resulted in criminal proceedings compared with one in four crimes generally.[48] Such restrictions undoubtedly result in a skewed sample of cases for which convictions are obtained, containing incidents which conform closely to the stereotypical image of sexual assaults involving blameless victims.

However, it would be wrong to conclude that there have been no significant shifts in judicial thinking over the last decade. Ostensibly the most important development has been in relation to marital rape. Traditionally rape was not a crime which could be committed by a husband on a wife, unless the incident took place after the couple had been divorced or legally separated.[49] Yet research suggests that rape within marriage is widespread, perhaps involving one in seven married women at some time during their married lives.[50] Three key Scottish cases were instrumental in fundamentally altering that judicial perception. They have been hailed as shining examples of the ability of Scots law to move with the times and to accommodate social changes through judicial decision-making rather than legislative provision. (This contrasted with the situation in England and Wales where it was not until 1991 that marital rape was recognised as a crime.[51]) In *Duffy*[52] and *Paxton*[53] the parties were living apart at the time the alleged rape took place but their separation was de facto and not de jure. In the landmark case of *Stallard*[54] the parties were cohabiting. The High Court permitted the trial to proceed in all three cases on the basis that the complainer had suffered an assault in each case and that the law must provide a remedy for that. To find a justification for decontextualising sexual penetration from the marriage bond the bench effectively desexualised the crime of rape. The Lord Justice-General appears to have expressed the views of his fellow judges as well as himself when he stated that "rape has always been essentially a crime of violence and indeed no more than an aggravated assault". The evidence suggests that physical violence beyond anything required for penetration was present in each of these cases. This reclassification enabled the judges to move away from the minefield of heterosexual mores to the more familiar and comfortable ground of the use of force. However, the juries did not find it so easy to shrug off the particular context in which the alleged offences took place and failed to return a "guilty" verdict in any of these cases.

This review provides the backdrop to a consideration of sentencing in sexual assault cases. But before such cases are analysed and the images of women presented in them are explored it is important to consider how judges make sentencing decisions in Scotland.

SENTENCING IN SCOTLAND

[I]t is, I think, of prime importance that sentences passed should not be so far out of touch with the expectations of ordinary law-abiding citizens as to create discontent. However forward thinking the penologists, criminologists and bureaucrats in government departments may be, their views should not be allowed to prevail so as to impose a sentencing regime which is incomprehensible or unacceptable to right-thinking people generally.[55]

The Lord Chief Justice's remarks to a Scottish audience were made shortly before sentencing in sexual assault cases in Scotland became the subject, for the first time, of public debate, when Judy, the victim of a violent sexual attack, chose the Conservative Party Conference as the venue for criticising the decision of the Appeal Court in relation to her case.[56]

According to one commentator, Lord Taylor considered that "major reform of sentencing practice should be resisted in Scotland because it would interfere with essential judicial discretion".[57] As the leading textbook on sentencing reveals,[58] judges in Scotland enjoy far more unfettered discretion than their English counterparts.[59] Appeals against sentence, for instance, rarely involve detailed case-by-case analysis or appeals to precedent.[60] Indeed, the High Court has sought to discourage Sheriffs from drawing on similar cases in their sentencing decisions. The High Court does not offer general guide-lines for judges to apply in relation to particular types of offences. The limits on sentencers' discretion in Scotland derive from the jurisdiction of the particular court, the penalties prescribed in legislation for specific offences and some general legislative provisions.

In relation to those offences which form the subject-matter of this article - rape, assault with intent to rape and indecent assault - there are no statutory penalties since these are all offences at Common Law[61] and the High Court is competent to try any of these crimes. Rape as a Plea of the Crown can only be tried in the High Court which can impose any sentence up to life imprisonment. The Sheriff Court, sitting as a court of solemn procedure with a jury, can impose a custodial sentence of up to two years imprisonment or an unlimited fine. If the sheriff regards these powers as inadequate in indictment cases the case may be remitted to the High Court for sentence. On summary procedure when the sheriff sits alone the maximum custodial sentence is three months and the maximum fine (where this is not prescribed by statute) is £1,000. In addition sentencers in all courts are required to secure a Social Background Report when the offender is either under twenty-one[62] or has not previously served time in custody[63] and it appears that a custodial sentence may be the appropriate penalty. Accused persons who are not legally represented must be informed of their right to apply for legal aid before a custodial sentence can be passed.[64]

A clear preference has been expressed by the High Court, both in sentencing appeals[65] and extra-judicially,[66] for an individualised approach to sentencing. Recent research on sentencing by sheriffs appears to have confirmed the impression that sentences vary considerably between different sheriffdoms and has emphasised the need for more information for sentencers.[67] It has been agreed that a database should be established to supply information on similar cases. However, this will not lay down guide-lines or express principles to be followed in sentencing so that the ways in which Scottish judges choose to exercise their discretion at the sentencing stage are likely to remain unclear. Occasionally, judges do make the rationale underlying their decisions explicit (as in a recent case of a woman convicted of "plagium" or child-stealing[68]) but this is rare. Instead, uncertainty in sentencing is likely to be managed through "patterned responses", which depend on the application of stereotypes, including assumptions based on gender.[69]

It is interesting to apply to the Scottish sentencing system the three factors presented by Mossman[70] as central to the construction of legal knowledge: defining boundaries, prescribing relevance and drawing analogies. This framework excludes the subjective nature of experience, limits the nature of evidence and uses precedent to outlaw alternative perspectives. However, none of them apparently apply to Scottish criminal procedure after conviction. Pleas in mitigation, background reports and the judge's decisions on the appropriate sentence contain precisely that information which is out-of-bounds before conviction. Precedents are rarely cited and, at least in theory, significant opportunities are given for subjective accounts to be given. While in Frankel's terms sentencing may be a "wasteland of the law" it does offer opportunities for individualised decision-making which are not present in any other part of the criminal justice system.[71]

In relation to sexual assaults Scottish courts have taken note of factors similar to those laid down in the guide-lines issued by the English Court of Appeal in rape cases.[72] For instance, Chambers and Millar point to previous convictions and excessive use of force including a weapon as aggravating factors in sexual assault cases.[73] Although judgments in Scottish cases are much terser and less developed, the starting point of five years in a rape case is seen by the judiciary and commentators as the appropriate figure in Scotland and in England and Wales.[74] Recent research suggests that there are marked similarities in outcome between the two jurisdictions.[75]

As a general rule Scottish courts have refused to countenance any discount for a guilty plea following the case of *Strawhorn v. McLeod*,[76] regarding it as an "irrelevant consideration" in sentencing which restricts the judge's discretion and is objectionable in principle. However, in practice it is clear that pleas of guilty are frequently offered in the hope that, by sparing distress to witnesses, the offender will be given a lighter sentence and this is frequently used as a plea in mitigation.[77]

Statistical analysis shows that both the likelihood of a custodial sentence and the length of that sentence have increased over the last twenty years. In 1973, for instance, forty per cent of sexual assaults tried in Scottish courts resulted in a term of imprisonment or detention. By 1992 this figure had increased to fifty-two per cent.[78] Unlike the trends in relation to reported crime this is a greater increase than that for crimes generally over the period. It is more difficult to obtain information on the length of sentence but a comparison with figures collected by Chambers and Millar for 1981 and unpublished material[79] shows a marked increase in sentence length. Nevertheless, only about fifty per cent of offenders convicted of rape between 1986 and 1991 received a custodial sentence of five years or more.

A recent Scottish Office report has accepted that "there may be public concern about the leniency of sentences imposed for some serious crimes. Rape and sexual assault are the crimes most frequently cited in this latter context."[80] This concern has received extensive coverage in Scotland recently as the result of the "Judy" case, where the victim became the focus of both government and media attention. Her views were sought by the Press on the outcome of subsequent cases, she featured in several television reports and she was invited to join the Scottish Crime Prevention Council.[81] It is clear that the five year norm for rape laid down in *Billam*[82] is not being implemented in over a third of all rape cases.[83]

IMAGES OF WOMEN

> Femininity is routinely constituted within a number of discourses which circumscribe not only a woman's behaviour but also the images which she has of herself and her relationships with other people.[84]

An impassioned debate is taking place within feminist discourse, a "contest over knowledge",[85] about the interpretation of female experience within criminal law and practice. First, there is concern about the masculinisation of domestic violence and sexual assault, where a predominantly male judiciary applies the standard of the reasonable man to events which are grounded in gender relationships. Provocation provides a good example of such reasoning and this is particularly so in Scotland, where judges have steadfastly refused to abandon the traditional requirements of immediate response in hot blood to manifest physical violence.[86] The definition of the defence of provocation laid down by Hume in 1797 is still the prevailing one. It must involve "a sudden impulse of resentment" in response to provocation "suffered upon the spot".[87] While the Scottish judiciary are willing to accept rape within marriage they are not prepared to acknowledge the very real difficulty which female partners may experience in responding directly and contemporaneously to violence. This apparent paradox is in fact perfectly logical since the underlying rationale in both cases is that marital rape is an aggravated form of assault and should be treated in the same way as the majority of assaults processed by the courts, which take place between males. Power imbalances between men and women and in particular between male and female cohabitants are thereby removed from consideration and the focus is on the conventional approach to defences in cases of violent crime.[88] The political becomes privatised and loses its sting, collective experiences are personalised and lose their power.

Second, there is conflict within the feminist arena itself about the appropriateness of universalising women's experiences. The influential French psychoanalyst, Luce Irigaray, while recognising that women do not constitute a "class" and that their demands may be contradictory, nevertheless considers that:

> [t]he first issue facing liberation movements is that of making each woman 'conscious' of the fact that what she has felt in her personal experience is a condition shared by all women, thus *allowing that experience to be politicized*.[89]

On the other hand, Jackson[90] and others have argued strongly that this kind of feminist discourse is imperialistic, seeking to impose on very diverse groups and individuals a monolithic view of reaction and experience. Black women, women with disabilities, women living in rural areas, working-class women become invisible. Instead an educated, urban, middle-class, white elite determine and control the definition of women. In effect, domination by men is replaced with domination by a small but powerful group of women. While the female stereotypes designed by the law and by feminism are radically different they nevertheless both deny the individual experience of women. Legal discourse itself polarises and creates false opposites, "binary divisions" of male and female, guilty and not guilty. The images of women portrayed in the sentencing of sex offenders reflect this binary division, producing at best oversimplistic generalisations and at worst crude caricatures of women's experiences of sexual assault.

1. The wronged woman

Traditionally in sexual assault cases sentences have reflected the prevailing attitude among the judiciary towards acceptable behaviour in heterosexual relationships and also their assessment of the impact of the sexual assault on the woman. Yet increasingly reported incidents of rape involve acquaintances or even intimates.[91] The "commonsense view" that rape by strangers is more painful to women is not universally supported by research findings. Indeed some studies consider that the more intimately acquainted the victim is with the offender the more painful the impact.[92] According to Home Office studies, the closer the relationship between offender and victim the shorter the sentence.[93] Research in Scotland supports this.[94] The sample of 1992 cases broadly reflects this with longer sentences being imposed in cases involving strangers. However, some interesting variations from this pattern emerge which suggest that changes in the status of women may have had an impact on judicial attitudes.

First the image of women within marriage appears to have changed dramatically over the last ten years. The traditional notion that a married woman could not be raped by her husband, which has held sway in most Western jurisdictions for centuries, was overturned in Scotland by the trio of cases already discussed.[95] However, the impact of such a relationship on the sentence was not tested in any of those cases because the outcome was either a not guilty or a not proven verdict. Indeed one of the High Court judges was at pains to point out that a wife could still forgive her husband and that that should have an effect both on culpability and on sentence.

> Our decision does not deprive a wife of the right to forgive or to tolerate or to change her mind. If a wife does change her mind after complaining of rape to the criminal authorities there is little doubt that a prosecution of her husband would not be insisted upon.[96]

The sample of cases analysed in this chapter included four instances of sexual assault either within marriage or where a couple was cohabiting. Four years was held to be the appropriate sentence for rape by a former cohabitant on the mother of his daughter,[97] even though she did not wish to bring the case to court. Lord Prosser indicated that, while it was right to take the victim's view into account, the offender's behaviour had been "vicious" and involved serious non-sexual assault also. The case of *X v H.M.Advocate*[98] involved an estranged husband, the father of the victim's children. The "normal" sentence for rape, five years, was not considered excessive by the Appeal Court, which supported the trial judge's obiter remarks that "no man can rape a woman with impunity no matter what relationship exists between them".[99] In *Campbell* several charges of rape against cohabitants resulted in a sentence of nine years, in spite of the fact that the cohabitants resumed living with the offender after each had been raped.[100] The Appeal Court clearly did not take the view in these cases that either forgiveness or resumption of cohabitation after the crime merited a lighter sentence. In *S v H.M.Advocate*[101] the court went even further. Here a sentence of two years six months for assault with intent to rape was appealed on the grounds that the offender had desisted when requested by his wife to do so and that the relationship was continuing. While the trial judge considered "on reflection" that the sentence was unduly severe this view was not shared by the Appeal Court bench which upheld the sentence.

While these cases are important it would be wrong to assume that they reflect an acceptance on the part of the judiciary that non-consensual sexual intercourse between husband and wife or cohabitants is equivalent to the crime of rape. In each the court was quick to point out that the incidents showed extreme physical violence. The issue was not so much the right of a wife or cohabitant to refuse intercourse, rather a reinterpretation of the offending behaviour as a serious assault which happened to be perpetrated as part of a sexual encounter. This desexualising of rape provides a useful way of bringing an otherwise ambiguous area into safe waters, equating the criminal behaviour with the numerous physical assaults committed by males on males. This is not to deny that the wife and the cohabitant have both benefited from this development but to advise against unreserved enthusiasm. In effect, the raped wife or cohabitant is replaced by the male victim of assault and the uncomfortable connotations of sexuality and male-female exploitation are thereby lost. It remains to be seen whether "normal" sexual intercourse will be viewed in the same light.

Some developments can also be seen in other relationships between rape victims and offenders outside cohabitation. The court seem to have acknowledged that a prior relationship between the parties is not automatically a mitigating factor in sentencing. Thus in *Stewart* where a divorcee was raped after she accepted a lift from a man she met at a casino a sentence of five years was imposed.[102] (It should be noted, however, that the offence was accompanied by extreme extraneous violence and that the victim had thirteen injuries when medically examined, including a black eye and internal bleeding.) Where a young man raped an eighteen year-old at a birthday party after asking her outside four years in prison was regarded as the appropriate sentence even though the offender was under twenty-one and had no previous convictions.[103]

Cases which the defence portray as "ambiguous" may nevertheless be regarded by the court as matters meriting a custodial sentence. For instance, where the victim had had sex willingly with another party in the offender's flat and the offender then raped her anything less than five years was seen as inadequate.[104] The offender's plea of "no real injury" was rejected. However, the court was at pains to note that the victim had not encouraged or contributed to the offence. In *MacKinnon* the victim had been staying with the offender but they had had no prior sexual relationship. She got into bed with him to keep warm and was then subjected to attempted rape. Twelve months was held not to be excessive.[105] In none of these cases did the court accept that there had been any previous sexual connection between the parties. The women were viewed as "wronged" and therefore deserving of the court's protection.

The final area which appears to have been opened up by recent cases is sexual assault at work. The case of *Caring*, for instance, where an employer was prosecuted for a series of indecent assaults against his female employees over several months, resulted in a custodial conviction of nine months even though the accused had no previous convictions.[106]

2. The wounded woman

> 'True' rape in popular imagination involves the use of weapons, the infliction of serious injury and occurs in a lonely place late at night ... the 'true' rape victim was not voluntarily in the place where the rape took place, fought to the end and has bruises to show for it.[107]

The importance of violence is not only central to the definition of sexual assault but also of immense practical and symbolic significance to female victims.

> According to the criminal justice system rape, in and of itself, does not necessarily warrant a heavy sentence; it is the use of other coercive acts which contribute to sentencing decisions.[108]

The absence of signs of physical force may make corroboration of the sexual assault more difficult and encourage prosecutors not to proceed. Clear evidence of force extraneous to the sexual assault serves to undermine the so-called "rape myths":

> It is hard to imagine that a woman could enjoy being raped, when, in about 80 per cent of the cases, it involves some form of physical violence ... [M]ost of the rape victims were subjected to at least minor violence, half were threatened with physical harm, and a third received some form of injury ... [T]o the woman involved, the attack might justifiably be seen as a *life-threatening* situation.[109]

In certain jurisdictions, such as Canada, rape is no longer defined as a gender-specific crime and can be committed by a person of either sex on a person of either sex. The essence of the new crime of rape in the Canadian Criminal Code is that it is graded according to the degree of physical violence used.[110] According to psychological studies this is more likely to encourage juries to see the victim as blameless, unlike the position where rape is conceptualised as a sexual act.[111]

In the 1970s feminists sought to establish sexual assaults against women and rape in particular as crimes of violence and thus to liberate them from undesirable associations with female sexuality. Brownmiller's definition of rape as "a conscious process of intimidation by which all men keep all women in a state of fear"[112] is the most potent example and may have been influential in modifying the legal and public view of rape. From a very different perspective Foucault[113] also recommended the desexualisation of rape as part of his general enterprise to deconstruct sexuality. However, this approach may prove counterproductive, and writers like MacKinnon have argued strongly against it.[114]

> To reject forced sex in the name of women's point of view requires an account of women's experience of being violated by the same acts both sexes have learnt as natural and fulfilling and erotic.[115]

Recent research suggests that male rape produces just as traumatic effects on its male victims as heterosexual rape does on female survivors.[116] However, on a social and political level sexual assaults on women constitute something more than individual experience of pathological criminality. They are rooted in the structure of power relations between men and women, in which female sexuality is denied autonomy. It appears from research studies that men see violence and intimacy as closely intertwined.[117] Violence can be sexually stimulating and/or it can be a route to obtaining sex.[118] As Kelly has shown, rape and other forms of sexual assault fall along a continuum which also encompasses so-called "normal" heterosexual behaviour.[119] It is not necessary to accept MacKinnon's elision of the differences between rape and heterosexual intercourse in order to acknowledge that male sexuality presents a problem for women and is central to our understanding of sexual assaults committed by men against women.[120]

Definitions of violence may also present problems for women who have been sexually assaulted. Scots criminal law retains a notion of violence which is derived from the culture of the late eighteenth century. It focuses on overt actions or immediate threats of physical strength. It omits power imbalances between parties in a violent confrontation and neglects the very real possibility of different meanings and perceptions of violence, particularly for women.

Research has suggested that sexual assaults involving extreme physical violence may be more easily dealt with by the victim than assaults where the behaviour is less obviously violent and more ambiguous. Victims may find it difficult to segregate themselves from the latter type of incident and to bracket it off from their everyday lives. It is clear from the level of sexual harassment in society that such ambiguous events are commonplace. For the victim the choice is a stark one "either she suffers the trauma of a brutal rape or she is accused of complicity if she does not".[121]

Within the sample cases, those attracting longer sentences frequently involved acts of physical violence in addition to the sexual assault itself, including threats to use, or the use of, a weapon, usually a knife. In one case the indictment describes how the accused jumped on the victim and seized her by the throat, threatening to kill her if she did not do as he wished.[122] His appeal against an eight year sentence for rape was dismissed. In another case a sentence of ten years imprisonment for attempted rape was upheld where the offender had threatened the victim with violence and "place[d] her in such a state of fear and alarm for her safety that she was unable to resist".[123] The offender's appeal against a five year sentence was dismissed where he had induced the victim at knife-point to accompany him into woods and had then committed an indecent assault on her.[124] Eighteen months was not regarded as an excessive sentence in a case of indecent assault where the offender had torn the victim's blouse, causing bruising and lacerations.[125]

Conversely in several cases the defence sought to rely on the absence of physical injury, the fact that no weapon was used or that the victim suffered no serious physical damage as mitigating factors.[126] With a few notable exceptions[127] no attempt was made by either the prosecutor or the judge to explore the victim's understanding of violent behaviour.[128] Instead physical violence was seen as particularly malign and damaging, in line with Scots legal tradition and their own male perceptions.

3. The weak woman

"Woman is delicate, soft, submissive, dependent and virtuous ... man is strong, competent, courageous and protective towards her."[129] This image of woman is intimately bound up with the ethics of chivalry on the one hand and the rule of male dominance on the other. It was used to justify the exclusion of women from public life in Victorian times[130] and to assert a husband's right to chastise his wife.[131] It is particularly pertinent still in the field of sexual assault against women, as Catharine MacKinnon explains:

> Vulnerability means the appearance/reality of easy sexual access; passivity means receptivity and disabled resistance enforced by trained physical weakness; softness means pregnability by something hard.[132]

The image of the weak woman also dovetails neatly with the passive victim, a stereotype fostered not only by influential victimologists but also by practitioners.[133] However, this is not a blanket description which can be applied to all women. It does not, for instance, cover prostitutes or women who exist independently from men but rather "the chaste matron and the virgin spinster, their own or their peers' wives and daughters".[134] It is inextricably linked to the "ideology of familialism which construes [particular classes of] women as legitimate objects of 'husbandly' respect, pity, and protection".[135] The converse of protection is submission and women who choose not to submit lose the benefits of such protection.

It is clear from the sample that the courts are particularly keen to protect the elderly, the young and the respectable from the depredations of men. Assaults on defenceless old ladies,[136] innocent young women[137] and respectable wives and mothers[138] tend to attract the more severe sentences. The courts also consider that men occupying positions of "trust", on whom women must depend, such as taxi-drivers and doctors, should be punished more severely.[139] Contrary to all the statistical evidence which suggests that women are most likely to be assaulted by acquaintances or intimates in their own homes, judges seek to shield women from attacks in public places or after forced entry to the victim's home. Two cases which illustrate these points and which were featured many time in press coverage of sexual assaults merit further consideration.

Judy, a mother of three and an active campaigner for the Scottish Conservative Party was attacked and robbed in her home by a man who posed as a priest. He struck her with a poker, punched her repeatedly and committed a series of sexual assaults on her. The trial judge imposed a sentence of life imprisonment for the protection of the public but this was overturned on appeal and replaced by a six year custodial sentence on the grounds that the accused was not a danger to the public. Nevertheless, the court had in fact imposed a longer sentence than the average of five years which might have been expected. Lord Cowie noted that the court was influenced, inter alia, by the "nature and circumstances of the indecent assault".[140] Here was a woman who represented many other women deserving of the law's protection. "Judy", the victim, courageously expressed her concern about several aspects of the case through the media. In one newspaper article she reflects back to the judges the image of the woman in need of protection by asking whether "these three judges [would] be happy to leave their wives and daughters in a room with Cronin".[141]

The other victim of sexual assault who figured prominently in media coverage over the period of the research was a sixteen year-old girl who was raped by a man almost twice her age whom she did not know. She had been a virgin and the assault had been discovered when her mother read her diary. Her parents reported the matter to the police and the accused, a well-known local restauranteur, was convicted. His Counsel sought to influence the sentence by claiming that this "prepossessing young woman showed all the signs of being able to put this behind her and lead a life without the kind of mark that certain other victims of rape might suffer".[142] Both the trial judge and the Appeal Court refused to accept that submission and jailed the accused for five years. Lord Milligan, the trial judge, noted particularly the age of the girl and implicitly suggested that the sentence would have been longer had it not been for the fact that the accused had no previous convictions.[143]

4. The wifely woman

An interesting and somewhat paradoxical image of woman which is introduced by the defence in many pleas in mitigation and in appeals against sentence generally is the supporting, controlling influence which "good" wives, cohabitants or mothers may exert on wayward men. This is a particularly powerful image in sexual assault cases presenting women as the rescuers of men from themselves, providing women with a redeeming role in taming male sexuality. For example, in *Martin*[144] the fact that the accused had been living with a woman for three years was noted as a factor which should be set against the sentence of ten years for rape which had been imposed at first instance. Again in *Doherty*[145] the defence noted that the accused was married and the father of a child.[146] In an unusual twist, the defence in *Townsley*[147] referred to the appellant's family circumstances, emphasising that a baby would be shortly born to his wife following artificial insemination and that she was "looking forward to setting up a family unit with the appellant again many years hence in spite of all he [had] done in the past".[148] Where the female partner had at first reacted unfavourably to the accused's conduct but they were subsequently reconciled the defence considered that this should be brought to the court's attention.[149] Conversely, in several cases the defence appeared to suggest that the failure of a wife to play her wifely role contributed to the commission of the indecent assault since the couples had been temporarily separated at the time.[150]

GIVING WOMEN A VOICE

The images described in this chapter are not simply of academic interest. They help to inform and shape decisions made by judges about sentencing in sexual assault cases. They also obscure, distort and replace the descriptions which individual women themselves might otherwise present of their experiences. Such powerful stereotypes may exacerbate the difficulties which many women already have in making their own assessment, in trusting their own being.[151] Within the court many groups have problems in articulating their experience because of the hierarchy of discourses which elevates one discourse and disqualifies others. Women are likely to be doubly disadvantaged in this situation.[152]

Attempts to develop criteria for harmfulness in criminal law have not dealt adequately with the safeguarding of the interests of different groups. Instead, the courts impose a particular worldview, based on notions of harm derived from a male, white elite. Attempts have been made to develop standard ratings for quality of life which could be applied in sentencing but these are still in their infancy.[153] In any case fears have already been expressed in Scotland by both the judiciary and the Lord Advocate about the role of the victim in sentencing.[154] Sentencing policy continues to be based on "the judge's assessment of what is appropriate in the interests of punishment and general deterrence in respect of the offence".[155] It is therefore impossible for statements of opinion to be made by victims in Scottish criminal trials which will affect sentencing, as happens routinely in the United States.[156] It is unclear whether victim impact statements, which permit the victim either in person or by completing a standard form to describe the effect of the crime on her, would be admissible in Scotland.[157] Chambers and Millar consider that sexual assault victims do not want to be involved directly in sentencing but that they would value "more say" prior to conviction, particularly in relation to acceptance of guilty pleas by the Crown. Several women in their sample had specific points which they wanted to make known prior to sentence, such as the impact of the crime upon them, but were unable to do so.

> It is of course open to the prosecutor to draw to the attention of the court matters relevant to sentencing over and above the circumstances of the commission of the offence. Nevertheless, complainers may have wanted to put to the court matters which the prosecutor would not have thought strictly relevant in this context.[158]

The powerful victim lobby in the United States has, according to its critics, not been successful in its aim of ensuring victim involvement at all stages of the criminal process.[159] Instead it has been hijacked by harsh law and order politics which may have created "the illusion of power" and may hurt the victims more than benefit them.[160] Would there be any advantage to a female victim of sexual assault in being able to describe the physical, material but above all psychological and emotional effects of the crime on her?[161]

Studies of how women view themselves and their bodies have shown that their vision is a highly fragmented one "lacking a sense of autonomy in the world and feeling carried along by forces beyond their control".[162] Those who have been sexually assaulted and who are already routinely disqualified from involvement in legal discourse may feel doubly silenced. Giving such women the opportunity to articulate their experience may produce:

> a rich mix of consciousness of alternative social and cultural worlds, together ... with resistance and protest against conditions perceived to be diminishing and denying of autonomy and fulfilment.[163]

Solveig Dahl's study of raped women provides a valuable representation of how some women experience rape. Speaking through the women's own voices she describes the violation of physical safety, human worth, of sexual boundaries, of personal control over their bodies and their lives, of trust which rape entails. The evidence produced at sexual assault trials will generally deal only with the first of these effects.[164]

> That rape and fear of rape can be an instrument of social control over women is not conjecture when one studies the consequences of rape in the lives of the victims. The experience restricts their behaviour, their freedom to move around, tó love and to interact with other people.[165]

The ways in which women might be permitted to present these descriptions, whether directly to the court, through their own Counsel, as a written report or in a standard form, are central to qualifying those discourses as authentic and also legitimate. The purpose for which this information would be collected might inevitably be symbolic rather than instrumental and the whole exercise might either become an empty ritual or promise far more to the victim than could ever be achieved in practice. However, the idea seems to offer a significant, if limited opportunity to challenge the absence of female discourse in law. At present in order to discover women's voices we have to adopt a process which:

> involves listening not only to who speaks and in what circumstances, but who does not speak and why ... to trace the ways in which women ... 'represent' themselves. This entails discerning where or how they break through the discourses that have circumscribed their perceptions of the causes and the nature of sexual violation and contributed to what amounts to a cultural cover-up.[166]

If the "injury of rape lies in the meaning of the act to its victim"[167] is there not value in exploring the possibility of giving voice to that experience in the court-room?

NOTES

1. (1829) *Edinburgh Political and Literary Journal,* 14 March.
2. F.Heidensohn, "The Deviance of Women: A Critique and an Enquiry" (1968) XIX *Brit. J. Sociol.* 160.
3. C.Smart, *Women, Crime and Criminology, A Feminist Critique* (1977).
4. M.Chesney-Lind, "Judicial Enforcement of the Female Sex Role: The Family Court and the Female Delinquent" (1973) 8 *Issues in Criminology* 197.
5. D.Klein, "The Etiology of Female Crime: A Review of the Literature" in *The Female Offender,* ed. L.Crites (1976).

6.   J.Scutt, "Role-conditioning Theory: An Explanation for Disparity in Male and Female Criminality" (1976) 19 *Aust. and N.Z. J. of Crim.*

7.   S.Edwards, *Women on Trial* (1984) at p.13.

8.   P.Carlen et al., *Criminal Women* (1985).

9.   M.Eaton, *Justice for Women?* (1986).

10.   A.Worrall, *Offending Women: Female Lawbreakers and the Criminal Justice System* (1990).

11.   A useful review is given in P.Carlen, *Women, Crime and Poverty* (1988) chapters 1 and 4.

12.   'A.Morris, *Women, Crime and Criminal Justice* (1987). See also D.Farrington and A.Morris, "Sex, Sentencing and Reconviction" (1983) 23 *Brit. J. Criminology* 229.

13.   See I.Nagel, "Sex Differences in the Processing of Criminal Defendants" in *Women and Crime*, eds. A.Morris and L.Gelsthorpe (1981); D.Farrington and A.Morris, *ibid.*, n.12.

14.   M.Eaton, "Mitigating Circumstances - Familiar Rhetoric" (1983) 11 *Int. J. Sociology of Law* 385; C.Kruttschnitt, "Respectable Women and the Law" (1982) 23 *The Sociological Quarterly* 221.

15.   F.Heidensohn, *Gender and Crime* (1985) at p.93.

16.   J.Donzelot, *The Policing of Families* (1979).

17.   E.Parsons, *Social Rule: A Study of the Will to Power* (1916) at pp.1-2.

18.   For useful English studies, see B.Toner, *The Facts of Rape* (1977); Z.Adler, *Rape on Trial* (1987).

19.   Criminal Procedure (Scotland) Act 1975, ss.141A, 141B, 346A, 346B as amended by the Law Reform (Miscellaneous Provisions) (Scotland) Act 1985, s.36. For a research study on the effectiveness of this legislation, see B.Brown et al., *Sexual History and Sexual Character Evidence in Scottish Sexual Offence Trials* (1992).

20.   D.Weisstub, "Victims of Crime in the Criminal Justice System" in *From Crime Policy to Victim Policy*, ed. E.Fattah (1986) at p.197.

21.   C.Smart, *Feminism and the Power of Law* (1989) at p.26.

22.   See *H.M.Advocate v. McKenzie* 1990 S.L.T. 28.

23.   The sample was drawn from all reported appeal cases between 1982 and 1993 where there was a conviction for rape, assault with intent to rape or indecent assault committed by a male on a female aged sixteen or over; a total of forty-one cases.

24.   Taken from *The Scotsman, The Herald, The Courier* from January 1992 to June 1993; a total of twenty-seven cases. See K.Soothill and D.Soothill, "Prosecuting the Victim? a Study of Reporting of Barristers' Comments in Rape Cases" (1993) 32 *Howard Journal* 12; K.Soothill and S.Walby, *Sex Crime in the News* (1991) for studies of newspaper reporting of sexual assault cases.

25.   The old form of the charge is assault with intent to ravish.

26.   In G.Gordon, *Criminal Law of Scotland* (1992), the most authoritative text on Scots criminal law, rape is defined, at p.883, as "carnal knowledge of a female by a male person obtained by overcoming her will".

27.   See C.Smart, "Penetrating Women's Bodies: The Problems of Law and Medical Technology" in *Gender, Power and Sexuality*, eds. P.Abbott and C.Wallace (1991).

28. S.Edwards, *supra*, n.7 at p.4.

29. A broader definition may also lead to increases in the number of convictions and the length of sentence. See C.Goldberg-Ambrose, "Unfinished Business in Rape Law Reform" (1992) 48 *J. Soc. Issues* 173.

30. C.Gane, *Sexual Offences* (1992) at p.4. For a proposal to abolish indecent assault in England and Wales and create a new crime of sexual assault, see G.Sullivan, "The Need for a Crime of Sexual Assault" [1989] *Crim. L.R.* 331.

31. L.Kelly, *Surviving Sexual Violence* (1988).

32. See A.Morris, *supra*, n.12, chapter 7.

33. See an interesting analysis of the serial rapist in the United States which came to "the chilling conclusion that a serial rapist is no more different than the man next door" and that with such a "heterogeneous sample, an exact profile is hard to obtain" (J.Allison and L.Wrightsman, *Rape: The Misunderstood Crime* (1993) at p.25). See also Government Statistical Service, "Statistics on Rape 1977-87" (1989) *Home Office Statistical Bulletin*, which states that there is no evidence that rapists form a distinct specialised subgroup of offenders.

34. F.Smart, *Neurosis and Crime* (1970) at p.39.

35. C.Smart, *supra*, n.21, at p.162.

36. L.Smith, *Concerns about Rape*, Home Office Research Study No.106 (1989).

37. For example, between 1989 and 1993 less than a third of women who contacted the Rape Crisis Centre in Dundee had reported the matter to the police (Dundee Rape Crisis Centre, *10 Years of Crisis* (1994)).

38. See M.Burman and S.Lloyd, *Police Specialist Units for the Investigation of Crimes of Violence against Women and Children in Scotland* (1993).

39. Scottish Office, *Criminal Statistics Scotland 1980-1982 Cmnd 9403* (1984) Table 2.2; Scottish Office, *Recorded Crime in Scotland* (1992) Cr/J/1993/2.

40. Crime surveys are not a satisfactory way of assessing the "real" rate of sexual assaults but the figures from local crime surveys such as the Islington Crime Survey do provide evidence of underreporting. See T.Jones et al., *The Islington Crime Survey* (1986). For a discussion of difficulties associated with crime surveys and sexual assaults see S.Walklate, *Victimology* (1989) chapter 2.

41. G.Chambers and A.Millar, *Investigating Sexual Assault* (1983) and *Prosecuting Sexual Assault* (1986).

42. R.Harper and A.McWhinnie, *The Glasgow Rape Case* (1983).

43. The complainer subsequently brought a successful private prosecution. See *X v. Sweeney and Ors.* 1982 S.C.C.R. 161.

44. *Supra*, n.19.

45. Brown et al., *supra*, n.19.

46. *DPP v. Morgan* [1976] A.C. 182.

47. *Meek and Others v. H.M.Advocate* 1982 S.C.C.R. 613; *Jamieson v. H.M.Advocate* 1994 S.C.C.R. 181. For a useful comparison of English and Scots law generally in relation to rape, see P.Ferguson, "Controversial Aspects of the Law of Rape: An Anglo-Scottish Comparison"

in *Justice and Crime*, ed. R. Hunter (1993) 190.

48. Scottish Office, *supra*, n.39; Scottish Office, *Criminal Proceedings in Scottish Courts 1992* (1993) Cr/J/1993/8.

49. There are numerous articles on this topic, including, for instance, R.Shiels, "Marital Rape in England and Wales" (1991) *Scolag Bulletin* 7. For a useful review of the issues before changes were introduced, see J.Scutt, "To Love, Honour and Rape with Impunity: Wife as Victim of Rape and the Criminal Law" in *The Victim in International Perspective*, ed. H.Schneider (1982).

50. D.Russell, *Rape Within Marriage* (1982).

51. *R v. R* [1991] 4 All E.R. 481. Prior to the *R* case it had been considered by some judges that legislation would be required to make marital rape unlawful. In 1975 an attempt had been made to alter the law in s.1(3) Sexual Offences Amendment Bill but this was defeated.

52. 1983 S.L.T. 7.

53. 1984 J.C. 105.

54. 1989 S.C.C.R. 248.

55. Lord Justice Taylor, "Address given at the Annual Conference of the Law Society of Scotland" (1993) *Journal of the Law Society of Scotland* 129.

56. It is, of course, legally incorrect to ascribe ownership of a criminal case to the victim. But it is interesting to note that this case became associated in the public mind with the name of the complainer, Judy, rather than the offender, Cronin. See *Cronin v. H.M.Advocate* 1993 S.C.C.R. 158.

57. N.Hutton and C.Tata, "Reform of Sentencing Practice" (1993) *J.L.S.S.* 230.

58. G.Nicholson, *Principles of Sentencing in Scotland* (1992). See also A.Stewart, *The Scottish Criminal Courts in Action* (1990); D.Kelly, *Criminal Sentences* (1993).

59. Until 1993 the prosecutor in Scotland could not appeal against a sentence which was regarded as too lenient. This has been amended by s.42 of the Prisoners and Criminal Proceedings (Scotland) Act which came into force on 1 October 1993. It was welcomed by the Labour spokesperson on Scottish Affairs, Maria Fyfe, particularly in relation to sexual attacks on women.

60. Although a recent Scottish Office Report sought views on the desirability of sentencing guide-lines. See Scottish Office, *Sentencing and Appeals* (1993).

61. Unlike the situation in England and Wales much of Scottish criminal law remains non-statutory. For discussion of the impact of this, see G.Gordon, *supra*, n.26.

62. Criminal Procedure (Scotland) Act 1975, ss.207(3), 41(3).

63. Criminal Justice (Scotland) Act 1980, s.42.

64. Criminal Justice (Scotland) Act 1980, s.41; *Milligan v. Jessop* 1988 S.C.C.R. 137.

65. See *Law v. H.M.Advocate* 1988 S.C.C.R. 347; *Forrest v. H.M.Advocate* 1988 S.C.C.R. 481.

66. See N.Hutton and C.Tata, *supra*, n.57.

67. N.Hutton and C.Tata, *ibid.*

68. *Nicholson v. H.M.Advocate* 1991 S.C.C.R. 606.

69. See C.Albonetti, "An Integration of Theories to Explain Judicial Discretion" (1991) 38

Social Problems 247.

70.   M.J.Mossman, "Feminism and Legal Method: The Difference It Makes" (1986) 3 *Aust. J. of Law and Society* 30.

71.   M.Frankel, "Lawlessness in Sentencing" (1971) 41 *Cincinnati Law Review* 1.

72.   See *Billam* (1986) 8 Cr. App. R. (S) 48; *Khaliq* (1993) 14 Cr. App. R. (S) 233. For a useful analysis of sentencing in rape cases in England and Wales see J.Temkin, *Rape and the Legal Process* (1987) at pp.16-23. It is clear from statistical evidence that *Billam* has had an impact on the length of sentences in rape cases. In 1985, according to Home Office statistics for England and Wales, forty-five per cent of rape convictions resulted in imprisonment for five years or more, by 1987 that figure had increased to eighty per cent. See C.Lloyd and R.Walmsley, *Changes in Rape Offences and Sentencing* (1989) H.O.R.S. No.105.

73.   G.Chambers and A.Millar, *supra*, n.41.

74.   See G.Nicholson, *supra*, n.58, at pp.246-8.

75.   See P.Robertshaw, "Sentencing Rapists: First Tier Courts in 1991-2" [1994] *Crim. L.R.* 343, where custodial sentences of less than three years were awarded in about ten per cent of all rape cases in both jurisdictions over the period 1989-1991.

76.   1987 S.C.C.R. 413.

77.   For a recent article on the practice in England and Wales, see P.Robertshaw, "The Guilty Plea Discount: Rule of Law or Role of Chance?" (1992) 31 *Howard Journal* 53. It is thought that a Criminal Justice Bill for Scotland in 1995 will include discounts for guilty pleas.

78.   Scottish Office (1993) *supra*, n.48, Table 10(b).

79.   Analysed for the author by the Civil and Criminal Justice Statistics Unit, Scottish Office Home and Health Department.

80.   Scottish Office, *supra*, n.60, at p.39.

81.   Certain cases in England also provoked criticism of an over lenient judiciary, as in *Attorney-General's Reference No. 3 of 1993* [1993] *Crim. L.R.* 472 where a fifteen year-old boy convicted of rape was put under a supervision order for three years. The Appeal Court decided that only a custodial sentence could be justified and imposed two years with some reduction for the "double jeopardy" effect upon the offender of an appeal against lenient sentence.

82.   *Billam, supra*, n.72.

83.   Scottish Home Office and Health Dept., *supra*, n. 79.

84.   P.Carlen and A.Worrall, *Gender, Crime and Justice* (1987) at p.2.

85.   See K.O'Donovan, "Law's Knowledge: The Judge, the Expert, the Battered Woman and her Syndrome" (1993) 20(4) *J. of Law and Society* 427. See also M.Fox "Legal Responses to Battered Women who Kill" in this volume.

86.   For a review of recent case-law, see *Brodie v. H.M.Advocate* 1993 S.C.C.R. 371.

87.   D.Hume, *Commentaries on the Law of Scotland Respecting Crimes* ed. B. Bell (1844 4th ed., reprinted 1986) at p.239.

88.   See also the very narrow definition of coercion in Scots law which requires that the accused show that the crime was committed in order to avoid imminent death or serious injury:

G.Gordon, *supra*, n.26; M.Jones and M.Christie, *Criminal Law* (1992) at pp.162-166; R.McCall Smith and D.Sheldon, *Scots Criminal Law* (1992) at pp.136-138.

89.   L.Irigaray, *This Sex Which is Not One* (1985) at p.164.

90.   E.Jackson, "Contradictions and Coherence in Feminist Responses to Law" (1993) 20 *J. Law and Society* 398.

91.   See C.Lloyd and A.Walmsley, *supra*, n.72, showing that whereas forty-seven per cent of offenders were strangers to their victims in 1973 by 1985 that figure had dropped to thirty-nine per cent. Smith's study of rapes reported within two London boroughs during 1984-6 suggests that thirty-nine per cent involved men well known to the victim and twenty-nine per cent involved brief acquaintances.

92.   See, for instance, M.Baurmann, "Sexuality, Violence and Emotional After-effects: A Longitudinal Study of Victims of Forcible Rape and Sexual Deviance in Cases Reported to the Police" in *Developments in Crime and Crime Control Research*, eds. K.Sessar and H.J.Kerner (1991).

93.   See L.Smith, *supra*, n.36; C.Lloyd and R.Walmsley, *supra*, n.72.

94.   G.Chambers and A.Millar, *supra*, n.41, at p.69. For a judicial view, see Judge Michael Addison's recent comment about a rape case involving acquaintances: "[t]his is not in my view the more serious type of rape - that is the rape of a total stranger" ((1993) *The Herald*, 11 August).

95.   See *Duffy* 1983 S.L.T. 7; *Paxton* 1984 J.C. 105; *Stallard* 1989 S.C.C.R. 248.

96.   *Stallard, ibid.*, at p.474.

97.   *H.M.Advocate v. Ward* reported in (1992) *The Scotsman*, 26 November, at p.12.

98.   *X v. H.M.Advocate* reported in (1993) *The Scotsman*, 12 January, at p.2.

99.   *Ibid.*, per Lord Caplan.

100.   *Campbell v. H.M.Advocate* 1993 Greens Weekly Digest (G.W.D.) 33.

101.   *S v. H.M.Advocate* 1992 G.W.D. 13.

102.   *H.M.Advocate v. Stewart* reported in (1993) *The Dundee Courier*, 26 June, at p.7.

103.   *H.M.Advocate v. McKie* reported in (1993) *The Scotsman*, 20 February, at p.5.

104.   *Robinson v. H.M.Advocate* 1988 G.W.D. 13.

105.   *MacKinnon v. H.M.Advocate* 1989 G.W.D. 12. It should be noted that the court doubted whether the sentence was in fact adequate but felt unable to impose a longer sentence because there was insufficient evidence to prove rape.

106.   *Caring v. H.M.Advocate* 1989 G.W.D. 15.

107.   A.Morris, *supra*, n.12, at p.165.

108.   J.Hanmer and S.Saunders, *Women, Violence and Crime Prevention* (1993) at p.57.

109.   R.Wright, "Rape and Physical Violence" in *Sex Offenders in the Criminal Justice System*, ed. D.West (1980) at p.100.

110.   See Canadian Federal-Provincial Task Force, *Justice for Victims of Crime* (1983) at p.30; P.Begin, "Rape Law Reform in Canada" in *Crime and its Victims*, ed. E.Viano (1989).

111.   See P.Pollard, "Judgments about Victims and Attackers in Depicted Rapes" (1992) 31 *Brit. J. Soc. Psy.* 307; K.McCaul et al., "Understanding Attributions of Victim Blame for Rape: Sex,

Violence and Foreseeability" (1990) 20 *J. App. Soc. Psy.* 1.

112.   S.Brownmiller, *Against Our Will: Men, Women and Rape* (1973) at p.15.

113.   M.Foucault, *The History of Sexuality: An Introduction* (1982).

114.   See also V.Bell, "Beyond the 'Thorny Question': Feminism, Foucault and the Desexualisation of Rape" (1991) 19 *Int. J. Socio. of Law* 83.

115.   C.MacKinnon, *Towards a Feminist Theory of the State* (1989) at p.160.

116.   M.King and G.Mezey, *Male Victims of Sexual Assault* (1992).

117.   C.Gilligan, *In a Different Voice* (1982) at p.39 et seq.

118.   See L.Holmstrom and L.Burgess, *The Victims of Rape: Institutional Reactions* (1983) introduction.

119.   L.Kelly, *supra*, n.31.

120.   See E.Jackson, "Catharine MacKinnon and Feminist Jurisprudence: A Critical Appraisal" (1992) 19 *J. Law and Society* 195; C. Smart, *supra*, n.21, chapter 2.

121.   T.McCahill et al., *The Aftermath of Rape* (1979) at p.65.

122.   *H.M.Advocate v. Conlon* 1981 S.C.C.R. 141.

123.   *Barbour v. H.M.Advocate* 1982 S.C.C.R. 195.

124.   *Smith v. H.M.Advocate* 1993 G.W.D. 33.

125.   *Rae v. H.M.Advocate* 1992 G.W.D. 18.

126.   See, for instance, *Curley v. H.M.Advocate* 1989 G.W.D. 23, where the fact that the victim's injuries were minor contributed to a reduction in the sentence from ten to six years.

127.   For instance, Lord Stewart in *Barbour v. H.M.Advocate supra*, n.123 takes a more enlightened approach, noting that the victim was "humiliated". His analysis, which heralded a more liberal attitude to the absence of resistance on the part of the sexual assault victim, nevertheless also speaks of the offender "misusing" the victim; begging the question whether there are legitimate ways in which a woman can be "used".

128.   See, for instance, the complaints made by the victim in *Cronin v. H.M.Advocate* 1993 S.C.C.R. 158, about the Appeal Court judges' analysis of the indecent assaults which she experienced (reported in (1993) *Scotland on Sunday*, 23 May, at p.9).

129.   J.Chapman and M.Gates, *The Victimisation of Women* (1978) at p.18.

130.   See A.Sachs and J.Hoff Wilson, *Sexism and the Law: A Study of Male Beliefs and Legal Bias in Britain and the United States* (1978).

131.   See S.Edwards, "Male Violence Against Women: Excusatory and Explanatory Ideologies in Law and Society" in *Gender, Sex and the Law*, ed. S.Edwards (1985).

132.   C.MacKinnon, "Feminism, Marxism, Method and the State" (1980) 6 *Signs* 530.

133.   For a fuller discussion, see E.Stanko, *Intimate Intrusions: Women's Experience of Male Violence* (1985).

134.   See S.Atkins and B.Hoggett, *Women and the Law* (1984) at pp.66-67.

135.   A.Worrall, *supra*, n.10, at p.90.

136.   For instance in *Wotherspoon v. H.M.Advocate* 1989 G.W.D. 2 the accused was convicted on two charges of assault with intent to ravish against elderly women and received a custodial sentence of six years in spite of the fact that the trial judge considered that "the sentence on

reflection had been unduly severe". In *Langston v. Friel* 1992 G.W.D. 10 the seventy-five year-old victim was described as "a defenceless old lady".

137.   In spite of the fact that evidence as to the victim's previous sexual history is generally inadmissible the fact that the victim is a virgin is clearly regarded as significant in sentencing. See *Townsley v. H.M.Advocate* 1986 S.C.C.R. 248; *Di Lucca v. H.M.Advocate* 1994 unreported.

138.   In *Rorrison v. H.M.Advocate* 1989 G.W.D. 34 the accused raped the victim, described as a "young mother", in her own bed after forcing his way into her house late at night. Eight years was not regarded as excessive although the accused appeared to have no previous record. In *Innes v. H.M.Advocate* reported in (1993) *The Herald*, 10 June, at p.2 the accused had committed an indecent assault on a woman in similar circumstances in front of her young daughter. While no mention is made of the impact of this attack on the woman it is noted that the child "needed medication" for eighteen months after the offence. The accused, who had a previous conviction for rape, was sentenced to seven years imprisonment.

139.   See *H.M.Advocate v. Hepburn* reported in (1993) *The Scotsman*, 2 March, at p.7, where the accused posed as a taxi-driver. See also *Hussain*, a case reported in (1993) *The Scotsman*, 12 July, where a doctor committed indecent assaults on female patients under the guise of medical examinations. He was given a three month custodial sentence partly on the grounds that his actions constituted a "breach of trust". Several of his victims did not consider that the sentence was long enough to reflect the seriousness of his offences. In contrast to these two cases a prison officer who was convicted on five counts of indecent assault and had three other indecent assault charges reduced to assault or breach of the peace was given 240 hours community service. The majority of the assaults had been committed on young women with whom he worked at Perth Prison while he was at work (*H.M.Advocate v. Moran* reported in (1993) *The Scotsman*, 21 May, at p.8).

140.   *Cronin, supra,* n.56.

141.   (1993) *Scotland on Sunday,* 16 May. There are no permanent judges in Scotland who are women. In 1993 the first woman was appointed to the High Court in a temporary capacity.

142.   (1994) *Scotland on Sunday,* 16 February.

143.   (1994) *The Scotsman,* 11 February; *Di Lucca v. H.M.Advocate.* 1994 unreported.

144.   *Martin v. H.M.Advocate.* 1987 G.W.D. 17.

145.   *Doherty v. H.M.Advocate* 1988 G.W.D. 39.

146.   See also *Watson v. H.M.Advocate* 1993 G.W.D. 4; *Rae v. H.M.Advocate* 1992 G.W.D 18.

147.   *Townsley v. H.M.Advocate* 1986 S.C.C.R. 248.

148.   *Ibid.,* at p.250.

149.   *Derret v. Lockhart* 1990 G.W.D. 14.

150.   *Tennant v. H.M.Advocate* 1993 G.W.D. 1; *H.M.Advocate v. Dewar* reported in (1993) *The Herald,* 24 April, at p.7.

151.   S.Griffin, "Rape: The All-American Crime" (1971) *Ramparts* September.

152.   C.Smart, *supra,* n.21.

153.   A.von Hirsch and N.Jareborg, "Gauging Criminal Harm: A Living-Standard Analysis"

(1991) 11 *Oxford Journal of Legal Studies* 1.

154.   See *H.M.Advocate v. McKenzie, supra*, n.22, in which the trial judge sought the views of the victim of attempted rape as to whether a custodial sentence was the appropriate penalty. On appeal by the Lord Advocate, using the rarely invoked procedure of Bill of Advocation to seek review of irregularities in the proceedings, the Appeal Court held that it was entirely wrong that the victim should be asked her views. She had no expertise in sentencing and her opinion was of no relevance to the judge's decision.

155.   *McKenzie, ibid.*, at p.33.

156.   See D.Kelly, "Victim Participation in the Criminal Justice System" in *Victims of Crime: Problems, Policies and Programs*, ed. A.Lurigio et al. (1990) at p.172.

157.   It has been suggested that such information could be included in the Social Enquiry Report and the victim could be interviewed by court social workers. A commentator on the *McKenzie* case does not believe that it renders victim impact statements inadmissible. See R.Wilson, "The Victim in the Criminal Justice System" (1990) *S.L.T.(News)* 8.

158.   G.Chambers and A.Millar, *supra*, n.41, at pp.77-78.

159.   See L.Henderson, "The Wrongs of Victims' Rights" (1985) 37 *Stanford L.R.* 937; R. Elias, *Victims Still: The Political Manipulation of Victims* (1993).

160.   R.Elias, *ibid,* at p.89.

161.   See A.Ashworth, "Victim Impact Statements and Sentencing" [1993] *Crim. L.R.* 498, for a strong argument against their use in England and Wales.

162.   E.Mark, *The Woman in the Body* (1989) at p.194.

163.   E.Mark, *ibid.*

164.   S.Dahl, *Rape - A Hazard to Health* (1993) at p.55.

165.   S.Dahl, *ibid.*, at p.145.

166.   L.Higgins and B.Silver, *Rape and Representation* (1991) at pp.3-4.

167.   C.MacKinnon, *supra*, n.115, at p.160.

11 International Human Rights and Body Politics

FIONA BEVERIDGE AND SIOBHAN MULLALLY

Despite continued and widespread criticism of appeals to rights and rights-based concepts as a tool for addressing the oppression of women, international human rights practice displays a marked reluctance to abandon this familiar form and its associated baggage. Indeed the label "human rights", used to connote all areas of international legal discourse concerning the condition of individuals and/or groups in an individual v. State context,[1] presupposes in a remarkable way the pre-eminence of the rights formula as a tool for redress. The gender neutral discourse of international human rights law claims to apply to all human beings equally, however the difficulties experienced in accommodating women's "differences" within that discourse and in articulating or responding to harms experienced uniquely by women serve to reveal its underlying gendered nature. Women's human rights have been marginalised, both institutionally and conceptually, from national and international human rights movements; abuse of women's human rights has been perceived as a cultural, private or individual issue, not a political matter requiring State action.[2] The main international organs have dealt with violations of women's human rights only in a marginal way, while women's bodies have been rendered almost invisible within mainstream human rights law. This exclusion of women's bodies is apparent both in the failure of international human rights law to respond to violence against women and in the lack of any clear understanding or consensus on a woman's right to bodily integrity.

Central to the silencing of women's voices in international human rights forums is the public/private dichotomy of international law: "modern international law rests on and reproduces various dichotomies between the public and private spheres, and the 'public' sphere is regarded as the province of international law".[3]

The objective of this essay is to examine existing feminist critiques of "rights" and to consider their relevance in relation to questions of body politics in international human rights law. Three major groups of writings will be examined. First, jurisprudential critiques of the pre-eminence of the rights discourse will be examined, with particular focus on problems associated with the invocation of rights or rights-based concepts in relation to body politics. Secondly, challenges to the assumed or claimed universality of applicability or utility of human rights concepts will be explored. The issue of cultural relativism may be seen by some as of particular relevance in the area of body politics, though that viewpoint itself entails the making of deep assumptions about the public/private division, which will be discussed. Thirdly, critiques of current international human rights law and practice will be examined, and in particular the claims that women's concerns remain invisible within this discourse. Consideration will be given to the treatment of rape, domestic violence and female genital mutilation within international human rights forums. Finally, the possibility of including a "right to bodily integrity" into mainstream human rights instruments will be examined.

RIGHTS AND BODY POLITICS

If feminism can be defined as a tradition of questioning, then body politics questions have been the subject matter of much of this questioning. Inevitably, perhaps, this has been seen to involve engagement with the law, either to change already existing laws which are seen as oppressive or to harness the power of law/legal protection as a strategy to secure gains for women. The relationship between "body politics" questions and law has been problematic on a number of levels - criticisms have ranged from general critiques of law (for its maleness, sexism, irrelevance) to specific critiques regarding the appropriateness of law as a medium for the regulation of body politics. Much of the discussion has centred around the usefulness of rights law as a strategy for improving the position of women. This section reviews some of these arguments as they relate specifically to body politics questions.

One body of criticism relates to the *form* of rights discourse epitomised by the perpetual opposition of "rights" to corresponding duties, freedoms, powers and privileges. Essentially rights are portrayed as the property of individuals (or occasionally groups), property which under the law serves within the context of identified relationships to privilege the bearer in some way against interference from other individuals or legal entities. In rights discourse it is necessary to accord priority to conflicting rights, powers and privileges: hence the task facing claimants of a right is twofold - first, they must identify themselves as within the category recognised as being in possession of the claimed right; and secondly, they must establish that in the particular context their claimed right or privilege should be accorded priority over the conflicting claims.[4] A number of critics have argued that the assumption upon which this rights discourse is predicated of a society of free-willed individuals, motivated by self-interest, perpetually seeking prioritisation of their own claims (rather than accommodation, negotiation or some other form of compromise) is false, either because it misrepresents the way in which individuals operate generally,[5] or because it misrepresents the way in which women in particular operate (i.e. that it is inherently sexist).[6]

In reality rights discourses, it is argued, oversimplify complex power relations. Rights are generally formulated in individual terms; although the invocation of rights to sexual equality may therefore solve an occasional case of inequality for individual women, the position of women generally remains unchanged. As Chinkin et al. have put it:

> [r]ights discourse is taxed with reducing intricate power relations in a simplistic way. The formal acquisition of a right, such as the right to equal treatment, is often assumed to have solved an imbalance of power. In practice, however, the promise of rights is thwarted by the inequalities of power.[7]

The discourse of rights, it is argued, presupposes a world of autonomous individuals starting a race or making "free" choices; it takes no account of the various factors implicated in women's oppression, assuming instead that the acceptance of rights claims is sufficient to make the "competition" fair.

This concept of the self as essentially separate from and antagonistic towards others conflicts with competing cultural conceptions of the self as "essentially connected" to others and as embedded in existing social practices and roles. Rawls summarises the liberal view of the self by saying that "the self is prior to the ends which are affirmed by it", that is, the self is prior to its socially given roles and relationships, and is free only if it is capable of holding these features of its social situation at a distance and judging them according to the dictates of reason. A number of feminist writers, reiterating the criticisms voiced by communitarians, believe that this is a false view of the self. It ignores the fact that the self is "embedded" or "situated" in existing social practices and that we cannot always stand back and opt out of those roles and relationships. Sandel[8] argues that we cannot view ourselves as independent, independent in the sense that our identity is never tied to our aims and attachments:

> [W]ithout great cost to those loyalties and convictions whose moral consists partly in the fact that living by them is inseparable from understanding ourselves as the particular persons we are - as members of this family or community or nation or people, as bearers of this history, as sons and daughters of that revolution, as citizens of this republic.[9]

West[10] also takes a view of the self as embodied in its societal context. She argues that women's view of themselves is fundamentally different from that of men, because of their different biological make-up. She describes the liberal view of the self, which she argues is subscribed to by most modern political theory, as "the separation thesis". As an alternative to this she proposes "the connection thesis". Her argument runs as follows:

> Women are actually or potentially materially connected to other human life. Men aren't. This material fact has existential consequences. While it may be true for men that the individual is 'epistemologically and morally prior to the collectivity', it is not true for women. The potential for material connection with the other defines women's subjective, phenomenological and existential state, just as surely as the inevitability of material separation from the other defines men's existential state.[11]

This thesis, she argues, underlies both "radical" and "cultural" feminism. It is women's potential for material connection that constitutes the fundamental material difference between women and men and it is the rediscovery of this difference that distinguishes radical and cultural feminism from liberal feminism.

The recognition of women's material state of connection has led feminist theorising down different avenues. For cultural feminists, women's connectedness to the other is the source of women's different morality, women's "different voice" and "different ways of knowing". According to Gilligan, "intimacy and the ethic of care constitute the entailed values of the existential state of connection with others, just as autonomy and freedom constitute the entailed values of the existential state of separation from others for men."[12] For radical feminists, however, that same potential for connection is identified as being the source of women's oppression and women's connectedness with the "other" is above all else invasive and intrusive:

> [W]omen's potential for material 'connection' invites invasion into the physical integrity of our bodies, and intrusion into the existential integrity of our lives.[13]

Thus pregnancy itself is perceived as an assault on the physical integrity and privacy of the body.

These differences of opinion are often translated from the theoretical level to the level of strategy. There is common ground in the observation that neither the values that follow from women's potential for material connection with others nor the dangers attendant to that state are recognised by the Rule of Law;[14] women's experiences of their own bodies are excluded from legal discourse. But while cultural feminism leads to a rejection of the language of rights because of its failure to take account of the "essential connectedness" of the self, radical feminism (as characterised by West) frequently resorts to rights strategies to protect women's reproductive freedom and bodily integrity. Arguments for reproductive freedom, for instance, have frequently been founded on a claimed "right to privacy". These arguments, however, have been cast in the terms of the existing (male) discourse: West points out that rape is understood to be a harm, and is punished as such, only when it involves some other harm: where, for example it is accompanied by violence that appears in a form men understand. Similarly she argues that unwanted pregnancy is not understood as a "foetal invasion", an attack on a woman's bodily integrity.[15] The last twenty years she argues has seen a substantial amount of feminist law reform, primarily in the areas of rape, reproductive freedom, and pregnancy rights in the workplace. However, these reforms have often been won by characterising women's injuries as analogous to injuries men suffer. The time has now come, she says, to rearticulate these new rights "in such a way as to reveal, rather than conceal their origin in women's distinctive existential and material state of being."[16]

The individualistic concept of the self on which rights discourse is based has led to problems for feminists particularly in relation to body politics; its underlying logic seems to lead them to conclusions which are unpalatable. The self is abstracted not only from its social, economic and cultural context but also from the physical body of the subject herself. This seems to invite recognition of the right of the subject herself to do what she wants with her body - a position which can then be interpreted variously to include the "right to choose" in relation to abortion, the right to consent to a wide range of non-essential "medical" practices (cosmetic surgery, body alteration, fertility treatments) as well as sporting and sexual practices (from boxing to sadism).[17] The view of the subject as an abstract disembodied "self" does little to assist in drawing lines between such practices and seems to lead to conclusions unacceptable to many feminists.

The response to this apparent dilemma has often been to resort to a concept of autonomy or privacy to justify particular claims of right in determining the "treatment" of the body, yet as MacKinnon and others have pointed out, this reproduces and reinforces the public/private divide when it should instead be dismantled.

As indicated above, further criticism of rights-based dialogue has centred on the claim that rights themselves, or the legal systems within which they operate, are inherently sexist. MacKinnon argues that sexuality is defined, at present, in terms of dominance and submission, specifically male dominance and female submission. She works by analogy with Marxism: "[s]exuality is to feminism what work is to Marxism, that which is most one's own, yet most taken away".[18] Female sexuality is distorted and manipulated to meet the interests of a sex which does not share female interests. The alienation of female sexuality has particular significance, because MacKinnon argues that it is a woman's defining characteristic; it provides female identity - one becomes a woman through the experience of sexuality. In a male dominated society, sexuality is defined by men, the dominant class, in their interests. Women are defined and come to identify themselves as sex objects. The organised expropriation of female sexuality for male use, has material consequences for women: rape, pornography, sexual harassment. Legal reforms through rights strategies are inadequate to challenge what MacKinnon sees as being an all-pervasive system of male domination and female submission. She quotes the laws regulating rape as an example.[19] Focusing on the issue of consent, she argues, fails to recognise that consent to traditional heterosexual relations in a patriarchal society is not "real". Just as Marx used the tools of historical materialism to destroy the myth that workers are freely contracting wage labourers, MacKinnon uses the notion of sexual objectification to destroy the myth that consent in sexual relations is or can be "freely" given. She goes on to make the even stronger claim that rights strategies are inherently limited because the law itself is fundamentally gendered. She argues that the law is "male", not merely substantively, but also formally. Substantively, the law is male, in that it sees and treats women the way men see and treat women. Formally, the law is male, in that its claims to objectivity and neutrality reflect a masculine mode of thinking. Attempting to protect women's bodily integrity through rights strategies is limited then, not merely by the substantive content of law but also by its very form. MacKinnon states:

> [w]hen the state is most ruthlessly neutral, it will be most male; when it is most sex blind it will be most blind to the sex of the standard being applied. ... The law is objective, therefore male.[20]

This critique echoes many of the arguments advanced by feminists against rights strategies, including in particular, the work of Carol Gilligan. Gilligan draws attention to the fact that the masculine mode of thinking deemed to be unemotional, impersonal and objective coincides with expectations of justice and sound moral judgment.[21] Her starting point is the position articulated by Freud, that women have a lesser moral sense than men:

> I cannot evade the notion, though I hesitate to give it expression, that for women the level of what is ethically normal is different from what it is in men. Their super-ego is never so inexorable, so impersonal, so independent of its emotional origins as we require it to be in men ... they show less sense of justice than men, ... they are less ready to submit to the great exigencies of life, ... they are more often influenced in their judgements by feelings of affection or hostility.[22]

Gilligan challenges the presumption that this "feminine" mode of thinking is a more unreliable form of ethical judgment. She argues that there are two moral codes, the feminine one based on caring and the maintenance of relationships and networks, and the masculine based on a more abstract systemisation of rights and rules. For women, a moral problem is identified as arising:

> from conflicting responsibilities rather than from competing rights, and would require for its resolution a mode of thinking that is contextual and narrative rather than formal and abstract. This conception of morality as concerned with the activity of care, centres moral development around the understanding of relationships, just as the conception of morality as fairness ties moral development to the understanding of rights and rules.[23]

Thus Gilligan claims that women argue in a "different voice" or as Friedman puts it there is "a division of moral labour" along the lines of gender:

> The genders have ... been conceived in terms of special and distinctive moral projects. Justice and rights have structured male moral norms, values and virtues, while care and responsiveness have defined female moral norms, values and virtues.[24]

The differences, however, are not attributable to biological differences so much as to the psycho-social development of female children. Supporters of Gilligan's views have argued that feminists, rather than working within the prevailing norms of "justice and rights", should develop a care-based approach, or what has become known as an "ethic of care". The care ethic, it is argued, while initially developed in the context of private relationships, has public significance, and should be extended to public affairs.[25]

Gilligan's arguments have not been accepted without some controversy. Her thesis repeats many of the attempts of Western political philosophy to distinguish the intuitive, emotional, particularistic dispositions said to be required for women's domestic life, from the rational, impartial and dispassionate thought said to be required for men's public life. Early feminist theorising devoted a great deal of energy to repudiating these claims. Disagreement exists therefore, as to whether or not these different modes of moral reasoning correlate with gender divisions. However, whether or not the care-based approach reflects a peculiarly feminine mode of moral reasoning, there remains the question of whether there is a care-based approach to moral questions that competes with the ethic of justice, and if there is whether it is a superior approach. In advocating the adoption of an "ethic of care", it is argued that it is an approach to moral problems that can better accommodate the concerns arising from those experiences that are uniquely female, in particular issues relating to control over the female body.

Gilligan herself is equivocal as to the consequences of recognising the existence of an ethic of care. While she does not propose that the feminine mode of thinking is superior, she does argue that what she calls the different voice of women's experience and judgment should be heard alongside the male voice.[26] However, the modes of moral reasoning outlined by Gilligan are not usually seen as being complementary. Rather they are perceived as being not only competing but also often conflicting modes of reasoning. Both Carol Pateman[27] and Susan Okin[28] have argued that the exclusion of women from the public sphere is not incidental. The integrity and working order of the public sphere they argue, actually depends on the exclusion of women; women's particularistic dispositions, while functional for family life, are seen as subversive of the impartial justice required for public life. Thus it is argued that the care-based approach cannot be easily "added on" to the dominant mode of moral reasoning with its emphasis on rights and rules.

Rights discourse has also been criticised by feminists because of what is perceived as the inherent indeterminacy of rights claims. Unresolved normative conflicts abound within theories of rights and determinate criteria for resolving such conflicts are often not available. Resorting to rights strategies, it is argued, raises the spectre of provoking competing and often conflicting rights claims which potentially limit a woman's autonomy and control over her body to an even greater extent. Rights may produce counter claims to other rights including, inter alia, foetal rights, children's rights and men's rights to decide whether or not a biological offspring is born. Kingdom, for example, has argued that:

> [i]f feminists claim that a woman has the right to reproduce, there is no obvious reason why that right should not be claimed for men too, and on traditional liberal ground of equality it would be difficult to oppose that claim.[29]

Another limitation on rights discourse, less seldom addressed, concerns its bluntness as an instrument. It has already been noted that rights discourse reduces complex power relations to a simplified form. For strategic reasons, this may be appropriate in certain contexts (though some would reject this): however its appropriateness to certain subject matters or types of conflict must surely be doubted. All else being equal, and it seldom is, some conflicts, either because of the nature of the relationships involved, or because of the nature of the subject matter, cannot be reduced satisfactorily to the paradigmatic paired oppositions of free-willed self-interested individuals of rights discourse.

Conflicts over the body involve issues of immense social, political, economic, sexual and psychological complexity. The body is a complex social construct, whose meaning and significance changes from place to place and time to time (and sometimes very rapidly). Cultural diversity in the treatment of the body is immense. Women's bodies in particular have been a site of struggle, definition and control and are extensively regulated and confined by societal mores and norms.

Law has played an important part in this process:

> Law has been deeply interested in things corporeal ... it has defined them as specific sites of activity over which the law should have jurisdiction.[30]

Now, in apparent disregard for the wide variety of forms of legal regulation and control utilised already in respect of the body, we seem often to attempt to squeeze all conflicts into the narrow confines of rights discourse. The limitations of such an approach are self-evident and, even without doubts about the inherent maleness of law, would be a high-risk strategy.[31]

Rights discourse has also been noted to be inherently liable to manipulation by existing power groups. Smart cites the example of the right to family life under the European Convention on Human Rights, relied on by unmarried fathers to claim rights over children on a par with those claimed by married fathers.[32] Even feminists who do not share the radical feminist critique of law as a system of male power seem to accept the need for constant vigilance to prevent the "hijacking" of rights discourse by powerful interest groups. De Gama, for example, seems to imply that appropriations of "rights" and other legal discourses by powerful groups must be challenged by feminists, but she stops short of offering any strategy to do this.[33] There are also criticisms as to the course which rights dialogue has taken in various contexts to date. For instance, it has been argued by Lindgren that the invocation of a right to privacy to protect a woman's right to choose in relation to reproductive freedom has had the unfortunate consequence of also protecting certain established privileges which would have been better dismantled.[34]

For some, these mistakes have left a heritage which requires radical and wholesale dismemberment if rights discourse is to be effectively harnessed by women in the future. For others, less radical solutions are suggested: writing women "in" to "rights of man" charters, introducing certain gender specific rights, or aspects to rights, into the existing discourse, or supplementing the rights discourse with other measures designed to better equip women to invoke rights and rights-based discourses. Such views are dismissed by many more radical critics as doomed to failure, for reasons indicated above.

1. The public/private divide
The exclusion of women's accounts of their experiences from legal discourse has been facilitated by the public/private dichotomy of liberal theory and practice. Criticisms of the public/private divide have been central to feminist critiques of the liberal State. Carol Pateman has argued that the "dichotomy between the public and the private ... is, ultimately, what the feminist movement is all about."[35] Contemporary liberalism expresses its commitment to liberty by sharply separating the public power of the State from the private relationships of civil society, and by

setting strict limits on the State's ability to intervene in private life.[36] However, as Pateman notes, this division between private and public spheres is constructed as a division within the world of men. Civil society is conceptualised by liberal theory in abstraction from domestic life, and so the latter remains "forgotten" in theoretical discussion. The domestic sphere is thus rendered invisible within liberal theory and practice.[37]

Failure to apply concepts of rights and justice to the domestic sphere reflects the lingering influence of pre-liberal ideas about the "naturalness" of the traditional family. The traditional family is seen as a bastion of civilisation and a precondition for social stability and so remains immune to judicial reform.[38] The idea of the domestic sphere as constituting a separate sphere to which the concept of justice is not appropriate is accepted also by Rawls. He suggests that the concept of an independent self distinct from its values and ends may not be appropriate when considering one's "personal affairs" or family ties.[39] This leads one to Sandel's conclusion:

> As the independent self finds its limits in those aims and attachments from which it cannot stand apart, so justice finds its limits in those forms of community that engage the identity as well as the interests of the participants.[40]

For these reasons and others, the domestic sphere has not been subjected to the same tests of justice as the public sphere. Rights discourse has generally failed to transcend this notion of "separate spheres of justice" and has instead concerned itself with problems arising within the "public" rather than the domestic sphere.

Difficulties in articulating harms suffered by women within this conceptual framework have been exacerbated by the legal recognition of a right to privacy. The right to privacy is a derivation of the classical liberal values of freedom and autonomy. It separates the personal or the intimate from the public sphere, where the "public" includes both State and civil society. It serves to remove a sphere of action from the regulation or control of the State.

Privacy was first utilised by feminists in the US in the case of *Griswold v. Connecticut*[41] to gain a ruling that laws which denied access to contraception to married women violated the constitutional right of privacy. Initially this ruling was welcomed by feminists as a victory. However, it has since become clear that the right to privacy is a double-edged sword which has frequently been used to depoliticise many of the harms suffered by women. The sphere of action protected by the right to privacy has often been defined by the structure of the traditional family unit, complete with its power imbalances. Thus, for example, violence and rape within the family have traditionally been subjected to different tests of justice than similar acts committed outside that context. The public/private divide has been identified as central to this state of affairs; hence much feminist debate has focused on how to challenge this concept.

Gavison[42] distinguishes between "internal" and "external" critiques of the public/private divide. Internal critiques purport that a given version of the public/private distinction is wrong or mistaken (which creates negative effects) and should be reconstructed (to avoid these negative effects). "Beyond this general criticism, however, this challenge acknowledges that the distinction can be used in beneficial ways."[43] External critiques challenge the distinction itself, claiming "that there is no useful, helpful or valid way to draw the distinction."[44] MacKinnon states:

> For women the measure of the intimacy has been the measure of the oppression. This is why feminism has had to explode the private. This is why feminism has seen the personal as political. The private is public for those for whom the personal is political. In this sense, for women there is no private, either normatively or empirically.[45]

In support of this view MacKinnon cites the example of *Roe v. Wade* and the invocation of a right of privacy in the context of abortion, arguing that the concept of privacy has been instrumental in maintaining women's oppression:

> [T]he very place, the body; the very relations, heterosexual; the very activities, intercourse and reproduction; and the very feelings, intimate - form the core of what is covered by privacy doctrine. From this perspective, the legal concept of privacy can and has shielded the place of battery, marital rape, and women's exploited labour; has preserved the central institutions whereby women are *deprived* of identity, autonomy, control and self-definition.[46]

Body politics questions lie at the core of the distinction between these two positions. For "internal" critics certain matters, "intimate" or "personal", ought to remain private: they assume that within a private sphere, properly defined, women will be able to act autonomously and freely. Law should seek to protect women from undue pressure within this autonomous sphere and provide effective remedies where autonomy is infringed; consent is often seen as a key tool in defining autonomous action. Body politics questions are very often regarded as falling inside this sphere of intimacy.

For external critics the personal is political (or public) and the label "private" merely a tool of oppression:

> When the law of privacy restricts intrusions into intimacy, it bars change in control over that intimacy. The existing distribution of power and resources within the private sphere will be precisely what the law of privacy exists to protect.[47]

Rights serve to draw a distinction between public and private fields. Rights can render certain matters private, either through silence (the failure of law to specifically recognise particular claims), or through the invocation of a "privatising" right (privacy, autonomy, freedom). Thus some claims are protected at the expense of others, by rendering some of the claims involved invisible to law.[48] To leave the body in a "private" or "intimate" sphere, beyond legal control, is therefore to replicate the "invisibility" of women and women's bodies in dominant discourses of rights. Gender neutral rights discourses fail to take account of the deeply gendered nature of society: they are predicated on a public/private divide which is not gender neutral.

The dichotomies between public and private and between the State and civil society are reproduced in international law through traditional doctrines of State responsibility and a focus within international human rights law on direct State violations of individual rights. Harms suffered by women at the hands of private individuals or within the family have been placed outside of the conceptual framework of international human rights. Feminists have argued that a failing of international human rights norms is that by not recognising the gendered consequences of their application they render invisible particular problems suffered by women:

> The differences in the nature and the level of threats to the enjoyment of their rights to life and to bodily integrity that women and men face justify the conclusion that women and men do not enjoy these rights on an equal basis, which is the promise held out to women by the major human rights instruments.[49]

Where the particular problems faced by women have been addressed in the substance of human rights instruments, the instruments (and related enforcement mechanisms) have generally been located on the periphery of the international human rights process.[50]

The complexity of the debate is multiplied, however, in the international context as the argument finds an echo in the debate over cultural relativism.

2. Cultural relativism

Rights discourse has been attacked because of its universalistic claims and inherent "essentialism". Attempts to promote universal standards on "women's rights" have met with hostility and have often been perceived as threats to traditional practices and traditions. Whilst liberal human rights advocates justify their discipline by reference to the basic humanity of individuals - and therefore presume the universal applicability of the standards they promote - cultural relativists see morality as a product of culture - and therefore liable to differ in different places and at different times. From this latter perspective it is easy to view the entire international human rights enterprise as imposed morality, and in the current international situation as neo-colonialist.

As Donnelly points out,[51] between radical cultural relativism and radical universalism there is a continuum of positions "involving varying mixes of relativism and universalism". The question in relation to the enforcement of human rights law is whether there is sufficient consensus on universal standards of treatment of individuals and groups to make the whole enterprise viable. For feminists the problem has been that while the international community has by and large succeeded in reaching such a consensus regarding the behaviour of public officials, little consensus has been achieved on the behaviour of individuals in a non-official or "private" capacity.[52] In practice this means that the harms typically suffered by women are left out of human rights charters. Either they are committed by private individuals and hence beyond their scope or they are simply not addressed in the varying investigating, reporting and adjudicating forums which operate these instruments. Yet when women have sought to query this, to seek enlargement of the area of consensus, the cry of cultural relativism has been raised.

Many of the questions with which this collection is concerned - private violence, rape, body alterations, reproduction - are questions in respect of which the "defence" of culture has been pleaded. This is a reflection of the extent to which the body in general, and women's bodies in particular, are the subject of societal construction and regulation: a cultural construct. The question is therefore one which is of great significance in this context. Feminists are deeply divided on the matter of cultural relativism. While some have argued that, "[t]he cry against 'interference in culture' is used as a defense of men's rights, not of women's; it is used to avoid creating a 'national shame' over the behaviour of one sex toward the other, at the expense of the second sex",[53] others have pointed to the cultural specificity of rights discourse. The concept of human rights, it is argued, is a peculiarly western construct.[54] In particular, it is argued that the concept of the self underlying human rights discourse is derived from the modern western tradition of liberal individualism. The liberal concept of the self as essentially separate from and existing in an antagonistic relationship to others, conflicts with competing cultural conceptions of the self as "essentially connected" to others and as embedded in existing social practices and roles. Thus some commentators have argued that: "whereas Western conceptions are based on the autonomous individual, African conceptions do not know such individualism".[55] Sandra Harding notes the curious coincidence of African and feminine "world views". This world view is characterised by "a conception of the self as intrinsically connected with, as part of, both the community and nature".[56] Anne Bunting points out in a recent article that cultural relativism in human rights scholarship has much in common with anti-essentialist tendencies in feminist theory. Feminist theorists have long warned against the essentialising tendencies of using universal categories such as the category "woman", arguing that to do so is to ignore the specificities of race, class and sexuality.[57]

Engle attempts to address this failing by introducing the "Exotic Other Female".[58] She argues that advocates of women's human rights, though failing to acknowledge her existence, imagine and make assumptions about the "woman" in "other" cultures who engages in or condones practices, in Engle's example clitoridectomy, which the advocate opposes:

> Implicit in this label is the assumption that the Exotic Other Female, or at least her needs and desires, are not totally accessible to someone outside her culture. ... In discussing the Exotic Other Female, I do not mean to essentialize her; she is only that where she is merely imagined and not engaged.[59]

Engle's exhortation to the advocates of women's human rights is a plea, however, not a manifesto: she does not attempt to define or describe the engagement process which she advocates. This is the point at which a schism opens up between the views of postmodernists and others. Acknowledging the existence of the Exotic Other Female is not problematic: the difficulty lies in assessing the consequences of doing so.

For some, the consequence of recognising cultural differences between women means no more than that feminists should be "cautious and contingent"[60] in advocating universalistic solutions. This view does not undermine the universalistic claim of human rights discourse, but advocates shaping that discourse in such a way that space remains for diversity between cultural groups. The immediate retort of radical feminists is that this space, a new form of private space, will be colonised by powerful (male) interest groups. Here the argument is identical to the argument made in relation to privacy: since everywhere women are at the bottom it is women who will suffer from any attempt to accommodate cultural difference in international human rights documents. Thus radical feminism is portrayed as unable to "engage" the Exotic Other Female.[61] Engle describes this as paradoxical:

> It might seem that those advocates most critical of what they see as the 'maleness' of the international human rights framework would be most able to take into account women's differences, since they would not be tied to formal universal norms as embodied in 'male' international human rights doctrine. It happens, though, that the radical feminists ... do not generally even acknowledge the existence of the Exotic Other Female.[62]

This is only paradoxical, however, if radical feminism is also claiming to represent all women's concrete and lived experiences. Given the impossibility of a unifying

254 International Human Rights and Body Politics

category, "women" or "women's experiences", such a claim clearly cannot be sustained. Engle herself does not specify what "engagement" with the "Exotic Other Female" would entail. If it is to require respect for the diversity of women's experiences, this cannot be ensured from within a relativist position. As has been pointed out on many occasions, if one begins from a position that there are no universal moral truths or values, there cannot be any ground for asserting the value of "tolerance". Such a position is clearly contradictory.

The need to respect the diversity of women's experiences arises not only at the international level but also within the confines of national boundaries. This diversity cannot, therefore, be used as an argument to confine the feminist project to national jurisdictions. To do so would be to abandon the "other-regarding" nature of the feminist project. It would also limit the solidarity of the feminist movement to the confines of the nation state, propping up the international legal defence of non-interference in domestic affairs of the State, and thereby reinforcing the public/private divide of international law which feminists have fought hard to transcend.

One possible way out of this apparent dilemma is to recognise that the form of rights discourse, the language of rights, is not universal and need not be so. What may be asserted in the form of a rights claim in one society may be asserted in a more familiar form in another society. Concepts such as Pannikar's "homeomorphic equivalent"[63] come to mind here. This would enable feminism to allow space for diversity between cultural groups without abandoning the international agenda of the feminist project. At present the human rights organs established to monitor the reporting procedures of international legal instruments such as the Women's Convention (discussed below) do not confine themselves to the limiting language of rights but rather recognise the various ways in which particular values and norms may be protected. Specifying the substance of such international legal norms will of course still raise many problems. However, to abandon the project would remove access to international forums that may be of assistance to women who seek to move beyond the confines of what they perceive as oppressive traditional practices within their communities.

INTERNATIONAL HUMAN RIGHTS LAW

The rules making up the body of law referred to as international human rights law are couched in gender-neutral terms. The International Bill of Rights[64] as well as the numerous other Conventions and Declarations making up mainstream human rights law provide that everyone is entitled to the rights provided for without any distinction on grounds, inter alia, of sex. No distinction is made between the nature of human rights violations suffered by women and men. This assumes of course, as

MacKinnon points out, that distinction is the problem and lack of distinction the solution.[65]

The guarantees set out in the Bill of Human Rights may be interpreted so as to include protection against those injuries or assaults experienced mainly by women. Until recently, however, this has not occurred. In addition, where physical assault such as rape has been explicitly prohibited, it has not been punished as such. The failure to recognise the uniqueness of women's reproductive capacities and biological make-up, has rendered it impossible for mainstream human rights law to adequately protect the right to bodily integrity or security of the person where the subject of the rights claim is a woman. What have been perceived as "women's human rights" have been marginalised both institutionally and conceptually, from national and international human rights law.

Within the UN system, a separate institutional structure has been established to deal with violations of women's human rights. The culmination of this process was the adoption of the UN Convention on the Elimination of all Forms of Discrimination Against Women[66] which represented the first significant challenge to a vision of human rights which had traditionally excluded much of women's experience. Its adoption also underlined the exclusion of women from mainstream human rights law and the gendered nature of what claims to be an impartial and neutral body of rules. MacKinnon points out that the paradigm of human rights violations is based on experiences of men, not women. What masquerade as universal standards, in reality, serve to protect only sectional interests, in this case the interests of men. Such guarantees of sex equality as do exist assume that equality is best achieved by treating women "the same as" men; the specificities of women's concrete, lived experiences are thereby excluded:

> Women are violated in many ways that men are not, or rarely are; many of these violations are sexual and reproductive. ... [T]his abuse occurs in forms and settings and legal postures that overlap every recognised human rights convention but is addressed, effectively and as such, by none. What most often happens to women escapes the human rights net. Abuses of women as women rarely seem to fit what these laws and their enforcing bodies have in mind.[67]

Although the right to freedom from torture, inhuman and degrading treatment and the right to liberty and security of the person, both widely recognised by international human rights law, would seem to cover any form of physical assault against a woman, they have not traditionally been applied to such cases. Even where a particular form of assault, such as rape, has been explicitly excluded by the rules of humanitarian law, it has not usually been punished as such.

Rape by soldiers has been prohibited by the law of war for centuries and those transgressing those rules have been subjected to capital punishment under national military codes. However, in many instances it has been suggested that rape by soldiers has been permitted, either as an instrument of policy or as an encouragement for soldiers.[68] No mention of rape as a war crime[69] was made in the Nuremberg Charter and no prosecutions for rape took place in the Nuremberg trials. It was, however, prosecuted in Tokyo as a war crime. This lack of consistency shines through also in the fourth Geneva Convention[70] and the Additional Protocols[71] which, although explicitly and categorically prohibiting rape, do not list rape 'among the "grave breaches" subject to universal jurisdiction.[72] Following the extensive media coverage of the systematic practice of rape in the former Yugoslavia and its use as an instrument of "ethnic cleansing", a number of declarations were made proclaiming rape to be a "war crime", a "grave breach under customary international law and the Geneva Conventions"[73] and a "crime against humanity". The Statute of the International Tribunal established to prosecute those responsible for violations of international humanitarian law committed in the former Yugoslavia, lists rape as a crime against humanity.[74]   The Vienna Declaration and Programme of Action adopted by the World Conference on Human Rights states that violations of the human rights of women in situations of armed conflict are violations of the fundamental principles of international human rights and humanitarian law and further provides that all violations of this kind, including in particular murder, systematic rape, sexual slavery, and forced pregnancy, require a "particularly effective response".[75]

Meron suggests that the recognition of rape as a war crime may lead also to its recognition as torture or inhuman treatment contrary to international human rights law.[76] The prohibition of torture is clearly open to this interpretation as also is the right to liberty and security of the person propounded by both the Universal Declaration and the Covenant on Civil and Political Rights. As traditionally interpreted the right to security of the person protects an individual against arbitrary arrest or detention. It is uncertain, however, to what extent it protects against mutilation of the human body. It has been argued that if the right to security of the person is interpreted in conjunction with the protection of privacy, a broad category of physical integrity could thereby be protected.[77]

The implementation of other rights, in particular those outlined in the 1966 International Covenant on Economic, Social and Cultural Rights (ICESCR) would greatly strengthen women's status. However, as Shelley Wright[78] has pointed out, economic and social rights have been marginalised from mainstream human rights practice in the same way that "women's rights" have been. The enforcement mechanisms established under both the ICESCR and the Women's Convention are far weaker than those concerned with the protection of what are rather arbitrarily categorised as civil and political rights.[79]

The failure of mainstream human rights law to respond to "harms" suffered uniquely or mainly by women reveals the gendered nature of its apparently neutral and impartial guarantees. These standards are supplemented by a separate body of norms and institutional structures governing what are identified as "women's human rights". Even within that system, however, the extent to which the specificities of women's concrete experiences are taken into account is limited.

The adoption of the 1979 UN Convention on the Elimination of all Forms of Discrimination Against Women was the culmination of work begun in 1974 by the UN Commission on the Status of Women. Dissatisfaction with the impact of existing instruments led from the mid-1960s to increasing efforts to develop international instruments providing a global conceptualisation of the human rights of women and containing concrete measures of implementation and supervision. These efforts led in 1967 to the adoption of the Declaration on the Elimination of All Forms of Discrimination Against Women[80] and resulted in 1979 in the adoption of the Convention. The Convention falls far short of what many feminists would have hoped for both in terms of its substance and the mechanisms established for its enforcement; the only enforcement mechanism envisaged by the Convention is the reporting procedure. Unlike the 1966 Convention on the Elimination of All Forms of Racial Discrimination[81] (CERD) on which the Women's Convention is closely modelled, no provision is made for individual complaints or inter-state complaints.[82] In addition, the number and scope of reservations entered by States Parties has rendered the Convention largely ineffective.[83] Many of these reservations invoke the primacy of traditional customs and practices and/or religious law, in particular the Shari'a.[84] Again, unlike CERD, no procedure is established for determining whether such reservations are compatible with the "object and purpose" of the Convention.[85] They have, therefore, largely remained unchallenged.

In its substance the Convention continues the "equal treatment" approach found in mainstream human rights law, that is, the belief that equality is best achieved by extending to women the same rights as are available to men. Discrimination is defined in Article 1 as:

> any distinction, exclusion or restriction made on the basis of sex which has the effect or purpose of impairing or nullifying the recognition, enjoyment or exercise by women, irrespective of their marital status, on a basis of equality of men and women, of human rights and fundamental freedoms in the political, economic, social, cultural, civil or any other field.

Again the belief that distinction is the problem and lack of distinction the solution is reiterated. This serves only to reinforce existing norms and values without in any way subverting the inherently gendered nature of the existing rules. Temporary "special measures" may be adopted under the Convention in order to eliminate any distinctions that have resulted from pre-existing discriminatory practices and to "accommodate" women's child-bearing capacities within the structures of the workplace. However, such measures are open to the criticism advanced by MacKinnon and others that this "special treatment" approach attempts to "compensate" women for their lack of correspondence with men, thereby reinforcing the belief that the male standard is the norm against which we are all to be measured.

A significant omission from the Convention is the failure to explicitly address the issue of violence against women. In fact, apart from some references to reproduction and the needs of pregnant women within the workplace, women's bodies are largely absent from the text of the Convention. Despite the reference to a range of social structures that are identified as contributing to discrimination against women, including, inter alia, apartheid, racism, foreign occupation and domination and interference in the internal affairs of States, no reference is made in either the Preamble or the main text to violence against women. Nor is any attempt made to articulate a right to bodily integrity. An attempt was made to correct this omission at the eighth session of CEDAW (Committee on the Elimination of All Forms of Discrimination Against Women). The Committee adopted a general recommendation[86] on violence against women stating, inter alia, that the Convention requires States Parties to protect women against violence of any kind occurring within the family, at the work place or in any other area of social life. It also recommended that States should include in their periodic reports to the Committee information about legislation in force to protect women against the incidence of all kinds of violence, and any other measures adopted to eradicate this violence.[87] This was followed in 1990 by a general recommendation on female circumcision.[88] The Committee "expressed its concern" about the continuation of the practice of female circumcision and other traditional practices "harmful to the health of women", and recommended that States Parties take appropriate and effective measures with a view to eradicating the practice of female circumcision. Its practice was not condemned as a violation of women's human rights, but rather identified as harmful to women's health. In 1992 the Committee adopted a comprehensive recommendation on violence against women.[89] In its general comments, the Committee stated that the definition of discrimination contained within the Convention included gender-based violence and defined such violence as, "violence that is directed against a woman because she is a woman or that affects women disproportionately". The particular rights and freedoms identified as being violated by the existence of gender-based violence included:

(a)   The right to life;
(b)   The right not to be subject to torture or to cruel, inhuman or degrading treatment or punishment;
(c)   The right to equal protection according to humanitarian norms in time of

international or internal armed conflict;
(d)   The right to liberty and security of person;
(e)   The right to equal protection under the law;
(f)   The right to equality in the family;
(g)   The right to the highest standard attainable of physical and mental health;
(h)   The right to just and favourable conditions of work.

Further, it was stated that traditional attitudes by which women are regarded as subordinate to men perpetuate widespread practices involving violence, such as female circumcision; the effect of such practices on women's mental and physical integrity, the Committee stated, was to deprive them of the equal enjoyment, exercise and knowledge of human rights and fundamental freedoms. This was a significant move beyond the stance adopted in its previous recommendation on female circumcision. Finally, it was recommended that all States Parties should ensure that laws against family violence and abuse, rape, sexual assault and other gender-based violence give adequate protection to all women, and respect their integrity and dignity. Implicit within this recommendation is clearly an acceptance of a right to bodily integrity.

The identification of gender-based violence as a violation of a woman's human rights was reiterated in the Vienna Declaration and the Declaration on the Elimination of Violence against Women.[90] Paragraph 30 of the Vienna Declaration identified discrimination against women as a gross and systematic violation of human rights. Paragraph 38 stresses the particular importance of working towards the elimination of violence against women in public and private life. Of particular interest is the reference to the need to eradicate any conflicts which may arise between the rights of women and the harmful effects of certain traditional or customary practices. The World Conference called upon the General Assembly to adopt the UN draft Declaration on the Elimination of Violence against Women;[91] this was duly adopted by the General Assembly without a vote on 20 December 1993. In the Declaration the General Assembly recognises "the urgent need for the universal application to women of the rights and principles with regard to equality, security, liberty, integrity and dignity of all human persons." Violence against women is defined as:

> any act of gender-based violence that results in, or is likely to result in, physical, sexual or psychological harm or suffering to women, including threats of such acts, coercion or arbitrary deprivation of liberty, whether occurring in public or in private life.

As Christine Chinkin points out, the reference to violence as "gender-based" emphasises the "specificity" of the problem: "[i]n other words, the right is not an adaptation of a right built on male experience".[92] Rape (including marital rape), female genital mutilation and any form of violence within the family are all specifically identified as being prohibited by the Declaration. Another step taken by the Declaration is its clarification in Article 4 that custom, tradition or religion cannot be used as a justification to avoid eliminating violence against women. The reference to "female genital mutilation" and "other traditional practices harmful to women" was included over the protest of some Islamic nations, particularly the Sudan.[93] A clear attempt is also made to transcend the public/private dichotomy of international law. Violence occurring within the general community and in the family as well as any form of violence "perpetrated or condoned" by the State is within its scope. Article 4(c) exhorts States to:

> [e]xercise due diligence to prevent, investigate and, in accordance with national legislation, punish acts of violence against women, whether those acts are perpetrated by the State or by private persons.

It thus clearly departs from the traditional doctrine of State responsibility with its almost exclusive emphasis on the public sphere. Chinkin, however, points out that the main text of the Convention avoids making any clearly stated nexus between violence and human rights. Violence against women is defined in Articles 2 and 3 without any reference to human rights while Article 3 refers to human rights but not to violence against women. This, she argues, reflects the strong opposition to describing violence against women as a violation of human rights which was expressed, in particular, by the United States and Sweden during the 1992 inter-sessional meeting of the Commission on the Status of Women. It was argued that human rights provide protection from actions in which there is direct State involvement and to extend rights discourse to cover "private" behaviour would reduce the status of the whole human rights canon.[94] Nonetheless, the Declaration is clearly an improvement on previous legal instruments. A further step towards the integration of "women's rights" into the mainstream human rights agenda was the approval of the appointment of a special rapporteur on violence against women.[95]

While the symbolic importance of these recent developments should be recognised, it must also be remembered that the instruments within which these advances have been made do not in themselves give rise to any binding legal obligations.[96] At most they could be said to form part of the growing body of *lex ferenda* in the international sphere. This, coupled with the lack of adequate enforcement mechanisms under the Women's Convention, ensures that women's bodies and the concerns and issues arising therefrom remain marginalised within international human rights forums.

WOMEN'S RIGHTS AND HUMAN RIGHTS

The potential of human rights discourse as a venue for addressing the harms suffered by women is a matter of debate concerning both the substance and the form of that discourse. Substantively it is argued that human rights practice and doctrine reflects the needs and interests of the male sex. "Adding women in" to that body of rules would reinforce what are inherently male norms and values. This might hold true particularly where "adding in" means simply assimilating women into existing norms and practices. In any case existing human rights documents already hold out the promise of equal treatment and have been shown to be no sure foundation for the effective realisation of that promise. More far-reaching attempts to subvert the gender bias of those rules by "accommodating women's differences" also lead to difficulties; varying interpretations exist as to what those differences are and what consequences should follow from the recognition of such differences. As is clear from the debate on cultural relativism, women's experiences cannot be easily translated into universally applicable rules.

Some feminists have argued that any attempt to "add women into" human rights doctrine is an inherently flawed enterprise; the adversarial nature of rights discourse distorts and fails to address many of the concerns that arise especially with regard to issues surrounding the female body. The assertion of a rights claim frequently provokes competing and often conflicting rights claims leading to apparently indeterminate debates which, many feminists argue, detract attention from the underlying inequalities in power between the disputing parties. Furthermore, as Smart points out, "the acquisition of a right in a given area may create the impression that a power difference has been resolved."[97] In addition it may be seen to legitimate existing inequalities. Such inequalities as do persist are then attributed to "natural" sex differences or different "free" choices.

As to the form of human rights theory and practice, the feminist critique of its public/private dichotomy is well-documented. However, feminists differ in their response; while some have called for greater regulation of the "private" sphere, others have pointed to the lack of autonomy in many women's lives and the need for protection from the "invasiveness" of the family and the community. The danger in this latter approach is that it leaves open a space that may be vulnerable to colonisation by powerful male interests.

Despite these difficulties, however, many feminist writers are reluctant to abandon the discourse of rights. The reasons are many and varied. Elsewhere in this volume Elizabeth Kingdom argues, in support of Patricia Williams, that the critiques of rights advanced, inter alia, by the Critical Legal Studies (CLS) movement neglect the motivational power of rights discourse.[98] Williams herself stresses the symbolic importance of an assertion of a rights claim,[99] echoing Carol Smart; "[t]o couch a claim in terms of rights is a major step towards a recognition of a social wrong";[100] the claim is immediately made visible within the public sphere and conferred with an air of legitimacy reserved for assertions of rights. The power of rights discourse to render visible issues and concerns previously silenced is in itself a strong attraction for feminists. Although the recognition of a woman's right to autonomy and self-determination may be a double-edged sword, it has served in some instances to protect women from interference by the State. It is because of this that challenges to women's abortion rights, for example, are perceived as threats to a woman's autonomy and reproductive "freedom".

From the perspective of activists the point made by Elizabeth Kingdom in this volume that rights discourse is "ineluctable" must be recognised. The prevalence of rights discourse, particularly within international law, means that feminists cannot avoid articulating their claims in the language of rights if those claims are to be acknowledged in international legal fora. It is for these reasons that many feminists have been reluctant to accept the "all or nothing" approach to rights discourse advocated by some CLS scholars.[101]

The existing international human rights discourse, where women's concerns are not directly addressed in the mainstream but instead are confined to the margins where the forms of protection are weaker, contributes to and reinforces the invisibility of women. This effect is important both on a symbolic and on a practical level, since international human rights law at times forms an important influence on domestic law.

There are, therefore, many reasons why feminists might seek to utilise international human rights law. The concluding section of this chapter considers how many of the issues discussed above might be addressed at the level of strategy, if an attempt were made to "write in" women's rights to mainstream human rights documents. These questions of strategy are discussed in relation to a proposed "right to bodily integrity".[102] The idea of such a right has long been regarded by feminists as desirable. More recently, the impetus for securing such a right could be said to have been renewed by the focus in the Vienna Declaration on violence against women and the attention which this issue received in the General Assembly Resolution on Violence Against Women. The attention of the international community has also been drawn to the systematic use of rape as a weapon by the warring factions in the Bosnian conflict. Suzanne Gibson has pointed out that rape has not throughout most of recorded history been a crime against women. She argues that "it has, significantly however, been a heinous crime against men: a humiliation inflicted upon a nation, an affront to a man's pride as guardian of his women, a desecration of all that man holds dear." We must, she argues, "vigorously reject arguments which seem to be derived from discourses around the interests of the nation state, the chastity of Muslim women, the sanctity of the Islamic family, the humiliation of Bosnian men, or anything remotely similar"; objections to war rape must be unambiguously founded upon women's right to physical autonomy and bodily integrity. Such a stance, she admits, seems to be precisely the stance of the liberal humanist discourse of human rights.[103] Although Gibson advocates the recognition of a right to bodily integrity she does not go on to specify its content. In the next section, we will try to draw out the parameters of such a right.

In choosing to confine the remaining discussion to the proposed "right to bodily integrity" we do not intend to suggest that the inclusion of such a right is the only way in which feminists should seek to bring body politics questions into existing human rights documents. There is clearly scope for gains to be made by raising awareness within both supervisory and judicial bodies, where these exist, of the failures of existing human rights law and mechanisms to address the issues which concern women, and by seeking to bring about change in these fora. Another legitimate and important area of debate for feminists, concerns the extent to which the gender-specific human rights measures and mechanisms discussed above ought to be strengthened.[104]

It should also be recognised that the effectiveness of any body politic right is affected by a wide range of socio-economic factors such as health policies, literacy and economic situation. Our purpose in proposing a "right to bodily integrity" is to explore its potential as a tool which might be used by women in present and future struggles, in combination with other tools, to address the situation of women.

A RIGHT TO BODILY INTEGRITY

It is immensely difficult to cast such a right so that it can be of use to women seeking to assert control and choice over their bodies in the wide variety of cultural settings in which such struggles can be imagined. The right must be specific enough to make its meaning and its subject evident to those who will be charged with implementing or overseeing the application of the instrument in question, since experience has shown that gender neutral language and general formulations of rights are liable to be interpreted so as to exclude that which is the concern primarily of women.[105] Yet it must be general enough to accommodate the wide range of body politics struggles which feminists would seek to assist. Specificity is to be avoided if it entails taking a narrow and unquestioning cultural perspective of "women" and "women's bodies" but this is not to say that no moral judgments should be made over the practices common in cultures other than one's own. Specificity is also to be avoided if its effect is to freeze meanings of what it is to be female. Law, for this purpose at least, should be regarded as process rather than as a static set of normative statements. And it is to assist in the shaping of that process in a variety of settings that the "right to bodily integrity" must be proposed.

From the analysis above it can be concluded that "privatising" rights should be avoided where possible in favour of a positive statement of the right to bodily integrity against specified harms. Moreover a specific effort should be made to ensure that international law's own version of the public/private divide is overcome. This would entail placing States under a firm positive obligation to promote and maintain the conditions under which bodily integrity can be realised and to provide effective means of redress where bodily integrity is infringed. Most importantly, the State must be obliged to protect bodily integrity from interference by private individuals. A model for this can be seen in the General Assembly Resolution on Violence Against Women.[106] There is no reason why this obligation - to protect against violations by "private" individuals - should not be incorporated into the definition of the right to bodily integrity.

On a more general note, consideration should be given as to whether the specific content of the "right to bodily integrity" should be gender neutral or not. There are dangers in any course which involves recognising explicitly that women are especially vulnerable to particular forms of harm. This would be regarded by many feminists as sending out undesirable signals about women's vulnerability, perpetuating images of women as victims. However, there are other ways to ensure that a "right to bodily integrity" reflects the experiences of women: the right might incorporate specific references to areas of body politics with which women have been concerned: reproduction, domestic violence, rape, female circumcision, to mention a few. Consideration ought to be given as to whether attention should be drawn specifically to these or other areas of concern as a means to ensure that the right cannot be "confined" in its interpretation or application, so as to exclude the concerns of women. Of course, there is a difficulty in this, that the more the specific content of the right is detailed, the less likely it is to avoid the charge of cultural relativism and the less flexible it will be as a tool for adoption in future struggles.

An alternative approach, perhaps less attractive, might be to focus on procedural rather than substantive aspects of the right to bodily integrity. Under this approach, aspects such as access to advice and information, education and questions such as consent and choice might be addressed. Many feminist critics of rights strategies would dismiss this as inadequate to empower women in any real sense. Catharine MacKinnon, for example, attacks the focus on consent in the law of rape, arguing that it is impossible for consent to be "freely" given in a society where sex discrimination is all-pervasive. Alan Gewirth, however, in outlining his theory of rights, suggests that the test of consent could be a strong one.[107] An individual could not be said to be "freely" consenting where that individual is starting from a economically or socially disadvantaged position. States would therefore be placed under a duty to take positive action to correct past discrimination. While this might seem to lend itself more to "progressive implementation" than to immediate judicial enforcement, it should not be dismissed solely for this reason - State reporting mechanisms under existing human rights instruments provide opportunities for State delegates to be questioned about the allocation of resources to "positive action" and/or "affirmative action" programmes.

Would anything be achieved by the "writing in" of a "right to bodily integrity" to existing human rights documents? At minimum, it is suggested, its inclusion would signify, to governments and to the international public at least, that a value is placed on the human body within the value system which those documents represent. It would indicate that the body is a subject of protection, from interference of some sorts. If the right is cast as an *individual* right, it would go some way to prevent practices affecting women being subsumed into group or collective rights, such as the right to family or freedom of religion, or at least provide some element of balance.

The further that it was found to be acceptable to proceed in specifying the content of the "right to bodily integrity", the more it could be made apparent what the types of harm were to be tackled - hence, the more it would become apparent that *women's* bodies are valued and that *women* are to be protected from the harms from which *women* suffer. As can be seen from the discussion of rape in the humanitarian law context above, this would not guarantee any improvement in the condition of women; however, it would provide a tool for those seeking to ensure that such improvement does materialise.

It is not possible to foresee to any degree the fate which might befall such a right once it became embedded in mainstream human rights documents. At the jurisprudential level, the interpretation and application of existing rights has at times followed unforeseen paths. One particular feature of human rights law which should be mentioned here is the interplay in jurisprudential discourse between different rights. A right to bodily integrity might, for instance, have some impact on the interpretation of the existing right to equal treatment under the law. Constant vigilance would be required on the part of feminists to ensure that maximum capital was made of any opportunities thus presented. Constant vigilance would also be required to ensure that the bodies charged with the supervision and implementation of the human rights instruments in question, in their dialogue with States Parties on the "right to bodily integrity", addressed the harms suffered by women.

NOTES

1. The label is used here to refer to the body of international law commonly referred to as international human rights law, where the obligations can be said to arise from the bare humanity of the "victim" (including specific areas of concern such as refugee law), but excluding that area traditionally referring to the treatment of "aliens" or non-nationals where the obligations can be explained as deriving from the nationality of the individuals in

question.

2.   C.Bunch, "Women's Rights as Human Rights: Toward a Re-Vision of Human Rights" (1990) 12 *Human Rights Quarterly* 486, at p.489.

3.   H.Charlesworth et al., "Feminist Approaches to International Law" (1991) 85 *A.J.I.L.* 613, at p.625.

4.   See, for example, De Gama's analysis of the consequences of according legal recognition to the foetus as a locus of rights (K.De Gama, "A Brave New World? Rights Discourse and the Politics of Reproductive Autonomy" in *Feminist Theory and Legal Strategy*, eds. A.Bottomley and J.Conaghan (1993) 114, at pp.116-119).

5.   B.Cossman, "A Matter of Difference: Domestic Contracts and Gender Equality" (1990) 28 *Osgoode Hall Law J.* 303, at p.332: "[t]he liberal conception of the self is individualistic and atomistic. The self is posited as a separate, autonomous unit capable of free choice. The voluntaristic self exists prior to its aims and attachments - it is a self unconstituted by its relationships with others".

6.   See, for example, C.Gilligan, *In a Different Voice* (1982).

7.   H.Charlesworth et al., *supra*, n.3, at p.635.

8.   M.J.Sandel, "Justice and the Good" in his *Liberalism and Its Critics* (1984) 159.

9.   M.J.Sandel, *ibid.*, at p.172.

10.   R.West, "Jurisprudence and Gender" (1988) 55 *University of Chicago Law Rev.* 1, reprinted in K.Bartlett and R.Kennedy, *Feminist Legal Theory: Readings in Law and Gender* (1991) 201.

11.   R.West, *ibid.*, at p.207.

12.   R.West, *ibid.*, at p.210.

13.   R.West, *ibid.*, at p.208.

14.   R.West, *ibid.*, at p.230.

15.   R.West, *ibid.*, at pp.230-231.

16.   R.West, *ibid.*, at p.232.

17.   See L.S.Bibbings, "Female Circumcision: Mutilation or Modification?" in this volume for further discussion on this point.

18.   C.MacKinnon, "Feminism, Marxism, method and the state: an agenda for theory" (1982) 7 *Signs* 515. For further discussion of this point and the subsequent arguments in this section see C.Smart, *Feminism and the Power of Law* (1989) chapter 4.

19.   C.MacKinnon, "Feminism, Marxism, method and the state: toward feminist jurisprudence" (1983) 8 *Signs* 635.

20.   C.MacKinnon, *ibid.*, at p.658.

21.   J.Rawls, for example, sees his concept of justice as an Archimidean point that "is not at the mercy, so to speak, of existing wants and interests." J.Rawls, *A Theory of Justice* (1972) at p.261.

22.   S.Freud, *On Sexuality* (1977) at p.342.

23.   C.Gilligan, *supra*, n.6, at p.19.

24.   M.Friedman, "Beyond Caring: The De-moralization of Gender" (1987) supplementary

vol.13 *Canadian Journal of Philosophy* 87, at p.94.

25. See generally W.Kymlicka, *Contemporary Political Philosophy: An Introduction* (1990) at p.264.

26. C.Gilligan, *supra*, n.6.

27. C.Pateman, "The Disorder of Women: Women, Love and the Sense of Justice" (1980) 91 *Ethics* 20.

28. S.Okin, "Thinking Like a Woman" in *Theoretical Perspectives on Sexual Difference*, ed. D.Rhode (1990).

29. E.Kingdom, "The Right to Reproduce" (1986) *Medicine, Ethics and Law* 32 (13th Annual Conference of the Association for Legal and Social Philosophy, Leeds, 4-6 April).

30. C.Smart, *supra*, n.18, at pp.92-93. See generally C.Smart, *supra*, n.18, chapter 5, "Law, Power and Women's Bodies".

31. For a discussion of the inadequacies of the "conflict" model in respect of maternal and foetal rights, see H.Draper, "Women, Forced Caesarians and Antenatal Responsibilities" and C.Wells, "Maternal Versus Foetal Rights" both in *Body Politics: Control versus Freedom: the role of feminism in women's personal autonomy*, (1993) Feminist Legal Research Unit, University of Liverpool, Working Paper No. 1.

32. C.Smart, *supra*, n.18, at pp.145-6.

33. K.De Gama, *supra*, n.4.

34. R.J.Lindgren, "Rethinking the Grounds for Reproductive Freedom" in *Women's Rights and the Rights of Man*, eds. A.J.Arnaud and E.Kingdom (1990) 109.

35. C.Pateman, "Feminist Critiques of the Public/Private Dichotomy" in *Feminism and Equality*, ed. A.Phillips (1987) 103.

36. W.Kymlicka, *supra*, n.25, at p.251.

37. C.Pateman, *supra*, n.35, at p.107.

38. *Meyer v. Nebraska* (1923) 262 U.S. 390.

39. J.Rawls, "Kantian Constructivism in Moral Theory" (1980) 77 *Journal of Philosophy* 515, at p.544.

40. M.J.Sandel, *supra*, n.8, at p.174.

41. (1965) 381 U.S. 49.

42. R.Gavison, "Feminism and the Public/Private Distinction" (1992) 45 *Stanford Law Review* 1.

43. R.Gavison, *ibid.*, at p.3.

44. R.Gavison, *ibid.*

45. C.MacKinnon, *Towards a Feminist Theory of the State* (1989) at p.191.

46. C.MacKinnon, *Feminism Unmodified* (1987) at p.101.

47. C.MacKinnon, *ibid.*

48. *Roe v. Wade* (1973) 410 U.S. 113.

49. A.Byrnes, "Women, Feminism and International Human Rights Law - Methodological Myopia, Fundamental Flaws Or Meaningful Marginalisation" (1992) 12 *Australian Yearbook of International Law* 205, at p.217.

50. See below, at n.66 and accompanying text.

51.   J.Donnelly, *Universal Human Rights in Theory and Practice* (1989) p.109.

52.   Under the traditional international law doctrine of State responsibility, the State is only liable for the shortcomings and failings of its own officers. For an account see, for example, I.Brownlie, *Principles of Public International Law* (1990) Part VIII, at p.446 *et infra*.

53.   G.Ashworth, *Of Violence and Violation: Women and Human Rights* (1986) at p.8.

54.   A.Pollis and P.Schwab, "Human Rights: A Western Construct with Limited Applicability" in *Human Rights: Cultural and Ideological Perspectives*, eds. A.Pollis and P.Schwab (1979) 1.

55.   I.Shivji, *The Concept of Human Rights in Africa* (1989) at p.12.

56.   S.Harding, *The Science Question in Feminism* (1986) at p.170.

57.   A.Bunting, "Theorizing Women's Cultural Diversity in Feminist International Human Rights Strategies" (1993) 20 *Journal of Law and Society* 6.

58.   K.Engle, "Female Subjects of Public International Law: Human Rights and the Exotic Other Female" (1992) 26 *New England Law Review* 1509.

59.   K.Engle, *ibid.*, at p.1512.

60.   B.Cossman quoted in A. Bunting, *supra*, n.57, at p.18.

61.   K.Engle, *supra*, n.58, at pp.1518-20: "The radical feminist positions of these critics do not, I believe, make them incapable of accepting that women disagree, even about clitoridectomy. Rather, they focus so much on the subordination of women by men that they tend to generalize the extent to which all women have an interest in overcoming men's power. ... Were (these) critics to confront the fact that females disagree about clitoridectomy, they would likely assign 'false consciousness' to those whom they consider do not recognize their own oppression".

62.   K.Engle, *ibid.*, at p.1512.

63.   R.Pannikar distinguishes homeomorphism from analogy. Rather, he says, homeomorphism "represents a peculiar functional equivalence discovered through a topological transformation; it is a kind of existential analogy." R.Pannikar, *The Intra-religious Dialogue* (1978) at p.xxii. See also R.Pannikar, "Is the notion of human rights a western concept?" (1982) 120 *Diogenes* 75.

64.   The term is employed to refer collectively to the Universal Declaration on Human Rights (G.A.Res. 217A 1111) GAOR 3rd Ses., Part I, Resolutions, p.71, the International Covenant on Civil and Political Rights 1966 (999, UNTS 171; UKTS 6 (1977), Cmnd. 6702) (and Optional Protocols) and the International Covenant on Economic, Social and Cultural Rights 1966 (993 UNTS 3; UKTS 6 (1977), Cmnd. 6702).

65.   C.MacKinnon, "Crimes of War, Crimes of Peace" in *On Human Rights*, eds. S.Shute and S.Hurley (1993) 83, at pp.100-101.

66.   G.A.Res. 34/180 of 18 December 1979. As of 1 January 1994 130 States had ratified the Women's Convention.

67.   C.MacKinnon, *supra*, n.65, at p.85.

68.   See generally T.Meron, "Rape as a crime under international humanitarian law" (1993) 87 *American Journal of International Law*, 424 at pp.425, quoting the *Report of Walter Kalin on the Situation of Human Rights in Kuwait under Iraqi Occupation*, UN Doc.

E/CN.4/1992/26, at pp.47-48.

69.   T.Meron defines war crimes as crimes "against the conventional or customary law of war that are committed by persons 'belonging' to one party to the conflict against persons or property of the other side". The perpetrator, as the Nuremberg jurisprudence makes clear, need not necessarily be a soldier. Attacks committed by persons against other persons belonging to the same side are not considered war crimes.

70.   Convention Relative to the Protection of Civilian Persons in Time of War, August 12 1949, Art. 27, 6 UST 3516, 75 UNTS 287.

71.   Protocol Additional to the Geneva Conventions of 12 August 1949 and Relating to the Protection of Victims of International Armed Conflicts, opened for signature 12 December 1977, Arts. 76(1) and 85, 1125 UNTS 3, 16 ILM 1391 (1977) [Protocol 1]; Protocol Additional to the Geneva Conventions of 12 August 1949 and Relating to the Protection of Victims of Non-International Armed Conflicts, opened for signature 12 December 1977, Art. 4(2)(e), 1125 UNTS 609, 16 ILM 1442 (1977) [Protocol II].

72.   See generally F.Krill "The Protection of Women in International Humanitarian Law" (1985) 25 *International Review of the Red Cross* 337, at p.341.

73.   In a letter from the US Department of State on 27 January 1993, the Department stated unequivocally that rape was already a war crime or a grave breach under the Geneva Conventions and customary international law and that the legal basis for prosecuting troops for rape was, therefore, already well established. Letter from Robert A. Bradtke, Acting Assistant Secretary for Legislative Affairs, to Senator Arlen Specter, quoted in T.Meron, *supra*, n.68, at p.427, n.22.

74.   UN Doc. S/25704 Annex, Art. 5 (1993). This statute was approved by Security Council Resolution 827 adopted by the Security Council on 25 May 1993, reprinted in (1993) 32 *I.L.M.* 1203, at pp.1203-1205.

75.   Vienna Declaration and Programme of Action, paragraph 38. For the full text of the Declaration, see UN Doc. A/CONF.157/23 (1993), reprinted in (1993) 32 *I.L.M.* 1661.

76.   T.Meron, *supra*, n.68, at p.428.

77.   See generally R.Lillich, "Civil Rights" in *Human Rights in International Law*, ed. T.Meron (1984) 115, at p.124, quoted in K.Brennan, "The Influence of Cultural Relativism on International Human Rights Law: Female Circumcision as a Case Study" (1989) 7 *Law and Inequality* 367, at p.388, n.104.

78.   S.Wright, "Economic Rights and Social Justice: A Feminist Analysis of Some International Human Rights Conventions" 12 *Australian Yearbook of International Law* 241. Danilo Turk, the special rapporteur on the realisation of economic, social and cultural rights appointed by the Sub-Commission on Prevention of Discrimination and Protection of Minorities, noted in his first progress report that "women tend, on the whole, to enjoy many economic, social and cultural rights to a far lesser degree than men, in all regions of the world." (*Realization of Economic, Social and Cultural Rights, Preliminary Report by the Special Rapporteur*, UN Doc. E/CN.4.Sub.2/1990/19, at p.14.)

79.   The only enforcement mechanisms established under the ICESCR and the Women's

Convention are the reporting procedures which rely heavily on the good-will of the States Parties. Unlike the 1966 Covenant on Civil and Political Rights, no provision is made for individual or inter-state complaints. For a detailed discussion of the enforcement mechanisms established under the Women's Convention, see A.Byrnes, "The Other Human Rights Treaty Body: The Work of the Committee on the Elimination of Discrimination Against Women" (1988) 14 *Yale Journal of International Law* 1.

80.　G.A.Res. 2263 (XXIX) of 7 November 1967.

81.　G.A.Res. 2106 A (XX) of 21 December 1965.

82.　The Vienna World Conference recommended that the Commission on the Status of Women and CEDAW examine the possibility "of introducing a right of petition through the preparation of an optional protocol." (Vienna Declaration and Programme of Action, *supra*, n.75, at para. 40.)

83.　For the full text of the reservations, see United Nations, *Multilateral Treaties Deposited with the Secretary-General* (1993).

84.　See, for example, the general reservation entered by Egypt to Article 2 of the Convention: "The Arab Republic of Egypt is willing to comply with the content of this article provided that such compliance does not run counter to the Islamic Shari'a." For a detailed discussion of reservations to the Women's Convention, see R.Cook, "Reservations to the Convention on the Elimination of All Forms of Discrimination Against Women" (1990) 30 *Virginia Journal of International Law* 643; B.Clark, "The Vienna Convention Reservations Regime and the Convention on Discrimination Against Women" (1991) 85 *American Journal of International Law* 281.

85.　Article 20(2) of CERD provides that: "A Reservation shall be considered incompatible or inhibitive if at least two thirds of the States Parties to this Convention object to it." The Women's Convention provides for no such procedure. In Article 28(2) it states simply that: "A reservation incompatible with the object and purpose of the present Convention shall not be permitted". However, no criteria are established for determining the compatibility or otherwise of a reservation. In addition, a number of States have entered reservations to Article 29 of the Convention which provides for the jurisdiction of the International Court of Justice for the settlement of disputes arising out of the Convention.

86.　Article 21 of the Women's Convention authorises the Committee to make "suggestions and general recommendations based on the examination of reports and information received from the States Parties". Like the general comments adopted by the Human Rights Committee under the International Covenant on Civil and Political Rights, CEDAW's general recommendations are not binding on States Parties.

87.　General Recommendation No.12 (eighth session, 1989), GAOR, 44th Session, Supp. No.37 (A/44/38), 1989.

88.　General Recommendation No.14 (ninth session, 1990), GAOR, 45th Session, Supp. No.38 (A/45/38), 1990. See also the study of the Special Rapporteur on Traditional Practices Affecting the Health of Women and Children, E/CN.4/SUB.2/1989/42 of 21 August 1989 and the study of the Special Working Group on Traditional Practices, E/CN.4/1986/42, 1986.

89. CEDAW General Recommendation No.19, GAOR, 47th Session, Supp. No.38 (A/47/38), 1992.

90. G.A.Res. 48/103, of 20 December 1993.

91. The initial draft of the declaration was prepared at an expert group meeting in November 1991 (*Report of the Expert Group Meeting on Violence Against Women*, UN Doc. EGM/VAW/1991/1). The Commission on the Status of Women (CSW) revised the experts' draft at an intersessional meeting in August 1992, and adopted the revised draft at its regular session in March 1993 (*Report of the Commission on the Status of Women on its thirty-seventh session*, UN Doc. E/1993/27-E/CN.6/1993/18, at p.11).

92. C.Chinkin, "Women's Rights as Human Rights under International Law" paper presented at the W.G.Hart Legal Workshop (1994).

93. C.Chinkin, ibid.

94. C.Chinkin, ibid.

95. The Commission on Human Rights approved the appointment of a special rapporteur on violence against women in its resolution on "The Question of Integrating the Rights of Women into the Human Rights Mechanisms of the United Nations and the Elimination of Violence Against Women", 4 March 1994, E/CN.4/1994/L.11/Add.3, at para.6.

96. The recognised sources of international law are listed in Article 38(2) of the Statute of the International Court of Justice, See generally, J. Harris, *Cases and Materials in International Law* (1991) chapter 2.

97. C.Smart, *supra*, n.18, at p.144.

98. E.Kingdom, "Rights and Body Politics" in this volume, at pp.12-13.

99. P.Williams, *The Alchemy of Race and Rights* (1990).

100. C.Smart, *supra*, n.18, at p.143.

101. See, for example, E. Schneider, "The Dialectics of Rights and Politics" in *At the Boundaries of Law: Feminism and Legal Theory*, eds. M.A.Fineman and N.S.Thomadsen (1991) 301.

102. Those already trying mentally to locate this within existing catalogues of rights might find it helpful to consider this new right as a fundamental civil right, complementary, perhaps, to the existing right to liberty and security of person (or perhaps as an antidote to the construction which has generally been placed on that right).

103. S.Gibson, "The discourse of Sex/War: Thoughts on Catharine MacKinnon's 1993 Oxford Amnesty Lecture" (1993) 1 *Feminist Legal Studies* 188.

104. See, for example, S. Coliver "United Nations Machineries on Women's Rights: How Might They Better Help Women Whose Rights are Being Violated?" in *New Direction in Human Rights*, eds. E.L.Lutz et al. (1989) at p.25; T. Meron, "Enhancing the Effectiveness of the Prohibition of Discrimination Against Women" (1990) 84 *American Journal of International Law* 213.

105. The right to bodily integrity, covering rape, domestic violence and female circumcision, could arguably have been addressed in various aspects in the context of deliberations on the right to life, the right to freedom from torture and inhuman or degrading treatment or punishment and on the right to liberty and security of the person inter alia.

106.   *Supra*, n.91.
107.   A.Gewirth, *Reason and Morality* (1978) at p.290.

Bibliography

Abdalla, R.H.D. (1982), *Sisters in Affliction: Circumcision and Infibulation of Women in Africa*, (Zed: London).

Adams, P. and Cowie, E. (1990), *The Woman in Question*, (Verso: London).

Adler, Z. (1987), *Rape on Trial*, (Routledge: London).

Albonetti, C. (1991), "An Integration of Theories to Explain Judicial Discretion", 38 *Social Problems* 247.

Allen, H. (1987), *Justice Unbalanced: Gender, Psychiatry and Judicial Decisions*, (Open University Press: Milton Keynes).

Allen, H. (1988), "One Law for All Reasonable Persons?", 16 *International Journal of the Sociology of Law* 419.

Allen, H. (1990), "At the Mercy of her Hormones: Premenstrual Tension and the Law", in Adams, P. and Cowie, E. (eds.), *The Woman in Question*, (Verso: London).

Allison, J. and Wrightsman, L. (1993), *Rape: The Misunderstood Crime*, (Sage: London).

Armstrong, S. (1991), "Female Circumcision: fighting a cruel tradition", 2 February *New Scientist* 42.

Arney, W. (1982), *Power and the Profession of Obstetrics*, (University of Chicago Press: Chicago).

Ashworth, A. (1976), "The Doctrine of Provocation", 35 *Cambridge Law Journal* 292.

Ashworth, A. (1990), "Reforming the Law of Murder", *Criminal Law Review* 75.

Ashworth, A. (1993), "Victim Impact Statements and Sentencing", *Criminal Law Review* 498.

Ashworth, G. (1986), *Of Violence and Violation: Women and Human Rights*, (Change: London).

Atiya, N. (1982), *Five Egyptian Women Tell Their Stories*, (Syracuse University Press: New York).

Atkins, C. and Hoggett, B. (1984), *Women and the Law*, (Basil Blackwell: Oxford).

Badran, M. and Cook, M. (eds.) (1990), *Opening the Gates: A Century of Arab Feminist Writing*, (Virago: London).

Bainham, A. (1987), "Handicapped Girls and Judicial Parents", 103 *Law Quarterly Review* 334.

Bainham, A. (1987), "Wardship: effect and uses - medical treatment", 137 *New Law Journal* 518.

Bainham, A. (1991), "Care after 1991 - a reply", *The Journal of Child Law* 99.

Bandalli, S. (1992), "Battered Wives and Provocation", 142 *New Law Journal* 212.

Bandalli, S. (1992), "Provocation from the Home Office", *Criminal Law Review* 716.

Barr, M.W. and Maloney, E.F. (1921), *Types of Mental Defectives*, (Lewis: London).

Barron, J. (1990), *Not Worth The Paper...? The Effectiveness of Legal Protection for Women and Children Experiencing Domestic Violence*, (Women's Aid Federation: Bristol).

Baurmann, M. (1991), "Sexuality, Violence and Emotional After-effects: A Longitudinal Study of Victims of Forcible Rape and Sexual Deviance in Cases reported to the Police" in Sessar, K. and Kerner, H.J. (eds.), *Developments in Crime and Crime Control Research*, (Springer Verlag: New York).

Begin, P. (1989), "Rape Law Reform in Canada" in Viano, E. (ed.), *Crime and its Victims*, (Hemisphere: Washington D.C.).

Bell, C. and Fox, M. (1994), *"A Tragedy of Two Women": Contextualising the Dynamics of Woman-Killing*, (Unpublished Conference Paper presented at the SLSA Conference: Nottingham).

Bell, V. (1991), "Beyond the 'Thorny Question': Feminism, Foucault and the Desexualisation of Rape", 19 *International Journal of the Sociology of Law* 83.

Bell, V. (1993), *Interrogating Incest: Feminism, Foucault and the Law*, (Routledge: London).

Berk, R.A. et al. (1992), "The Deterrent Effect of Arrest: A Bayesian Analysis of Four Field Experiments", 57 *American Sociological Review* 698.

Bettelheim, B. (1962), *Symbolic Wounds: Puberty Rights and the Envious Male*, (2nd ed.) (McMillan: New York).

Bibbings, L. and Alldridge, P. (1993), "Sexual Expression, Body Alteration, and the Defence of Consent", 20 *Journal of Law and Society* 356.

Birch, H. (ed.) (1993), *Moving Targets: Women, Murder and Representation*, (Virago: London).

Blackburn, R. and Taylor, J. (eds.) (1991), *Human Rights for the 1990's: legal, political and ethical issues*, (Mansell: London).

Bordo, S. (1993), *Unbearable Weight: Feminism, Western Culture and the Body*, (University of California Press: Berkeley).

Boulware-Miller, K. (1985), "Female Circumcision: Challenges to the Practice as a Human Rights Violation", 8 *Harvard Women's Law Journal* 155.

Bowker, L. (1983), *Beating Wife Beating*, (Lexington Books: Lexington, Massachusetts).

Boyle, C. et al. (1981), *A Feminist Review of Criminal Law*, (Ministry of Supply and Services: Canada).

Brahams, D. (1987), "Court Powers and the Mentally Handicapped", 84 *Law Society Gazette* 867.

Brannen, J. and Moss, P. (1990), *Managing Mothers: Dual Earner Households after Maternity Leave*, (Unwin Hyman: London).

Brazier, M. (1990), "Down the Slippery Slope", 6 *Professional Negligence* 25.

Brazier, M. (1992), *Medicine, Patients and the Law*, (Penguin: Harmondsworth).

Brennan, K. (1989), "The Influence of Cultural Relativism on International Human Rights Law: Female Circumcision as a Case Study", 7 *Law and Inequality: a Journal of Theory and Practice* 367.

Bridgeman, J. (1992), "Hunger Strikes and Children's Rights", 25 *Trouble and Strife* 36.

Bridgeman, J. (1993), "Demanding Reproductive Control?" in Feminist Legal Research Unit (ed.), *Body Politics: Control versus Freedom*, (Faculty of Law, University of Liverpool: Liverpool).

Bridgeman, J. (1993), "Old enough to know best?", 13 *Legal Studies* 69.

Bringer Cross, M. (1982), "The Expert as Educator: A Proposed Approach to the use of Battered Woman Syndrome Expert Testimony", 35 *Vanderbilt Law Review* 741.

Brown, B. et al. (1992), *Sexual History and Sexual Character Evidence in Scottish Sexual Offence Trials*, (H.M.S.O.: Edinburgh).

Browne, A. (1987), *When Battered Women Kill*, (The Free Press: New York).

Brownlie, I. (1990), *Principles of Public International Law*, (4th ed.) (Oxford University Press: Oxford).

Brownmiller, S. (1973), *Against Our Will: (Men, Women and Rape)*, (Penguin: Harmondsworth).

Bryan, M. (1993), "Two cheers for welfare: the Marion case and sterilisation in Australia", 5 *Journal of Child Law* 40.

Brygger, M.P. and Edleson, J.L., "The Domestic Abuse Project: A Multi Systems Intervention in Woman Battering", 2 *Journal of Interpersonal Violence* 324.

Bryson, V. (1992), *Feminist Political Theory: An Introduction*, (Macmillan Press: Basingstoke).

Bunch, C. (1990), "Women's Rights as Human Rights: Toward a Re-Vision of Human Rights", 12 *Human Rights Quarterly* 489.

Bunting, A. (1993), "Theorizing Women's Cultural Diversity in Feminist International Human Rights Strategies", 20 *Journal of Law and Society* 6.

Burman, M. and Lloyd, S. (1993), *Police Specialist Units for the Investigation of Crimes of Violence against Women and Children in Scotland*, (H.M.S.O: Edinburgh).

Buss, E. (1986), "Getting Beyond Discrimination: A Regulatory Solution to the Problem of Fetal Hazards in the Workplace", 95 *Yale Law Journal* 577.

Butler, J. (1990), *Gender Trouble*, (Routledge: London).

Byrnes, A. (1988), "The Other Human Rights Treaty Body: The Work of the Committee on the Elimination of Discrimination Against Women", 14 *Yale Law Journal of International Law* 1.

Byrnes, A. (1992), "Women, Feminism and International Human Rights Law - Methodological Myopia, Fundamental Flaws Or Meaningful Marginalisation", 12 *Australian Yearbook of International Law* 205.

Callahan, D. (1986), "How technology is reframing the abortion debate", *Hastings Center Report* 33.

Callery, M. (1990), "In the Best Interest of the Children", 13 *Harvard Women's Law Journal* 383.

Campling, J. (1981), *Images of Ourselves: Women with Disabilities Talking*, (Routledge Kegan Paul: London).

Canadian Federal-Provincial Task Force (1983), *Justice for Victims of Crime*.

Carlen, P. (1988), *Women, Crime and Poverty*, (Open University Press: Milton Keynes).

Carlen, P. and Worrall, A. (1987), *Gender, Crime and Justice*, (Open University Press: Milton Keynes).

Carlen, P. et al. (1985), *Criminal Women*, (Polity Press: Cambridge).

Carson, D. (1989), "The Sexuality of People with Learning Difficulties", *Journal of Social and Welfare Law* 354.

Carty, A. (1990), "Introduction: Post-Modern Law" in Carty, A. (ed.), *Post-Modern Law: Enlightenment, Revolution and the Death of Man*, (Edinburgh University Press: Edinburgh).

Chalker, R. and Downer, C. (1992), *A Woman's Book of Choices: Abortion, Menstrual Extraction, RU-486*, (Four Walls Eight Windows: New York).

Chamberlain, G. (1984), *Pregnant Women at Work*, (Royal Society of Medicine: London).

Chambers, G. and Millar, A. (1983), *Investigating Sexual Assault*, (H.M.S.O.: Edinburgh).

Chambers, G. and Millar, A. (1986), *Prosecuting Sexual Assault*, (H.M.S.O.: Edinburgh).

Chapkis, W. (1986), *Beauty Secrets*, (The Women's Press: London).

Chapman, J. and Gates, M. (1978), *The Victimisation of Women*, (Sage: New York).

Charlesworth, H., Chinkin, C. and Wright, S. (1991), "Feminist Approaches to International Law", 85 *American Journal of International Law* 625.

Charlesworth, H. (1993), "The Australian Reluctance about Rights", 31 *Osgoode Hall Law Journal* 195.

Chatterton, D. (1987), "The powers of the courts in respect of the mentally handicapped", 84 *Law Society Gazette* 2441.

Chernin, K. (1981), *Womansize: The Tyranny of Slenderness*, (The Women's Press: London).

Chesler, P. (1993), "A Woman's Right to Self-Defense: the case of Aileen Carol Wuornos", 66 *St John's Law Review* 933.

Chesney-Lind, M. (1973), "Judicial Enforcement of the Female Sex Role: The Family Court and the Female Delinquent", 8 *Issues in Criminology* 197.

Child Poverty Action Group (1994/1995), *Rights Guide to Non-means-tested Benefits*, (Child Poverty Action Group: London).

Chinkin, C. and Wright, S. (1993), "The Hunger Trap: Women, Food and Self-determination", *Michigan Law Journal* 262.

Chinkin, C. (1994), "Women's Rights as Human Rights under International Law", (Unpublished Conference Paper presented at the Hart Legal Workshop).

Cipparone, R. (1985), "The Defense of Battered Women Who Kill", 135 *University of Pennsylvania Law Review* 427.

Coester, M. (1993), "The protection of the embryo in German family law", 5 *Journal of Child Law* 88.

Coleman, T. (1992), "Body Manipulations", 17 *Body Art* 32.

Coliver, S. (1989), "United Nations Machineries on Women's Rights: How Might They Better Help Women Whose Rights are Being Violated?" in Lutz, E.L., Hannum, H. and Burke, K.J. (eds.), *New Directions in Human Rights*, (University of Pennsylvania Press: Philadelphia).

Collins, R. (1977), "Language, History and the Legal Process: A Profile of the Reasonable Man", 8 *Rutgers-Camden Law Journal* 311.

Conaghan, J. (1993), "Pregnancy and the Workplace: A Question of Strategy?" in Bottomley, A. and Conaghan, J. (eds.), *Feminist Theory and Legal Strategy*, (Blackwell: Oxford).

Cooper, D. (1994), "Productive, Relational and Everywhere?: Conceptualising Power and Resistance within Foucauldian Feminism", 28 *Sociology* 435.

Corea, G. (1988), *The Mother Machine: Reproductive Technologies from Artificial Insemination to Artificial Wombs*, (The Women's Press: London).

Cossey, D. (1982), *Abortion and Conscientious Objection*, (Birth Control Trust: London).

Cossman, B. (1990), "A Matter of Difference: Domestic Contracts and Gender Equality", 28 *Osgoode Hall Law Journal* 303.

Coughlin, A. (1994), "Excusing Women", 82 *University of California Law Review* 1.

Craft, A. (1987), *Mental Handicap and Sexuality: Issues and Perspectives*, (Costello: Tunbridge Wells).

Crenshaw, K.W. (1988), "Race, Reform and Retrenchment: Transformation and Legitimation in Antidiscrimination Law", 101 *Harvard Law Review* 1331.

Culliton, K.M. (1993), "Finding a Mechanism to Enforce Women's Right to State Protection from Domestic Violence in the Americas", 34 *Harvard International Law Journal* 507.

Dahl, S. (1993), *Rape - A Hazard to Health*, (Oxford University Press: Oxford).

Daly, M. (1991), *Gyn/Ecology: The Metaethics of Radical Feminism*, (The Women's Press: London).

Daud, S. (1993), "Abortion, contraception and ethnic minorities" in Newman, K. (ed.), *Progress Postponed: Abortion in Europe in the 1990s*, (International Planned Parenthood Federation: London).

Davies, V. (1991), *Abortion and Afterwards*, (Ashgrove Press: Bath).

Davis, K. (1991), "Remaking the She-Devil: A Critical look at Feminist Approaches to Beauty", 6 *Hypatia* 21.

De Cruz, S.P. (1988), "Sterilization, Wardship and Human Rights", 18 *Family Law* 6.

De Gama, K. (1993), "A Brave New World? Rights Discourse and the Politics of Reproductive Autonomy" in Bottomley, A. and Conaghan, J. (eds.), *Feminist Theory and Legal Strategy*, (Blackwell: Oxford).

"Developments - Medical Technology and the Law, Section III: State Intervention During Pregnancy" (1990), 103 *Harvard Law Review* 1556.

Dell, S. (1982), "Diminished Responsibility Reconsidered", *Criminal Law Review* 809.

Dickens, B.M. (1966), *Abortion and the Law*, (MacGibbon and Kee Ltd: Bristol).

Diduck, A. (1993), "Child protection and foetal rights in Canada", 5 *Journal of Child Law* 133.

Diduck, A. (1993), "Legislating Ideologies of Motherhood", 2 *Social and Legal Studies* 461.

Dobash, R.E. and Dobash, R.P. (1979), *Violence against Wives*, (New York Free Press: New York).

Dobash, R.E. and Dobash, R.P. (1992), *Women, Violence & Social Change*, (Routledge: London).

Donnelly, J. (1989), *Universal Human Rights in Theory and Practice*, (Cornell University Press: New York).

Donzelot, J. (1979), *The Policing of Families*, (Hutchinson: London).

Doran, S. (1991), "Alternative Defences: 'The Invisible Burden' on the Trial Judge", *Criminal Law Review* 878.

Dorkenoo, E. and Elworthy, S. (1992), *Female Genital Mutilation: Proposals for Change*, (2nd ed.) (Minority Rights Group: London).

Douglas, G. (1991), *Law, Fertility and Reproduction*, (Sweet & Maxwell: London).

Douzinas, C. and Warrington, R. (1991), "'A Well-Founded Fear of Justice': Law and Ethics in Post-Modernity", 2 *Law and Critique* 115.

Downer, C. (1984), "Through the Speculum" in Arditti, R. et al. (eds.), *Test-Tube Women: What Future For Motherhood?*, (Pandora Press: London).

Doyal, L. (1994), "Managing Conception: Self-insemination and the Limits of Reproductive Freedom", 22 *Policy and Politics* 89.

Draper, H. (1993), "Women, Forced Caesarians and Antenatal Responsibilities" in Feminist Legal

Research Unit (ed.), *Body Politics: Control versus Freedom: the role of feminism in women's personal autonomy*, (Faculty of Law, University of Liverpool: Liverpool).

Dreyfus, H. and Rabinow, P. (1982), *Michel Foucault: Beyond Structuralism and Hermeneutics*, (The Harvester Press: Brighton).

Duncan, S. (1994), "Law as Literature: Deconstructing the Legal Text", V *Law and Critique* 3.

Duncan, S. (1994), "'Disrupting the Surface of Order and Innocence': Towards a Theory of Sexuality and the Law", 2 *Feminist Legal Studies* 3.

Dundee Rape Crisis Centre (1994), *10 Years of Crisis*, (RCC: Dundee).

Dworkin, R. (1986), *Law's Empire*, (Fontana: London).

Easteal, P. (1993), "Sentencing Those Who Kill Their Sexual Intimates: An Australian Study", 21 *International Journal of the Sociology of Law* 189.

Eastman, N. (1992), "Abused Women and Legal Excuses", 142 *New Law Journal* 1549.

Eaton, M. (1983), "Mitigating Circumstances- Familiar Rhetoric", 11 *International Journal of Sociology of Law* 385.

Eaton, M. (1986), *Justice for Women?*, (Open University Press: Milton Keynes).

Eber, L.P. (1981), "The Battered Wife's Dilemma: To Kill or To Be Killed", 32 *The Hastings Law Journal* 895.

Edelman, B. (1979), *Ownership of the Image: Elements for a Marxist Theory of Law*, (Routledge Kegan Paul: London).

Edwards, S. (1984), *Women on Trial*, (Manchester University Press: Manchester).

Edwards, S. (1985), "Gender 'Justice': Defending Defendants and Mitigating Sentence" in Edwards, S. (ed.), *Gender, Sex and the Law*, (Croom Helm: London).

Edwards, S. (1985), "Male Violence Against Women: Excusatory and Explanatory Ideologies in Law and Society" in Edwards, S. (ed.), *Gender, Sex and the Law*, (Croom Helm: London).

Edwards, S. (1987), "Provoking her Own Demise: From Common Assault to Homicide" in Hanmer J. and Maynard M. (eds.), *Women, Violence and Social Change*, (Macmillan: London).

Edwards, S. (1988), "Mad, bad or pre-menstrual", 140 *New Law Journal* 456.

Edwards, S. (1990), "Battered women who kill", 140 *New Law Journal* 1380.

Edwards, S. (1992), "Battered woman syndrome", 142 *New Law Journal* 1350.

Eekelaar, J. (1993), "White Coats or Flax Jackets? Doctors, children and the Courts - Again", 109 *Law Quarterly Review* 182.

Ehrenreich, B. and English, D. (1979), *For Her Own Good: 150 Years of the Experts' Advice to Women*, (Pluto Press: London).

Eisenstein, H. and Jardine, A. (eds.) (1990), *The Future of Difference*, (Rutgers University Press: New Brunswick, New Jersey).

El Dareer, A. (1982), *Women, Why Do You Weep? Circumcision and its Consequences*, (Zed: London).

El Saadawi, N. (1980), *The Hidden Face of Eve: Women in the Arab World*, translated by Hetata, S., (Zed: London).

Elias, R. (1993), *Victims Still: the Political Manipulation of Victims*, (Sage: London).

Engle, K. (1992), "Female Subjects of Public International Law: Human Rights and the Exotic Other Female", 26 *New England Law Review* 1509.

Equal Opportunities Commission (1993), *Women and Men in Britain 1993*, (H.M.S.O: London).

Ewing, C.P. (1987), *Battered women Who Kill: Psychological Self-Defense as Legal Justification*, (Lexington Books: Lexington, Masachusettes).

Faigman, D.L. (1987), "Discerning Justice When Battered Women Kill", 39 *Hastings Law Journal* 207.

Faludi, S. (1992), *Backlash: The Undeclared War Against Women*, (Chatto & Windus; London).

Fargher, T. (1985), "The Police Response to Violence against Women in the Home" in Paul J. (ed.), *Private Violence and Public Policy*, (Routledge Kegan Paul: London).

Farrington, D. and Morris, A. (1983), "Sex, Sentencing and Reconviction", 23 *British Journal of Criminology* 229.

Farsides, C.C. (1992), "Body Ownership" in McVeigh, S. and Wheeler, S. (eds.), *Law, Health and Medical Regulation*, (Dartmouth: Aldershot).

Feldman, D. (1987), "Rights, Capacity and Social Responsibility", 16 *Anglo-American Law Review* 97.

Fennel, P. (1990), "Inscribing Paternalism in the Law: Consent to Treatment and Mental Disorder", 17 *Journal of Law and Society* 29.

Ferguson, P. (1993), "Controversial Aspects of the Law of Rape: An Anglo-Scottish Comparison" in Hunter R. (ed.), *Justice and Crime*, (T & T Clark: Edinburgh).

Ferris, P. (1966), *The Nameless: Abortion in Britain Today*, (Hutchinson: London).

Finemanz, M.A. and Thomasden, N.S. (eds.) (1991), *Boundaries of Law: Feminism and Legal Theory*, (Routledge: London).

Finger, A. (1984), "Claiming all of our Bodies: Reproductive Rights and Disabilities" in Arditti, R. et al. (eds.), *Test-Tube Women: What Future For Women?*, (Pandora Press: London).

Fletcher, J. (1979), *Morals and Medicine*, (2nd ed.) (Princeton University Press: Princeton).

Fortin, J.E.S. (1988), "Legal Protection for the Unborn Child", 51 *Modern Law Review* 54.

Fortin, J.E.S. (1988), "Sterilisation, the Mentally Ill and Consent to Treatment", 51 *Modern Law Review* 634.

Fortin, J.E.S. (1988), "Can You Ward a Foetus?", 51 *Modern Law Review* 768.

Foucault, M. (1982), *The History of Sexuality: An Introduction*, (Penguin: London).

Foucault, M. (1991), *Discipline and Punish: The Birth of the Prison*, (Penguin: London).

Francome, C. (1986), *Abortion Practice in Britain and the United States*, (Allen and Unwin: London).

Frankel, M. (1971), "Lawlessness in Sentencing", 41 *Cincinnati Law Review* 1.

Franklin, S., (1991), "Fetal fascinations: new dimensions to the medical-scientific constructions of fetal personhood" in Franklin, S., Lury, C. and Stacey, J. (eds.), *Off-Centre: Feminism and Cultural Studies*, (Harper Collins Academic: London) 190.

Franklin, S., Lury, C. and Stacey, J. (eds.) (1991), *Off-Centre: Feminism and Cultural Studies*, (Harper Collins Academic: London).

Fredman, S. (1994), "A Difference With Distinction: Pregnancy and Parenthood Reassessed", 110 *Law Quarterly Review* 106.

Freeman, M. (1987), "For Her Own Good", 84 *Law Society Gazette* 949.

Freeman M. (1990), "Care after 1991" in Freestone D. (ed.), *Children and the Law*, (Hull University Press: Hull).

Freud, S. (1977), *On Sexuality*, (Penguin: Harmondsworth).

Friedman, M. (1987), "Beyond Caring: The De-moralization of Gender", 13 (supplementary) *Canadian Journal of Philosophy* 87.

Frug, M.J. (1992), "A Postmodern Feminist Legal Manifesto (An Unfinished Draft)", 105 *Harvard Law Review* 1045.

Fudge, J. (1989), "The Effect of Entrenching a Bill of Rights upon Political Discourse", 17 *International Journal of the Sociology of Law* 445.

Fyfe, W. (1991), "Abortion Acts: 1803 - 1967" in Franklin, S., Lury, C. and Stacey, J. (eds.), *Off-Centrè: Feminism and Cultural Studies*, (Harper Collins Academic: London) 160.

Gallagher, J. (1987), "Prenatal Invasions and Interventions: What's Wrong with Fetal Rights?", 10 *Harvard Women's Law Journal* 9.

Gane, C. (1992), *Sexual Offences*, (Butterworths: Edinburgh).

Gardner, S. (1992), *Substance Abuse during Pregnancy*, (Social Work Monographs, University of East Anglia: Norwich).

Garfinkel, P. and Garner, D. (1982), *Anorexia Nervosa: A Mulitdimensional Perspective*, (Brunner/Mazel: New York).

Gavison, R. (1992), "Feminism and the Public/Private Distinction", 45 *Stanford Law Review* 1.

Gelles, R.J. (1993), "Family Violence" in Hampton, R.L. et al. (eds.), *Family Violence Prevention and Treatment*, (Sage: Newbury Park, California).

Gelles, R.J. and Cornell C.P. (1990), *Intimate Violence in Families*, (Sage: London).

Gerwith, A. (1978), *Reason and Morality*, (University of Chicago Press: Chicago).

Gevins, A. (1983), "Tackling Tradition: African Women Speak out Against Female Circumcision" in Davis, M. (ed.), *Third World: Second Sex*, (Zed: New York).

Gibson, S. (1993), "The Discourse of Sex/War: Thoughts on Catharine MacKinnon's 1993 Oxford Amnesty Lecture", 1 *Feminist Legal Studies* 188.

Gilligan, C. (1982), *In a Different Voice: psychological theory and women's development*, (Harvard University Press: Cambridge, Massachusetts).

Goldberg-Ambrose, C. (1992), "Unfinished Business in Rape Law Reform", 48 *Journal of Social Issues* 173.

Goodrich, P. (1993), "Writing Legal Difference: Helena Kennedy's *Eve was Framed: Women and British Justice* and Luce Irigaray's *J'aime à toi: equissé d'une felicité dans l'histoire*", 4 *Women: A Cultural Review* 317.

Gordon, G. (1992), *Criminal Law of Scotland*, (Greens: Edinburgh).

Gordon, L. (1980), "Review of James Mohr's Abortion in America: the Origins and Evolutions of National Policy", 13 *Journal of Social History* 514.

Government Statistical Service (1989), *Statistics on Rape 1977-87*, 4 Home Office Statistical Bulletin.

Graycar, R. and Morgan, J. (1990), *The Hidden Gender of Law*, (The Federation Press: Leichhardt, New South Wales.).

Greenwood, V. and Young, J. (1976), *Abortion in Demand*, (Pluto Press: London).

Griffin, S. (1971), "Rape: The All-American Crime", September *Ramparts*.

Grubb, A. and Pearl, D. (1987), "Sterilisation and the Courts", 46 *Cambridge Law Journal* 439.

Grubb, A. and Pearl, D. (1989), "Sterilisation - Courts and Doctors as Decision Makers", 48 *Cambridge*

Law Journal 380.

Gunn, M. (1988), "T v T", 5 *Journal of Social Welfare Law* 336.

Halpern, J., Midge, L. and Hickman, J. (1993), "Pregnancy as a source of bias in performance appraisals", 14 *Journal of Organizational Behaviour* 649.

Hanmer, J. and Maynard, M. (1987), *Women, Violence and Social Change*, (Macmillan: London).

Hanmer, J. (1989), "Women and Policing in Britain" in Hanmer, J. et al. (eds.), *Women, Policing and Male Violence: International Perspectives*, (Routledge Kegan Paul: London).

Hanmer, J. and Saunders, S. (1993), *Women, Violence and Crime Prevention*, (Avebury: Aldershot).

Harding, S. (1986), *The Science Question in Feminism*, (Open University Press: Milton Keynes).

Harper, R. and McWhinnie, A. (1983), *The Glasgow Rape Case*, (Hutchinson: London).

Harris, C.C. (1985), "The Cultural Decision-Making Model: Focus Circumcision", 6 *Health Care for Women International* 27.

Harris, J. (1991), *Cases and Materials in International Law*, (4th ed.) (Sweet and Maxwell: London).

Hedley, R. and Dorkenno, E. (1992), *Child Protection and Female Genital Mutilation: Advice for Health, Education, and Social Work Professionals*, (Minority Rights Group, with support from the Department of Health: London).

Heidensohn, F. (1968), "The Deviance of Women: A Critique and an Enquiry", XIX *British Journal of Sociology* 160.

Heidensohn, F. (1985), *Gender and Crime*, (Macmillan: London).

Hellum, A. (1993), "New Reproductive Technology in an Ecological Perspective" in Hellum, A. (ed.), *Birth Law*, (Scandinavian University Press: Oslo).

Henderson, L. (1985), "The Wrongs of Victims' Rights", 37 *Stanford Law Review* 937.

Herman, D. (1994), *Rights of Passage: Struggles for Lesbian and Gay Legal Equality*, (Toronto University Press: Toronto).

Higgins, L. and Silver, B. (1991), *Rape and Representation*, (Columbia: New York).

Hilbert, A.M. (1994), "The Irish Abortion Debate: Substantive Rights and Affecting Commerce Jurisprudential Models", 26 *Vanderbilt Journal of Transnational Law* 1117.

Hindell, K. and Simms, M. (1971), *Abortion Law Reformed*, (Peter Owen: London).

Hirst, P. and Kingdom, E. (1979/80), "On Edelman's Ownership of the Image", *20 Screen* 135.

Holmstrom, L. and Burgess, L. (1983), *The Victims of Rape: Institutional Reactions*, (Wiley: New York).

Horder, J. (1992), *Provocation and Responsibility*, (Clarendon Press: Oxford).

Horder, J. (1992), "Provocation and Loss of Self-Control", 108 *Law Quarterly Review* 191.

Hornstein, F. (1984), "Children by Donor Insemination: A New Choice for Lesbians" in Arditti, R. et al. (eds.), *Test-Tube Women: What Future For Motherhood?*, (Pandora Press: London).

Hosken, F. (1982), "The Hosken Report: Genital and Sexual Mutilation of Females", *Women's International Network News*, (Women's International Network News: Lexington, Massachusetts).

Howard, R. (1984), "Womens Rights in English Speaking Sub-Saharan Africa" in Welch, C. and Melker, R. (eds.), *Human Rights and Developmant in Africa*, (State U N.Y. Press: New York).

Human Fertilisation and Embryology Authority (June 1993), *Code of Practice* (H.F.E.A.: London).

Human Fertilisation and Embryology Authority (July 1994), *Donated Ovarian Tissue in Embryo*

Research and Assisted Conception Report (H.F.E.A.: London).

Hume, D. (1844, reprinted 1986), *Commentaries on the Law of Scotland Respecting Crimes*, Bell B. (ed.), (4th ed.) (Stair Society: Edinburgh).

Hussain, A. (1981), "Foucault's History of Sexuality", 5&6 *m/f* 169.

Hutton, N. and Tata, C. (1993), "Reform of Sentencing Practice", *Journal of the Law Society of Scotland* 230.

Irigaray, L. (1985), *This Sex Which is Not One*, (Cornell University Press: New York).

Irigaray, L. (1993), *Je, tu, nous: Toward a Culture of Difference*, (Routledge: London).

Jackson, E. (1992), "Catharine MacKinnon and Feminist Jurisprudence: A Critical Appraisal", 19 *Journal of Law and Society* 195.

Jackson, E. (1993), "Contradictions and Coherence in Feminist Responses to Law", 20 *Journal of Law and Society* 398.

Jackson, J. (1992), "Law's Truth, Lay Truth and Lawyers' Truth: The Representation of Evidence in Adversary Trials", 3 *Law and Critique* 29.

Jenkins, A. (1960), *Law for the Rich*, (Victor Gollancz: London).

Johnsen, D. (1986), "The Creation of Fetal Rights: Conflicts with Women's Constitutional Rights to Liberty, Privacy and Equal Protection", 95 *Yale Law Journal* 599.

Jones, A. (1990), *Women Who Kill*, (Victor Gollancz: London).

Jones, M. and Christie, M. (1992), *Criminal Law*, (Greens: Edinburgh).

Jones, T. et al. (1986), *The Islington Crime Survey*, (Gower: Aldershot).

Joshi, H. (1992), "The Cost of Caring" in Glendinning, C. and Millar, J. (eds.), *Women and Poverty in Britain in the 1990s*, (Harvester Wheatsheaf: New York).

Kamerman, S., Kahn, A. and Kingston, P. (1983), *Maternity Policies and Working Women*, (Columbia University Press: New York).

Kane, A. (1990), "Anti-abortionists defeated", 7 *Socialist Action* 18.

Kasian, M. et al. (1993), "Battered women who kill: jury simulation and legal defenses", 17 *Law and Human Behaviour* 289.

Kelly, D. (1990), "Victim Participation in the Criminal Justice System" in A. Lurigio et al. (eds.), *Victims of Crime: Problems, Policies and Programs*, (Sage: New York).

Kelly, D. (1993), *Criminal Sentences*, (T & T Clark: Edinburgh).

Kelly, L. (1988), *Surviving Sexual Violence*, (Polity Press in association with Basil Blackwell: London).

Kelman, M. (1981), "Interpretive Construction in the Criminal Law", 33 *Stanford Law Review* 591.

Kennedy, H. (1992), *Eve Was Framed: Women and British Justice*, (Chatto & Windus: London).

Kenyatta, J. (1953), *Facing Mt Kenya: The Tribal Life of the Kikuyu*, (Secker and Warburg: London).

Keown, J. (1988), *Abortion, Doctors and the Law: Some Aspects of the Legal Regulation of Abortion in England from 1803 to 1982*, (Cambridge University Press: Cambridge).

King, M. and Mezey, G. (1992), *Male Victims of Sexual Assault*, (Oxford University Press: Oxford).

Kingdom, E. (1991), *What's Wrong with Rights? Problems for Feminist Politics of Law*, (Edinburgh University Press: Edinburgh)

Kingdom, E. (1992), *Problems with rights*, (Unpublished Conference Paper presented at the European University Institute: Florence).

Kirsta, A. (1994), *Deadlier Than the Male: Violence and Aggression in Women*, (Harper Collins: London).

Klein, D. (1976), "The Etiology of Female Crime: A Review of the Literature" in Crites, L. (ed.), *The Female Offender*, (D.C. Heath: Lexington, Massachusetts).

Klein, D. and Kress, J. (1981), "Any Woman's Blues: a Critical Overview of Women, Crime and the Criminal Justice System" in Platt, T. and Takagi, P. (eds.), *Crime and Social Justice*, (Macmillan: London).

Klein, R.D. (1984), "Doing It Ourselves: Self Insemination" in Arditti, R. et al. (eds.), *Test-Tube Women: What Future for Motherhood?*, (Pandora Press: London).

Klein, R.D. (1985), "What's 'New' about the 'New' Reproductive Technologies" in Corea, G. et al. (eds.), *Man-Made Women: How New Reproductive Technologies Affect Women*, (Hutchinson: London).

Koso-Thomas, O. (1987), *The Circumcision of Women: A Strategy for Eradication*, (Zed: London).

Krill, F. (1985), "The Protection of Women in International Humanitarian Law", 25 *International Review of the Red Cross* 337.

Kruttschnitt, C. (1982), "Respectable Women and the Law", 23 *The Sociological Quarterly* 221.

Kymlicka, W. (1990), *Contemporary Political Philosophy: An Introduction*, (Clarendon Press: Oxford).

Lacey, N. (1994), "Abstraction in Context", 14 *Oxford Journal of Legal Studies* 255.

Lacey, N. (1994), "Government as Manager, Citizen as Consumer", 57 *Modern Law Review* 534.

Langer, R. (1989), "Battered Women and the Criminal Injuries Compensation Board: *Re A.C.*", 55 *Saskatchewaan Law Review* 453.

Law Commision Report No.207 (1992), *Domestic Violence and Occupation of the Family Home*, (H.M.S.O.: London).

Lee, R.G. and Morgan, D. (1988), "Sterilisation and Mental Handicap: Sapping the Strength of the State?", 15 *Journal of Law and Society* 229.

Ley, N.J. (1993), *Drink Driving Law and Practice*, (Sweet and Maxwell: London).

Lillich, R. (1984), "Civil Rights" in Meron, T. (ed.), *Human Rights in International Law*, (Clarendon Press: Oxford).

Littleton, C. (1989), "Women's Experience and the Problem of Transition: Perspectives on Male Battering of Women", (1989) *University of Chicago Legal Forum* 23.

Lindgren, J. (1990), "Rethinking the Grounds for Reproductive Freedom" in Arnaud A-J. and Kingdom E. (eds.), *Women's Rights and the Rights of Man*, (Aberdeen University Press: Aberdeen).

Liu, A. (1991), *Artificial Reproduction and Reproductive Rights*, (Dartmouth: Aldershot).

Lloyd, C. and Walmsley, R. (1989), *Changes in Rape Offences and Sentencing*, HORS No.105 (H.M.S.O.: London).

Lorber, S. (1984), "Legal Considerations of Reproductive Hazards in Industry in the United Kingdom" in Chamberlain, G. (ed.), *Pregnant Women at Work*, (Royal Society of Medicine: London).

Lord Justice Taylor (1993), "Address given at the Annual Conference of the Law Society of Scotland", *Journal of the Law Society of Scotland* 129.

Lowe, N. and Juss, S. (1993), "Medical Treatment - Pragmatism and the Search for Principle", 56 *Modern Law Review* 865.

Luckhaus, L. (1985), "A Plea for PMT in the Criminal Law" in S. Edwards (ed.), *Gender, Sex and the*

Law, (Croom Helm: London).

MacKinnon, C. (1980), "Feminism, Marxism, method and the state", 6 *Signs* 530.

MacKinnon, C. (1982), "Feminism, Marxism, method and the state: an agenda for theory", 7 *Signs* 515.

MacKinnon, C. (1983), "Feminism, Marxism, method and the state: toward feminist jurisprudence", 8 *Signs* 635.

MacKinnon, C. (1987), *Feminism Unmodified: Discourses on Life and Law*, (Harvard University Press: Cambridge, Massachusetts).

MacKinnon, C. (1989), *Towards a Feminist Theory of the State*, (Harvard University Press: Cambridge, Massachusetts).

MacKinnon, C. (1993), "Crimes of War, Crimes of Peace" in Shute, S. and Hurley, S. (eds.), *On Human Rights (The Oxford Amnesty Lectures 1993)*, (Basic Books: New York).

Macpherson, C.B. (1962), *The Political Theory of Possessive Individualism*, (Clarendon Press: Oxford).

Maguigan, H. (1991), "Battered Women and Self-Defense: Myths and Misconceptions in Current Reform Proposals", *University of Pennsylvania Law Review* 379.

Mahoney, M. (1991), "Legal Images of Battered Women: Redefining the Issue of Separation", 90 *Michigan Law Review* 1.

Maidment, S. (1987), "Sterilisation of Minors", 137 *New Law Journal* 468.

Maier-Katkin, C. and Ogle, R. (1993), "A Rationale for Infanticide Laws", *Criminal Law Review* 902.

Mark, E. (1989), *The Woman in the Body*, (Open University Press: Milton Keynes).

Marks, E. & Courtvron, I.de. (eds.) (1981), *New French Feminisms*, (The Harvester Press: Brighton).

Marshall, S. (1994), "Whose Child is it Anyway?" in Morgan, D. and Douglas, G. (eds.), *Constituting Families: a Study in Governance*, (Franz Steiner Verlag: Stuttgart).

Martin, N. (1987), "Re B (a minor)", *Journal of Social Welfare Law* 369.

Martinson, D. et al. (1991), "A Forum on *Lavallee v. R*: Women and Self-Defence", 25 *University of British Columbia Law Review* 23.

Mason, J.K. (1990), *Medico-Legal Aspects of Reproduction and Parenthood*, (Dartmouth: Altershot).

Masson, J. (1993), "Re W: appealing from the golden cage", 5 *Journal of Child Law* 37.

"Maternal Rights and Fetal Wrongs: The Case against the Criminalization of 'Fetal Abuse'" (1988), 101 *Harvard Law Review* 994.

McArthur, K. (1989), "'Through Her Looking Glass': Premenstrual Syndrome on Trial", 47 *University of Toronto Faculty of Law Review* 825.

McCahill, T. et al. (1979), *The Aftermath of Rape*, (Lexington Books: Lexington, Massachusetts).

McCall Smith, R. and Sheldon, D. (1992), *Scots Criminal Law*, (Butterworths: Edinburgh).

McCaul, K. et al. (1990), "Understanding Attributions of Victim Blame for Rape: Sex, Violence and Foreseeability", 20 *Journal of Applied Social Psychology* 1.

McColgan, A. (1993), "In Defence of Battered Women Who Kill", 12 *Oxford Journal of Legal Studies* 508.

McNay, L. (1992), *Foucault and Feminism*, (Polity Press: Cambridge).

McNeil, M. (1991), "Putting the Alton Bill in context" in Franklin, S., Lury, C. and Stacey, J. (eds), *Off-Centre: Feminism and Cultural Studies*, (Harper Collins Academic: London).

McRae, S. (1991), *Maternity Rights in Britain: the experience of women and employers*, (Policy Studies

Institute: London).

McSherry, B. (1993), "The Return of the Raging Hormones Theory: Premenstrual Syndrome, Postpartum Disorders and Criminal Responsibility", 15 *Sydney Law Review* 292.

MENCAP (1989), *Competency and Consent to Medical Treatment: Report of the Working Party on the Legal, Medical and Ethical Issues of Mental Handicap Convened by MENCAP, The Royal Society for Mentally Handicapped Children and Adults*, (Mencap: London).

Meron, T. (1990), "Enhancing the Effectiveness of the Prohibition of Discrimination Against Women", 84 *American Journal of International Law* 213.

Meron, T. (1993), "Rape as a crime under international humanitarian law", 87 *American Journal of International Law* 425.

Mihjalovich, M. (1987), "Does Plight Make Right: The Battered Woman Syndrome, Expert Testimony and the Law of Self-Defense", 62 *Indiana Law Journal* 1253.

Miller, A. (1987), *For Your Own Good - The Roots of Violence in Child Rearing*, (Virago: London).

Miller, L. (1993), "Two Patients Or One? Problems of Consent in Obstetrics", 1 *Medical Law International* 97.

Millns, S. (1993), "Homosexual Rights and Wrongs under the European Convention on Human Rights: A Question of Privacy or Equality?" in Jackson, B.S. and McGoldrick, D. (eds.), *Legal Visions of the New Europe*, (Graham & Trotman Ltd: London).

Minow, M. (1990), "Words and the Door to the Land of Change: Law, Language and Family Violence", 43 *Vanderbilt Law Review* 1665.

Minow, M. (1987), "Interpreting Rights: an Essay for Robert Cover", 96 *Harvard Law Journal* 1860.

Mohanty, C.T., Russo A. and Torres L. (1991), *Third World Women and the Politics of Feminism*, (Indiana University Press: Indianapolis).

Morgan, D. (1990), "F v. West Berkshire Health Authority", *Journal of Law and Society* 204.

Morgan, D. and Lee, R.G. (1991), *Blackstone's Guide to the Human Fertilisation and Embryology Act 1990*, (Blackstone Press: London).

Morgan, D. and Nielson, L. (1992), "Dangerous Liaisons? Law, Technology, Reproduction and European Ethics" in McVeigh, S. and Wheeler, S. (eds.), *Law, Health and Medical Regulation*, (Dartmouth: Aldershot).

Morris, A. (1987), *Women, Crime and Criminal Justice*, (Basil Blackwell: Oxford).

Morris, A. and Nott, S. (1991), *Working Women and the Law: Equality and Discrimination in Theory and Practice*, (Routledge: London).

Morris, A. and Nott, S. (1992), "The Legal Response to Pregnancy", 12 *Legal Studies* 54.

Mossman, M.J. (1986), "Feminism and Legal Method: The Difference it Makes", 3 *Australian Journal of Law and Society* 30.

Murphy, C. (1981), "Objections to Western Conceptions of Human Rights", 9 *Hofstra Law Review* 433.

Myers, J. (1992), "Nonmainstream Body Modification", 21 *Journal of Contemporary Ethnography* 267.

Myers, R.A. et al. (1985), "Circumcision: Its Nature and Practice Among Some Ethnic Groups in Southern Nigeria", 21 *Social Science and Medicine* 581.

Nadel, J. (1993), *Sara Thornton: The Story of a Woman Who Killed* (Victor Gollancz: London).

Naffine, N. (1990), *Law and the Sexes: Explorations in Feminist Jurisprudence*, (Allen & Unwin:

Sydney).

Nagel, I. (1981), "Sex Differences in the Processing of Criminal Defendants" in Morris, A. and Gelsthorpe, L. (eds.), *Women and Crime*, (Cambridge University Press: Cambridge).

Neave, M. (1992), "From Difference to Sameness - Law and Women's Work", 18 *Melbourne University Law Review* 768.

Nedjati, Z.M. (1978), *Human Rights under the European Convention*, (North Holland Publishing Company: Amsterdam).

Nelken, D. (1987), "Critical Criminal Law", 14 *Journal of Law and Society* 105.

Neustatter, A. and Newson, G. (1986), *Mixed Feelings: The Experience of Abortion*, (Pluto Press: London).

Nicholson, G. (1992), *Principles of Sentencing in Scotland*, (2nd ed) (Green: Edinburgh).

Nicolson, D. and Sanghiv, R. (1993), "Battered Women and Provocation: The implications of *R v. Ahluwalia*", *Criminal Law Review* 728.

Nielson, L. (1994), *Procreative Tourism, Genetic Testing and the Law*, (Unpublished Conference Paper presented at ISFL Conference: Cardiff).

Norrie, A. (1993), *Crime, Reason and History*, (Weidenfeld and Nicholson: London).

Norrie, K. (1989), "Sterilisation of the Mentally Disabled in English and Canadian Law", 38 *International Comparative Law Quarterly* 387.

Nsiah-Jefferson, L. (1989), "Reproductive Laws, Women of Color and Low Income Women", 11 *Women's Rights Law Reporter* 15.

O'Connor, S.D. (1991), "Portia's Progress", 66 *New York University Law Review* 1546.

O'Donovan, K. (1984), "The Medicalisation of Infanticide", *Criminal Law Review* 259.

O'Donovan, K. (1985), *Sexual Divisions in Law*, (Weidenfield and Nicholson: London).

O'Donovan, K. (1991), "Defences for Battered Women Who Kill", 18 *Journal of Law and Society* 219.

O'Donovan, K. (1993), "Law's Knowledge: The Judge, The Expert, The Battered Woman and Her Syndrome", 20 *Journal of Law and Society* 427.

Oakley, A. (1984), *The Captured Womb: A History of the Medical Care of Pregnant Women*, (Blackwell: Oxford).

Ogbourne, D. and Ward, R. (1989), "Sterilization, The Mentally Incompetent and the Courts", 18 *Anglo-American Law Review* 230.

Okin, S. (1990), "Thinking Like a Woman" in Rhode, D. (ed.), *Theoretical Perspectives on Sexual Difference*, (Yale University Press: New Haven).

Oliver, M. (1993), *The Politics of Disablement*, (Macmillan: London).

Olsen, F. (1991), "Statutory Rape: A Feminist Critique of Rights Analysis" in Bartlett, K.T. and Kennedy, R. (eds.), *Feminist Legal Theory: Readings in Law and Gender*, (Westview Press: Oxford).

Orbach, S. (1993), *Hunger Strike: The Anorectic's Struggle as a Metaphor for Our Age*, (Penguin: London).

Outshoorn, J. (1988), "Abortion Law Reform: a Woman's Right to Choose?" in Buckley, M. and Anderson, M. (eds.), *Women, Equality and Europe*, (Macmillan: London).

Packer, H. (1968), *The Limits of the Criminal Sanction*, (Stanford University Press: Stanford,

California).

Paglow, M. (1984), *Family Violence*, (Praeger Press: New York).

Pannikar, R. (1982), "Is the notion of human rights a western concept?", 120 *Diogenes* 75.

Pannikar, R. (1978), *The Intra-religous Dialogue*, (Harvard University Press: Cambridge, Massachusetts).

Parsons, E. (1916), *Social Rule: A Study of the Will to Power*, (Putnam: New York).

Pateman, C. (1980), "The Disorder of Women: Women, Love and the Sense of Justice", 91 *Ethics* 20.

Pateman, C. (1987), "Feminist Critiques of the Public/Private Dichotomy" in A. Phillips (ed.)', *Feminism and Equality*, (Blackwell: Oxford).

"Paternity leave" (1994), 55 *Equal Opportunities Review* 14.

Petchesky, R.P. (1984), *Abortion and Woman's Choice: The State, Sexuality, and Reproductive Freedom*, (Longman: New York and London).

Petchesky, R.P. (1987), "Foetal images: the power of visual culture in the politics of reproduction" in Stanworth, M. (ed.), *Reproductive Technologies: Gender, Motherhood and Medicine*, (Polity Press: Cambridge).

Phillips, A. (ed.) (1987), *Feminism and Equality*, (Basil Blackwell: Oxford).

Pollard, P. (1992), "Judgments about Victims and Attackers in Depicted Rapes", 31 *British Journal of Social Psychology* 307.

Pollis, A. and Schwab, P. (1979), "Human Rights: A Western Construct with Limited Application" in Pollis, A. and Schwab, P. (eds.), *Human Rights: Cultural and Ideological Perspectives*, (Praeger: New York).

Poynter R. and Martin, C. (1993), *Rights Guide to Non-Means-Tested Benefits*, (16th ed.) (Child Poverty Action Group: London).

Radford, J. (1991), "Sterilization Versus Segregation: Control of the 'Feebleminded', 1900-1938", 33 *Social Science and Medicine* 448.

Radford, L. (1993), "Pleading for Time: Justice for Battered Women Who Kill" in Birch, H. (ed.), *Moving Targets: Women, Murder and Representation*, (Virago: London).

Ramazanoglu, C. (1989), *Feminism and the Contradictions of Oppression*, (Routledge: London).

Randles, T. (1991), "The Alton Bill and the media's consensual position" in Franklin, S., Lury, C. and Stacey, J. (eds.), *Off-Centre: Feminism and Cultural Studies*, (Harper Collins Academic: London).

Rawls, J. (1972), *A Theory of Justice*, (Oxford University Press: Oxford).

Rawls, J. (1980), "Kantian Constructivism in Moral Theory", 77 *Journal of Philosophy* 515.

Renteln, A. (1984), "The Unanswered Challenge of Relativism and the Consequences for Human Rights", 7 *Human Rights Quarterly* 514.

"Rethinking (M)otherhood: Feminist Theory and State Regulation of Pregnancy" (1990), 103 *Harvard Law Review* 1325.

Rhoda, H. (1984), "Women's Rights in English Speaking Sub-Saharan Africa" in Welch, C. and Meltzer, R. (eds.), *Human Rights and Development in Africa*, (State U N.Y. Press: New York).

Rhoden, N. (1986), "The Judge in the Delivery Room: The Emergency of Court-Ordered Caesarian", 74 *California Law Review* 1951.

Rhoden, N.K., "Late abortions and technological advances in fetal viability: some legal considerations",

17 *Family Planning Perspectives* 160.

Roberts, A. and Guelff, A. (eds.) (1994), *Documents on the Laws of War*, (Oxford University Press: Oxford).

Roberts, D. (1991), "Punishing Drug Addicts Who Have Babies: Women Of Color, Equality And The Right Of Privacy", 104 *Harvard Law Review* 1419.

Roberts, D. (1992), "The Future of Reproductive Choice for Poor Women and Women of Color", 14 *Women's Rights Law Reporter* 305.

Robertshaw, P. (1992), "The Guilty Plea Discount: Rule of Law or Role of Chance?", 31 *Howard Journal* 53.

Robertshaw, P. (1994), "Sentencing Rapists: First Tier Courts in 1991-2", *Criminal Law Review* 343.

Rothman, B.K. (1989), *Recreating Motherhood*, (Norton: London).

Rubinstein, M. (1992), "Understanding pregnancy discrimination: a framework for analysis", 42 *Equal Opportunities Review* 22.

Russell, D. (1982), *Rape Within Marriage*, (Collier Books: New York).

Rutherford, F. (1989), "The proposal for a European Directive on parental leave: some reasons why it failed", 17 *Policy and Politics* 301.

Ryan, J. and Thomas, F. (1987), *The Politics of Mental Handicap*, (2nd ed.) (Free Association Books: London).

Sachs, A. and Wilson, J.H. (1978), *Sexism and the Law: A study of male beliefs and legal bias in Britain and the United States*, (Martin Robertson: Oxford).

Sandel, M.J. (1982), *Liberalism and the Limits of Justice*, (Cambridge University Press: Cambridge).

Sandel, M.J. (1984), *Liberalism and Its Critics*, (Blackwell: Oxford).

Sanderson, L.P. (1981), *Against the Mutilation of Women: the struggle to end unnecessary suffering*, (Ithaca Press: London).

Savane, M.A. (1979), "Why We Are Against the International Campaign", 40 *International Child Welfare Review* 38.

Saxton, M. (1984), "Born and Unborn: The Implications of Reproductive Technologies for People with Disabilities" in   Arditti, R. et al. (eds.), *Test-Tube Women: What Future For Motherhood?*, (Pandora Press: London).

Schneider, E. (1980), "Equal Rights to Trial for Women: Sex Bias in the Law of Self-Defense", 15 *Harvard Civil Rights-Civil Liberties Law Review* 623.

Schneider, E. (1992), "Particularity and Generality: Challenges of Feminist Theory and Practice in Work on Woman-Abuse", 67 *New York University Law Review* 520.

Schneider, E. (1991), "The Dialectics of Rights and Politics" in Fineman, M.A. and Thomadsen, N.S. (eds.), *At the Boundaries of Law: Feminism and Legal Theory*, (Routledge: London).

Schuller, R. and Vidmar, N. (1992), "Battered woman syndrome evidence in the court room: a review of the literature", 16 *Law and Human Behaviour* 273.

Science and Technology Sub Group (University of Birmingham) (1991), "Feminism and abortion: pasts, presents and futures" in Franklin, S., Lury, C. and Stacey, J. (eds.), *Off-Centre: Feminism and Cultural Studies*, (Harper Collins Academic: London).

Scottish Office (1984), *Criminal Statistics Scotland 1980-1982*, Cmnd 9403 (H.M.S.O.: Edinburgh).

Scottish Office (1993), *Recorded Crime in Scotland 1992*, CrJ/1993/2 (H.M.S.O.: Edinburgh).

Scottish Office (1993), *Criminal Proceedings in Scottish Courts 1992*, Cr/J/1993/8 (H.M.S.O.: Edinburgh).

Scottish Office (1993), *Sentencing and Appeals*, (Scottish Office: Edinburgh).

Scroggie, F. (1990), "Why do parents want their children sterilised? A broader approach to sterilisation requests", 2 *Journal of Child Law* 35.

Scott, J.A. (1990), *Women and the Law: Commentary and materials*, (Law Book Co.: North Ryde, New South Wales).

Scutt, J. (1976), "Role-conditioning Theory: An Explanation for Disparity in Male and Female Criminality", 19 *Australia and New Zealand Journal of Criminology*.

Scutt, J. (1982), "To Love, Honour and Rape with Impunity: Wife as Victim of Rape and the Criminal Law" in Schneider, H. (ed.), *The Victim in International Perspective*, (De Gruyter: New York).

Scutt, J. (1990), "Women's Bodies, Patriarchal Principles" in Scutt, J. (ed.), *The Baby Machine*, (Merlin Press: London).

Seriaux, A. (1985), "Droit naturel et procréation artificielle: quelle jurisprudence?", *Recueil Dalloz-Sirey* (chronique) 53.

Shandall, A.A. (1967), "Circumcision and Infibulation of Females", 5 *Sudan Medical Journal* 179.

Shapiro, T.M. (1985), *Population Control Politics: Women, Sterilization and Reproductive Choice*, (Temple University Press: Philadelphia).

Shaw, J. (1990), "Sterilisation of Mentally Handicapped People: Judges Rule OK?", 53 *Modern Law Review* 91.

Sheehy, E. et al. (1992), "Defending Battered Women on Trial: The Battered Woman Syndrome and its Limitations", 16 *Criminal Law Journal* 369.

Sheldon, S. (1993), "'Who is the Mother to Make the Judgment?': the Constructions of Woman in English Abortion Law", 1 *Feminist Legal Studies* 3.

Sheldon, S. (1994), "The British Abortion Act (1967) - A Permissive Reform?", (European University Institute Working Papers Law No. 94/2).

Sherman, L.W. and Berk, R.A. (1984), "The Specific Deterrent Effects of Arrest for Domestic Assault", 49 *American Sociological Review* 261.

Sherman, L.W. and Smith, D. (1992), "Crime, Punishment and Stake in Conformity: Milwaukee and Omaha Experiments", 57 *American Sociological Review* 680.

Shiels, R. (1991), "Marital Rape in England and Wales", *Scolag Bulletin* 7.

Shivji, I. (1989), *The Concept of Human Rights in Africa*, (CODESRIA Book Series: London).

Shone, M. (1987), "Mental Health - Sterilization of Mentally Retarded Persons - *Parens Patriae* Power: *Re Eve*", 66 *Canadian Bar Review* 635.

Showalter, E. (1991), *Sexual Anarchy: Gender and Culture at the Fin de Siècle*, (Bloomsbury: London).

Shute, J. (1992), *Life-size*, (Martin Secher & Warburg Ltd: England).

Slack, A.T. (1988), "Female Circumcision: A Critical Appraisal", 10 *Human Rights Quarterly* 437.

Smart, C. (1977), *Women, Crime and Criminology, A Feminist Critique*, (Routledge Kegan Paul: London).

Smart, C. (1989), *Feminism and the Power of Law*, (Routledge: London).

Smart, C. (1991), "Penetrating Women's Bodies: The Problems of Law and Medical Technology" in P. Abbott and C. Wallace (eds.), *Gender, Power and Sexuality*, (Macmillan: London).

Smart, C. (1992), *Regulating Womanhood: Historical Essays on Marriage, Motherhood and Sexuality*, (Routledge: London).

Smart, C. (1992), "The Woman of Legal Discourse", 1 *Social and Legal Studies* 29.

Smart, F. (1970), *Neurosis and Crime*, (Duckworth: London).

Smith, J.C. and Hogan, B. (1992), *Criminal Law*, (7th ed.) (Butterworths: London).

Smith, L. (1989), *Concerns about Rape*, Home Office Research Study No. 106 (H.M.S.O.: London).

Smith-Rosenberg, C. (1979), "The Hysterical Woman: Sex Roles and Role Conflict in 19th-Century America", 39 *Social Research* 652.

Soothill, K. and Soothill, D. (1993), "Prosecuting the Victim? a Study of Reporting of Barristers' Comments in Rape Cases", 32 *Howard Journal* 12.

Soothill, K. and Walby, S. (1991), *Sex Crime in the News*, (Routledge: London).

Spallone, P. (1989), *Beyond Conception: The New Politics of Reproduction*, (MacMillan Education Ltd: Basingstoke).

Stanko, E. (1985), *Intimate Intrusions: Women's Experience of Male Violence*, (Routledge: London).

Stanley, L. and Wise, S. (1993), *Breaking Out Again*, (Routledge: London).

Stanworth, M. (1987), "The Deconstruction of Motherhood" in Stanworth.M. (ed.), *Reproductive Technologies: Gender, Motherhood and Medicine*, (Polity Press: Cambridge).

Steinberg, D.L. (1991), "Adversarial politics: the legal construction of abortion" in Franklin, S., Lury, C. and Stacey, J. (eds.), *Off-Centre: Feminism and Cultural Studies*, (Harper Collins Academic: London).

Stewart, A. (1990), *The Scottish Criminal Courts in Action*, (Greens: Edinburgh).

Struble, C. (1983), "Protection of the Mentally Retarded Individual's Right to Choose Sterilization: The Effect of the Clear and Convincing Evidence Standard", 12 *Capital University Law Review* 413.

Sullivan, G. (1989), "The Need for a Crime of Sexual Assault", *Criminal Law Review* 331.

Taylor, L. (1986), "Provoked Reason in Men and Women: Heat-of-Passion Manslaughter and Imperfect Self-Defense", 33 *U.C.L.A. Law Review* 1679.

Temkin, J. (1987), *Rape and the Legal Process*, (Sweet and Maxwell: London).

Thar, A. (1982), "The Admissibility of Expert Testimony on Battered Wife Syndrome: An Evidentiary Analysis", 71 *Northwestern University Law Review* 348.

The Home Affairs Committee (1992), *Report on Domestic Violence: Minutes of Evidence*, (H.M.S.O.: London).

Thevos, M. (1984), *The Painted Body*, (Rizzoli International: New York).

Thomas, A. (1987), "For Her Own Good - A Reply", 84 *Law Society Gazette* 1196.

Thomson, J.J. (1990), *The Realm of Rights*, (Harvard University Press: Cambridge, Massachusetts).

Thornton, R. (1993), "Minors and Medical Treatment - Who Decides?", 52 *Cambridge Law Journal* 34.

Toner, B. (1977), *The Facts of Rape*, (Hutchinson: London).

Tushnet, M. (1984), "An Essay on Rights", 62 *Texas Law Review* 1375.

Vale, V. and Juno, A. (eds.) (1989), *Modern Primitive*, (RE/Search Publications: San Francisco, California).

Van Dijk, P. and G.J.H. van Hoof (1990), *Theory and Practice of the European Convention on Human Rights*, (Kluwer: Deventer).

Viano, E. ed. (1989), *Crime and its Victims*, (Hemisphere: Washington D.C.).

Victim Support/National Inter-Agency Working Party Report (1992), *Domestic Violence*, (Victim Support: London).

Von Hirsch, A. and Jareborg, N. (1991), "Gauging Criminal Harm: A Living-Standard Analysis", 11 *Oxford Journal of Legal Studies* 1.

Walker, A. (1992), *Possessing The Secret of Joy*, (Jonathon Cape: London).

Walker, A. and Parmar, P. (1993), *Warrior Marks: female genital mutilation and the sexual binding of women*, (Jonathon Cape: London).

Walker, L. (1979), *The Battered Woman*, (Harper & Row: New York).

Walker, L. (1984), *The Battered Woman Syndrome*, (Springer Publishing: New York).

Walker, L. (1989), *Terrifying Love: Why Battered Women Kill and How Society Responds*, (Harper Collins: New York).

Walklate, S. (1989), *Victimology*, (Unwin Hyman: London).

Warnock, M. (1984), *A Question of Life: The Warnock Report on Human Fertilisation and Embryology*, (Basil Blackwell: Oxford).

Wasik, M. (1982), "Cumulative Provocation and Domestic Killing", *Criminal Law Review* 29.

Weisstub, D. (1986), "Victims of Crime in the Criminal Justice System" in E. Fattah (ed.), *From Crime Policy to Victim Policy*, (Macmillan: London).

Wells, C. (1990), "Domestic Violence and Self-Defence", 140 *New Law Journal* 1380.

Wells, C. (1993), "Maternal Versus Foetal Rights" in Feminist Legal Research Unit (ed.), *Body Politics: Control versus Freedom: the role of feminism in women's personal autonomy*, (Faculty of Law: University of Liverpool: Liverpool).

Wells, C. (1994), "Patients, Consent and Criminal Law", *Journal of Social Welfare and Family Law* 65.

West, R. (1991), "Jurisprudence and Gender", reprinted in Barlett K. and Kennedy R., *Feminist Legal Theory: Readings in Law and Gender* (Westview Press: Oxford).

Whitford, M. (1991), *Philosophy in the Feminine*, (Routledge: London).

Whitford, M. (ed.) (1993), *The Irigaray Reader*, (Blackwell: Oxford).

Whitty, N. (1993), "Law and the Regulation of Reproduction in Ireland", XLIII *University of Toronto Law Journal* 851.

Williams, G. (1958), *The Sanctity of Life and the Criminal Law*, (Faber and Faber: London).

Williams, G. (1994), "The Fetus and the 'Right to Life'", 53 *Cambridge Law Journal* 71.

Williams J. (1991), "Gender Wars: Selfless Women in the Republic of Choice", 66 *New York University Law Review* 1559.

Williams, P. (1990), *The Alchemy of Race and Rights*, (Virago: London).

Wilson, R (1990), "The Victim in the Criminal Justice System", *Scot's Law Times (News)* 8.

Wing, A.K. (1994), "Custom, Religion and Rights: the Future Legal Status of Palestinian Women", 35 *Harvard International Law Journal* 149.

Winn, D. (1988), *Experiences of Abortion*, (Macdonald Optima: London).

Wolf, N. (1990), *The Beauty Myth*, (Vintage: London).

Wollman, L. (1973), "Female Circumcision", 20 *Journal of the American Society of Psychosomatic Dentistry and Medicine* 4.

Women of Europe (1990), *Childcare in the European Communities 1985-1990*, (European Commission: Brussels).

Worrall, A. (1990), *Offending Women: Female Lawbreakers and the Criminal Justice System*, (Routledge: London).

Wright, R. (1980), "Rape and Physical Violence" in West, D. (ed.), *Sex Offenders in the Criminal Justice System*, (Cambridge Institute of Criminology: Cambridge).

Wright, S. (1988-89), "Economic Rights and Social Justice: A Feminist Analysis of Some International Human Rights Conventions", 12 *Australian Yearbook of International Law* 241.

Yeo, S. (1991), "Provocation Down Under", 141 *New Law Journal* 1200.

Yeo, S. (1993), "Resolving Gender Bias in Criminal Defences", 19 *Monash University Law Review* 104.

Yllo, K. (1988), "Political and Methological Debates in Wife Abuse Research" in Yllo, K. and Bograd, M. (eds.), *Feminist Perspectives on Wife Abuse*, (Sage: Newbury Park, California).

Young, A. (1990), *Femininity in Dissent*, (Routledge: London).

Index